Abraham Lincoln's Honored Dead
at the
Gettysburg National Cemetery

Abraham Lincoln's Honored Dead
at the
Gettysburg National Cemetery

★ ★ ★ ★ ★

Profiles of the 2,000 Soldiers with Names Preserved for Their Gravestones

JAMES A. CHRISTIAN

PALMETTO
PUBLISHING
Charleston, SC
www.PalmettoPublishing.com

Copyright © 2024 by James A. Christian

All rights reserved

No portion of this book may be reproduced, stored in a retrieval system, or transmitted in any form by any means–electronic, mechanical, photocopy, recording, or other–except for brief quotations in printed reviews, without prior permission of the author.

Cover photograph of President Abraham Lincoln bare headed and seated on the speaker's platform after delivering his Gettysburg Address

Paperback ISBN: 9798822972858
eBook ISBN: 9798822972865

To Nina

Preface

Whenever I have been in Gettysburg, I have usually tried to visit the National Cemetery. I have always found walking the grounds there reposeful. Of course, this has largely to do with my respect for history and the historical fact that some 160 years ago, our 16th American President rose at this cemetery's dedication to eulogize these honored dead of the Gettysburg battle and to articulate the meaning of their sacrifice.

During my past visits to the cemetery, I have walked the rows of gravestones, pausing at the graves of the few soldiers whose war experiences at Gettysburg I knew something about. However, my sensibilities are such that I have wished that I knew something about the war experiences and preceding lives for many, many more of these buried men.

So, it was that two years ago during a visit to the cemetery, I thought of writing a book that would profile the lives of all the soldiers in the cemetery—or more exactly, the 2,000 soldiers out of the total 4,000 who had been fortuned with having their names preserved for their gravestones.

The first task I would confront would be to come to the cemetery with a copy of the *1865 Report of the Select Committee Relative to the Soldiers' National Cemetery Report* in hand. This *Report* gives a row-by-row, space-by-space sequential listing of every grave in the cemetery, providing either the name and army unit affiliation of the soldier buried there or the notation that the grave was occupied by an unknown. The *Report* would provide the framework for my research. I would take the *Report* to the cemetery and walk grave by grave, comparing the name written in the *Report* with the name inscribed on the headstone and then making pen notations in my *Report* copy of the variances. The organization of my book would then be to present my profiles in this same sequencing order as these checked names appearing in the *Report*, which of course would mean presenting the profiles in the same sequencing order as the soldiers lay buried in the cemetery.

In my notetaking walks along the rows of graves, I would find scores of variances between the names in the *Report* and the names on the headstones. Some of the variances were simple, as with a headstone only reporting the soldier's first initial whereas the *Report* gave the soldier's first name. Other variances were more problematic, as with the spellings of surnames, especially as tended to occur with Germanic or Irish surnames. Also, I would find in further research that there was often not one "correct" surname spelling. And the thought that came to me was that if my book was to have some usefulness for people checking for Gettysburg ancestors buried in this famous cemetery, these surnames would have to have some close recognizability to the surname variations known to these people. Purposefully then, many of the soldier's profiles in my book would first report the actual headstone name, reported underneath this with one, or even two alternately spelled surnames.

I would pause here to relate a singular event that I experienced the first day I arrived at the cemetery ready to pen notes of these headstone name spellings in the margin of my *Report* copy. That mid-November 2022 afternoon I had observed that I was alone in the cemetery. As I began walking along the first row of graves in the Connecticut state plot, the already unseasonably cold afternoon abruptly gave way to a blanketing, but oddly silent snowfall. This event caught me very much off guard. As the snowflakes began to wet the pages of my open *Report* book copy, I felt disappointment that I would have to put off this research on its very first day. But then I had a different thought that perhaps this weather anomaly was a kind of omen. Although not a subscriber to the notion of Gettysburg ghosts, I pondered whether the dead under these plots were acquiring cognizance of my intention to tell their stories and this weather blast were not the recoil of their reawakened death agonies. Be this a wholly fanciful notion or not, I had never before beheld the cemetery lovelier—or lonelier.

To properly pay homage to the sacrificed lives of these honored dead, I would need to make certain that their profiles in my book were about more than just what army unit the soldier belonged to, where the soldier had been wounded, and what date the soldier died. The kind of detailed personal information I would want to reference in my profiles would require access to primary historical documents. This detailed personal information must include: what were the communities or countries these men had come from, what had been their pre-enlistments occupations; what promotions, demotions, enemy captures, woundings had occurred prior to coming to Gettysburg. Going beyond where a soldier had been wounded and when the soldier died, my profiles must report the wound care these men received in field hospitals, their amputations and their disease complications. Finally, I would want to search through the archived dependents' pension applications to report the impact of these men's deaths on their bereft family members left behind—in particular, for the men's dependent widowed mothers and the now-widowed wives and fatherless children.

Once I determined to pursue this research in this degree of intimate detail, I was fortunate that I resided only a short forty-minute subway ride to the main National Archives Research Center in downtown Washington, D.C. My research here would take me nearly twenty months of daily visits to complete. And by the conclusion of this period, through some Internet searches, but mainly by hands-on, personal review of archival documents, I had reviewed some 2500 army service records and over 700 U.S. Pension files for dependent applicants.

The open availability afforded every American to view soldier's actual muster cards, enlistment papers, medical descriptive lists and pension file documents is a wondrous bequest of the National Archives and Records Administration agency. I wish to acknowledge here a number of National Archives employees who have been extremely helpful and supportive during my research. Chief among these individuals has been Dennis Edelin, Reference Chief, who besides being an incredible resource on the Civil War holdings at the Archives, also excelled at going into the back records rooms and finding that one misfiled record that the regular file pullers had failed to locate. Other Archives employes whose assistance I wish to acknowledge here are Archives specialist Katherine Vollen, Archives technician Carolyn Grier, Bridgette Banks, and Paul Harrison, Archives records managers Sean Williams (retired) and Tenisha Wagstaff, Archives specialist supervisor LaTesha Wagstaff and specialists Maria Mairena, Jesse Wilinski, Denise Smith, Ernest Anim, Shea Lawson, Jessica Shainker, Will Johnson, and the late Alison Gavin.

Of course, my greatest appreciation for support during this project must go to my wife, Nina.

From my first broaching the idea of this project with her, she has been and remained supportive. While not nearly the Civil War enthusiast as her husband, she had previously proved herself quite the supportive partner in accompanying me on the innumerable past trips up from Maryland to attend Battle of Gettysburg events. Now, closing upon two years since I began this project, she has all this while lovingly allowed me the absented evening and weekend hours to work on this book—hours that we might have otherwise spent in mutually enjoyable pursuits as a couple. She remains my greatest fan (as I hers) and my happy co-adventurer in the enriching experiences of art, culture, and European travel, in those welcome respites I could break away from my research.

I must also acknowledge here my two adult children, Jason and Jana Christian, who through this project have also been supportive of "Dad doing his Civil War thing." Finally, I mention here my sister, Melva Christian, whose positive feedback and encouragement following my previous Civil War publications have been also deeply appreciated.

James Christian
November 2024

Prologue

That November 18, 1863 day that President Abraham Lincoln stepped down onto the platform at the Gettysburg train station, he had in his mind to deliver a profoundly affirmational address on human mortality and sacrifice, national purpose and rededication. So important had it been to Lincoln to give this address that he had left Washington the day before the scheduled ceremonies in order to make certain his presence in town on the date. Leaving Washington at this moment involved some risk for Lincoln that he could be away, if the condition of his seriously-ill son, Tad, back at the White House, were to take a turn for the worst. Only twenty-one months earlier, the Lincolns had experienced the devastating loss of their cherished eleven-year-old son, Willie, due to typhoid.

This risk notwithstanding, Abraham Lincoln felt the need to attend and to speak at this Gettysburg National Cemetery dedication. As President and Commander-in-Chief, Lincoln held command responsibility for the men killed and now being reinterred here. Nor did Lincoln regard this command responsibility perfunctorily. During his two summers of residence at the Soldier's Home Cottage, Lincoln had been known to walk the rows of freshly-dug graves at the neighboring Soldier's Home Cemetery in reverent reflection. Lincoln understood the immovable weight of grief that these soldiers' deaths must mean for fathers, mothers, siblings, wives and young children in so many American homes.

In the main address of the dedication ceremonies, the celebrated orator Edward Everett extolled how the ceremonial treatment being afforded Gettysburg "honored graves," compared favorably with this burial ceremony accorded the Greek "fallen martyrs," following the Greeks' victorious Battle of Marathon 2,400 years in the past. In contrast, Lincoln, in his remarks, spoke plainly of the men as the "honored dead." Lincoln had experienced too much tragic death in his early years and now during these war years to find in death any cause for glorification. What mattered now, Lincoln suggested, was "for us the living" to be dedicated to the unfinished work which those men who had fought at Gettysburg "had so nobly advanced." In the minds of everyone in the crowd that day, that unfinished work meant the favorable conclusion of the war.

However, immediately in the next sentence, Lincoln called for dedication to "the great task remaining before us," wording suggestive of a challenge more substantial than just the favorable concluding of the war. Lincoln keyed on the notion that for the dead of Gettysburg not to have died in vain would require more than merely the restitution to the nation to what it had been. This was Lincoln's evocation of "a new birth of freedom," or in so many words, his call for a renewed national dedication to cherishing, expanding, and defending our not imperishable democracy.

This great task of remembrance and renewed dedication remains with us, the living.

Keys to the Profiles

The soldiers' profiles are presented to match the position of each soldier's burial location, as it would be encountered walking right to left in the burial row. This grave number will be identical to that cited in other data bases for the cemetery. However, the rows in this book are designated differently. In 1863, as disinterred soldiers from the fields were being reburied in the National Cemetery, the outer rims of each state's plots were filled first. This outermost row was designated Row A with successive rows being designated B, C, etc. In this book, the rows are first designated numerically with Row 1 corresponding to the first row of graves behind the state's plot marker. Hence, taking the Connecticut plot as an example, Section A in other data bases becomes Row 3 in this book. Correspondingly, Row 1 in this book corresponds to Section C in the other data bases.

In the tables in this book, each soldier's entry begins with his row and space designation. To the right of this is given the exact name inscription on the soldier's grave. Beneath these inscribed names, where needed, are given the soldier's name with a corrected or preferred spelling or otherwise the soldier's name with his first and/or middle names specified in substitution for the mere initials appearing on the inscription.

To the right of the soldier's name information is given the age of the soldier at his death. If known from documented birthdates, these ages are given exactly. However, as a consequence of soldiers giving only their ages, and not their actual birthdates, upon enlisting into the army, the majority of these ages at death can only be approximated. Of course, a percentage of soldiers enlisting in the army were minors, who falsely gave their ages at enlistment as 18. However, checks of 1850 and 1860 U.S. Census records together alongside online genealogical records, do allow approximate age of death determinations for these soldiers.

To the right of these death age determinations are given the soldier's regiment, calvary or artillery unit and company assignment, usually only as inscribed on the actual headstone. In some cases where the inscribed unit assignment is in error, I have corrected the errors, but not routinely. Confederate soldiers, who were mistakenly buried in the National Cemetery, are identified.

To the right of the unit assignment entries are the mini-profiles reporting the following: birth date or year; country, state or town of birth; residence and occupation prior to entering the army; enlistment month and year; service history, including promotions, court martials, captures or woundings prior to Gettysburg; casualty date and character of wound sustained at Gettysburg; hospitalizations details, particularly amputations; date of death; details on family and/or dependents left behind, particularly as reported in referenced WC (Widow's certificates). Both these Widow's certificates and the Dependent Mothers' certificates have been mined to yield important information, such as the names of soldiers' wives and children with their ages at the date of the soldier's death, similarly the names and ages of the soldiers' parents at the dates their dependent pension applications were filed.

Given this voluminous set of information, it is inevitable that there will be some factual and transcription errors. As these errors are identified, corrections will be forthcoming in subsequent editions of this book. A particular effort has been placed on correcting reporting the WC file numbers, as individuals with active Fold3.com accounts can access the full files of pension documents by typing in the WC###### into the Fold3.com search field.

The first row of the Pennsylvania tables are notable for absent dates of deaths for almost all the men profiled in the row. This follows my preference for only noting ages at death for soldiers whose deaths occurred in relation to the battle. Beginning primarily in the 1880's, certain Pennsylvanian veterans, many of whom had not even served during the Civil War, were extended the honor of being buried in what had become the first row of the state plot. The appropriateness of these post-Civil War burials in Pennsylvania plot and of the few others in the Ohio and U.S. Infantry plots, can certainly be debated. However, to have omitted profiling these veterans in the burial spaces where they plainly lie would have been even more inappropriate.

Offered below are two soldiers' profiles from the Pennsylvania plot, presented with an explanation of common abbreviations used in these profiles.

Row/space	Soldier's name	Age at Death	Unit Assigned	Personal and Service History Profile
R4#60	JOHN METZ	25-26	68 Inf A	B ~1837 Philadelphia, PA. R same. Occ laborer. E Aug 62 private. C Jul 2. D Aug 18. Survivor (WC20708): Eliza 25 (M Aug 62); 1 ♀- Hannah 11 months.
R4#61	E T GREEN ELI T GREEN	~24	CONFED VA 14 Inf E	B ~1839 VA. Occ saddler. E May 61 private. C Jul 3: GSW fracturing forearm bones just below elbow→amp. Admitted to Camp Letterman hospital on Aug 7. D Aug 15.

Abbreviations

1. Row (R) and space (#) position designate the soldier's grave location with his state plot.
2. Soldier's name exactly as inscribed on his cemetery gravestone, followed underneath with any corrected spelling or with first or middle names specified and substituting for initials on the inscriptions. MN = middle name. Also, when there is uncertainty between any two or three possible correct spellings of a soldier's name, the most probable spelling is highlighted with bold lettering. In most instances, the soldier's name as it has appeared on the muster cards within his service file are viewed more definitely. Definitive spellings are also established by the occasional finding of a soldier's signed enlistment paper.
3. D = the soldier's date of death. Only a month and day are given, as no deaths from the Gettysburg battle occurred after 1863. There can be no 100% accurate reporting as regards the exact date that each of these soldiers died, nor the exact wound that would prove fatal. Preference as to reporting the date a soldier died is given to the date appearing in the soldier's service file. Not uncommonly, two different dates are reported in the soldier's military service file as to what exact date the soldier died. However, in this book, preference is given to the information presented in these service files.
4. Ages at death are approximate, based on extrapolations of the age the soldier reported upon enlisting into the army. Soldiers gave ages, not dates of birth in enlisting into the army. As an example, if a soldier killed in July 1863 had truthfully reported his enlistment age as 18 upon entering into the army in April 1861, then his age at death will be reported at approximately 20. As another example, if a soldier killed in July 1863 had reported his enlistment age as 21 upon entering the army in August 1862, then his age at death will be reported as 21-22.
5. Unit assignments are first identified by their unit number, then "Inf" for infantry, "Cav" for cavalry, and "Art" for artillery, followed by a company or battery assignment. Other utilized abbreviations utilized here are "Indpt" for Independent and "Btn" or "Bat" for battalion. Confederate soldiers are identified by "CONFED."

6. In the Pennsylvania section, "PRC" stands for Pennsylvania Reserve Corps. This corps of infantry regiments was organized and funded by the Pennsylvania state legislature to accommodate the thousands of Pennsylvanian men desiring army enlistment, but whose numbers exceeded what the Federal quotas for the state's enrollment had allowed for. These Pennsylvania Reserve Corps units would ultimately receive federal acceptance and would be renamed Pennsylvania Volunteers with new unit designations.
7. A summary of the most common abbreviations utilized in the profile section are as follows:
    - B = year born (usually as approximated by the soldier's reported age at enlistment) followed by state (and town, if known) or followed by foreign country that soldier was an immigrant from.
    - R = residence given at soldier's enlistment or else as can be affirmed in the 1860 U.S. Census. The spelling of town names are as they appear in enlistment records. No effect has been given to correcting these spellings. Some towns appearing in enlistment records no longer exist.
    - E = enlistment year and month followed by the soldier's rank upon enlisting, as in E Apr 61 private. A city or town name in parentheses is used when no pre-enlistment residence is known, as here E (Philadelphia, PA) Apr 61.
    - Occ = reported occupation prior to enlisting or a prior occupation reported in the Census records.
    - C = casualty date at Gettysburg with nature of mortal wounding specified, if given in military records.
    - Amp = amputation.
    - D = date in 1863 that soldier died
    - KIA = killed in action.
    - WC = Widow's Certificate, the designation given generically to all successful pension claimants. Widow's certificate, where followed by a file number (i.e., WC123456), documents a successful pension request. A paid subscription to Fold3.com allows viewing of each pension application's complete file of submissions. "WC not online" denotes an unavailable pension file on File3.com, either because the file was not copied from the National Archives original file or that original file is lost.

- W = wife, then followed by marriage month and year, as here (M mo/yr).
- Chn = children. Each dependent child's name and sex are given, along with the child's age as of the date his father died.
- ReM = Widow's remarriage, if occurred, reported with year of remarriage, as here (ReM year).
- M = mother, usually widowed, with her age given as of the year she submitted a dependent mother's pension application. WC, generically, the Widow's Certificate, in each case where a file number is reported (i.e., WC123456) documents a successful pension request. A paid subscription to Fold3.com allows viewing of each pension application's complete file of submissions, that is, unless the WC is specifically reported in the tables as not being online.

8. Camp Letterman was a massive tent hospital established northeast of the city and serving as a central receiving hospital. It was intended to draw in the wounded soldier care from the dozens of dispersed field hospitals, churches, establishments, and homes where these men had been emergently receiving care since the end of the battle.

9. **Please note that the WC's reported in the tables should be presumed to have been filed in 1863, unless otherwise noted.** On many occasions, a widowed mother of a killed Gettysburg soldier might submit an application for pension support many years after 1863. In these instances, the date that application was filed is reported along with her age at the time of the application.

Table of Contents

Connecticut	1
Delaware	5
Illinois	8
Indiana	10
Maine	18
Maryland	29
Massachusetts	32
Michigan	52
Minnesota	72
New Hampshire	77
New Jersey	82
New York	90
Ohio	160
Pennsylvania	175
Rhode Island	220
Vermont	223
West Virginia	229
Wisconsin	232
U. S. Infantry	239

Connecticut

R1#1	PATRICK DUNN	30-31	27 Inf D	B ~1832 Ireland. R Wallingford, New Haven Co., CT. Occ farmer. E Sep 62 private. C Jul 2. D Jul 4.
R2#1	ALFRED H DIBBLE	25	14 Inf G	B 1/3/1838 Westbrook, New Haven Co., CT. R same. Occ farm laborer. E Jun 62 private. C Jul 2: GSW to right shoulder. D Jul 5. Survivors (WC98888): W Calista 24 (M June 60|ReM 1865); 1 ♂- Willy 2.
R2#2	NELSON HODGE	25-26	14 Inf I	B 1837 Glastonbury, Hartford Co., CT. R Coventry, Tolland Co., CT. Occ dresser. E Jul 62 private. Captured 12/16/62 at Fredericksburg. Sent to regiment from Camp Parole on 5/15/63. C Jul 3: GSW to left knee. D Jul 23. Survivors (WC44301): W Mary 25 in 1864 (M Oct 60); no chn.
R2#3	JAMES CASSIDY	44-45	20 Inf C	B ~1818 Ireland. R Hartford, CT. Occ laborer. E Aug 62, private. W Jul 3: wounds to thigh and abdomen. D Jul 13. Survivor (WC92083): W Elizabeth 45 (M Aug 45); no chn.
R2#4	JOEL C DICKERMAN	22	20 Inf I	B 9/22/1840 Hamden, New Haven Co., CT. R same. E Aug 62 corporal. KIA Jul 3.
R2#5	CHARLES H ROBERTS[1]	24	20 Inf F	B 5/20/1839 NYC. R Newtown, Fairfield Co., CT. Occ mechanic. E Aug 62 private. Promoted to corporal in Aug 62. Resigned rank, returned to private in Nov 62. C Jul 3: shot in left lung. D Jul 8 or 9. Survivors (WC12862): W Eliza 24 (M Feb 60); 2 ♀- Jennie 2, Alice 7 months.
R2#6	DANIEL H PURDY	21	17 Inf C	B 6/10/1842 Paterson, Passaic Co., NJ. R Danbury, Fairfield Co., CT. Occ carpenter. E Aug 62 private. C Jul 1: wounded in left shoulder and lung. D Jul 15. Survivor (WC304215): M Mrs. Deborah Purdy ~70 in 1890 (Alson Purdy affirmed too old and feeble to support wife).
R2#7	JAMES FLYNN	35-36	17 Inf E	B ~ 1827 Ireland. R Westport, Fairfield Co., CT. Occ farmer. E Aug 62 private. C Jul 2: severe wound to left arm. D Jul 14. Survivors (WC15934→WC156798 neither online) W Catherine 27 (M Feb 55, died Dec 71); 2 ♂- John 5, Thomas 2.

---

1 **Identity question.** There were two Charles Roberts in the 20th Connecticut Infantry killed at Gettysburg, one with the middle initial H and the other with the middle initial F. Charles F. Roberts was a member of Company K. Here the fact that headstone for Charles H. Roberts accurately identifies him as a member of Company F should confirm that it is his remains are in this grave. Interestingly, Charles F. Roberts was killed in action on July 3rd, as had been Corporal Joel Dickerman, the 20th Connecticut soldier interred just to the left of Charles F. One would expect that these two soldiers killed on the same July 3rd date would have received battlefield burials in proximity to each other and then been transferred together to the National Cemetery. However, Charles H. Roberts died July 8th or 9th, likely at a field hospital where the likelihood of a surviving accurate headboard was much greater than with battlefield burials.

R2#8	___ WILLIAMS DAVID WILLIAMS[2]	~27	CONFED NC 20 Inf D	B ~1836 Columbus Co., NC. 1860: R same; occ working on father's farm. E Jun 61 private. KIA Jul 1.
R2#9	JOHN W METCALF	21-22	17 Inf F	B ~1841 England. R Norwalk, Fairfield Co., CT. Occ wool sorter. E Aug 62 private. KIA Jul 2.
R2#10	WILLIAM CANNELLS WILLIAM **CANNELL**	30	ME 16 Inf F	B 2/16/1833 Gorham, Cumberland Co., ME. R same. Occ laborer. E Jul 62 private. KIA Jul 1: wounded in side.
R3#1	WILLIAM E WILSON	~29	27 Inf D	B ~1834. R New Haven, CT. E Apr 61 private. Jan 63: promoted to corporal. KIA Jul 2.
R3#2	JOSEPH PUFFER (MN WILLIAM)	22	14 Inf I	B 8/18/1840 Coventry, Tolland Co., CT. R same. Occ mechanic. E Jul 62 private. KIA Jul 3.
R3#3	WILLIAM D MARSH[3] (MN DOTY)	17	14 Inf G	B 1/24/46 Madison, New Haven Co., CT. R same. Occ sailor. E Aug 62 private. KIA instantly Jul 3.
R3#4	MOSES G CLEMENT	29	14 Inf G	B 8/3/1833 Norwich, Windsor Co. VT. R Guilford, New Haven Co., CT. Occ farm laborer. E Jul 62 private. KIA Jul 3: killed by an enemy battery. Survivor (WC17852): W Jane 35 (M Dec 58); no chn.
R3#5	S CARTER SIDNEY CARTER, JR[4]	31	CONFED SC 14 Inf A	B 5/28/1832 Darlington, SC. R same. Occ farmer/slave owner, 6 slaves: 29 to 6mos. E Sep 61 sergeant. Feb 62 promoted to 2nd lieutenant Oct 62 wounded, home on leave. Jan/Feb 63 home on furlough. C Jul 1: bullet in.to chest. D Jul 8. Survivors: W Hester Ellen Carter 26 (M Oct 55); 3 chn: 2 ♀- Minnie 7, Ida 6 & 1 ♂- Horace 4.
R3#6	EDWARD B FARR	19-20	27 Inf F	B ~1843 CT. R New Haven, CT. Occ clock maker. E Aug 62 private. D Jul 2 of wounds.

---

    2 **Confederate in the Cemetery**. Samuel Weaver, contracted for the reburial of Union soldiers in the new National Cemetery, wrote David Wills to assert that *"**there has not been a single mistake made** in the removal of soldiers to the Cemetery by taking the body of a rebel for a Union soldier (my bold italics)."* However, quite to the contrary, David Williams, identified here within the Connecticut Union plot, is one of nine generally-accepted Confederates, who were mistakenly buried in the National Cemetery. David Williams, a soldier in the North Caroline regiment referenced above, is one of these nine known mistakenly buried Confederates.

    3 **Minor at death**. According to a birth record, William Marsh was 16 when he enrolled into the army and 17 when he was killed instantly on July 3rd.

    4 **Confederate in the Cemetery**. Lieutenant Sidney Carter is another of the nine identified Confederates mistakenly buried in the National Cemetery. In 1978, Bessie Mell Lane published "Dear Bet," a collection of 34 letters Sideny Carter sent home to his wife, Ellen (nicknamed Bet) Carter, during his 22-month service in the Confederate army. The letters are intelligent, thoughtful and tender. Carter appears to be the only one of the nine mistakenly-buried Confederates, who owned slaves. The Darlington County, SC slave schedules in the 1860 U.S. Census report that he owned seven slaves, an adult couple in their twenties and five boys, aged fifteen to six months.

R3#7	MICHAEL CONFREY	37-38	27 Inf F	B ~1825 Ireland. R New Haven, CT. Occ saloon keeper. E Sep 62 private. Survivors (WC11483): W Epsey 45 (M Jan 55); 2 ♂- William 12, Daniel 10. D Jul 2 of wounds.
R3#8	JOHN D PERRY[5]	43-44	20 Inf F	B ~1819 CT. R New Haven, CT. Occ laborer. E Aug 62 private. KIA Jul 3. Survivors (WC88600); 1 ♀- Jane 6 (from 1st marriage- Harriet); Sarah 29 (3rd wife M Sep 62 | ReM 1865).
R3#9	BERNARD MULVEY	21-22	20 Inf I	B ~1841 Ireland. R Hamden, New Haven Co., CT. Occ mechanic. E Aug 62 private. KIA Jul 3
R3#10	FRANK J BENSEN	29-30	17 Inf C	B ~1833 Sherman, Fairfield Co., CT. R Brookfield, Fairfield Co., CT. Occ laborer. E Aug 62 private. C Jul 1: GSW. D Jul 17. Survivor (WC144610): W Jane 30 (M Sep 56); no chn.
R3#11	JOSEPH WHITLOCK (MN SILLICK)	21-22	17 Inc C	B 1841 Ridgefield, Fairfield Co., CT. R same. Occ farmer. E Jul 62 private. C Jul 1: wounded in lower right arm→amp. D Jul 16.

---

5 **Soldier's Three Marriages, Two Wives**. The 1863 widow's pension application for John Perry highlights this soldier's unusual marital history prior to enlisting into the army. John Perry married Harriet Hope in July 1854, then was divorced from her in October 1859. From this first marriage came Perry's only acknowledged offspring, Jane, born June 19, 1857. The couple would remarry in July 62, then divorce again eight weeks later on September 2, 1862. On September 6, 1862, Perry then married Sarah Bundy. The new couple's time together would be indeed truncated. On September 8, 1862, Perry mustered-in to the 20th Connecticut regiment and would be killed-in-action ten months later on July 3rd.

Memorial Marker to Jedediah Chapman, Captain 27th Connecticut Infantry, at the west end of the Wheatfield

★ ★ ★ ★ ★

Originally placed alongside the Wheatfield Road in the 1880's, this stone tablet holds the honor of being the oldest unaltered battlefield marker on the field. The diminutive 27th Connecticut regiment charged into the Wheatfield on July 2nd with only 75 men and would sustain nearly 50% casualties during its fighting. Jeremiah Chapman has a burial site in the Grove Street Cemetery in New Haven, Connecticut.

Delaware

R1#1	JAMES DOUGHERTY	25-26	1 Inf I	B ~1837 Ireland. R Wilmington, DE. Occ mason. E Sep 61 private. C Jul 2: wounds to right leg and left ankle. D Jul 3.
R1#2	S CASEY STEPHEN **CAREY**[6]	~31	2 Inf A	B ~1832 Ireland. R Middleton, New Castle Co., DE. Occ laborer. E May 61 private. C Jul 2. D Jul 3. Survivors (WC102628): W Mary ~41 in 1867 (M Jan 50); 2 ♀- Bridget 12, Mary 10.
R2#1	PETER BOSTER PETER **BOSTLER**	~21	2 Inf A	B ~1842 NYC. E (Dover, DE) May 61 private. C Jul 2. D Jul 9.
R2#2	JACOB STILES JACOB **STEITZ**	~44	2 Inf A	B ~1819 Philadelphia, PA. E (Philadelphia) May 61 private. Promoted to corporal on 3/1/62. C Jul 2: severe wound to right leg→amp. D Jul 8.
R2#3	__ DOWNEY			No killed Delaware soldier with this or similar name found in military sources.
R2#4	SERGT JACOB BOYD[7]	~26	2 Inf I	B ~1837 Cecil Co., MD. R Linwood, Delaware Co., DE. Occ blacksmith. E Oct 61 sergeant. Jul/Aug→Nov 62: absent on recruiting service. Appointed color sergeant of Company I. C Jul 2: wounded in the leg→amp. D Jul 6. Survivors (WC33164): W Elizabeth 23 (M Nov 61); 1 ♂- Jacob 7 months.
R2#5	A HUHN ADAM HUHN	23-24	1 Inf A	B ~1839 Philadelphia, PA. 1860: R Wilmington, New Castle Co., DE; occ brickmaker. E Aug 61 corporal. Jun 62: reduced to private for an unspecified infraction. Wounded 12/13/62 at Fredericksburg. Jan/Feb 63: absent in the hospital. C Jul 2. D Jul 3.
R2#6	LIEUT. GEO G PLANK GEORGE G PLANK	~29	2 Inf E	B ~1834 Germany. Occ druggist. Commissioned 2nd lieutenant (Philadelphia) Jun 61. Feb 63: served as hospital steward. KIA Jul 2.
R3#1	CORP W STONG WILLIAM STONG	~35	2 Inf D	B ~1828 PA. R Philadelphia, PA. 1850 occ: paper stainer. E June 61 private. Desertion and return from desertion on 4/2/62. Promoted to corporal on 1/1/63. KIA Jul 2. Survivors (WC22352): W Anna 34 (M Jan 48); 2 chn: 1 ♂- Harry 13 & 1 ♀- Clara 11.

---

6 **Delayed pension approval**. After initially being denied a widow's pension, Mrs. Mary Casey did eventually qualify for a pension in 1867 at a time Mrs. Casey and her two girls were residing back in Ireland.

7 **Color Sergeant's death**. Jason Boyd was serving as color sergeant for the 2nd Delaware Infantry Company I when mortally wounded on July 2nd.

R3#2	SERGT T SEYMORE THOMAS **SEYMOUR**	20-21	1 Inf B	B ~1842 Philadelphia, PA. R Wilmington, DE. Occ laborer. E Sep 61 private. Promoted to corporal on 3/19/62. Promoted to sergeant on 3/28/63. KIA Jul 3: struck directly in the chest by a 12-lb cannonball.
R3#3	WILLIAM DORSEY	22-23	1 Inf D	B ~1840 Philadelphia, PA. Occ farmer. E (Milford, DE) Sep 61 private. KIA Jul 3
R3#4	JOHN B SHEETS JOHN B **SHEETZ**	22-23	1 Inf D	B ~1840 Philadelphia, PA. Occ farmer. E (Milford, DE) Sep 61 private. Promoted to corporal on 9/28/62. Apr 63: absent on furlough. KIA Jul 3.
R3#5	T. P. CAREY THOMAS PAYNTER CAREY	21-22	1 Inf E	B 1841 Sussex Co., DE. Occ farmer. E (Georgetown, Sussex Co. DE) Sep 61 private. Wounded 12/13/62 at Fredericksburg. Jan/Feb 63: present with regiment. KIA Jul 3: shot in head.
R3#6	JOHN BLACK JOHN S BLACK	~21	1 Inf K	B ~1842 NJ. Occ farmer. E (Wilmington, DE) Oct 61 private. Captured 12/14/62 at Fredericksburg. Returned to duty from Camp Parole on 5/15/63. D Jul 3 of wounds.
R3#7	SERGT M CAVANAGH MICHAEL **CAVANAUGH**	25	2 Inf G	B 12/3/37 Ireland. E (Philadelphia) Jul 61 private. Sep/Oct 61: promotion to corporal. May 63: promotion to sergeant. KIA Jul 2 or D Jul 3.

> I YIELD HIM UNTO HIS
> COUNTRY AND HIS GOD

86th New York Monument in the Rose Woods

★ ★ ★ ★ ★

The Only Gettysburg Monument Featuring a Woman, Idealizing the Sacrifices of Women like the wife of Lieutenant Colonel Bra Chapin, their commanding officer who had been killed at Chancellorsville in May 1863.

Illinois

War with Spain

#1	O R KLEINKE 3 MO Inf D War with Spain			B ~1869 Chicago, IL. R same. Occ detective. E May 1998 private. Court martialed for AWOL on 7/11-13/98 and sentenced to forfeit $10 of pay. Admitted 8/10/1998 with typhoid fever to hospital at Camp Meade, PA. Died 8/25/1898 of bowel perforation (age 29). Remains directly transferred for interment in the Gettysburg National Cemetery. Survivors (WC486061): W Margaret 29 (M Mar 91); 1 ♂- Charles 3.
#2	HARRY PRAGER 2 Tenn Inf H (Spanish American War)			B ~1868 Memphis, TN. R Dyersburg, Dyer Co., TN. Occ blacksmith. E May 1898 private. May/Jun 1898: promotion to corporal. Detached to Santiago, Cuba from 7/15/1898. Died of an unspecified disease on 8/18/1898 (age 30). His remains were transferred for interment in the Gettysburg National Cemetery, occurring 9/19/98.
#3	O H THWEATT OTHER H THWEATT 2 Tenn Inf A (Spanish American War)			B ~1876 Hodgenville, LaRue Co., KY. R Nashville, TN. E Jun 1898 private. Admission to Camp Meade 2nd Corps hospital on 9/21/1898 and transferred on 9/24/1898 to the City Hospital at Harrisburg, PA. Died of typhoid fever on 10/13/1898 (age 22). His remains were buried on 10/15/1898 in the Gettysburg National Cemetery.
#4	JACOB J NOEL JACOB J **NOELL**[8] (71 Illinois Inf B)			B ~1843 Gettysburg, PA. E (Shannon, Carroll Co., IL) Jul 62 private. D/C 10/29/1862. Died 1/2/1901 (age 67).
R1#1	J WALLIKECK **ERNST WALLISCHECK**	38-39	82 Inf H	B ~1824. R Highland, IL. E Aug 62, private. Wounded and taken prisoner Jul 1: GSW to left knee. D Aug 6 at Seminary General Hospital.
R1#2	JOHN ELLIS	~23	12 Cav G	B ~1840. R Hancock, IL. E Jan 62 private. Mar 62: detached for daily duty as a hospital nurse. C Jul 1: severe wound in right arm→amp. D Aug 19.
R1#3	CHARLES W MINER[9] (MN WILLIAM)	19	70 NY Inf C	B 2/4/1844 Kewanee, Henry Co. IL. Occ farm laborer. E (Paw, Van Buren Co., MI) Apr 61 private. Captured 8/29/62 at 2nd Manassas. Deserted from Camp Parole 9/23/62. Returned from desertion 3/13/63. KIA Jul 2.

---

8 **Hometown burial honors**. Jacob Noell, born in Gettysburg, served one hundred days in an Illinois regiment. As a Gettysburg native and veteran, he received a post-Civil War burial in the National Cemetery.

9 **Identity question**. The Charles W Miner buried without a regimental notation within the Illinois plot is likely Charles William Miner of the 70th NY Regiment, as there is no record of any similarly-named Illinois soldier who was present at Gettysburg.

R1#4	DAVID DIEFFEUBAUGH DAVID DONER **DIFFENBAUGH** or **DEFIBAUGH**	27	8 Cav G		B 8/28/1835 Lancaster Co., PA. R Freeport, IL. Occ painter. E Sep 61 private. KIA Jul 1: shot in head while serving as orderly to Col. William Gamble, one of General Buford's brigade commanders. Survivors (WC40988→WC165190 not online): W Elizabeth 26 (M Aug 57| ReM 1867); 1 ♂ - George 3.
R1#5	JOHN ACKERMAN JOHN **ACKERMANN**[10]	~28	82 Inf K		B ~1835 Switzerland. R Chicago, IL. E Aug 62 private. May 63: promoted to corporal. D Jul 3 of wounds.

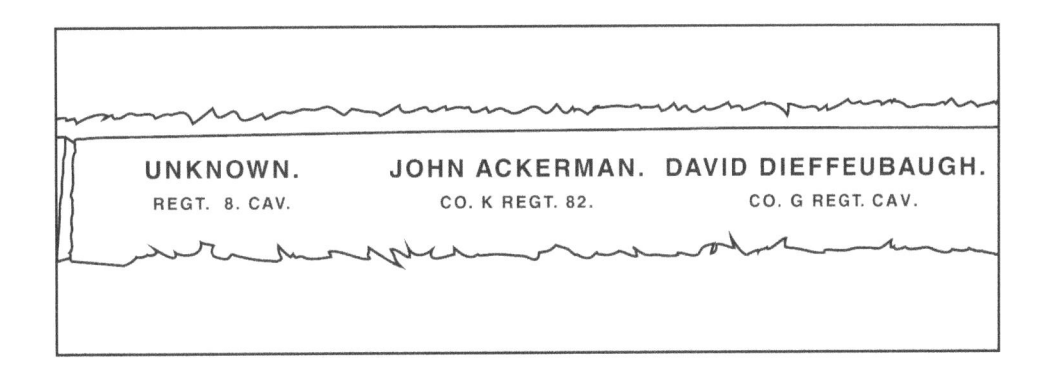

```
UNKNOWN.          JOHN ACKERMAN.   DAVID DIEFFEUBAUGH.
REGT. 8. CAV.     CO. K REGT. 82.  CO. G REGT. CAV.
```

Cemetery row segment in the Illinois plot

★ ★ ★ ★ ★

The 82nd Illinois Infantry reported 4 men killed at Gettysburg. Typical of the recovery and identification of bodies for the cemetery, only two of these men are buried with their names preserved.

---

10 **Death premonition**. In his service in prior battles, John Ackermann had proved himself a brave officer. However, seized upon by a death premonition on July 1st, Corporal Ackermann pleaded with his captain that he be excused from accompanying his company into the town streets at the base of Cemetery Hill, a dangerous mission risked to dislodge snipers there. Held back, he was paradoxically killed by an exploding Confederate shell that struck him on the unfortunate exact location on Cemetery Hill where he stood awaiting the return of his company.

Illinois 9

Indiana

R1#1	H. S. BROWN HENRY S BROWN	~25	14 Inf I	B ~1838 MD. R Vermillion Co, IN. Occ farm laborer. E June 61 private. Promoted to corporal during service. KIA Jul 2.
R1#3	A LISTER ABRAHAM LISTER[11]	~19	27 Inf F	B ~1844 Morgan Co., IN. R same. Occ farmer. E Sep 61 private. Wounded and captured 5/25/62 at Winchester, VA. Paroled on 9/13/62 at Aiken's Landing, VA. Returned to regiment on 10/9/62. Wounded in May 63 at Chancellorsville. KIA Jul 2: shot through the head during skirmishing. Survivor (WC32927): M Mrs. Nancy Lister 50 (widow of John Lister).
R1#8	THOMAS J WASSON	20	19 Inf B	B 2/2/1843 Richmond, Wayne Co., IN. R Wayne Co., IN. E Jul 61 private. Wounded 8/8/62. Aug/Sep 62: absent, in hospital. Mar/Apr 63: promoted to corporal. KIA Jul 1: shot in head.
R1#9	WM W STORY WILLIAM WALLACE STORY	24	3 Cav F	B 3/25/1839 Jefferson Co., OH. R Jefferson Co., IN. Occ miller. E Aug 61 private. C Jul 1: wound to left chest. D Jul 10.
R2#1	SERGT JEREMIAH DAVIS	21-22	20 Inf H	B ~1841 Dayton, Montgomery Co., OH. Occ farmer. E (Lafayette, Tippecanoe Co., IN) Sep 61 private. Mar/Apr 62: promoted to corporal. Promoted to sergeant on 11/1/62. KIA Jul 2.
R2#3	FRANCIS WALLACE	~29	14 Inf C	B ~1834 PA. 1860 R: Brown twp, Martin Co., IN. R Martin Co., IN. Occ farmer. E May 62 private. C Jul 2: shot in back. D Jul 4. Survivors (WC35273): Mary 20 (M Apr 60); 1 ♂ - William 2.
R2#4	R PAVY **HENRY CLAY** PAVY	22	3 Cav B	B 7/7/41 Switzerland Co., IN. R same. Occ farmer. E Feb 62 private. C Jul 1: wound to left elbow. D Jul 22.
R2#5	J ROBINSON JAMES ROBINSON	25-26	7 Inf K	B ~1837 Ireland. R Dearborn Co., IN. E (Lawrenceburg, Dearborn Co., IN) Aug 61 private. KIA Jul 3. Survivors (WC203164→WC293922 neither online) M Mrs. Martha Robinson 68 in 1879│ died 1881 (Daniel Robinson affirmed unable to support due to old age and physical disability│ he qualifies in 1881).

---

[11] **Soldier killed during skirmishing.** Abraham Lister was killed instantly by a shot to the head during skirmishing July 2nd for the 19th Indiana regiment. Out in the field beyond a regimental formation, the "cat and mouse" rouses of skirmishing could be instantly deadly for a soldier.

R2#6	F. W. SMITH FREDERICK W SMITH	26-27	27 Inv K	B ~1836. R Huntingburg, Dubois Co., IN. E Sep 61 private. C Jul 3: GSW to the right chest. D Jul 25.
R2#7	H AMBROSE HARRISON AMBROSE[12]	24	20 Inf H	B 6/15/1839 Ligonier, Westmoreland Co., PA. Height 6'8". 1860 R: Warren, Clinton Co., IN. R Marion Co., IN. Occ cabinet maker. E Oct 61 private. C Jul 2: compound fracture wound to left leg→amp. D Sep 8 from pyemia complication.
R2#8	A J CRABB ANDREW T CRABB	22-23	20 Inf D	B ~1840 OH. 1860: R Prairie, Warren Co., IN; occ farm laborer. R Fountain Co., IN. E Jul 61 private. Promoted to corporal during service. C Jul 2: wound to right knee. D Sep 20.
R2#9	SERGT GEO W BATCHELOR GEORGE W BATCHELOR	27-28	27 Inf H	B ~1835 OH. R Indianapolis, IN. 1860 occ: school teacher and farmer. E Sep 61 sergeant. Captured on 5/24/62 at Winchester, VA. Exchanged around 12/15/62. KIA Jul 3.
R2#10	WILLIAM TILLOTTSON	21	14 Inf I	B 12/5/41 Terre Haute, IN. R Vermillion Co., IN. Occ day laborer. E Jun 6 private. Wounded on 9/17/62 at Antietam. Jan/Feb 63: absent, in general hospital in NYC. Mar/Apr 63: returned to duty. KIA Jul 2.
R3#1	J K FLETCHER JOHN PARKER FLETCHER	~25	27 Inf F	B ~1838 IN. R Morgan Co., IN. Occ community school teacher, farmer. E Sep 61 corporal. Promoted sergeant on 2/13/63. KIA instantly Jul 3: chest wound.
R3#2	JESSIE WILLS JESSIE **WELLS**	23-24	27 Inf C	B ~1839 Clinton Co., IN. R same. Occ wagon maker. E Sep 61 private. Captured on 5/24/62 at Winchester, VA. Paroled on 9/19/62 at Aiken's Landing. KIA Jul 3: GSW to head. Survivor (WC86379): M Mrs. Ruth Wells 58 (widow of John Wells).
R3#3	SAMUEL R LEWIS[13]	17	27 Inf D	B ~1846 Lawrence Co., IN. R Bedford, Lawrence Co., IN. Occ farmer, miller. E Sep 61 drummer. Rank change to private on 10/20/61. KIA Jul 3: by reason of rifle ball breaking his neck.
R3#4	JOHN D NOBLE (MN DENNISON)	20-21	27 Inf K	B 1842 Dubois, Dubois Co., IN. R Knox Co., IN. Occ farmer. E Sep 61 private. KIA Jul 3.

---

12 **Tallest confirmed soldier in Cemetery**. At 6 feet 8 inches height, private Harrison Ambrose was a full foot above the height of the average Civil War soldier. He is also the tallest documented soldier buried in the National Cemetery.

13 **Minor at death**. Samuel Lewis's reported ages of 4 and 14 for the successive August 1850 and July 1860 U.S. Censuses attest to the strong likelihood that Samuel was not 18 at his September 1861 enlistment, but actually no older than 16. Perhaps due to an unit suspicion that he had been a minor, Samuel was enrolled in the unit as a drummer, an army position commonly allowed for underaged enlistees. However, in October, Samuel was promoted to an infantry private position. When Samuel was violently killed on July 3rd, he was likely only 17.

R3#5	JAMES CHAPMAN JAMES M CHAPMAN	23-24	27 Inf E	B ~1839 Parke Co., IN. R same. Occ farmer. E Sep 61 private. Wounded 8/9/62 at Cedar Mountain, VA on 8/9/62. Wounded on 9/17/62 at Antietam. Absent, in hospital through Jan/Feb 63. Promoted to corporal during service. KIA Jul 3. Survivor (WC89299): M Mrs. Nancy Chapman 49 (widow of Justice Chapman).
R3#6	J D LYNN JOSEPHUS DANIEL LYNN	21-22	27 Inf D	B ~1841. R Fayette, IN. E Sep 61 private. D Jul 3 of wounds. Survivor (WC14475): W Sally 29 (M Mar 61| ReM Jun 64); no chn.
R3#7	THOMAS J LETT (MN JEFFERSON)	19-20	27 Inf H	B 1843 Crawford, IN. R Jennings Co., IN. E Sep 61 private. KIA Jul 3.
R3#10	E McKNIGHT ELIJAH McKNIGHT	24	27 Inf F	B 2/22/39 Washington Co., IL. R New Philadelphia, Washington Co., IN. Occ farmer. E Sep 62 corporal. Wounded on 9/1762 at Antietam. Captured with imprisonment 12/20/62 at Bardstown, VA. Paroled between 12/20/62 and 1/10/63. Promoted to sergeant on 4/11/63. KIA Jul 3.
R3#11	D T DAVID DANIEL T DAVID	25-26	27 Inf G	B ~1837 Brown Co., IN. R same. Occ farmer. E Sep 61 private. Wounded on 9/17/62 at Antietam. KIA Jul 3.
R4#1	JOHN SHEHAN[14] ORDERLY GEN GIBBONS	38	Orderly	B 12/31/1824 Ireland. E May 55 private. KIA Jul 3, killed instantly by either the signal shell or an early shell initiating the July 3rd Confederate cannonade.
R4#2	A G WRIGHT **DANIEL** G WRIGHT	~24	20 Inf A	B 1839 Botetourt Co, VA. R Miami City, Miami Co., IN. Occ blacksmith. E Jul 61 private. C Jul 2: GSW to left hip. D Jul 21.
R4#3	C E WISHMYER CHARLES E **WISHMERE**	20-21	27 Inf A	B ~1842 Hancock Co., IN. R Indianapolis, IN. Occ farmer. E Sep 61 private. Wounded on 8/9/62 at Cedar Mountain, VA. Sep/Oct 62: hospitalized in Alexandria, then Newark, NJ. C Jul 3: hand wound. D Jul 16: tetanus complication.
R4#4	L C ANTRIM LEVI COLUMBUS ANTRIM OR ANTHRUM	23-24	27C	B ~1839 OH. R Brown Co, IN. Occ farmer. E Sep 61 private. KIA Jul 3.

---

14 **Identity question**. John Shehan would be a common name for an Irish army enlistment soldier. This individual with this birthdate is based on a Fold3.com posting.

R4#5	D C CALVIN DANIEL JAMES COLVIN[15]	33-34	27 Inf C	B 1829 Bartholomew Co., IN. R same. Occ laborer. E Sep 61 private. C Jul 3: wounded in right knee. D Jul 6. Survivors (WC102200): W Rebecca 31 (M Jul 53 | ReM 1866); 5 chn (4 ♂ and 1 ♀): Andrew 9, twins George Washington & Martha Washington 5, John 4, Corrilius 2. .
R4#6	JOHN TICE	~21	20 Inf A	B ~1842 Willistown, Chester Co., PA. R Miami Co, IN. Occ farmer. E Jul 61 private. Promoted to corporal on 7/1/62. KIA Jul 2.
R4#7	ORD SERGT E TUMEY* ELIJAH TUMEY[16]	34-35	27 Inf D	B 1828 Mercer Co., KY. R Lawrence Co., IN. Occ farmer, cooper. E Sep 61 private. Promoted to sergeant on 3/20/62. Wounded 8/9/62 at Cedar Mountain, VA. Wounded 9/17/62 at Antietam. C3 Jul 3: GSW to right knee. D Jul 6. Survivors (WC14474→WC155932 neither online): W Mary 36 (M Sep 54 | ReM 1865); 6 chn: 2 ♂ (with 1st wife Mahala) William 15, Henry 14 | 3 ♂ & 1 ♀ (with 2nd wife Mary): Thomas 6, George 4, Theodore 6 months & 1 ♀ Emeline 7.
R4#8	LEVI BULLA	~20	20 Inf G	B ~1843. R Tippecanoe Co., IN. E Jul 61 private. KIA Jul 2.
R4#9	JAMES W WHITLOW	23-24	19 Inf B	B 1839 KY. R Wayne Co, IN. Occ day laborer. E Jul 61 private. C Jul 1. D Jul 5.
R4#10	JESSE SMITH	20	3 Cav D	B ~May 1843 Dearborn, IN. R same. Occ farmer. E Feb 62 private. KIA Jul 1.
R4#11	GEORGE BALES[17]	25-26	27 Inf A	B ~1837. R New Salem, Rush Co., IN. E Sep 61 private. KIA Jul 3: GSW to heart. Survivors (WC18655→WC154356): W Nancy 28 (M Jan 59 | ReM 1868): 2 chn: 1 ♀ - Sophonia 19 months and Nancy approximately 7 months pregnant with 1 ♂ George, who would be born on 9/22/63). [18]
R4#12	T HUNT THADDEUS HUNT	~19	27 Inf A	B 1844 Hendricks Co., IN. R Amo, Hendricks Co., IN. E Sep 61 private. Wounded slightly in right arm on 5/03/63 at Chancellorsville, VA. KIA Jul 3.

---

15 **Soldier's choice of children's names shows his patriotism.** In the 19th century, ordinary citizens could honor U.S. Presidents or other admired leaders by giving the names of these men to their children. Daniel Colvin took this convention one step further by naming his twins born in 1859 George Washington Colvin and Martha Washington Colvin. His death at Gettysburg would leave his widow with five children under the age of ten.

16 **Soldier's choice of children's names shows his patriotism.** With his new wife Mary, Elijah Tumey named his first two children: first, Thomas Jefferson Tumey in 1857, then George Washington Tumey in 1859 (readers may make what they want out of this ordering).

17 **Soldier killed reportedly under a flag of truce.** A FindAGrave posting reports that George Bales was killed instantly while attempting under a flag of truce to retrieve a wounded man from the field.

18 **Soldier's widow seven-months pregnant with couple's second child at soldier's death.** Mrs. Nancy Bales was pregnant with couple's second child, George, who would be born 9/22/63.

Indiana 13

ID	Name	Age	Unit	Details
R5#1	P UMPHILL PETER **UMPHRESS** or **UMPHREYS**	21-22	27 Inf D	B ~1841. R Bryantsville, Lawrence Co., IN. Occ farmer. E Sep 61 private. Wounded on right cheek on 5/3/63 at Chancellorsville, VA. C Jul 3: wounded on the right side. D Jul 4. Survivor (WC16814): M Mrs. Bethiah Umphreys 42 (widow of John Umphreys).
R5#2	J GILMORE JOSEPH SHIELDS **GILMORE**[19]	35	27 Inf I	B 6/23/1828 Preble Co., OH. R Putnam Co., IN. Occ farmer. E Sep 61 sergeant. Reduced to private on 3/28/62 for an unspecified infraction. C Jul 3: wounded severely in right side. D Jul 4. Survivors (WC23799): W Rebecca 33 (M Mar 56 | ReM 1868); 3 chn: 2 ♀- Mary 6 and Josie (Rebecca approximately 5 months pregnant with Josie, who would be born on 12/18/63) & 1 ♂ John 4.
R5#3	E STALLUP ELI **STALCUP**	21-22	27 Inf K	B ~1841 IN. R Jasper, Pike Co., IN. Occ farmer. E Sep 61 private. KIA Jul 3 GSW to the head.
R5#4	J GARDNER JACOB **GARDNER**	~29	27 Inf K	B 1834 Germany. R Jaspar, Pike Co., IN. Occ farmer, plasterer. E Sep 61 private. private. C Jul 3: severe wound to left leg→amp. D Jul 28.
R5#5	SILAS UPHAM	38	19 Inf G	B 1/9/1825 Butler, Wayne Co., NY. R Elkhart Co., IN. E Jul 61 private. Promoted to corporal during service. C Jul 1. D Jul 13.
R5#6	JOHN E WEAVER (MN EDWARD)	~21	3 Cav D	B 1842 IN. R Switzerland Co., IN. Occ wagon maker. E Feb 62 private. C Jul 1: severe wound left leg→amp. D Aug 30.
R5#7	SERGT A C LAMB ALONZO H **LAMB**	~22	20 Inf E	B ~1841 VT. R Laporte Co., IN. Occ farm laborer. E Jul 61 corporal. Promotion to 1st sergeant during service. C Jul 2: shot through chest with fracture of vertebrae. D Jul 4 or 6.
R5#8	SERGT G H REDRICK GEORGE H **REDDICK**	~30	20 Inf F	B 1833 IL. R Cass Co., IN. Occ tinner. E Jul 61 corporal. Promotion to sergeant during service. C Jul 2: severe wound in left leg→amp. D Jul 6.
R5#9	P A BUSSARD PHILIP A **BUSSARD**	20	20 Inf K	B 8/7/42 Bedford PA. R White Co., IN. Occ farm laborer. E Jul 61 private. Promotion to corporal during service. C Jul 2. D Jul 4 or 8.
R5#10	J WILLIAMS **ISAAC** WILLIAMS	~20	20 Inf B	B ~1843. R Lake Co., IN. E (Lafayette, Tippecanoe Co., IN) Jul 61 private. C Jul 2: wounded in abdomen. D Jul 5.

---

19 **Soldier's widow five month's pregnant with couple's second child at soldier's death.** Mrs. Rebecca Gilmore was pregnant with the couple's third child, Josie, who would be born 12/18/63.

R5#11	C SHOWALTER CHRISTOPHER SHOWALTER	24-25	27 Inf A	B ~1838 PA. R Putnam Co., IN. Occ farm laborer. E Sep 61 private. Wounded in right leg on 9/17/62 at Antietam. Promoted to corporal on 9/17/62. Deserted regiment on 2/15/63 and returned to regiment on 5/27/63. C Jul 3: wounds to the left arm and right thigh. D Jul 22. Survivor (WC94695 not online): M Mrs. Sarah Showalter ~40 in 1867 (widow of Jacob Showalter).
R5#12	E HOLT **LYFUS** HOLT	23-24	27 Ind G	B ~1839 IN. R Martin Co., IN. Occ farm laborer. E Aug 62 private. C Jul 3: wounded in the head. D Jul 22.
R6#1	H K 6 H			No killed Gettysburg Indiana soldier with these initials identified in military sources.
R6#2	JOSHUA RICHMOND	19	20 Inf B	B ~Jun 1844 Canada. E (Indianapolis, IN) Aug 62 private. Occ farmer. Detached to ambulance service 10/16/62 →Jan/Feb 63. KIA Jul 2.
R6#3	GEORGE SYLVESTER GEORGE **EDGERSTON**[20]	~21	20 Inf B	B ~1842 Winfield, Lake Co., IN. R Lake Co., IN. E Jul 61 private. KIA Jul 2.
R7#1	LIEUT R JONES RICHARD JONES	22-23	19 Inf B	B ~1840 IN. R Centerville, Wayne Co., IN. Occ farm laborer. E Jul 61 corporal. Promoted to sergeant during service. Commissioned 2nd lieutenant on 3/15/63. KIA Jul 1: wound to head.
R7#2	SERT T DOUGHERTY THOMAS **DAUGHERTY**	23-24	19 Inf K	B ~1839 Warren Co., OH. R Delaware Co., IN. Occ farmer. E Jul 61 private. Promoted to corporal on 1/25/62. Promoted to sergeant on 11/1/62. KIA Jul 1.
R7#3	JAMES STICKLEP JAMES **STICKLEY**	26-27	19 Inf C	B 1836 OH. R Randolph Co., IN. Occ day laborer. E Jul 61 private. KIA Jul 1: GSW to abdomen.
R7#4	W HOOVER WILLAM HOOVER	24-25	19 Inf C	B ~1838 Dark Co., OH. R Randolph Co., IN. Occ farmer. E Jul 61 private. KIA Jul 1: GSW to the head.
R7#5	ALEXANDER BURK	22-23	19 Inf C	B ~1840 Randolph Co., IN. E Dec 61 private. KIA Jul 1: GSW to the groin.

---

20 **Identity question.** There is no killed George Sylvester at Gettysburg, 20th Indiana infantry or otherwise, in military sources. There was, however, a George Edgerton of the 20th Indiana Company B, who was killed at Gettysburg. The burial at this to the immediate left of Joshua Richmond, a soldier of the 20th Indiana Company B, allows speculation that this is George Edgerton who has been misidentified on this gravestone.

R7#6	R CLARK **REUBEN CLARK**[21]	~32	19 Inf C	B ~1831 Wayne Co., IN. R Randolph Co., IN. Occ carpenter. E Jul 61 private. KIA Jul 1: GSW to head.
R7#7	A SULGROOF **ELKANAH SULGROVE**[22]	27-28	19 Inf F	B ~1835 IN. R Marion Co., IN. E Jul 61 private. Occ farm laborer. Nov/Dec 62: promoted to corporal. KIA Jul 1: shot through the breast, causing instant death. Survivor (WC34045): M Mrs. Lucinda Potter 50 (widow of Jacob Sulgrove and of 2nd husband Daniel Potter).
R7#9	PETER L FOUST **PETER LUDWIG FOUST**[23]	28-29	19 Inf C	B ~1834 Randolph Co., IN. R same. Occ farmer. E Aug 62 private. KIA Jul 1: GSW to head. Survivors (WC95141): W Sarah 24 (M Jun 56| ReM 1865); 2 chn: 1 ♀- Elizabeth 4 & 1 ♂- Peter, Jr. 7 months.
R7#10	WILLIAM SIMMONS	43-44	19 Inf E	B ~1819 OH. R Delaware Co., IN. Occ laborer. E Jul 61 private. KIA Jul 2. Survivors (WC21082): W Sarah ~40 (M Sep 49); 1 ♂ Samuel William Simmons 13.
R7#11	SERGEANT J FERGUSON **BJAMES M FURGASON**	19-20	19 Inf H	B ~1843 Johnson Co., IN. R same. Occ blacksmith. E Jul 61 musician. Rank change to private on 9/1/61. Nov/Dec 62: promoted to corporal. Promoted to sergeant on 1/1/63. Apr 63: 15-day furlough. KIA Jul 1: GSW to head. Survivor (WC40545): M Mrs. Mary Furgason 53 in 1864 (widow of William Furgason).
R7#12	WESLEY SMITH	22-23	20 Inf A	B ~1840 OH. R Miami Co., IN. E Jul 61 private. KIA Jul 2.
R7#13	AMOS D ASHE AMOS D **ASH**	~29	20 Inf A	B ~1834 Bedford, PA. R Miami Co., IN. Occ carpenter. E Jul 61 private. Detached as a teamster: Aug→Oct 62 and Jan 63. KIA Jul 2.
R7#14	JOHN SAGER JOHN M SAGER	20-21	20 Inf A	B ~1842. R Miami Co., IN. E Jul 61 private. KIA Jul 2.

---

21 **Birth year question**. An Ancestry.com family tree gives Reuben Clark's birthdate in April 1833. However, Clark's enlistment card in his service file records that he reported his age as 30 at his July 1861 enlistment.

22 **Mother's pension approval comes too late**. Mrs. Lucinda Potter had been dependent on portions of the army pay sent to her by her oldest son, Elkanah Sulgrove. On August 1, 1863, Mrs. Potter initiated the procedure for qualifying for a dependent mother's pension. Due to administrative delays, her eligibility for a pension would not be accepted until November 1864. This acceptance would provide little comfort to Mrs. Potter, who had died prematurely the previous month at age 51 due to emphysema.

23 **Soldier's elderly, widowed mother informed she's ineligible for pension**. Peter Foust's widow, Sarah, remarried, would die in 1872, only nine years after he was killed at Gettysburg. However, a dependent minors' pension would continue to their children until the youngest, Peter Jr., reached age 16 in 1878. In 1887, Peter Foust's 85-year-old widowed mother, also Sarah Foust, applied to the U.S. Pension Office for a dependent mother's pension based on being impoverished and dependent on persons not obligated to her support. The Pension Office rejected her application, basically asserting that even in this non-concurrent circumstance, there could not be two separate pension-recipient parties.

16   Abraham Lincoln's Honored Dead at the Gettysburg National Cemetery

20th Indiana Infantry Monument in the Rose Woods, viewed from the John Wheeler boulder

★ ★ ★ ★ ★

Colonel John Wheeler, commanding the 20th Indiana Infantry, was shot from his horse July 2nd at site of this boulder. John Wheeler is buried at the Maplewood Cemetery in Crown Point, Lake County, Indiana.

Maine

R1#1	ALBION B MILLS[24]	16	16 Inf E	B 12/4/1846 Eaton, Carroll Co., NH. R Vassalboro, Kennebec Co., ME. E Aug 62 private. C Jul1: severe wound of right leg→ amp. D Oct 7.
R1#2	JOHN MERRIAM[25]	33	19 Inf D	B 10/11/29 Morrill, Waldo Co., ME. R same. Occ farmer. E Aug 62 corporal. C Jul 2: wound to left leg→amp. D Aug 15. Survivors (WC22728→WC78219)): W Hannah 34 (M May 58| ReM Mar 64): 1 ♂- Charles 6 months. John's brother Elisha receives guardianship of Charles following Hannah surrendering of her pension with her remarriage.
R1#3	ABIJAH CROSBY	37-38	19 Inf C	B ~1825 ME. R Benton, Kennebec Co., ME. Occ day laborer. E Aug 62 private. C Jul 2: severe wound to left leg→amp. D Jul 12.
R1#4	CORP R SCULLEY RICHARD SCULLEY	38-39	7 Inf K	B 1824 Canada. R Castleton, New Brunswick. E Aug 61 private. Promotion to corporal during service. C Jul 3. D Jul 4.
R1#5	CORP A H COLE AMOS HITCHINGS COLE	20	3 Inf F	B 7/14/42 Mercer, Somerset Co., ME. R Starks, Somerset Co., ME. 1860 occ: community school teacher. E Jun 61 private. Promoted to corporal on 9/01/61. KIA Jul 2.
R1#6	JOHN W JONES	~24	3 Inf B	B ~1839 Portland, ME. R Augusta, ME. E June 61 private. Captured at 7/21/61 at 1st Bull Run. C Jul 2. D Jul 4. Survivor (WC22729): W Rachel 27 (M Jul 62); no chn.
R1#7	HENRY S SMALL	~21	3 Inf S	B ~1842. R Bath, Sagadahoc Co., ME. E June 61 private. Promotion to sergeant major during service. KIA Jul 2.

---

24 **Minor at death**. Enlisting into the army on August 14, 1862, Albion Mills gave his age as 18. However, an Ancestry.com public family tree reports Mills' birthday reports his birthdate as December 4, 1846. This birthday agrees entirely with Mills' age of 13 given on the June 19, 1860 U.S. Census. This birthday would also mean that he was 15, not 18 at his army enlistment and further than he was only 16 when he would be killed at Gettysburg the following year.

25 **Soldier loses two young children the month before Gettysburg**. In June 1863, or one month prior to his mortal wounding at Gettysburg, John Merriam would lose his four-year-old son and his two-year-old daughter to medical illness. Only one infant son would survive him.

R1#8	CORP J L LITTLE JOHN LANGDON LITTLE[26]	24	3 Inf A	B 2/8/1839. R Bath, Sagadahoc Co., ME. Occ mariner. E Jun 61 private. Promotion to corporal during service. Kearny Cross recipient. KIA Jul 2.
R1#9	CALVIN H BURDIN	23	3 Inf I	B 1/15/1840. R Augusta, ME. E Jun 61 private. Captured at 1st Bull Run on 7/21/61. KIA Jul 2 or 3: killed instantly purportedly from a head wound fired by an enemy sharpshooter. Survivors (WC43984): M Mrs. Mary Burdin 49 (James Burdin III affirmed unable to perform labor).
R1#10	CAPT JOHN C KEEN JOHN COBURN **KEENE**	29	3 Inf K	B 1/19/34 Greene, Androscoggin Co., ME. R Leeds, Androscoggin Co., ME. Occ shoemaker. E Jun 61 private. Promoted to 1st sergeant. Promoted to captain during service. KIA Jul 2. Survivor (WC41630): 1 ♀- Annie 2 (W Josephine died 9/13/62).
R1#11	SERGT NELSON W JONES	~20	3 Inf I	B 1843 Palermo, Waldo Co., ME. R same. E Jun 61 private. Promoted sergeant in 1862. D Jul 2 of wounds. Survivors (WC19616): M Mrs. Hannah Jones 57 (Nelson Jones affirmed unable to perform labor).
R1#12	J BARTLETT			No Killed Gettysburg soldier with this name found in military sources.
R2#1	CAPT G D SMITH GEORGE D SMITH	27-28	19 Inf I	B ~1835 Readfield, Kennebec, ME. R Rockland, Knox Co., ME. 1860: occ music teacher. Commissioned 2nd lieutenant in Aug 62. Promoted to captain in 1863. KIA Jul 2: penetrating wound to left lung.
R2#2	JOSEPH D SIMPSON	36	20 Inf A	B 5/30/37 Quebec, Canada. R Waterville, Kennebec co., ME. Occ laborer. E Aug 62 private. C Jul 2: shot in neck. D Jul 3. Survivors (WC122219): W Henrietta 22 (M Mar 56| ReM 1868); 3 chn: 2 ♂- George 5, David 1 & 1 ♀- Paulena 3.
R2#3	MOSES DAVIS	34-35	20 Inf C	B ~1828. B Limington, York Co., ME. R Aroostook Co., ME. Occ farmer. E Aug 62 private. C Jul 2. D Jul 4.
R2#4	CORP S C BROOKINGS SAMUEL C BROOKINGS	21-22	19 Inf H	B 1841 Pittston, Kennebec Co., IN. R same. Occ farm laborer. E Aug 62 private. Promotion to corporal in 1863. D of wounds Jul 2 or 3. Survivor (WC23019): M Mrs. Lydia Brookings 49 (widow of Lewis Brookings).

---

26 **Kearny Cross recipient killed at Gettysburg**. Corporal John Little had been a Kearny Cross recipient. Although there are no Congressional Medal of Honor recipients buried in the Gettysburg National Cemetery, Corporal John Little had been a recipient of the prestigious Kearny Cross. Congressional Medals of Honor most commonly went to Union soldiers who succeeded in capturing a Confederate unit's flag during battle. Beginning in 1862, Kearny Crosses were awarded as tokens of unofficial acknowledgement to men in the III Corps 1st Division, who in the spirit of Major General Philip Kearny, had performed an act of extreme bravery in the face of the enemy.

R2#5	CORP W K WILLARD PINKHAM	44	20 Inf D	B 1/16/19 Bath, Sagadahoc Co., ME. R Charleston, Penobscot Co., ME. Occ farmer. E Aug 62 private. Promoted corporal during service. KIA Jul 2. Survivors (WC17740): W Abigail 52 (M Apr 43); 1 ♀- Mary 17.
R2#6	GEORGE S NOYES	28-29	20 Inf K	B 1834 Pownal, Cumberland Co., ME. R same. Occ farmer. E Aug 62 sergeant. KIA Jul 2: wounded in lungs.
R2#8	MICHAEL RARIDEN[27]	~37	4 Inf K	B ~1826 Ireland. R Belfast, Waldo Co., ME. Occ laborer. E Jun 61 private. C Jul 2: shot in left thigh. D Jul 24. Survivors (WC71093); 4 chn: 3 ♂- John 12, William 10, Thomas 6 & 1 ♀- Mary 8. (W Ellen M Mar 49| D Feb 63).
R2#9	SULLIVAN LUCE	22	5 Batt LA	B Oct 1840 ME. R Auburn, Androscoggin Co., ME. Occ shoemaker. E Dec 61 private. D Jul 3 of wounds.
R2#10	W H SMITH WILLIAM H SMITH	18	7 Inf K	B 4/21/45 Edmunds, Washington Co., ME. R same. Occ farmer. E Dec 62 private. C Jul 3: wound causing compound fracture of femur. D Sep 1.
R2#11	WILLIAM H DAY[28] WILLIAM HENRY DAY	19	17 Inf F	B 8/15/43 Brownfield, Oxford Co., ME. R same. E Aug 62 private. C Jul 2: wound to left shoulder. D Aug 31. Survivor (WC35562): M Mrs. Eliza Day 58 in 1864 (widow of Alvah Day).
R2#12	R FINCH 17 Inf E			A killed Gettysburg soldier in this regiment with this name or similar name not found in military sources.
R2#13	CROSBY R BROOKINGS	24	4 Inf G	B 7/24/39 Whitefield, Lincoln Co., ME. R Wiscasset, Lincoln Co., ME. Occ millman. E Jun 61 private. Captured at Bull Run on 7/21/61. Exchanged POW on 1/1/62. Promoted to sergeant in Jul 63. C Jul 2: shot in right knee. D Aug 7 of wound complicated by chronic diarrhea. Survivors (WC140165) M Mrs. Fanny Brookings 54 in 1869 (Samuel Brookings affirmed disabled).
R3#2	GOODWIN S IRELAND[29] (MN SILAS)	18-19	20 Inf H	B ~1844 Cooper, Washington Co., ME. R Presque Isle, Aroostook Co., ME. E Aug 62 private. KIA Jul 3.

---

27 **Soldier's death orphans his already motherless four children.** Michael Rariden's wife, Ellen, had predeceased him in February, 1863. With his death five months later, Rariden left four fully orphaned, pre-teen children.

28 **Soldier's mother loses him, then husband ten days later.** Mrs. Eliza Day's loss of her son William Day on Aust 31st had been tragically preceded just ten days earlier of her husband, Alvah Day.

29 **Brother and paternal uncle enlist with soldier on same day.** Enlisting August 29, 1862 into the 20th Maine along with Goodwin Ireland were his oldest brother John and a paternal uncle Otis, all three mustering into Company H. Otis Ireland would die of disease in December, 1862. John Ireland would survive the war and muster out of the regiment in 1865. Otis Ireland would die of disease during this service.

R3#4	ORRIN WALKER[30]			Misidentified soldier in grave
R3#8	CORP W S HODGDEN WILLIAM S **HODGDON**	16	20 Inf F	B 12/4/46 Embden, Somerset Co., ME. R same. E Aug 62 musician. Rank change to private during service. Promoted to corporal in 1863. D Jul 2 of wounds. Survivors (WC122347 not online): M Nancy ~36 (James Hodgdon affirmed disabled).
R3#9	CORP M C DAY MELVILLE C DAY	21-22	20 Inf G	B ~1841 ME. R Jefferson, Lincoln Co., ME. E Aug 62 private. Promoted corporal in 1863, served at color corporal. KIA Jul 2.
R3#10	SERGT CHAS W STEEL CHARLES WESLEY **STEELE**[31]	34	20 Inf H	B 5/29/29 ME. R Oakfield plantation, Aroostook Co., ME. Occ farmer. E Aug 62 sergeant. Promoted to 1st sergeant during service. C Jul 2: GSW to chest. D Jul 2. Survivor (WC12769): M Mrs. Abigail Steele 68 (widow of Rev. Joel Steele).
R4#1	SAMUEL O HATCH	29	17 Inf K	B 3/5/1834 Lewiston, ME. R same. Occ brickmaker. E Aug 62 private. D Jul 2 of wound in right side. Survivors (WC48757): 2 ♂- Willie 5, John 3 (from 1st wife Elvira, married Jun 56 and divorced Apr 61); W Asa 36 (M Jan 63).
R4#2	SERGT I N LATHROP ISAAC N LATHROP	24-25	20 Inf H	B ~1838 IL. R Bangor, ME. E Aug 62 private. Promoted to sergeant during service. C Jul 2: shot in abdomen. D Jul 5.
R4#3	BENJAMIN W GRANT	20-21	20 Inf F	B ~1842 ME. R Cornville, Somerset Co., ME. E Aug 62 private. Sick in hospital at Antietam 10/30→12/25/62. C Jul2: shot in abdomen. D Jul 5. Survivor (WC95737): M Mrs. Rachel Grant 47 in 1866 (Moses Grant affirmed disabled).
R4#4	CORP S C DAVIS SAMUEL C DAVIS	24-25	17 Inf B	B ~1838 ME. R Portland, ME. Occ farm laborer. E Aug 62 corporal. C Jul 2: wounded in left chest. D Jul 4.

---

30 **Misidentified soldier in grave**. Orin Walker's service record confirms that he was seriously wounded on Jul 2nd but that he was receiving care at the U.S. General Hospital at York, PA in Sep/Oct 63. The Frey burial book of battlefield burials notes the presence of his grave at the Jacob Weikert farm alongside others of the 20th Maine who had died there of their wounds. However, his service records reports that he was mustered out of the army in 1865. Finally, the 1880 U.S. Census shows him returned to his prewar residence in Stoneham, Maine.

31 **Did soldier really die suddenly from chest gunshot on Little Round Top**? An oft-repeated account of a sudden death at Gettysburg is that of Sergeant. Charles Steele exclaiming to his Capt. Joseph Land "I am going, Captain," immediately after receiving a minié ball to the chest. However, had Sergeant Steele died immediately from his wound, he would have been buried on Little Round Top. Rather, Jacob Frey's burial notebook reported that Steele was buried on the Jacob Weikert property, the site of the 5th Corps field hospital. This burial location suggests that Steele lingered enough time following being shot to be taken to the field hospital. Reviews of Civil War hospital logs often reveal soldiers lingering for days from wounds one might be inclined to think would have caused instant death, chest and head wounds being frequent examples of this situation. As a separate point of interest, Steele's father, Rev. Joel Steele, had been much-beloved Methodist circuit preacher, who died in 1846 when Charles was 17 years old.

R4#5	ROYAL RAND	38-39	17 Inf H	B ~1824 ME. R Windham, Cumberland Co., ME. Occ shoemaker. E Aug 62 private. C Jul 2: shot in abdomen. D Jul 3. Survivor (WC34794): W Mary 35 (M Oct 51); no chn.
R4#6	CHARLES E HERRIMAN CHARLES E **HARRIMAN**[32]	18	19 Inf E	B 1845 Bangor, ME. R Searsport, Waldo Co., ME. Occ working on father's farm. E Aug 62 private. C Jul 3: severe wound in left leg→ amp. D Jul 10.
R4#7	CORP G H WILLEY GEORGE H WILLEY	20-21	19 Inf H	B ~1842 ME. R Clinton, Kennebec Co., ME. Occ farmer. E Aug 62 corporal. C Jul 2. D Jul 24.
R4#8	WILLIAM H HUNTINGTON	34	16 Inf B	B 8/24/1828 Gardiner, Kennebec Co., ME. R same. Occ farm hand. E Aug 62 private. C Jul 1. D Jul 9.
R4#9	HARRISON PULLEN	18-19	16 Inf G	B 1844 ME. R Anson, Somerset Co., ME. Occ: working on father's farm. E Aug 62 private. C Jul 1. D Jul 18.
R4#10	EDWARD CUNNINGHAM	23-24	1 Cav L	B ~1839 ME. R Patten, Penobscot Co., ME. 1860: occ community school teacher. E Nov 61 private. KIA Jul 3: while serving as orderly to Gen. Doubleday, decapitated by a missile.
R4#11	M QUINT MONROE QUINT	~19	17 Inf B	B 1844 Conway, Carroll Co., NH. R Stow, Oxford Co., ME. Occ: working on father's farm. E Aug 62 private. KIA Jul 2.
R4#12	ALSBURY LUCE	19-20	3 Inf F	B ~1843 ME. R Norridgewock, Somerset Co., ME. Occ farmhand. E Jun 61 private. Wounded on 5/31/62 at Fair Oaks, VA. Desertion from regiment 1/21→26/63. KIA Jul 2. Survivor (WC83628): M Mrs. Mary Luce 55 in 1865 (widow of Alsbury Luce).
R4#13	CORP E FARRINGTON EBEN FARRINGTON	~26	3 Inf H	B 1837 ME. R Livermore, Androscoggin Co., ME. Occ factory operative. E Oct 62 private. Promotion to corporal. D Jul 2 of wounds. Survivor (WC16384): W Ann Elizabeth 25 (M Dec 61| ReM Jun 66); no chn.
R5#1	GEORGE F JOHNSON	~21	4 Inf K	B ~1842. R Windham, Cumberland Co., ME. E Jun 61 private. Feb 62→detached service for one year on western gunboat. C Jul 2: severe wound in left arm. D Jul 9.
R5#2	____ickels			No killer soldier could be identified with this scant information.

---

32 **Minor at enlistment**. Charles Harriman's ages of 5 and 15 on the successive August 1850 and June 1860 U.S. Census reports strongly supports that he was not 18, but likely 17 at his August 1862 enlistment. If accurate, Charles was likely only 18 when he would die at Gettysburg.

R5#3	CORP GEO W JONES GEORGE WASHINGTON JONES	33-34	17 Inf B	B ~1829. R Portland, ME. Occ brick mason. E Aug 62 private. Promoted to corporal IN 1862. C Jul 2: wounded in left thigh. D Jul 23. Survivor (WC24358): W Sarah 24 (M Nov 56| ReM Apr 84); 2 ♂- Albert 4, George E. Jones 2.
R5#4	SERGT E S ALLEN EBENEZER SMALL ALLEN	42	3 Inf D	B 2/21/1821 Bowdoin, Sagadahoc Co., ME. R Bath, Sagadahoc Co., ME. Occ carpenter. E Jun 61 corporal. Promoted to ordinance sergeant during service. Wounded 9/01/62 at Chantilly, VA. C Jul 2: severe wound to left leg→amp. D Aug 6 or 7. Survivor (WC104038): W Sophia 33 (M Feb 48); no chn.
R5#5	IRA L MARTIN (MN LEWIS)	23-24	17 Inf H	B ~1839 Sebago, Cumberland Co., ME. R same. 1860 occ: working on father's farm. E Aug 62 private. C Jul 2. D Aug 4. Survivor (WC137997): M Mrs. Sally Martin 62 in 1868 (widow of Robert Martin).
R5#6	JOHN F SHUMAN (MN FRANKLIN)	19	4 Inf K	B 8/11/1843 Belfast, Waldo Co., ME. R same. Occ: working on father's farm. E June 61 private. C Jul 2: severe wound in right arm→amp. D Jul 15.
R5#8	CORP B HOGAN BERNARD HOGAN	30	17 Inf D	B 1/11/33 Biddeford, York Co., ME. R Lewiston, Androscoggin Co., ME. Occ mill hand. E Aug 62 corporal. C Jul 2: wounded in left hip. D Jul 23. Survivors (WC22785): W Elizabeth (M Mar 53); 1 ♀- Florine 5.
R5#9	LIEUT G M BRAGG	19	4 Inf F	B 2/12/1844 Lincolnville, Waldo Co., ME. R same. Occ farm laborer. E Jun 61 corporal. Wounded at 2nd Bull Run on 8/29/62. Commissioned 2nd lieutenant on 1/1/63. Promoted to 1st lieutenant on Jul 2. C2 Jul 2. D Jul 5.
R5#10	WILLIAM H SHOVEY WILLIAM H **SHOREY**[33]	19-20	19 Inc F	B ~1843 ME. R Monmouth, Kennebec Co., ME. Occ farm laborer. E Jul-Aug 62 private. C Jul 2: GSW through right shoulder. D Jul 4. Survivor (WC23023): M Mrs. Sophronia Shorey 58 (widow of Joseph Shorey).
R5#11	JAMES ROBBINS	33-34	19 Inf D	B ~1829. R Belfast, Waldo Co., ME. Occ seaman. E Aug 62 private. C Jul 2. D Jul 4 or 5.

---

33 **Identity question.** Some sources report that Thomas T Rideout, rather than William H Shorey, is buried in this grave. However, Thomas Rideout did not even enlist into the 4th Maine infantry until 8/29/63.

R5#12	SERGT E C DOW ENOCH C DOW[34]	20	19 Inf E	B 12/5/1842 Prospect, Waldo Co., ME. Occ mariner. E (Stockton, Waldo Co., ME) Aug 62 private. KIA Jul 3: shot in head and leg.
R5#13	SERGT W S JORDAN WILLIAM S JORDAN[35]	22	20 Inf G	B 1/25/1841 Bangor, Penobscot Co., ME. 1860: R Veazie, Penobscot Co., ME; occ millman. E Jun 61 into 2nd ME Inf as a private. Wounded on 5/27/62 at Hanover Court House, VA. Jul 62: promoted to corporal. Promoted to sergeant during service. Transferred to 20th Maine on 5/20/63. C Jul 2: GSW to the left lung. D Jul 24.
R5#14	FRANK B CURTIS BENJAMIN FRANKLIN **CURTISS**	23	20 Inf F	B 11/28/1839 Wellington, Piscataquis, ME. R same. E Aug 62 private. Occ farmer. C Jul 2: Wounded in left arm. D Jul 11.
R5#15	ELFIN J FOSS	22-23	20 Inf F	B ~1840. R Embden, Somerset Co., ME. Occ farmer. E Aug 62 private. KIA Jul 2.
R5#16	LIEUT W L KENDALL WARREN LINCOLN KENDALL	26	20 Inf G	B 11/29/36 Waldo Co., ME. R Belfast, Waldo Co., ME. Occ carver. E Aug 62 corporal. Commissioned 2nd lieutenant in 1863. C Jul 2: wounds to throat and vertebrae. D Jul 5.
B6#1	SAMUEL L DWELLEY	24	17 Inf D	B 10/29/1838 ME. R Lewiston, Androscoggin Co., ME. Occ farmer. E Aug 62 private. C Jul 2: severe wound to right forearm. D Jul 9.
R6#2	FRANK COFFIN	18	19 Inf B	B 3/25/1845 Thorndike, Waldo Co., ME. R same. E Aug 62 private. C Jul 3: severe wound in leg→amp. D Jul 12.
R6#3	JAMES T HEAL MN THOMAS	27	19 Inf K	B 5/17/1836 Phippsburg, Sagadahoc Co., ME. 1860 R: same. Occ ship carpenter. E Aug 62 private. C Jul 3: shot in the head. D Jul 9. Survivors (WC118811): M Mrs. Cordelia Heal 60 in 1867 (Sumner Heal affirmed infirmed).

---

34 **Cemetery reenactment exercise**. As an exercise in reenactment, a Cemetery visitor might sit facing the gravestone of Sergeant Enoch Dow of the 19th Maine Infantry, Company E. Fifty-four years after Dow's death at Gettysburg, Alfred Stinson, who had served in the same regiment and company as Dow, composed a memorial note to be sent to Dow's sister. Dow wrote of how the two boys from Prospect, Maine had so bonded that they had "marched together, tented together, drank out of the same canteen." He also wrote how he and Dow had made a "solemn vow that we would stand by each other until one or the other was killed." When this day came for Dow, Stinson with the help of another comrade, buried Dow on the battlefield and marked his grave. Stinson then shared with Dow's sister an experience he had at her brother's gravesite fifty years after having buried him in the field. "I visited the National Cemetery, and as I was sitting there my thoughts drifted back to the night that I laid him away and my tears ran like rain." If one chooses to sit before the headstone of Sergeant Enoch Dow, it would be well to remember that while we today may see this grave and the thousands surrounding it at the National Cemetery as heroic sacrifices, the loss of these lives for the mothers, fathers, wives, children, comrades who knew them, would have been intensely painful and would ever remain so.

35 **Second Mainer's "three-year-man" dies on Little Round Top**. Sergeant William Jordan would have been one of the mutinous 2nd Maine "three-year-men" denied discharge with the disbandment of their regiment. In William Jordan's case, his extended service with Col. Joshua Chamberlain's 20th Maine on Little Round Top would cost him his life.

R6#4	LORING C OLIVER[36]	35	19 Inf K	B 9/1/1827 Georgetown, Sagadahoc Co., ME. R Phippsburg, Sagadahoc Co., ME. Occ mariner. E Aug 62 private. C Jul 2: severe wound in right leg→ amp. D Sep 11. Survivors (WC25701) W Mercy 32 (M Dec 49); 4 ♀: Delenda 12, Lepta 7, Zettella 5, Lizzie 14 months.
R6#5	SAMUEL B SHEA	30	19 Inf K	B 7/24/32 Georgetown, Sagadahoc Co., ME. R same. Occ farmer. E Aug 62 private. C Jul 2: wounded in chest or groin mortally. D Jul 9.
R6#6	CORP H F ARNOLD HOLLIS F ARNOLD	23-24	19 Inf H	B ~1839 Palermo, Waldo Co., ME. R same. Occ farm laborer. E Aug 62 corporal. KIA Jul 2. Survivors (WC100221): W Ellen 24 (M Dec 61| ReM 1866); 1 ♂- Arnold 8 months.
R6#7	SERGT J A DORMAN JESSE A DORMAN, SR	24-25	19 Inf H	B ~1838 Winslow, Kennebec Co., ME. R Canaan, Somerset Co., ME. Occ clothier. E Aug 62 sergeant. C Jul 2: shot in shoulder. D Jul 6. Survivors (WC83029): W Annie 21 (M Aug 62| ReM 1866); Jesse A Dorman, Jr. 3 months.
R6#8	GEORGE E HODGDON GEORGE **F** HODGDON	35-36	19 Inf C	B ~1827 ME. R Troy, Waldo Co., ME. Occ farmer. E Aug 62 private. C Jul 2: GSW to right arm. D Jul 26. Survivors (WC141744): W Mary 21 (M Apr 60| ReM 1869); 1 ♀- Lucy 2.
R6#9	CHARLES J CARROLL	18-19	19 Inf G	B ~1844 ME. R Windsor, Kennebec Co., ME. E Aug 62 private. C Jul 2. D Jul 26.
R6#10	RUEL NICKERSON **REUEL** NICKERSON	26-27	19 Inf E	B ~1836 ME. R Swanville, Waldo Co., ME. E Aug 62 private. C Jul 3: severe wound right arm→amp. D Jul 18.
R6#11	HUSHAI C THOMAS (MN CALVER)	21	19 Inf D	B 12/14/1841 Lincolnville, Waldo Co., ME. R Morrill, Waldo Co., ME. E Aug 62 private. C Jul 2. D Jul 21.
R6#12	JOHN F CAREY[37] (MN FRANK)	35-36	19 Inf I	B ~1827 ME. R Camden, ME. Occ laborer. E Aug 62 private. D Jul 2 or 3 of wounds. Survivors (WC16397): W Eliza 39 (M May 49); 9 chn: 1 ♀ Eveline 14 with 6 ♂ & 1 more ♀: Charles 12, John 9, twins Edward & Frederick 6, Benjamin 3, Willard 2, twins Nathaniel & Antionette 10 weeks.
R6#13	MOSES D EMERY	21-22	17 Inf B	R ~1841 ME. R Stow, Oxford Co., ME. 1860: occ: residing on father's farm, Stow, ME. E Aug 62 private. C Jul 2: wounded in left hip. D Jul 9.

---

36 **Widow experiences mental health challenge nine months after soldier's death.** In April 1864, A Mr. Obadiah Trask, was appointed guardian for the four girls following Mrs. Oliver being judged insane in a court proceeding. Fortunately, eight years later, Mrs. Trask's mental health had sufficiently recovered that her children could again be returned to her care.

37 **Soldier's death leaves his widow with nine children.** John Carey's death at Gettysburg would leave his wife with 9 underaged children, including two sets of twins, the younger set being only 10-weeks-old.

R6#14	FESSENDEN M MILLS FESSENDEN **S** MILLS	23-24	17 Inf C	B ~1839 Norway, Oxford Co., ME. R same. Occ farm laborer. E Aug 62 private. C Jul 2: wounded in head. D Jul 3.
R6#15	JOSEPH A ROACH[38]	22-23	3 Inf D	B ~1840 Brunswick, Cumberland Co., ME. R Bath, ME. Occ mariner. E May 62 private. C Jul 2: wounded in right leg→ amp. D Jul 11. Survivor (WC22777): W Mary Ann 21 (M Mar 62); no chn.
R6#16	ALLEN H SPRAGUE[39] (MN HERBERT)	~20	3 Inf E	B ~1843 St. Albans, Somerset Co., ME. R same. E Aug 61 private. Wounded and captured on 7/21/61 at 1st Bull Run on 7/21/61. Released 6/2/62 and sent to Washington, D.C. C Jul 2: wounded in right leg→amp. D Aug 3. Survivor (WC133910): F Jason Sprague 50 (disabled widower of Sophronia Sprague).
R6#17	JOHN S GRAY	~25	4 Inf D	B ~1838 ME. R Deer Isle, Hancock Co., ME. Occ fisherman. E June 61 private. Captured on 7/21/61 at 1st Bull Run. C Jul 2: wounded in left shoulder and right knee. D Jul 28. Survivors (WC113561): M Mrs. Lucy Gray 50 in 1867 (Oliver Gray affirmed disabled and unable to support wife).
R7#1	CORP F DEVEREUX FRANK DEVEREUX	22	16 Inf K	B 10/3/1840 Castine, Hancock Co., ME. R same. E Aug 62 private. Promotion to corporal during service. KIA Jul 1.
R7#3	GEORGE D MARSTON	29	16 Inf I	B 2/1/1834 North Paris, Oxford Co., ME. 1860: R Sumner, Oxford Co., ME; occ shoemaker. E Aug 62 corporal. KIA Jul 1.
R7#5	E BISHOP			No killed Gettysburg soldier with this name found in military sources.
R7#6	W H LOWE WILLIAM H **LOW**	20-21	19 Inf E	B ~1842 ME. R Frankfort, Waldo Co., ME. E Aug 62 private. KIA Jul 3.
R7#7	ALFRED P WATTERMAN ALFRED P **WATERMAN**	18	19 Inf D	B 9/10/1844 Belfast, Waldo Co., ME. R same. E Aug 62 private. Promoted to corporal during service. C Jul 2 or 3: GSW to head. D Jul 4. Survivor (WC92078): M Mrs. Rachael Waterman 45 in 1866 (widow of Joseph Waterman).
R7#8	SERGT A W LORD ALEXANDER WATSON LORD	35-36	19 Inf C	B ~1827 Vassalboro, Kennebec Co., ME. R Fairfield, ME. E Aug 62 private. Promotion to sergeant. KIA Jul 3. Survivors (WC133084): W Emeline 25; 3 chn: 2 ♀-Sarah 6, Mina 4 & 1 ♂- Ira 2.

---

38 **Widow's prior pension claim cancels out eligibility of soldier's elderly mother.** In 1893, Sylvester Roach, Joseph Roach's widowed father, at age 76 applied for a dependent pension. He would be denied based on the policy that there could be only one survivor pension recipient and that the soldier's wife, who was already receiving a pension, held preference.

39 **Prior to Gettysburg, soldier had been held for prolonged Confederate imprisonment.** Private Allen Sprague was wounded and captured July 21, 1861 at First Bull Run. Likely as delayed by an extended hospitalization, Sprague would not be released by the Confederates until June 1862.

R7#9	SERGT W E BURROWS WILLIAM L BURROWS	33	19 Inf I	B 10/5/1829 Rockland, Knox Co., ME. R same. Occ farmhand. E Aug 62 corporal. Promotion to sergeant in 1863. D Jul 3 of wounds. Survivors (WC16396): W Amanda 23 (M June 60| ReM 1865); 1 ♂ - Clifton 8 weeks.
R7#11	SERGT C F PERRY CHANDLER F PERRRY[40]	26-27	19 Inf I	B 1836 Minot, Androscoggin Co., ME. R South Thomaston, Knox Co., ME. Occ mariner. E Aug 62 private. Dec 62: promoted corporal. May 63: promoted to sergeant. D Jul 2 of wounds. Survivors (WC17752→WC155873 neither online): W Susan 22 (M Nov 60| ReM 1871); 2 ♀ - Sarah 2; Caroline 3 months.
R7#12	LOUIRA A KELLEY	19	19 Inf D	B 1/15/1844 ME. R Belfast, Waldo Co., ME. Occ laborer. E Aug 62 private. KIA Jul 3.
R7#14	CHARLES W COLLINS	19	19 Inf A	B 8/13/1843 Industry, Franklin Co., ME. 1860 R: New Sharon, Franklin Co., ME. R Starks, Somerset Co., ME; occ: laborer on father's farm. E Aug 62 private. KIA Jul 3.
R7#15	CORP A HANSON AUSTIN HANSON	19-20	17 Inf F	B 1843 ME. R Hiram, Oxford Co., ME. E Aug 62 private. Jan 63: promoted to corporal: C Jul 2 or 3: shot in abdomen. D Jul 2 or 3.
R7#16	ISAIAH V EATON[41] (MN VALENTINE)	32	4 Inf D	B 11/27/1830 Deer Isle, Hancock Co., ME. R same. Occ fisherman. E Jun 61 private into 4th ME infantry. Sep 61: transferred to 38th NY infantry. Transferred back to 4th ME infantry on 6/4/63. C Jul 2: severe wound to right leg→ amp. D Aug 18. Survivors (WC118959): W Susannah 28 (M Mar 51| ReM Oct 65); 6 chn: 4 ♀ - Lydia 12, Lavinia 8, Mary 6, Sarah 4 & 2 ♂ - Solomon 10, Isaiah 2.
R7#17	FRANK FAIRBROTHER	21	16 Inf G	B 4/19/1842 Somerset Co., ME. R Palmyra, Somerset Co., ME. E Aug 62 private. C Jul 1: wounded in right hip and abdomen. D Jul 9.

---

40 **Young Widow's 1871 remarriage to 72-year-old man**. Perhaps as necessitated by the disempowered state of women in pre-20th century America, Susan Chandler married a much older man eight years after Chandler Perry's death. On 4/16/1871, the 30-year-old widow married the 72-year-old widower, Levi Emery. At that time, Emery had nine surviving children from his first wife, the youngest of the nine being himself two years older than Susan. The excitement of a new young wife may possibly have been too much for Emery, who died sixteen months after marrying Sarah. The following year, Sarah, now 32, married Joseph Jackson, also 32. The couple had a long-lasting marriage, producing four offspring.

41 **Soldier's dying declaration**. Susannah Eaton's pension file includes a touching letter from a physician's wife, Mrs. Mary Germaine, who was working with the Sanitary Commission while her husband, Dr. Charles Germaine, was likely caring for the wounded. Mrs. Germaine wrote in the August 18th letter that she had been sitting Isaiah at his bedside when a letter sent by Susannah was brought in. Mrs. Germane wrote that at that moment Isaiah was unconscious and near death. However, Mrs. Germaine comforted Susannah that her husband had spoken of wanting to see her and his children once more, but that "if it was not God's will," he was "ready and willing to die."

Susannah Eaton's pension file also includes a witness letter that in October 1865, Susannah, seeking to better herself, injudiciously married a 42-year-old widower, William Blaster, who then chose to live separately and who refused to help support her children. The beleaguered Susannah in 1868 resigned the care of her children to a guardian.

R7#18	CORP R T NEWELL ROBERT THEODORE NEWELL	25	19 Inf D	B 2/11/1838 Searsmont, Waldo Co., ME. R Belfast, Waldo Co., ME. Occ laborer. E Aug 62 corporal. C Jul 2: severely wounded in right leg→amp. D Jul 16.	

Twentieth Maine Monument Atop Vincent's Spur

★ ★ ★ ★ ★

Alerted on July 2nd to the approach of Confederate troops to the unguarded Little Round Top ground, Colonel Strong Vincent, acting on his own authority, rushed his brigade into position on this hill, placing the 20th Maine regiment at the extreme end of this line. Vincent would be mortally wounded in the fighting that would follow and would die on July 7th, leaving behind a wife, Elizabeth, of two years and seven-months pregnant at his death. She would lose this child in infancy. Elizabeth would herself die in 1914, having never remarried. She is buried at the Erie Cemetery in Erie, Pennsylvania, with Vincent. (WC19397).

Maryland

R1#1	G W LOWRY GEORGE G LOWRY[42]	36-37	1 PHB Inf K	B ~1826 VA. R Berlin, Frederick Co., MD. E Dec 61 private. C Jul 3: shot in right lung. D Jul 5. Survivor (WC32337): W Ann 36 in 1864 (May 1851); no chn.
R1#2	JOHN CONNER JOHN CONNER, JR[43]	~19	1 PHB Inf F	B ~1844 VA. E Apr 62 private. KIA Jul 3: rifle ball entering skull just below the right eye (body found on the field July 4th). Survivor (WC125936): M Mrs. Jane Conner 54 in 1867 (widow of John Conner, Sr).
R1#3	DAVID KREBS (MN CEPHAS)	17	1 PHB Inf G	B 8/20/1845 MD. 1860: R Loudoun Co., VA; occ boatman. E Apr 62 private. KIA Jul 3.
R1#4	M F KNOTT MINION F KNOTT[44]	~23	CONFED MD 1 Inf F	B ~1840. Three-month enlistment in a Washington, D.C. militia unit in the spring of 1861. Enlistment in the Confederate 1st Maryland infantry possibly in the spring of 1863. C Jul 3: wounded on the left side and exiting near his spine. D Aug 24.
R1#5	FRANK BAXTER **FRANKLIN** BAXTER	20-21	1 PHB Inf D	B ~1842. E Oct 61 private. Captured and paroled 9/15/62 at Harper's Ferry, VA. C Jul 3: severely wounded in the right leg→amp. D Jul 26.
R1#6	JOHN W STOCKMAN	18-19	1 PHB Inf B	B ~1844 Frederick Co., MD. 1860 R: Jefferson, Frederick Co., MD. Occ farmer. E Aug 62 private. C Jul 3. D Jul 16.
R2#1	WILLIAM H EATON	22-23	1 ES[45] Inf E	B ~1840 Dorchester Co., MD. 1860 R: same. Occ farmer. E (Cabin Creek, Dorchester Co., MD) Oct 61 private. KIA Jul 3

---

42 **Soldier's wife loses fourth pregnancy fifteen days before he succumbs to his battle wound.** Mrs. Ann Lowry's pension application notes the loss of four children, occurring during pregnancy or in very early childhood. The couple's last loss was a same-day death of a girl on June 20, 1863.

43 **Irish-immigrant mother attests to being wholly dependent on son.** John Conner, Jr., son of Irish immigrant parents, appears on a 1860 Morgan County, VA Census as a 16-years-old. Mrs. Jane Connor's pension affidavit attest to the fact that she was wholly dependent on her young son for support, following the death of John Connor, Sr. in 1854.

44 **Confederate in the Cemetery.** Private Minion Knott is one of 9 identified Confederates mistakenly buried in the National Cemetery.

45 **Conflicted allegiance of border state Union regiment.** The 1st Maryland Eastern Shore Regiment was formed in 1861 primarily with the purpose of opposing Confederate sympathizers within the state. When the regiment was called up to contest Lee's 1863 incursion into Pennsylvania, one company of men, refusing to fight outside of Maryland, had to discharged from the regiment.

R2#2	G H BARGER GEORGE HENRY BARGER[46]	31	1 PHB Inf H	B 3/12/1832 MD. E Aug 62 private. C Jul 3: shot in right lung. D Jul 4. Survivors (WC133634): M Mrs. Mahala Barger 55 in 1867; 2 ♂- Charles 7, Theophilus 5 from wife Mary, M Apr 55, died 2/19/62.).
R2#3	A SATERFIELD ANDREW SATERFIELD	42-43	1 ES Inf H	B ~1820 MD. R Talbot Co., MD. Occ farm manager. E Sep 61 private. Detached service as hospital nurse during Jan/Feb 62 and during Sep/Oct 62. C Jul 3: GSW to right shoulder. D Jul 20. Survivors (WC108601): W Marietta 42 in 1865 (M Jan 45}; 1 ♂- Walter 3.
R2#4	JOSEPH BAILEY JOSEPHA **BAYLIS**	36-37	1 PHB Inf I	B ~1826. E Oct 1861 private. Captured and paroled 9/15/62 at Harper's Ferry. KIA Jul 3.
R2#5	TETER FRENCH	25-26	1 PHB Inf E	B ~1837. E Sep 61 private. C Jul 3: GSW to abdomen. D Jul 3 or 4.
R3#1	SOTHEY T STIRLING **SOUTHEY STERLING**	22-23	1 ES Inf K	B ~1840 MD. R Somerset Co., MD. Occ sailor (1860). E (Annamessex homeland, Somerset Co., MD) Nov 61 private. KIA Jul 3.
R3#3	WILLIAM P JONES	36-37	1 ES Inf B	B ~1826. R Dorchester Co., MD. E (Straits, Dorchester Co., MD) Sep 61 private. KIA Jul 3. Survivors: (WC132718): W Louisa 34 in 1865 (M May 51); 3 chn: 2 ♂- William 7, Goldsborough 5 & 1 ♀- Hester 3.
R3#4	EDWARD PRITCHART EDWARD **PRITCHETT**	22-23	1 ES Inf B	B ~1840 MD. R Dorchester Co., MD. E Sep 61. KIA Jul 3. Survivor (WC141192): M Mrs. Caroline Pritchett 54 in 1867 (widow of Henry Pritchett).
R3#7	R NEWTON GILSON RICHARD NEWTON **GILSON**[47] 1 PHB Cav C			B 1841 Frederick, MD. Occ student. E (Emmittsburg, Frederick Co., MD) Aug 62. private. Wounded and captured on 6/18/64 at Lynchburg, VA. D Aug 3, 1864. (age 22).
R3#8	H MILLER HENRY MILLER	37-38	1 PHB 1 Inf C	B ~1825. E (Frederick, MD) Aug 61 private. KIA Jul 3.

---

46 **Mother, please take care of my two boys while I'm gone.** George Barger chose to leave home to join a Maryland regiment only six months after Mary Barger, his wife and the mother of their two young boys, had died on 2/19/62. George Barger turned the care of his sons over to his own mother, Mrs. Mahala Barger, likely with the understanding that she would arrange full guardianship, were he to be killed in the war.

47 **1890 reburial into National Cemetery.** According to noted Gettysburg historian and NPS ranger John Heiser, the remains of Robert Newton Gilson, were taken from a Winchester, VA site and reburied at this National Cemetery site in April 1890. Heiser speculates that this relocation may have been at his family's request.

Maryland State Monument on the Taneytown Road

★ ★ ★ ★ ★

A Wounded Union and Wounded Confederate Soldier, Both Marylanders, Assist Each Other as They Seek Aid.

Massachusetts

R1#1	LIEUT SUMNER PAINE SUMNER EDWARD JACKSON PAINE[48]	18	20 Inf F	B 5/10/1845 Boston, MA. R same. Son of Boston lawyer, Charles Paine. Commissioned 2nd lieutenant as of April 23, 1863. KIA Jul 3.
R1#2	LIEUT HENRY HARTLEY	~29	1St Inf E	B ~1834 England. R Williamsburg, Hampshire Co., MA. Occ carver and gilder. E May 61 sergeant. Commissioned 2ndlieutenant by Gov. Andrews on 8/26/61. Promoted to 1st lieutenant on 8/21/62. Acting as Captain since 9/1/62. Absent on leave Mar 7→21/63. KIA Jul 2.
R1#12	GEORGE P ROUNDEY (MN PICKERING)	29-30	1st Co MA SS	B ~1833 ME. R Lynnfield, Essex Co., MA. Occ miner. E Sep 61 private. Oct 61: detailed extra duty as a gun wagon driver. Apr 63: detailed as brigade teamster. KIA Jul 3.
R1#13	J B NINGENT **ISAAC** B **NEWCOMB**, JR	42	22 Inf C	B 11/20/1820 Wellfleet, Barnstable Co., MA. R Boston, MA. Occ pianoforte maker. E Sep 61 private. Captured 6/27/62 at Gaines' Mill, VA. Paroled on 7/18/62. Promoted to corporal on 9/20/62. KIA Jul 2: wounds to left leg and abdomen. Survivors (WC16577): W Salome 42 (M Aug 59); 2 ♀ - Mary 13, Hattie 6.
R1#15	JAMES CRAMPTON	29-30	37 Inf K	B ~1833 Ireland. R Northampton, Hampshire Co., MA. Occ laborer. E Jul 62 private. C Jul 3: wounded in right thigh. D Jul 13.
R1#16	JOHN F MOORE	23-24	22 Inf K	B ~1839 MA. R Sturbridge, Worcester Co., MA. Occ farmer. E Sep 61 private. C Jul 2: wounded in hand. D Aug 22.
R1#17	C N REED CHARLES A REED	20	15 Inf H	B 8/10/1842 Grafton, Worcester Co., MA. R Upton, Worcester Co., MA. Occ shoemaker. E Jan 62 private. Wound in hand at Antietam 9/17/62. KIA Jul 2: wound to left chest.
R1#18	JOHN T BIXBY	19	15 Inf H	B 4/4/1844 Worcester, MA. R same. Occ machinist. E Aug 61 private. Wounded in the neck on 9/17/62 at Antietam on 9/17/62. Jul/Aug 63: detached following the battle to a Gettysburg hospital where he contracted typhoid fever. D Sep 12.

---

48 **Lieutenant killed only ten weeks after commission.** Sumner Paine left his class at Harvard at age 17 to accept a commission with the "Harvard Regiment", so called because it was officered largely by young Harvard graduates.

ID	Name	Age	Unit	Details
R1#19	S HINDEMAN **NAPOLEON B HINDMAN**[49]	~24	CONFED MS 13 Inf A	B ~1839 SC. 1860: R Winston Co., MS. Occ farm laborer. E May 61 for one year as a private. In May 62, enlistments under a Confederate conscription act were extended for two additional years. Detailed as a wagoner and teamster during service. C Jul 2. D Jul 2 or 19.
R1#20	G F LEONARD 13			No killed Gettysburg soldier with this name found in military sources.
R1#28	LIEUT J H PARKINS		37 Inf E	No killed Gettysburg soldier with this name found in military sources.
R1#29	LIEUT SHERMAN S ROBINSON[50]	20	19 Inf	B 7/25/1842 Deerfield, Rockingham Co., NH. R same. Occ shoemaker. E Jul 61 private. Promoted sergeant in Sep 61. Commissioned 2nd lieutenant in April 63. KIA Jul 3: killed by a shell. Survivor (WC137428): F Stephen Robinson 73 in 1866 (widower of Mary Robinson affirmed disabled by age and infirmities).
R2#1	SERGT HENRY C BALL	31	15 Inf F	B 1/12/1832 Sunderland, Franklin Co., MA. R Amherst, Hampshire Co., MA. Occ palm leaf worker. E Jul 61 corporal. Sep 61: promoted to sergeant. Wounded at Antietam on 9/17/62. Promoted 1st sergeant on 4/9/63. KIA Jul 3: GSW to left breast. Survivors (WC 10464): W Harriet 30 (M Jun 53 | ReM 1871); 2 ♀- Emma 7, Minnie 4.
R2#2	JOHN MARSH	27	15 Inf B	B 8/12/1835 Sandwich, Barnstable Co., MA. R Fitchburg, Worcester Co., MA. Occ palm leaf splitter. E Aug 61 corporal. Wounded in one leg on 9/17/62 at Antietam. KIA Jul 3: wounded in the head.
R2#3	MICHAEL FLINN MICHAEL **FLYNN**	~22	15 Inf E	B ~1841 Ireland. R Worcester, MA. Occ wiredrawer. E Jul 61 private. Detailed to Battery B 1st RI LA on 2/1/63. KIA Jul 2 while still serving on this detail. Survivors: (WC125596): M Mrs. Mary Flynn 60 in 1868 (John Flynn affirmed disabled due to old age).
R2#4	O STEVENS ORMAN STEVENS	30	15 Inf D	B 10/29/1832 Charlton, Worcester Co., MA. R same. Occ painter. E Jul 62 private. KIA Jul 2 or 3.

---

49 **Confederate in the Cemetery.** Napoleon Hindman is one of nine misidentified Confederates buried in the National Cemetery.

50 **Father's pension application reveals previous son lost in service.** The 73-year-old widower Stephen Robinson applied for a dependent father's pension in 1866. His application was prompted by the loss of support following the death of his son, Lieutenant Sherman Robinson. However, Stephen Robinson reported that he had also lost a second son in the war. On September 6, 1862, John H. Robinson had enlisted in the same 19th Massachusetts regiment, as had his younger brother. On October 30, 1862, he died of typhoid fever.

R2#5	GEORGE W CROSS[51]	22-23	15 Inf E	B ~1840 East Hanover, Grafton Co., NH. E 13th MA Co F. Jul 61 private. Deserted in Jan 62 when refused money to return from furlough. Mar/Apr 62: reenlisted in 15th MA infantry. Reported a deserter Sep 62, but found to have been sick in hospital. Rejoined company on 3/13/63. May/Jun 63: forfeited $5 from pay for straggling. KIA Jul 2: shell wound to chest.
R2#6	JOSEPH BARDSLEY	37-38	15 Inf I	B ~1825 England. R Grafton, Worcester Co., MA. Occ operative. E Jul 62 private. Wounded at Antietam on 9/17/62. Extended time in hospital on detached service serving as a nurse through 12/8/62. KIA Jul 2. Survivor (WC8957): W Mercy 53 (M Dec 53).[52]
R2#7	FRANCIS SANTUM	27-28	15 Inf I	B ~1835. R Webster, Worcester Co., MA. Occ farmer. E Dec 61 private. Absent, sick in hospital from Mar/Apr 62 through Nov/Dec 62. KIA Jul 3.
R2#8	FRANCIS A LEWIS (MN ALBERT)	23	15 Inf A	B 8/22/1839 Sterling, Worcester Co., MA. Occ farmer. E Jul 61 private. Promoted to corporal on 6/1/63. KIA Jul 3.
R2#9	GEORGE E BURNS[53] (MN EDWARD)	40	15 Inf G	B 1/31/23 Lenox, Berkshire Co., MA. R Sutton, Worcester Co., MA; occ operative. E Dec 61 private. Wounded at Antietam on 9/17/62. Mar/Apr 63: transferred to hospital in Philadelphia. Return to duty date not documented. C Jul 2. D Jul 14. Survivors (WC137751): 5 chn: 3 ♂ from 1st wife Mary (M 1848; died 1858) Charles 14, Eugene 13, Alanson 6 and 2 ♂ from 2nd wife Ann (M1858; died 8/15/63); George 4, James 2.
R2#10	GEORGE L BOSS	~21	15 Inf B	B ~1842 Worcester, Worcester Co., MA. R Fitchburg, Worcester Co., MA. Occ mechanic. E Jul 61 private. Absent sick with an unspecified condition: 10/30/62→March 63. C Jul 2: wounded in hip by shell. D Jul 5.
R2#11	SERGT E B ROLLINS EDWARD BEAN ROLLINS	35	15 Inf A	B 1/20/1828 Berlin, Washington Co., VT. R Leominster, Worcester Co., MA. Occ carpenter. E Jul 61 private. Promoted to corporal on 1/1/62. Promoted to sergeant on 12/1/62. KIA Jul 2: wounded in left breast. Survivors (WC11508): W Asenath 35 (M Nov 49); 4 chn: 3 ♀- Ada 10, Dana 5, Nina 16 months & 1 ♂- Lorenzo 8.

---

51 **Soldier refused request for money to return to regiment from furlough.** When Private George Cross was refused money by his 15th Massachusetts infantry regiment to return from a furlough, he responded by deserting and reenlisting in the 15th Massachusetts infantry regiment.

52 **Mother's boasts in pension application of seven sons then serving in the army.** In her second marriage in 1853, the widowed Mercy Remick, age 40, had married Joseph Bardsley, age 27. In her 1863 widow's application following his death, Mercy Bardsley declared that from the union with her first husband, she had 13 living children, of whom 7 were then serving in the Union army.

53 **Soldier's five boys lose him in July, mother in August.** Ann Burns's death from tuberculosis one month after George Burns died at Gettysburg would orphan the five boys. Burns' first wife, Mary, had also died of tuberculosis, as would Burns's 4th son, George, in 1867.

R2#12	JOHN GRADY	20	15 Inf I	B 9/17/1842 Ireland. R Webster, Worcester CO., MA. Occ shoemaker. E May 61 private. May/June 63: detached to service with Battery A 1st RI Light Artillery. KIA Jul 3: one leg carried away above the knee by a shell.
R2#13	N B BICKNELL NATHAN BICKNELL[54]	26	16 Inf C	B 4/27/1837 Westford, Middlesex Co., MA. R same. Occ yeoman. E Jul 61 private. Detached for service at Brigade HQ 3/3→6/23/63. KIA Jul 2. Survivors (WC151320 not online): M Mrs. Martha Bicknell 57 in 1869 (Ira Bicknell affirmed disabled).
R2#14	PIERCE HARVEY[55]	51	16 Inf B	B 12/17/11 New London, Merrimack Co., NH. R Boston, MA. Occ carpenter. E Aug 62 private. C Jul 2: wounded in foot. D Jul 17. Survivors (WC9905): W Catharine 52 (M Jun 38); 4 chn: 3 ♂- John 22, Thomas 19, Thaddeus 17 & 1 ♀- Catharine 13.
R2#15	G LAMBERT **GEORGE** EDWARD LAMBERT[56]	16	22 Inf F	B 2/12/1847 Dorchester, Boston, MA. R same. Occ fisherman. E Aug 61 private. C Jul 2: shot in the left thigh. D Jul 19.
R2#16	CALVIN S FIELD (MN STEARNS)	21	22 Inf B	B 9/4/1841 Northfield, Franklin Co., MA. R same. E Sep 61. C Jul 2: wounded in abdomen. D Jul 4.
R2#17	JOHN HICKEY	19-20	28 Inf C	B ~1843 Boston, MA. R same. Occ shoemaker. E Oct 61 private. C Jul 3. D Aug 16
R2#18	JOHN CASWELL	34-35	28 Inf G	B ~1828 Ireland. R Boston, MA. Occ hostler. E Dec 61 private. C Jul 2: wounded in both thighs. D Jul 29. Survivors (WC12415): W Elizabeth 32 (M Jun 51); 1 ♀ Elizabeth 11.

---

54 **Mother in pension application reports previous son lost in service**. Mrs. Martha Bicknell's dependent mother application emphasized with the Pension Office that Nathan's death meant the death of a second son in service with the 22nd MA Infantry. Her other son, James, had died of disease near Richmond in June 1862.

55 **Overaged at enlistment**. For his August 1862 enlistment, Pierce Harvey gave his age as 42. Census records, in agreement with an Ancestry.com family tree, indicate that he was actually 50, or five years beyond the prescribed upper-age limit for voluntary enlistment. At Gettysburg, Pierce Harvey had a son, John B. Harvey, who fighting with the 12th Massachusetts Infantry would be wounded July 3rd. John Harvey would survive this Gettysburg wound, but he would go on to be killed in the Wilderness in May 1864.

56 **Minor at death**. A Massachusetts town record gives George Lambert's date of birth as February 12, 1847. This birthdate is in agreement with George's reported ages of 3 and 13 on the successive August 1850 and August 1860 U.S. Census sheets. These sources attest that George was 14, not 18, at his 1861 enlistment and furthermore that he was only 16 when he was killed at Gettysburg.

R2#19	SERGT EDWARD MOONEY[57]	~40	28 Inf D	B ~1823 Ireland. R Boston, MA. Occ laborer. E Oct 61 sergeant. Reduced to rank of private for an unspecified reason. KIA Jul 3. Survivor (WC27338): W Jane 40 (M Feb 50); no chn.
R2#20	JOSEPH BEAL	28	33 Inf I	B 4/19/35 Hanson, Plymouth Co., MA. R North Bridgewater, Plymouth Co., MA. Occ shoe cutter. E Jul 62 private. C Jul 2: wounded in proximity of right eye. D Jul 31. Survivors (WC22694): W Maria 28 (M Dec 54); 1 ♀- Augusta 5.
R2#21	C H PIERCE CHARLES H PIERCE[58]	16	33 Inf E	B 7/22/46 Plymouth, MA. R Groton, Middlesex Co., MA. Occ farmer. E Jul 62 private. C Jul 2: wounded in left forearm. D Jul 7.
R2#23	GEORGE HILLS GEORGE H HILL[59]			Probably a misidentified soldier in grave. In July 1861, a George H. Hill, at age 20 did enlist into 13th MA infantry. This soldier fought and was captured at Gettysburg. He returned to his regiment after being paroled on 8/2/63. His service record shows him mustering out of the army in 1865.
R2#24	CORP PATRICK SCANNELL	22-23	19 Inf B	B ~1840 Ireland. R South Danvers, Essex Co., MA. Occ bleacher. E Dec 61 private. Promoted to corporal on 5/01/63. KIA Jul 3.
R2#25	SERGT A J BABCOCK ALONZO J BABCOCK	27-28	2 Inf H	B ~1835 Norwich, Windsor Co., VT. R Lowell, Middlesex Co., MA. Occ weaver. E May 61 private. Promoted to corporal on 12/22/61. Promoted to sergeant on 11/23/62. Promoted to 1st sergeant in Mar 63. C Jul 3: severe wound in left arm →amp. D Aug 6. Survivor (WC14291): W Abby 24 (M Feb 55); no chn.
R2#26	CORP JULES B ALLEN JULES R ALLEN	21-22	33 Inf D	B ~1841 MA. R Reading, Middlesex Co., MA. Occ cabinet maker. E Jul 62 private. Promoted to corporal on 6/20/63. KIA Jul 2: instant death from GSW through the heart. Survivor (WC90118): M Mrs. Lucy Jane Allen 58 (widow of Samuel Allen).
R2#27	CALVIN HOWE CALVIN HORR[60]	35	33 Inf I	B 9/12/1827 MA. R Freetown, Bristol Co., MA. Occ shoemaker. E Aug 62 private. KIA Jul 2: GSW to the head, died in a few minutes. Survivors (WC80464): W Mary 17 or 19 (M June 59| ReM Dec 64); 2 chn:1 ♀- Mary 3 & 1 ♂- John 20 months.

---

57 **Nature of charges warranting court martial are usually not noted in service records.** Edward Mooney on April 30, 1862 was court martialed from the rank of sergeant to private through his remaining term of service. The charge is not noted in the Mooney's service record. Regimental court martials were very common during the Civil War. The great majority of court martials referenced in the service records do not note the charge, likely suggesting that some court martial proceedings for relatively minor infractions were administered informally.

58 **Minor at death.** At his July 21, 1862 enlistment, Charles Pierce gave his age 18. However, a Massachusetts town record gives Charles birthdate as July 22, 1846. The 1846 birthyear is in agreement with Charles' given ages of 4 and 14 in the respective 1850 and 1860 U.S. Censuses. These sources attest that Charles was one day short of his 16th birthday at his 1861 enlistment and four days short of his 17th birthday when he died at Gettysburg.

59 **Misidentified soldier in grave.** Private George Hill was captured but not killed at Gettysburg. He survived the war, mustering out of the army in 1865.

60 **Soldier's death leaves behind teenage widow and two young children.** As a sign of the age, Mary Sullivan was 15 years old when she married the 28-year-old Calvin Horr in June 1859. With her husband's death at Gettysburg, she would be a teenage widow with a three-year-old daughter and a twenty-month-old son.

R2#28	E HOWE ELIJAH HOWE	40	33 Inf H	B 6/13/1823 Malborough, Middlesex Co., MA. R same. Occ farmer. E Jul 62 private. KIA Jul 2. Survivors (WC172405 not online); W Elizabeth 26 (M Apr 56| ReM 1874): chn: 2 ♂- George 6, Alvin 3.
R2#29	JEREMIAH DANFORTH 19 MA Inf C [Antietam reburial]			B 2/2/1818 Essex Co. MA. R Georgetown, Essex Co., MA. Occ shoemaker. E Aug 61 private. Wounded at Antietam on 9/17/62. D Dec 8, 1862 at Chambersburg (age 44). Survivors (WC4380): W Abigail 43 (M Apr 39); 7 chn: 3 ♂- Eben 23, George 14, Charles 14 & 4 ♀- Julia 16, Sarah 7, Annie 4, Abigail 3.
R2#30	CHARLES A TRASK 13 MA Inf K [Antietam reburial]			B ~1841 ME. R Southborough, Worcester Co., MA. Occ shoemaker. E Jul 61 private. Wounded at Antietam on 9/17/62: back wound. Died October 2, 1862 at Chambersburg (age ~22). Survivor (WC120943): F James Trask 52 (disabled widower of Martha Brown).
R2#31	CHARLES H WELLINGTON 13 MA Inf K {Antietam reburial]			B ~1838 Holden, Worcester Co., MA. R Upton, Worcester Co., MA. Occ bootmaker. E Jul 61 private. Wounded at Antietam on 9/17/1862: shoulder wound. Died October 2, 1862 (age ~24). Survivor (WC138724 not online): W Ann 23 (M Jul 60| ReM 1869); 1 ♀- Fanny 1.
R2#32	DANIEL HOLLAND	23-24	19 Inf D	B ~1839 Ireland. R Boston, MA. Occ laborer. E Jul 61 private. KIA Jul 3.
R2#33	P W PRICE PETER W PRICE	~34	28 Inf C	B ~1829 Wales. R Boston, MA. Occ bootmaker. E Oct 61 private. Promoted to sergeant on 9/1/62. Jan/Feb 63: in detention following charge of desertion. KIA Jul 2. Survivor (WC21554): W Margaret 35 (M Feb 60); no chn.
R2#34	GEORGE LAWTON	~22	16 Inf H	B ~1841 England. R Waltham, Middlesex Co., MA. Occ blacksmith. E June 61 private. Wounded at 2nd Bull Run on 8/29/62. KIA Jul 2.
R2#35	J COAKLEY JEREMIAH COAKLEY	~21	16 Inf A	B ~1842. E Jul 61 private. R Cambridge, Middlesex Co., MA. Occ glass blower. E Jul 61 private. Jul/Aug 61: left in Baltimore for hospitalization. Mar 62: discharged from hospital and sent home to Cambridge for a further 30-day sick leave to round out his convalescence. KIA Jul 2. Survivor (WC22133): M Mrs. Catherine Coakley 45 (widow of Timothy Coakley).
R3#1	J L JOHNSON JOHN T JOHNSON[61]	~17	CONFED MS 11 Inf K	B ~1846 (if given age 18 at enrollment truthful): MS. R Carroll Co., MS. Occ student. E Mar 62 private. Mortally wounded Jul 3.

---

61 **Confederate in the Cemetery dead as a minor**. John Johnson is one of nine misidentified Confederates mistakenly buried in the National Cemetery. Johnson's reported ages of 4 and 14 on the successive October 1850 and September 1860 U.S. Census sheets attest to the likelihood that he was not 18, but no older than 16 at his March 1862 enlistment. These Census dates also mean he was no older than 17 when he was killed at Gettysburg.

R3#2	JOSEPH MARSHALL JOSEPH A **MORRILL**	~24	11 Inf K	B ~1839 Danville, Caledonia Co., VT. E Jun 61 private. Occ molder. Hospitalized at Yorktown 5/6/62→Jul/Aug 62 for an unspecified condition. C Jul 2: GSW to left ankle. D August 2. Survivor (WC12447): W Jennie 23 (M Jun 61); no chn.
R3#3	JAMES E BUTLER **JOHN E BUTLER**[62]	~20	11 Inf D	B ~1843 Ireland. R Boston, MA. Occ glass blower. E Jun 61 private. KIA Jul 2. Survivor (WC12156): W Mary 17 (M 3/16/63); no chn.
R3#4	MICHAEL DOHERTY	~38	11 Inf A	B ~1825 Ireland. R Boston, MA. Occ stonecutter. E Jun 61 private. Wounded severely 5/5/62 at Williamsburg, VA. KIA Jul 2. Survivors (WC 24800): W Hanoria ~37 (M Nov 46); 3 ♀- Mary 14, Ann 6, Hanoria 2.
R3#5	LUCIUS STAPLES	~23	11 Inf A	B ~1840 Bedford, MA. R Burlington, Middlesex Co., MA. Occ carriage maker. E Jun 61 private. Captured at James River on 6/30/62 and paroled on 7/25/62. Sick, absent from regiment until returned on 4/13/63. KIA Jul 2.
R3#6	CORP EDWIN F TRUFANT (MN FRANKLIN)	25	11 Inf F	B 6/15/1838 NYC. R Weymouth, Norfolk Co., MA. Occ bootmaker. E June 61 private. Promoted to corporal on 9/1/62. KIA Jul 2. Survivor (WC64645): M Mrs. Charlotte Trufant 52 in 1865 (widow of Orin Trufant).
R3#7	CORP C R T KNOWLTON CHARLES RUSSELL TRAIN KNOWLTON[63]	25	11 Inf H	B 2/20/1838 Framingham, Middlesex Co., MA. R Ashland, Middlesex Co., MA. Occ carpenter. E Jun 61 private. Never promoted to corporal. Captured 7/21/61 at 1st Bull Run. Not paroled until 5/28/62. KIA Jul 2. Survivors (WC10499): W Maria 26 (M Feb 59 |ReM 1872); 1 ♂- Charles Edward Knowlton 16 months.
R3#8	SERGT WM SAWTELL **WILLIAM SAWTELL**	~22	11 Inf E	B ~1841 Boston, MA. R East Boston, MA. Occ pile driver. E Apr 61 private. Wounded and captured at 2nd Bull run on 8/29/62. Promoted to corporal on parole. May/Jun 63: promotion to sergeant. C Jul 2: severely wounded in abdomen and both thighs. D Jul 5.
R3#9	J S RICE **JOHN S RICE**	30-31	11 Inf K	B ~1832 Troy, Cheshire Co., NH. R Roxbury, Boston, MA. Occ carpenter. E Sep 61 private. C Jul2: wounded in hip. D Jul 15. Survivors (WC11519): W Agnes 27 (M May 54); 3 chn: 2 ♂- Amos 8, Frank 6 & 1 ♀- Hattie 2.

---

62 **Soldier fighting under an alias.** Mrs. Mary Butler's successful approval of a widow's pension had required that she persuade the Pension Office that her husband, John E. Butler, was using the alias James E. Butler when he enlisted into the army.

63 **Prior to Gettysburg soldier had been held for a prolonged Confederate imprisonment.** Private Charles Knowlton was captured July 21, 1861 at First Bull Run. His service record does not report an injury in this battle, but he may have been. He was not paroled by the Confederates until May 1862.

R3#10	SUMNER A DAVIS	24	11 Inf K	B 2/13/1839 Natick, Middlesex Co., MA. R Wayland, Middlesex Co., MA. Occ shoemaker. E May 61 private. Promoted to corporal in Apr 62. Wounded in the leg on 8/29/62 at 2nd Bull Run. C Jul 2: wound to abdomen. D Jul 15. Survivor (WC78901) M Mrs. Louisa Smith 44 in 1865 (abandoned by 2nd husband, Horace Smith).
R3#11	FRANCIS T FLINT FRANCIS **S** FLINT	18	11 Inf H	B 7/3/1844 Reading, Middlesex Co., MA. R North Reading, MA. Occ shoemaker. E Jun 61 private. Apr 62: promoted to corporal. Severely wounded on 5/5/62 at Williamsburg, VA. Returned from the hospital on 10/4/62. KIA Jul 2. Survivor (WC14763): M Mrs. Susan Flint 56 (Henry C. Flint intemperate and does little to nothing to support wife).
R3#12	JOHN BRODIE			Killed Gettysburg soldier with this name not found in Massachusetts records and military sources.
R3#13	SERGT WILLIAM CARR (MN REMINGTON)	23	12 Inf I	B 12/17/1839 Limerick, York Co., ME. R South Groveland, Essex Co., MA. Occ bootmaker. E Jun 61 private. Promotion to sergeant on 10/1/62. C Jul 1: severe wound to left leg→amp. D Jul 14.
R3#14	GEORGE F LEWIS	~24	12 Inf H	B ~1839 MA. R Weymouth, Norfolk Co., MA. Occ carpenter. E Jun 61 private. KIA Jul 3.
R3#15	HARDY P MURRAY (MN PHIPPIN)	20	12 Inf K	B 7/27/1842 Manchester-by-the-Sea, Essex Co., MA. R same. Occ mason. E Sep 61 private. C Jul 1: wounded in abdomen. D Jul 6. Survivor (WC87119 not online): M Mrs. Mary Murray 55 in 1866 (John Murray affirmed unable to support wife).
R3#16	CORP T H FENELON THOMAS H FENELON	~19	32 Inf G	B ~1844 MA. R Boston, MA. Occ bookkeeper. E May 62 corporal. Hospitalized early in term of service with an unspecified illness. C Jul 2. D Jul 4.
R3#17	WILLIAM D HUDSON WILLIAM **E** HUDSON	25	32 Inf H	B 6/26/1838 Framingham, Middlesex Co., MA. R same. Occ farmer. E Jul 62 private. C Jul 2. D Jul 3. Survivor (WC94511): M Mrs. Martha Hudson 67 (widow of Nathan Hudson).
R3#18	BARNEY CLARK **BARNARD** CLARK	~29	32 Inf G	B ~1834 Ireland. R Concord, Boston, MA. Occ laborer. E Jun 62 private. C Jul 2: wounded in the abdomen. D Jul 9. Survivors (WC114639): W Bridget 26 (M Aug 59| ReM Jan 64); 2 ♀- Mary 2, Margaret 1.

R3#19	SERGT J M HASKELL JAMES MADISON HASKELL	39	32 Inf A	B 7/24/1824 Augusta, ME. R Hingham, Boston, MA. Occ currier. E Apr 61 into 1st Battery MD Co A. Transferred to the 32nd MA Infantry. Jan 63: promoted to sergeant. C Jul 2: wounded in both legs→left leg amp. D Aug 25. Survivors (WC99062): M Mrs. Rachel Haskell 55 in 1866 (William Haskell affirmed unable to support his wife).
R3#20	ALVIN W LAMB (MN WILLIS)	21	32 Inf A	B 5/24/1842 Fitchburg, Worcester Co., MA. R same. Occ farmer. E Nov 61 private. C Jul 2: shot in right chest. D Jul 6.
R3#21	WILLIAM F BALDWIN (MN FRANKLIN)	19	32 Inf B	B 4/6/1844 Waltham, Middlesex Co., MA. R same. Occ farmer. E Nov 61 private. C Jul 2: wound to spine. D Jul 28.
R3#22	HENRY T WADE	~29	32 Inf E	B 1834 East Bridgewater, Plymouth Co., MA. R Braintree, Norfolk Co., MA. Occ bootmaker. E Dec 61 private. C Jul 2: wounded in left knee and right leg. D Jul 31. Survivor (WC48199): W Ann 25 (M June 56); no chn.
R3#23	CORP WM L GILLMAN WILLIAM **GILMAN**[64]	~29	32 Inf K	B ~1834 Greene County, NY. R Newton, Middlesex Co., MA. Occ clergyman. E Jul 62 corporal. Detached for hospital duty as a nurse 12/11/62→2/10/63. C Jul 2: wounded in left knee→amp. D Jul 30.
R3#24	DEMERICK STODDAR DEMERKCK **STODDER III**[65]	23	32 Inf F	B 11/23/1839 Hingham, Plymouth Co., MA. R same. Occ shoemaker. E Jul 61 private in 4th MA Infantry. Transferred to the 32nd infantry on 2/20/62. KIA Jul 2.
R3#25	CORP NATHANIEL MAYO	~25	32 Inf F	B ~1838 MA. R Boston, MA. Occ bootmaker. E Feb 62 private. Promoted to corporal on 3/01/63. KIA Jul 2: instantly killed by a minié ball.
R3#26	T J HEALEY THOMAS J **HEALY**	18-19	32 Inf G	B ~1844 Ireland. R Roxbury, Boston MA. Occ laborer. E Oct 62 private. KIA Jul 2: GSW to head. Survivor (WC25929): M Mrs. Ellen Healy 35 (widow of John Healy).
R3#27	JAMES H LEAVERNS JAMES HOWE **LEAVENS**[66] or LEVINES	F24	18 Inf A	B 2/16/1839 New Bedford, Bristol Co., MA. R same. Occ teamster. E Aug 61 private. Absent wounded 8/18→9/4/62. Promoted to sergeant on 2/1/63. KIA Jul 2. Survivor (123487): M Mrs. Almira Scott 54 in 1868 (separated from 2nd husband, James Scott, a "worthless, indolent man").

---

64 **Prior occupation a clergyman.** William Gilman had been a clergyman prior to entering the arm. A FindAGrave.com post recounts how a visitor to the barn where Gilman and a hundred other injured men were receiving care, found Gilman cheerfully proselytizing and encouraging all the wounded men in the barn.

65 **Soldier as an infant had lost seafaring father at sea.** Demerick's father, Demerick Stodder II, had been a sea schooner captain, who was lost at sea when Demerick was only 4 months old.

66 **Soldier had been cited for bravery at Fredericksburg.** Private James Levens was one of five men cited by their regimental colonel for bravery at the 1862 Battle of Fredericksburg.

Ref	Name	Age	Unit	Details
R3#28	SERGT G COFFIN GORHAM COFFIN	28	19 Inf A	B 4/21/1835 West Newbury, Essex Co., MA. R same. Occ shoemaker. E Aug 61 private. Promoted to corporal on 9/1/62. Wounded on 9/17/62 at Antietam. Promoted to sergeant on 11/1/62. KIA Jul 3.
R3#29	SERGT JOSEPH FORD	25	9 inf K	B 5/18/1838 Ireland. R Stoughton, Norfolk Co., MA. Occ bootmaker. E Jun 61 private. Promoted to sergeant on 7/5/61. Sent to hospital with typhoid fever on 7/6/62. Returned to regiment on 9/4/62. Promoted to 1st sergeant on 12/14/62. KIA Jul 2.
R3#30	EDWARD ROCHE EDMUND ROCHE	30	19 Inf E	B ~Sep 1832 Ireland. R Lynn, Essex Co., MA. Occ Morocco dresser. E Aug 62 private. KIA Jul 2. Survivors (WC11506): M Ellen 29 (M Nov 57 | ReM 1868); 2 chn: 1 ♀- Anna 4 & 1 ♂- John 7 months.
R3#31	CORP THOS W TUTTLE THOMAS W TUTTLE	19-20	19 Inf I	B ~1843 MA. R Boston, MA. Occ machinist. E Jul 61 private. Wounded on 6/25/62 at Fair Oaks, VA. Mar/Apr 63: returned to duty. Promoted to corporal on 5/1/63. KIA Jul 3.
R3#32	JEREMIAH WELLS (MN YOUNG)	36	19 Inf H	B 3/15/1827 Topsfield, Essex Co., MA. R same. Occ teamster. E Dec 61 private. Jan/Feb 62: detailed as wood chopper. Sick in hospital Sep 62→May 63. C Jul 3: shot in foot & leg→ amp. D Jul 21. Survivors (WC125423): W Frances 29 (M Jul 49 | ReM 1867); 1 ♀- Florence 8.
R3#33	CHARLES GURNEY	24	37 Inf E	B 3/18/1839 Plainfield, Hampshire Co., MA. R Cummington, Hampshire Co., MA. Occ farmer. E Aug 62 private. C Jul 3: wounded in both legs. D Jul 10.
R3#34	E BASSAMUNSON ENOS BESONCON	30	37 Inf B	B ~1833 France. R Sandisfield, Berkshire Co., MA. Occ collier. E Jul 62 private. C Jul 3: wound fracturing right femur. D Jul 27.
R3#35	ELISHA COVILLE ELIHU COVILL	18-19	37 Inf E	B 1844 Hatfield, Hampshire Co., MA. R same. Occ farmer. E Aug 62 private. C Jul 3: wound to left thigh. D Jul 22.
R4#1	CHARLES TRAYNOR CHARLES TRAYNER	~31	2 Inf I	B ~1832 Ireland. R Waltham, Middlesex Co., MA. Occ laborer. E May 61 private. Wounded and captured on 5/24/62 at Winchester, VA. Nov/Dec 62: returned to regiment. KIA Jul 3. Survivors (WC110793): W Bridget ~28 (M Dec 57); 2 chn: 1 ♀- Catharine 10 & 1 ♂- James 8.
R4#2	WILLIAM T BULLARD	37-38	2 Inf A	B ~1825 Oxford, Worcester Co., MA. R Boston, MA. Occ shoemaker. E Aug 62 private. KIA Jul 3. Survivors (WC56413): W Frances Josephine 38 in 1864 (M Oct 49); 2 chn: 1 ♂- Eugene 12 & 1 ♀- Eva 9.
R4#3	JOHN JOY	24-25	2 Inf I	B ~1838 Ireland. R Boston, MA. Occ waiter. E Aug 62 private. KIA Jul 3.

R4#4	PHILO H PECK[67] (MN HAWKES)	~20	2 Inf G		B 8/7/1842 Hawley, Franklin Co., MA. Occ laborer. E (Boston, MA) May 61 private. Detached as hospital attendant 11/28/61→4/11/62. Jan/Feb 63: sentenced in court martial proceeding to forfeit of $8 from pay for an unspecified infraction. KIA Jul 3. Survivor (WC138408): F Horace Peck 72 in 1869 (disabled widower of Clymena Peck).
R4#5	STEPHEN CODY	~28	2 Inf I		B ~1835 Ireland. R Boston, MA. Occ glazier. E May 61 private. Captured on 5/25/62 near Winchester, VA. Paroled on 9/13/62 at Aiken's Landing, VA. KIA Jul 3.
R4#6	RICHARD SEAVERS	~28	2 Inf H		B ~1835 Ireland. R North Easton, Boston, MA. Occ laborer. E May 61 private. Absent, sick in hospital with an unspecified condition: 10/22/62→May 63. KIA Jul 3.
R4#7	GEORGE BAILEY GEORGE M BAILEY	~25	2 Inf I		B ~1838 MA. R Wilmington, Middlesex Co., MA. Occ shoemaker. E May 61 private. Captured on 8/17/62. Paroled on 9/13/62 at Aiken's Landing. KIA Jul 3. Survivor (WC135914): M Mrs. Hannah Bailey 72 in 1868 (widow of Abner Bailey).
R4#8	ANDREW NELSON	19-20	2 Inf D		B ~1843 Lowell, Middlesex Co., MA. R same. Occ printer. E Oct 61 private. Mar/Apr 63: absent, sick in hosp. KIA Jul 3. Survivor (WC45034): M Mrs. Elizabeth Nelson 47 in 1864 (widow of James Nelson).
R4#9	JOHN DEER JOHN **DERR**	~30	2 Inf D		B ~1833 Germany. R Stockbridge, Berkshire Co., MA. Occ farmer. E May 61 private. Mar/Apr 63: absent sick in hospital. KIA Jul 3.
R4#10	CORP GORDON S WILSON	22	2 Inf G		B 4/18/1841 Salisbury, Merrimack Co., NH. R Plymouth, Grafton Co., NH. Occ clerk. E May 61 private. Detached Jul/Aug→Sep/Oct 62 for recruiting service. Promoted to corporal on 1/1/63. KIA Jul 3. Survivors (WC30776): M Mrs. Laura Wilson 38 (William Nelson affirmed to have physical disability).
R4#11	JOSEPH FURBUR JOSEPH HENRY **FURBER, JR.**[68]	32-33	2 Inf G		B ~1830 Westmoreland, Cheshire Co., NH. R Boston, MA. Occ teamster. E Oct 62 private. KIA Jul 3. Survivors (WC21726): W Mary 34 (M Nov 51| died 12/13/1863); 5 chn: 2 ♂- Joseph 11, John 3 & 3 ♀- Elizabeth 7, Edna 5, Mary 15 months.

---

67 **Father in pension application reports previous son killed in service**. The 72-year-old widower Horace Peck applied for a dependent father's pension in 1869. His application was prompted by the loss of support following the death of his son, Philo Peck. However, Horace Peck reported that he had also lost a second son in the war. Chauncey Peck, an enlistee of the 13th Massachusetts Infantry, had been killed in action on August 30, 1862 at 2nd Bull Run.

68 **Soldier's five children lose him in July, mother in December**. Joseph Furber's death at Gettysburg would leave his five young children without a father. Only five months later, these children would see their mother also die, a death attributed to anemia.

R4#12	COL CORP R J SADLER RUPERT J SADLER	20-21	2 Inf D	B ~1842 Ireland. R Lynn, Essex Co., MA. Occ machinist. E Oct 61 private. Promoted to corporal on 11/28/62. KIA Jul 3.
R4#13	FREDERICK MAYNARD	25-26	2 Inf D	B ~1837 MA. R Winchendon, Worcester Co., MA. Occ machinist. E May 61 corporal. Reduced from rank of corporal to private 5/1/62 on account of an unspecified offense. Detailed to pioneer corps 5/30/62→ Jul/Aug 62. KIA Jul 3.
R4#14	PATRICK HOEY PATRICK **HOYE**	19	2 Inf A	B ~Sep 1843 Ireland. R Lowell, Middlesex Co., MA. Occ carder. E May 61 private. Promoted to corporal on 5/12/63. KIA Jul 3.
R4#15	SERGT L C DURGIN **LEAVITT** C DURGIN[69]	19-20	2 Inf A	B ~1843 Beekmantown, Clinton Co., NY. E May 61 private. Promoted to corporal on 12/22/61. Serving as color corporal since 5/1/62. Promoted to color sergeant on 4/10/63. Casualty relief 4/27→5/6/63 for slight wounds of arm and leg. KIA Jul 3 "while gallantly bearing the colors." Survivors (WC90644): M Mrs. Deborah Durgin 62 in 1866 (Stephen Durgin affirmed unable to support wife).
R4#16	CORP WM MARSHALL WILLIAM MARSHALL	32-33	2 Inf C	B 1830 East Weare, Hillsborough Co., NH. R Boston, MA. Occ mechanic. E Aug 62 private. No service record documentation that soldier promoted to corporal. KIA Jul 3. Survivors (WC9894): W Delia 37 (M Nov 47); 3 chn: 1 ♀- Angelica 15 & 2 ♂- William 10, Emerson 9.
R4#17	CORP RUEL WHITTIER	27-28	2 Inf B	B ~1835 Mercer, Somerset Co., ME. R Lowell, Middlesex Co., MA. Occ carpenter. E May 61 private. Promoted to corporal 8/31/61. Hospitalized at Alexandria for an unspecified condition: 11/30/61→Jan/Feb 62. KIA Jul 3. Survivor (WC13211): M Mrs. Sarah Whittier 60 (widow of John Whittier).
R4#18	JAMES T EDMANDS JAMES T **EDMONDS**	~31	2 Inf I	B ~1832 Charlestown, Boston, MA. R Billerica, Middlesex Co., MA. Occ teamster. E May 61 private. Nov/Dec 61: court martial sentence to forfeit one-month's pay for an unspecified infraction. Wounded at Cedar Mountain 8/9/62 and hospitalized subsequently in Alexandria, VA. C Jul 3: wounds to leg and arm. D Jul 21.
R4#19	JOHN E FARRINGTON	21	2 Inf H	B 4/4/1842 Milford, Worcester Co., MA. R same. Occ laborer. E Aug 62 private. KIA Jul 3.
R4#20	PETER CONLAN	23-24	2 Inf 20	B ~1839 Ireland. R East Cambridge, Middlesex, MA. Occ laborer. E May 61 private. C Jul 3: wounded in neck. D Jul 11. Survivors (WC14282): M Mrs. Nancy Conlan 58 (Charles Conlan paralyzed and unable to work).

---

69 **Color Sergeant's death**. Sergeant Leavitt Durgin is one of very few confirmed color sergeants killed in the battle and buried in the National Cemetery.

R4#21	SIDNEY S PROUTY	~33	2 Inf A	B ~1830 Onondaga Co., NY. R Lowell, Middlesex Co., MA. Occ mason. E May 61 private. Dec 61: court martial sentence to forfeit 3 weeks' pay for an unspecified infraction. C Jul 3: wound to left thigh and right hip. D Jul 19. Survivor (WC92966): F Simeon Prouty 61 in 1866 (infirmed widower of Sabrina Prouty).
R4#22	F GOETZ FRITZ GOETZ	20	2 Inf C	B 8/30/1842 Germany. R Dorchester, Boston, MA. Occ laborer. E Aug 62 private. C Jul 3: GSW to left thigh. D Jul 6. Survivors (WC120047 not online): M Mrs. Barbara Goetz 53 in 1866 (Frederick Goetz affirmed disabled).
R4#23	CORP THEODORE S BUTTERS (MN STEPHEN)	22	2 Inf I	B 5/21/1841 Wilmington, Middlesex Co., MA. R same. Occ farmer. E May 61 private. Promoted to corporal on 4/10/63. C Jul 3: GSW to right leg→amp. D Jul 31. Survivor (WC252439 not online): M Mrs. Angeline Butters 68 in 1888 (Lorenzo Butters died in 1884).
R4#24	DAVID B BROWN	~34	2 Inf I	B ~1839 Scotland. R Boston, MA. Occ japanner (varnisher). E May 61 corporal. Court martial sentence on 7/3/61 to reduce rank to private and to forfeit one month's pay for an unspecified offense. Wounded and captured 8/9/62 at Cedar Mountain. Paroled on 9/13/62 at Aiken's Landing. Furlough granted 4/1-27/63 for an unspecified exigency. C Jul 3: wounded in abdomen. D Jul 21.
R4#25	WILLIAM H ELA	29-30	2 Inf D	B 1833 Boston, MA. R same. Occ printer. E Aug 62 private. Detailed as hospital attendant 11/9/62→3/3/63. C Jul 3: GSW to left side. D Jul 10.
R4#26	JAMES A CHASE[70] (MN ABNER)	29	2 Inf C	B 2/17/1834 Newbury, Essex Co., MA. R Hamilton, Essex Co., MA. Occ shoemaker. E May 61 private. Detailed as hospital nurse: 11/28/61→8/31/62. C Jul 3: GSW to left shoulder. D Jul 16. Survivors (WC10116): W Louisa 35 (M Jun54); 1 ♀- Mary Ann 8.
R4#27	CHARLES REIMAN CHARLES **KIERNAN**	~20	2 Inf F	B ~1843 NY. R Wenham, Essex Co., MA. Occ farmer. E May 61 private. Wounded on 9/17/62 at Antietam. C Jul 3. D Jul 13.
R4#28	AND. MOORE ANDREW T MOORE[71]	47-48	1 Inf F	B ~1815 Providence, RI. R Boston, MA. Occ frame maker. E Aug 62 private. Deserted from camp on 1/31/63. Returned to regiment from desertion on 4/12/63. KIA Jul 2. Survivors (WC10634): W Catharine 43 (M Jun 1840); 2 ♂- Andrew 11, George 3 months.

---

70 **Soldier's extended service as a hospital nurse.** James Chase was detailed as a hospital nurse for nine months of his twenty-six-month enlistment. His death on July 16th, likely in a field hospital, would leave behind a wife and eight-year-old daughter.

71 **Overaged at enlistment.** At his August 1862 enlistment, Andrew Moore gave his age as 43. However, the age he gave for the 1855 Massachusetts State Census was 40, which would have made his age at this enlistment 47, or two years beyond upper age restriction for voluntary enlistment, which was 45.

R4#29	LIEUT HENRY HARTLEY	~29	1 Inf E	B ~1834 England. R Williamsburg, NY. Occ carver and gilder. E May 61 sergeant. Promoted to 2nd lieutenant by Massachusetts Governor Andrew on 8/26/61. Promoted to 1st lieutenant on 8/21/62. Serving as acting captain since 9/1/62. Absence on leave 3/7-21/63 for unspecified exigencies. KIA Jul 2.
R4#30	FREDERICK S KRETTEL FREDERICK STICKNEY **KETTELL**	29	1 Inf E	B 11/27/1833 Boston, MA. R Boston, MA. Occ painter. E Aug 62 private. C Jul 2: wounded in thigh. D Aug 2. Survivors (WC34747): W Mary 35 (M Nov 59); 2 ♀- Irene 2, Bertha 6 months.
R4#31	GEORGE GOLDEN	35-36	1 Inf B	B ~1827 Portland, ME. R East Boston, MA. Occ cooper. E Aug 62 private. C Jul 2: GSW to right foot. D Jul 13. Survivors (WC33651): W Julia 37 in 1864 (M Nov 47); 3 ♀- Eliza 13, Julia 11, Alice 9.
R4#32	DAVID H EATON (MN HANSON)	31	1 Inf B	B 1/26/1832 Chesterville, Franklin Co., ME. R Boston, MA. Occ teamster. E Aug 62 private. Nov/Dec 61: detailed to pioneer corporals. C Jul 2: GSW to left thigh. D Jul 15. Survivors (WC89913): W Elizabeth 25 (M Apr 56/ReM Jan 64); 2 ♂ Charles 5, William 3.
R4#33	JACOB KESLAND[72]	28-29	1 Inf B	B ~1834 Denmark. R Boston, MA. Occ cooper. E Aug 62 private. C Jul 2. D Jul 10.
R4#34	SERGT E J McGINNIS EDWARD J **McGINNESS**	~24	1 Inf C	B ~1839 Boston, MA. R same. Occ caulker. E May 61 private. Promoted to corporal on 11/1/62. Promoted to sergeant on 2/1/63. KIA Jul 2: GSW to side. Survivor (10632): W Catharine 21 (M Mar 59); no chn.
R4#35	J MATTHEWS JAMES M **MATHEWS**	26-27	1 Inf D	B ~1836 Ludlow, Hampden Co., MA. R Montague, Franklin Co., MA. Occ painter. E Aug 62 private. KIA Jul 3: instantly killed by Minié ball to the head. Survivors (WC16575): W Adaline 32 (M Apr 59); 2 ♀: Maria 3, Adaline 20 months.
R4#36	SERGT WILLIAM KELREN	~32	1 Inf E	B ~1831 Portland, ME. R South Boston, MA. Occ teamster. E May 61 corporal Nov/Dec 62: present as sergeant. KIA Jul 2. Survivor (WC10753): W Mary 30 (M Nov 54); no chn.
R4#37	CORP HENRY EVANS	~26	1 Inf A	B ~1837 England. R South Boston, MA. Occ silversmith. E May 61 private. Promoted to corporal on 11/1/62. Furlough granted 3/10→30/63 for an unspecified exigency. KIA Jul 2. Survivors (WC33181): M Mrs. Mary Barker 58 in 1864 (Thomas Barker, 2nd husband, affirmed unable to perform labor).

---

72 **No widow's pension approval found in records**. The 1860 U.S. Census shows a Jacob Kissland, a 27-year-old cooper from Denmark, residing in Boston along with Mary, his 26-year-old Irish-born wife and their one-year-old girl, Mary. Whatever became of this wife and daughter is a mystery, as their names are not found among pension recipients, such as the death of a husband and father should have entitled them. Possibly, the wife and daughter preferred to return to Europe.

R5#1	ARTHUR MURPHY[73]	17	9 Indpt Batt MA LA	B ~1846 Boston, MA. R same. Occ clerk. E Jul 62 private. KIA Jul 2.
R5#2	JOHN W VERITY	~20	5th Art	B ~1843 NY. E Feb 62 into 10th Independent NY LA as a private. May 63: transferred to 5th MA LA. KIA Jul 2.
R5#3	EDWARD FROTHINGHAM		*5th Art*	No killed Gettysburg soldier with this name and assigned to a battery confirmed in military sources
R5#4	JOHN CRASSON JOHN **CROSEN**	20-21	9th Indpt Batt MA LA	B ~1842 Boston, MA. R same. Occ butcher. E Jul 62 private. KIA Jul 2.
R5#5	HENRY C BURRILL[74] 20 Inf H			Misidentified soldier in grave. Sergeant. Henry C Burrill. 20th MA Co H, was discharged with a disability in 1863 and lived into the 20th century.
R5#6	THOMAS KELLY	23-24	20 Inf A	B ~1839 Ireland. R Marblehead, Essex Co, MA. E Aug 61 private. Occ shoemaker. Captured 10/21/61 at Ball's Bluff, VA. Paroled on 2/20/62 at the James River, VA. Wounded on 9/17/62 at Antietam. Hospitalized Dec 62→Feb 63 with an unspecified condition. KIA Jul 3. Survivors (WC9511): W Ellen 30 (M May 59); 1 ♂- Thomas 2.
R5#7	GEORGE LUCAS	25	20 Inf D	B 10/8/1837 New Bedford, Bristol Co., MA. R same. Occ teamster. E Aug 61 private. Captured at Ball's Buff on 10/21/61. Paroled on 2/15/62 at the James River, VA. Hospitalized in Washington, D.C.: 12/25/62→ Jan/Feb 63. KIA Jul 3.
R5#8	ALIAS KRAFT **ALOIS** KRAFT	31-32	20 Inf C	B ~1831 Germany. R Boston, MA. Occ confectioner. E Jul 61 private. Wounded 10/21/61 at Ball's Bluff, VA. KIA Jul 3.
R5#9	T R GALLIVAN THOMAS R GALLIVAN	36-37	20 Inf F	B ~1826 Ireland. R Palmer, Hampden Co., MA. Occ farmer. E Aug 61 private. Mar/Apr 63: detached service with ambulance corporals. Sentenced on 6/20/63 by a court martial proceeding to forfeit $10 each of the following two months' pay based on a conviction for drunkenness on duty. KIA Jul 3. Survivors (WC20769): W Mary 45 (M Feb 40 in Ireland); 7 chn: 4 ♀- Fanny 22, Maria 18, Julia 13, Anna 11 & 3 ♂ - Henry 20, Robert 17, John 15.

---

73 **Death as minor.** Arthur Murphy's reported ages of 4 and 14 in the successive September 1850 and July 7, 1860 U.S. Censuses attest to the likelihood that Arthur was 16, not 18 at his July 1862 enlistment. He was likely 17 when he was killed. Arthur Murphy's Irish-born father, Daniel Murphy, reported his occupation as bridge architect in the 1860 U.S. Census. Daniel Murphy died in 1862, six months before his son would enlist into the army.

74 **Misidentified soldier in grave.** Sergeant Henry Burrill was discharged with a disability and would live into the 20th century.

R5#10	M KINARCH MICHAEL **KINNARK**	30-31	20 Inf H	B ~1832 Ireland. R Lynn, Essex Co., MA. Occ shoemaker. E Dec 61 private. Absent, sick in general hospital 8/15/62→Jan 63. KIA Jul 3.
R5#11	E BARRY EDWARD BARRY	24-25	20 Inf G	B ~1838 Ireland. R Boston, MA. Occ tailor. E Jul 61 private. Captured 11/21/61 at Ball's Bluff, VA. Paroled 6/2/62 at Washington, Beaufort Co., NC. Sent to Washington, D.C. on 9/26/62 62. KIA Jul 2. Survivors (WC15711): W Eliza 25 (M Nov 54| ReM Jan 64); 2 ♀- Mary 7, Ellen 3.
R5#12	SERGT GEORGE JOECKEL	26-27	20 Inf B	B ~1836 Boston, MA. R Roxbury, Boston, MA. Occ cabinet maker. E Jul 61 private. Promoted to corporal on 7/28/62. Wounded 9/17/62 at Antietam, subsequently hospitalized at Frederick. Sep/Oct 62: present as sergeant. KIA Jul 3: GSW to the head with instant death. Survivor (WC7575): M Mrs. Barbara Joeckel 53 (widow of Jacob Joeckel).
R5#13	PATRICK O'KEEFE **PETER KEEFE**	21-22	20 Inf F	B ~1841 Boston, MA. Occ mechanic. E Aug 61 private. KIA Jul 3.
R5#14	THOMAS DOWNEY	35-36	20 Inf E	B ~1827 Ireland. R Boston, MA. Occ stonecutter. E Aug 62 private. C Jul 3. D Jul 13. Survivors (WC28431): W Mary 38 (M May 39| ReM 9/26/64); 7 chn: 4 ♀- Elizabeth 15, Mary 7, Margaret 5, Susannah 2 & 3 ♂- Robert 13, John 9, Thomas 16 weeks.
R5#15	CORP JAMES SOMERVILLE	19-20	20 Inf E	B ~1843 Ireland. R Boston, MA. Occ sailor. E Jul 61 private. Captured 9/17/62 at Antietam. Paroled 10/6/62 at Aiken's Landing, VA. Promoted to corporal on 1/1/63. KIA Jul 3.
R5#16	WILLIAM INCH	32-33	20 Inf D	B ~1830 Ireland. R Boston, MA. Occ weaver. E Jul 62 private. KIA Jul 3.
R5#17	AUGUSTUS DEITLING AUGUSTUS **DETTLING** or DUTTLING	~21	20 Inf C	B 1842 Germany. R Boston, MA. Occ farmer. E Jul 61 private. KIA Jul 3.
R5#18	SERGT GEORGE F CATE	19-20	20 Inf A	B ~1843 Roxbury, Boston, MA. R same. Occ gas fitter. E Aug 61 private. Wounded in hand 6/30/62 at Nelson's farm. Jul/Aug 62: promotion to corporal. Promoted to sergeant on 12/21/62. Promoted to 1st sergeant on 4/15/63. KIA Jul 3. Survivor (WC9510): M Mrs. Louisa Cate 52 (widow of James Cate).
R5#19	CLEMENS WIESSENSEE CLEMENS **WEISSENSEE**	27-28	20 Inf B	B ~1835 Germany. R Boston, MA. Occ cabinet maker. E Jul 61 private. Captured 6/30/62 at the Battle of Nelson's Farm, Henrico Co., VA. Paroled 8/5/62, then absent, sick 8/22/62→Jan/Feb 63. KIA Jul 3.

R5#20	PATRICK QUINLIN PATRICK **QUINLAN**[75]	~30	20 Inf F	B ~1833 Ireland. R Boston, MA. Occ laborer. E Jul 61 private. Sep→Oct 61: performing daily duty as company cook. Oct 61: charged with loss of an overcoat while burying dead in VA. AWOL 12/15/61→Mar 62. Sep/Oct 62: absent, sick in general hospital. May 63: AWOL since 4/4/63. KIA Jul 3. Survivors (WC20173): Edward Quinlan (his brother?) 21 y/o; 3 chn: 2 ♀- Anne 11, Susan 8 & 1 ♂- Edward 5. (W Susan M Feb 52| died 4/14/63).
R5#21	G C PLANT GEORGE **L** PLANT[76]	38-39	20 Inf A	B 1824 England. R Boston, MA. Occ cutler. E Aug 61 private. Captured at Savage Station on 6/30/62. Jul/Aug 62: paroled, but having to be hospitalized into Jan/Feb 63. KIA Jul 3. Survivors (WC31962): W Ann 43 in 1864 (M Feb 44 in England and remaining resident in England): 1 ♀- Ann Jane ~5.
R5#22	HUGH BLAIN	~34	20 Inf H	B ~1829 Ireland. R Boston, MA. Occ draughtsman. E Jul 62 private. C Jul 3: wound to thigh. D Jul 10. Survivors (WC22155): W Janet 33 (M Jul 49); 4 chn: 3 ♀- Annie 10, Jessie 8, Caroline 7 & 1 ♂- Arthur 2.
R5#23	PATRICK MANNING	25-26	20 Inf D	B ~1837. R Royalston, Worcester Co., MA. Occ shoemaker. E Aug 61 private. C Jul 2: wounded in the wrist. D Jul 12.
R5#24	JOHN McCLARENCE JOHN **McCLANNEN**	24-25	20 Inf F	B ~1838 Glasgow, Scotland. Occ teamster. E (Readville, Boston, MA) Aug 61 private. Oct 62: detached to the Quartermaster Department bakery. Wounded 12/13/62 at Fredericksburg, VA. Jan 63: Employed building ovens for regiment. Mar/Apr 63: on extra duty as a baker. C Jul 3. D Jul 6.
R5#25	JOHN DIPPOLT *or* DIPPOLD	25-26	20 Inf B	B 1837 Germany. 1860: R Benzinger, Elk Co., PA; occ: farmer on farm with father. E Jul 61 private. C Jul 3. D Jul 14.
R5#26	HIRAM B HOWARD (MN BARTLETT)	25	20 Inf D	B 10/15/1837 Randolph, Norfolk Co., MA. R New Bedford, Bristol Co., MA. Occ butcher. E Jul 61 private. Detached service as brigade butcher 10/16/61 → May/June 62. Wounded at Antietam on 9/17/62. Sick at convalescent camp until returned to regiment on 4/22/63 (Had served as chief butcher while held at the camp). C Jul 2: wound to thigh→amp. D Jul 9.

---

75 **Soldier's three children lose mother in April, then him on July 3rd.** When Patrick Quinlin left his regiment on April 4 with an approved leave request, Patrick undoubtedly had the intention of returning home to Boston. Very likely Patrick had received some word that his wife Susan was dying. Following Susan's death on April 14, 1863, Patrick returned to his regiment. Eleven weeks after his wife's death, Patrick Quinlin would be killed at Gettysburg, leaving behind the couple's three young children.

76 "**Never will make a soldier.**" George Plant's regimental commander, complaining only two months into Plant's enlistment that Plant "never will make a soldier," attempted to detail him indefinitely to the Quartermaster's Department. His presence in the National Cemetery proves he knew how to die a soldier. An English immigrant, Plant's death left behind a wife and a 5-year-old daughter, both then residing back in England.

R5#27	EUGENE McLAUGHLIN	45-46	20 Inf F	B ~1817 Ireland. R Boston, MA. Occ carpenter. E Sep 61 private. Promoted to corporal during service. Wounded on the cheek by a spent ball on 5/31/62 at Fair Oaks, VA. C Jul 3: shell wound to the chest. D Jul 6. Survivors (WC32539): W Catharine 44 (M Oct 44); 1 ♂- George 15.
R5#28	CORP JOHN BURKE	33-34	20 Inf K	B ~1829 Ireland. R Springfield, Hampden Co., MA. Occ shoemaker. E Sep 61 private. Promoted to corporal during service. C Jul 3. D Aug 5 or 9. Survivors (WC13005→WC151317 neither online): Ellen 29 (M Nov 50| died 5/12/70 of typhoid pneumonia); 4 chn: 2 ♀- Mary 12, Cecilia 6 & 2 ♂- William 10, John 8.
R5#29	ALEXANDER AIKEN ALEXANDER **AKIN**	26-27	20 Inf D	B ~1836, Ireland. R New Bedford, Bristol Co., MA. Occ laborer. E Aug 61 private. Captured on 10/21/61 at Ball's Bluff, VA. Paroled 2/20/62 at James River, VA. Absent, sick on furlough since released from capture→Apr 62. Absent, sick in general hospital 8/15/62→ May/Jun 63. KIA Jul 2. Survivors (WC9904): W Mary 24 (M Oct 60); 1 ♂- Alexander 20 months.
R5#30	JAMES LANE[77]	~55	20 Inf F	B ~1808 Ireland. R South Boston, MA. Occ Laborer. E Aug 62. KIA Jul 3.: Survivors (WC12767): W Mary ~60 (M Jan 1833); no claimed chn.
R5#31	GEORGE F FALLS[78] Excelsior inf D	~20	74 NY Inf D	B 1843 MA. E May 61 private. KIA Jul 2
R5#32	GEORGE S WISE	~20	13 Inf D	B ~1843 Boston, MA. R same. Occ printer. E Jul 61 private. Sick in the hospital 8/31-11/9/61 with unspecified condition. C Jul 3: wound in one thigh. D Jul 12. Survivor (WC31098): M Mrs. Lovera Wise 44 (widow of George Wise).
R5#33	MICHAEL LAUGHLIN[79] or MICHAEL O'LAUGHLIN	23	13 Inf K	B ~1840 Ireland. R Shrewsbury, Worcester Co., MA. Occ shoemaker. E Jul 61 private. C Jul 2: GSW fracturing left leg near knee. D Nov 8. Survivor (WC17478): M Mrs. Margaret Laughlin 65 (widow of Patrick Laughlin).
R5#34	EDWIN FIELD	22	13 Inf B	B 6/30/1841 Chelsea, Suffolk Co., MA. R same. Occ clerk. E Jun 61 private. Sep/Oct 62→Jan/Feb 63: detached duty as brigade cattle guard. C Jul 1: GSW to left lung. D Jul 2.

---

77 **Overaged at enlistment.** James Lane's self-reported age of 46 in the July 1855 Massachusetts State Census and then of 53 in the July 1860 U.S. Census belie his claim that he was just at the recruitment upper-age limit of 45 when he enlisted.

78 **Birthyear question.** George Falls is found on the August 1850 U.S. Census as age 5. If this age were accurate, Falls could have been no older than 16 at his 1861 enlistment. However, other confirmatory sources would be required to definitely establish that he was underaged at his enlistment.

79 **Army makes a disreputable owed-money deduction on deceased soldier's final statement.** A Final Statement stoppage of $3.98 was made against any final pay due Michael O'Laughlin as of the date of his death. This numbingly callous stoppage was made to compensate the army for losses of his cartridge box plate, knapsack, coat straps and one-half shelter tent.

R5#35	JOHN M BROCK	23	13 Inf H	B Jun 1840 Mexico, Oxford Co., ME. R Natick, Middlesex Co., MA. Occ shoemaker. E Jun 61 private. Captured 8/30/62 at 2nd Bull Run. Paroled 10/13/62 at Centreville, Fairfax Co., VA. Held at parole camp 10/13/62→Jan/Feb 63 returned to duty. KIA Jul 1.
R5#36	FRANK A GOULD **FRANCIS** GOULD[80]	21	13 Inf K	B 7/28/1841 Clinton, Worcester Co., MA. R Southborough, Worcester Co., MA. Occ mechanic. E Jul 61 private. C Jul 1: wounded in hip. D Jul 14. Survivor (WC16584): M Mrs. Harriet Warner 49 (widow of Francis Gould and of 2nd husband Daniel Warner).
R5#37	CORP PRINCE A DUNTON	~22	13 Inf H	B ~1841 Hope, Knox Co., ME. R Natick, Middlesex Co., MA. Occ shoemaker. E Jun 61 private. Promoted to corporal on 4/1/63. C Jul 1: wounded in hip and and foot. D Jul 8.
R5#38	JOHN FLYE JOHN **FLY**[81]	~31	13 Inf K	B ~1832 New Portland, Somerset Co., ME. R Westborough, Worcester Co., MA. Occ blacksmith. E Jul 61 private. Absent, sick in Baltimore hospital 10/17/61→ 1/1/62. Detached service at brigade commissary department: 7/4/62→April 63. C Jul 1: wounded in leg severely. D Jul 27. Survivor (WC14189): W Harriet 23 (M May 60)5/6/60); (1 ♂- John Flye 13).
R5#39	SERGT EDGAR A FISKE	~27	13 Inf E	B ~1836 Millbury, Worcester Co., MA. R Roxbury, Boston, MA. Occ carpenter. E Jun 61 private. Removed from camp 9/30/61, sent to Baltimore general hosp. Returned to duty 10/31/61. Absent, sick Jul/Aug 62→2/6/63: hospitalized in Washington, D.C. with unspecified condition. C Jul 1: three wounds including in neck. D Jul 2. Survivor (WC20654): M Mrs. Mary Fiske 67 (widow of Benjamin Fiske).

---

80 **Court martial trial over allegedly stolen revolver.** At the end of an 1/5/63 court martial proceeding, Frank Gould was found not guilty of the embittered charge of having stolen the revolver of Private Charles F Rice of his same company. Private Rice would come through the Battle of Gettysburg uninjured. However, Rice would be killed May 8, 1864 at the Battle of Spotsylvania Court House, Virginia.

81 **Soldier's previous wife bumps soldier's widow from pension rolls.** In 1867, the widow's pension payments to Mrs. Harriet Fly were discontinued after a divorced wife of John Fly sought this pension for the support of John Flye, the soldier's adolescent son, whom existence had never been revealed to Harriet. Ultimately, in 1869, Harriet Fly again began receiving these payments based on the divorced wife being disqualified owing to her having remarried, and the son being disqualified owing to passing qualifying age of 16.

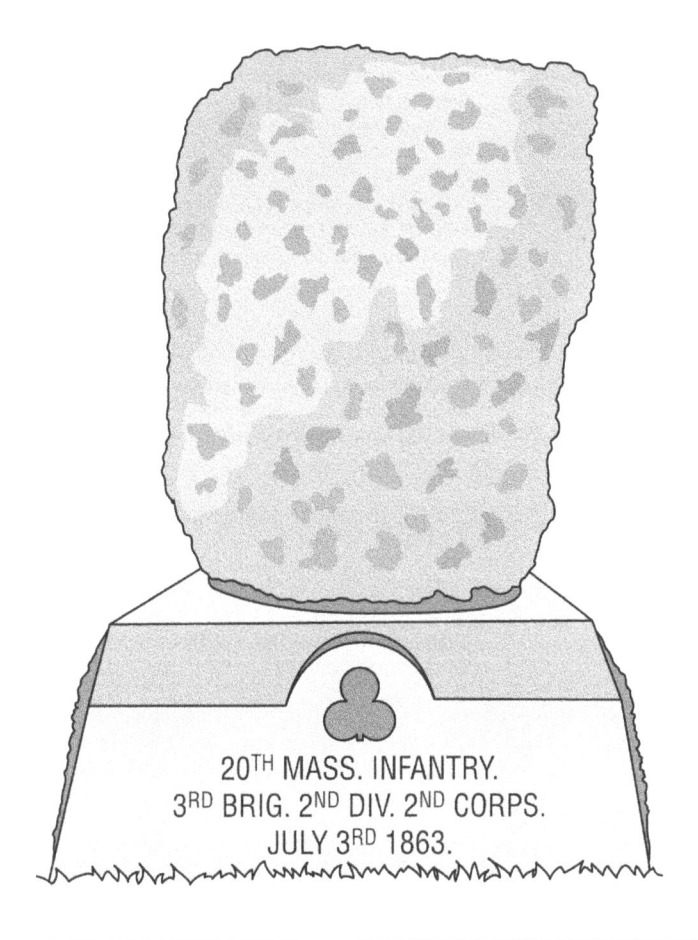

20TH MASS. INFANTRY.
3RD BRIG. 2ND DIV. 2ND CORPS.
JULY 3RD 1863.

20th Massachusetts Infantry Monument on Cemetery Ridge

★ ★ ★ ★ ★

A 30-ton Roxbury puddingstone, now the Massachusetts state stone, that the 20th Massachusetts veterans had erected with their monument, symbolizing their stalwartness at Gettysburg. Of the 300 men brought to battle July 3rd, the regiment would lose 30 killed and 94 wounded, most of these losses being incurred as the regiment reformed northward towards the copse of tress where Pickett's Charge had achieved a breech.

Michigan

R1#1	C J PATTIN CHARLES J **PATON**	22	24 Inf E	B ~1841 MI. R Detroit, MI. Occ laborer. E Jul 62 private. Detailed during the Battle of Gettysburg to serve with Battery B of 4th US. Artillery. C Jul 1. D Jul 5. Survivor (WC22912): M Mrs. Catherine Payton 55 (widow of Charles Pa).
R1#2	L W LAMPMAN LAWSON W LAMPMAN	~20	4 Inf K	B ~1843 NY. R Livingston Co., MI. E Jun 61 private. Wounded 6/27/62 at Gaines' Mill, VA. KIA Jul 2. Survivor (WC49510): M Mrs. Harriet Donley 47 in 1864 (widow of Frederick Lampman, remarried and divorced Hugh Donley).
R1#3	ARTEMUS CLARK **ARTIMUS H** CLARK[82] 5 Cav G			One of two gravestones inscribed for Artimus Clark, this Row 6 site initially appears in the 1865 Select Committee report for the Cemetery as the burial site of an unknown soldier. As pertains to this gravesite here and the gravesite in Row 6, Artimus Clark did not die during the Civil War. He died in 1904 (age 73) and was buried in the Byron Cemetery in Byron, Shiawassee County, Michigan.
R1#4	THOMAS SUGGET THOMAS **SUGGETT**	20-21	24 Inf G	B ~1842. R Detroit, MI. E Aug 62 corporal. C Jul 1: severe wound in leg→amp. D Jul 28.
R1#5	CHARLES RUFF	20	24 Inf D	B 6/18/1843 Nankin twp, Wayne Co., MI. R Dearborn, Wayne Co., MI. 1860 occ: farmer working on father's farm. E Aug 62 private. C Jul 1: shot in arm and left chest. D Jul 22.
R1#6	DAVID ROUNDS DAVID E ROUNDS	21	24 Inf D	B 8/25/1841 Dearborn, Wayne Co., MI. R Detroit, MI. 1860 occ: farmer working on father's farm. E Aug 62 private. Promoted to corporal on 2/7/63. KIA Jul 1.
R1#7	SERGT W H JACKSON WILLIAM H JACKSON	~22	4 Inf I	B ~1841 MI. R Detroit, MI. E Jun 61 sergeant. KIA Jul 2. Survivors (WC134309): M Mrs. Maria Jackson 46 in 1864 (George Jackson affirmed incapacitated).
R1#8	CORP R HOWE REUBEN HOWE[83]	27-28	5 Inf C	B 1837 NY. R Bridgeport, Saginaw Co., MI. E Aug 61 corporal. KIA Jul 2. Survivor (WC52956): W Mary 18 (M May 61| ReM1867), no chn.

---

82 **Misidentified soldier in grave.** Artimus Clark is one of the fourteen 5th Michigan Calvary soldiers who was not killed at Gettysburg. Clark, who has a gravestone here in Row 1 and another gravestone in Row 6, was discharged from the army with a disability in 1864.

83 **Soldier's two separate gravesites in Cemetery.** Corporal Reuben Howe has both a burial stone here in Row 1 and also at Row 3 site 2 of this Michigan plot. Determining which, if either of these two graves, holds Reuben Howe's remains does not seem possible.

R1#9	CHARLES CROUSE CHARLES CHRISTIAN **KRAUSS**	31	6 Cav A	B 4/5/1832 Germany. R Lowell, Kent Co., MI. E Aug 62 saddler. KIA Jul 2: killed in a mounted charge at the Battle of Hunterstown, PA. Survivor (WC109343): F Georg Krauss 68 in 1866 (widower of Fredericke Krauss affirmed incapable of supporting himself).
R1#10	WILLIAM C HARLAN	20	5 Inf F	B 4/15/1843 Chester, Delaware Co., PA. R Cascade, Kent Co., MI. E Sep 61 private. Promoted to corporal during service. Wounded on 5/3/62 at Fair Oaks, VA. C Jul 2. D Jul 12.
R1#11	SERGT FRANK A BARBOUR	~19	5 Cav A	B 1844 MI. R Pontiac, Oakland Co., MI. 1860: occ laborer. E Aug 62 private. Promoted to sergeant during service. C Jul 3: wound of intestines. D Jul 10. Survivor (WC170747 not online): M Mrs. Mary Barbour 54 in 1864 (widow of William Barbour).
R1#12	CORP WM A COLE[84]			One of two gravestones inscribed William Cole, this burial does not appear in the in the 1865 Select Committee report for the Cemetery. The inscription at this gravesite incorrectly identifies Clark as a member of the 5th Michigan Cavalry, rather than the 5th Michigan Infantry he was actually a member of. The Row 7 #4 gravestone incorrectly reports Cole's middle initial as H. However, it is easy to understand how such an inscription error from a headboard could have occurred. occurred. The Row 7 site must be regarded as Cole's likelier actual burial site.
R1#13	LIEUT F J DIATT[85] 5 Cav D			Misidentified soldier in grave. Misidentification could be for Lieut. Thomas J. Dean, 5th MA Cavalry Co. D, who was wounded at Gettysburg but survived the war.
R1#14	NOAH H FERRY Major 5 Regt Cav			Misidentified soldier or empty grave. The remains of Major Ferry, who was killed Jul 3 by a wound through his brain, were retrieved by his father, Rev. William Ferry, and transported back to Michigan for reburial in a Grand Haven cemetery.
R2#1	LIEUT B BROWN BUTLER BROWN	~27	16 Inf E	B 1836 Sullivan, Ashland Co., OH. R Adrian, Lenawee Co., MI. 1860 occ: clerk. Commissioned 2nd lieutenant in Aug 61. Promoted to 1st lieutenant on 9/28/62. KIA Jul 2. Survivors (WC100444) M Mrs. Ann Brown 52 in 1866 (Leonard Brown affirmed in very poor health).

---

84 **Misidentified soldier in grave.** Corporal William A. Cole is found to have two separate gravestones in the Michigan plot, one her in Row 1 and another in Row 7. This Row 1 burial site does not appear on the 1865 Committee report on the Cemetery. In addition, this Row 1 gravestone incorrectly identifies Clark as a member of the 5th Michigan Calvary instead of his actual 5th Michigan Infantry membership. The row 7 site is likelier Cole's actual burial site.

85 **Misidentified soldier in grave.** This is one of the several misidentified soldiers presumed to have been a member of the 5th Michigan Calvary. No Lieutenant F. J. Diatt of the 5th Michigan Calvary Company D is found in military sources. A Lieutenant Thomas J. Dean of the 5th Michigan Calvary Company D was wounded at Gettysburg but survived the war.

R2#2	LIEUT W JEWETT WALLACE JEWETT	~23	16 Inf K	B 1840 Saginaw, MI. R same. 1860 occ: law student. E Oct 61 sergeant. Promoted to sergeant major on 2/28/62. Promoted to lieutenant on 7/1/62. KIA Jul 2. Survivor (WC260730 not online): M Mrs. Azubah Jewett 75 in 1882 (widow of Eleazer Jewett).
R2#3	CHARLES McBRAHMIE CHARLES **McBRATNEE** or McBRATNIE	40	16 Inf D	B 1/3/1823 Scotland. 1860: R Thomas, Saginaw Co., MI; occ: farm laborer on widowed mother's farm. E Aug 61 private. Mar/Apr 62: promotion to corporal. Absent in hospital: Jul/Aug 62→3/26/63 with an unspecified condition. KIA Jul 2.
R2#4	ORIN D WADE[86] or OREN D WADE (MN DAVID)	24	3 Inf D	B 7/18/1838 Meigs Co., OH. R Ionia Co., MI. Occ farm laborer. E May 61 private. Rank change to bugler. Promoted to corporal during service. C Jul 2: wounded in chest. D Jul 3. Survivor (WC274830 not online): F Jonathan Wade 75 in 1889 (affirmed disabled widower of Margaret Wade).
R2#5	J HYDE **JOHN H KYDD**	21	4 Inf I	B 5/5/1842 Scotland. R Adrian, Lenawee Co., MI. 1860: occ carpenter. E Jun 61 private. Promotion to corporal, then sergeant during service. KIA Jul 2. Survivors (WC255384 not online): M Mrs. Margaret ~72 in 1887 (William Kydd unable to support wife).
R2#6	ASHER D ASHLEY A D **ARTLEY**	21-22	5 Inf F	B ~1841 PA. R Mottville twp, St. Joseph Co. MI. E Sep 62 private. KIA Jul 2.
R2#7	CHARLES THAYER	20-21	5 Inf I	B ~1842 OH. R Howell, Livingston Co., MI. 1860 occ: farm work on father's farm. E Sep 61 private. Promotion to corporal during service. KIA Jul 2. Survivor (WC8912): W Lizzie 20 (M Sep 62); no chn.
R2#8	GEORGE H MILLER G H **HILLEE**	34-35	5 Inf I	B ~1828 NY. R Brighton, Livingston Co., MI. E Aug 61 private. KIA Jul 2
R2#9	JOHN DOVER **JOHAN DORER** or DORAN	~41	5 Inf K	B ~1822 Switzerland. R Lapeer Co., MI. Occ farmer. E Mar 63 private. KIA Jul 2. Survivors (WC26682): W Mary 39 (M Apr 50); 1 ♂- Marshal 10.
R2#10	CHARLES SITS CHARLES **SITTS**	~19	1 Cav L	B 1844 Canada. R Almont, Lapeer Co., MI. 1860 occ: laborer. E Aug 61 private. C Jul 4: wounded at Fairfield Gap cavalry action. D Jul 4.

---

86 **Elderly father in pension application reports previous son killed in service**. The 75-year-old widower Jonathan Wade applied for a dependent father's pension in 1889. His application was prompted by the need for financial support which might have come from his son, Orin, had he survived the Civil War. Oren may have been serving as the regimental bugler when he was killed at Gettysburg. Jonathan Wade had also lost another son, Sylvanus Wade, who had been an enlistee of the 83rd Pennsylvania Infantry and who had been killed in action on June 27, 1862 at the Battle of Gaines' Mill, VA.

R2#11	WILLIAM BRENNAN	25	5 Cav B	B 7/4/1838 Hilltop, Grand Traverse Co., MI. R Georgetown, Ottawa Co., MI. E Aug 62 corporal. Nov/Dec 62: promotion to sergeant. C Jul 3: wounded at South Mountain near Monterey, MD. D Jul 5. Survivors (WC22811): W Mary 30 (M Oct 54); 3 chn: 2 ♂- Edwin 6, Willesbey 4 & 1 ♀- Charlotte 10 weeks.
R2#12	JOSEPH TUCKER JOSEPH W TUCKER	25	5 Inf I	B 3/23/1838 MI. R Mount Clemens, Macomb Co., MI. 1860 occ farm laborer. E Aug 62 private. KIA Jul 2.
R2#13	LIEUT J S McELHENY JAMES McELHENY	22-23	1 Cav	B 1840 Burnt Cabins, Dublin Twp, Fulton Co., PA. R Mattawan, Van Buren Co., MI. E Aug 61 corporal. Promoted to sergeant on 1/15/62. Commissioned lieutenant during service. KIA Jul 4 in calvary battle at Fairfield Gap, PA.
R2#14	JOSIAH G BOND (MN GODDARD)	30	16 Inf F	B 1/16/1833 York, Livingston Co., NY. 1860: R Cass Co., MI; occ laborer. E Aug 61 private. Promoted to corporal, then to sergeant during service. KIA Jul 2.
R2#15	SERGT H BARRET HUBBARD H **BARRETT**	27-28	16 Inf B	B ~1835 MI. R Ionia Co., MI. E Aug 61 corporal. Promoted to sergeant during service. KIA Jul 2.
R2#16	CORP H HART HORACE HART	22	6 Cav C	B 3/9/1841 Shiawassee, Shiawassee Co., MI. R New Haven, Lenox twp, Macomb Co., MI. 1860 occ laborer. E Aug 62 private. C June 30 at Hanover, PA. D Jul 3.
R3#1	CARLISLE BENNETT 1 Cav I			No killed Gettysburg soldier with this name found in military sources.
R3#2	CORP REUBEN HOWE[87]	25-26	5 Inf C	B 1837 NY. R Bridgeport, Saginaw Co., MI. E Aug 61 corporal. KIA Jul 2. Survivor (WC52956): W Mary 18 (M May 61 | ReM1867), no chn.
R3#3	S G HARRIS SIDNEY GILLESPIE HARRIS	19-20	7 Inf B	B 1843 Monroe Co., MI. R same. 1860 occ: working on farm of widowed mother. E Aug 61 private. KIA Jul 2.
R3#4	J S RIDER JOHN S RIDER	23-24	24 Inf B	B ~1839 MI. R Detroit, MI. 1860 occ mason. E Aug 62 private. C Jul 1: severe wound left arm→amp. D Jul 20. Survivors (WC92761): W Amelia Emeline 24 (M Oct 59 | ReM 1866); 1 ♂- George Harvey Rider 2.
R3#5	W WILLIAMS WILLIAM WILLIAMS	30-31	24 Inf B	B ~1832. R Dearborn, Wayne Co., MI. E Aug 62 private. C Jul 1: severe wound in the left leg→amp. D Jul 18.

---

87 **Soldier's two separate gravesites in Cemetery**. Corporal Reuben Howe has both a burial stone here in Row 3 and also at Row 1 site 8 of this Michigan plot. Determining which, if either of these two graves, holds Reuben Howe's remains does not seem possible.

ID	Name	Age	Unit	Details
R3#6	J McNISH JOHN McNISH	30-31	24 Inf F	B ~1832. R Detroit, MI. E Aug 62 private. C Jul 1. D Jul 23.
R3#7	SERGT E MOORE EDWARD MOORE	33-34	7 Inf A	B ~1829 Canada. Occ farmer. E (Port Huron, St. Clair Co., MI) Aug 61 private. Promoted to corporal in 1862. No service record documentation of promotion to sergeant. KIA Jul 2 reportedly while carrying the colors.
R3#8	CORP ALBERT SMITH	22-23	5 Inf D	B ~1840 MI. R Oakland Co., MI. 1860 occ farm laborer. E Aug 61 private. Promoted to corporal during service. KIA Jul 2: head wound. Survivor (WC38081): M Mrs. Mary Ann Smith 44 in 1864 (widow of James Smith).
R3#9	CAPT P GENEROUS PETER GENEROUS	~24	5 Inf B	B 1839 Mount Clemens, Macomb Co., MI. R same. 1860: occ bricklayer. E Aug 61 private. Commissioned 2nd lieutenant on 1/17/62. Captured 5/8/62 at Williamsburg, VA. Promoted to 1st lieutenant on 12/12/62. Promoted to captain on 9/16/62. KIA Jul 2.
R3#10	CHESTER McALEX CHESTER McAULEY	~24	5 Inf D	B ~1839 Ontario, Canada. R Arcada, Lapeer Co., MI. 1860 occ: farming working on father's farm. E Mar 63 private. KIA Jul 2.
R3#11	JOSEPH SUTTER	22-23	5 Inf E	B ~1840. R Wayne Co., MI. E Sep 61 private. KIA Jul 2.
R3#12	SERGT ALEX MOORE ALEXANDER MOREE	~22	5 Inf E	B ~1841. R Port Huran, St. Clair Co., MI. E Jun 61 sergeant. KIA Jul 2.
R3#13	LIEUT ALBERT SLAFTER	29	7 Inf E	B 9/15/1833 Ontario, Canada. R Tuscola Co., MI. 1860 occ farmer. E Aug 61 private. Promoted to sergeant on 4/15/62. Commissioned 2nd lieutenant on 5/01/63. KIA Jul 2: GSW through the head. Survivors (WC13052): W Ruth 27 (M Feb 55 | ReM 1867): 2 ♀- Mary 7, Florence 6.
R3#14	JOHN W BARBER (MN WOODWORTH)	19-20	1 LA Batt I	B ~1843 Fenner, Madison Co., NY. R Rome, MI. E Aug 62 private. KIA Jul 3.
R3#15	SERGT J M STEVENS JAMES MONROE STEVENS	24	16 Inf E	B 9/15/1838 Saint Clair Shores, Macomb Co., MI. R Macomb Co., MI. E Aug 61 private. Promoted to corporal on 7/15/62. Service record reports rank of sergeant at death. KIA Jul 2.

R3#16	J R HALL JAMES R HALL[88]	~20?	16 Inf D	B ~1843?. R Hillsdale Co., MI. E Aug 61 private. KIA Jul 2.
R3#17	CORP BECK JAMES **BECKETT**	~26	16 Inf I	B ~1837 England. Occ miller. E Apr 61 into 1st MI private. Hospitalized 8/31/62. E Sep 62 into 16th MI as sergeant. KIA Jul 2: GSW to head. Survivor (WC11096): W Anna 17 (M Nov 62 | ReM Sep 64); no chn.
R4#1	C W MARTIN CHARLES **A** MARTIN	~20	16 Inf C	B ~1843 MI. R Genesee Co., MI. 1860 occ farm laborer. E Jan 62 private. C Jul 2: shot in right leg→amp. D Jul 21. Survivor (WC16191): M Mrs. Ellen Martin 53 (Deserted by husband Jessie Martin several years in the past).
R4#2	C H HULMER CHARLES **W FULMER**	21	7 Inf G	B 6/13/1842 Ontario, Canada. R Lapeer Co., MI. E Aug 61 private. C Jul 3. D Jul 25.
R4#3	PETER LA VALLEY PETER **LEVALLEY**	26-27	5 Cav A	B ~1836 Canada. R Independence, Oakland Co., MI. Occ sailor. E Aug 62 private. KIA Jul 3. Survivor (WC677110 not online): W Catharine 23 in 1864 (M Dec 60 | ReM 1870); no chn.
R4#4	THOMAS MOTLEY	42-43	7 Cav G	B 1820. R Hampton, MI. E Dec 62 private. KIA Jul 3: GSW in abdomen.
R4#5	NELSON WATERS	20-21	7 Cav A	B ~1842 NY. 1860: R Silver Creek, Cass Co., MI; occ: farm laborer on father's farm. E (Pokagon, Cass Co., MI) Sep 62 private. KIA Jul 3.
R4#6	PHILIP WILCOX PHILIP WILCOX, JR	20-21	1 Cav L	B 1842 MI. R Almont, Lapeer Co., MI. E Aug 61 private. C Jul 3. D Jul 4. Survivor (WC16881): W Mary Jane 23 (M Feb 59); no chn.
R4#7	ROBERT HASTY ROBERT **HASTINGS**[89]	28-29	7 Cav I	B ~1834 Ireland. R Tecumseh, Lenawee Co., MI. 1860 occ farm laborer. E Dec 62 private. KIA Jul 3: instantly killed by being hit by a shell. Survivors (WC49676): W Anne 26 in 1864 (M Dec 1855 | ReM 1867) 3 chn: 2 ♀- Mary Ann 6, Johannah 20 months & 1 ♂- Robert 5.
R4#8	GEORGE HETCHLER	37-38	5 Cav E	B ~1825 NY. R Erin, Macomb Co., MI. 1860 occ farmer. E Aug 62 private. C Jul 3: wounded through the side. D Jul 6. Survivors (WC63100→WC102087 neither online): W Sarah 22 (M Apr 57 | ReM Feb 64); 3 chn: 1♀- Anna 5 & 2♂- William 2, Albert 1.

---

88 **Minor at death**? The James R. Hall, then residing in Hilldale County, Michigan, reported his age as 18 when enlisting into the 16th Michigan Infantry Regiment in August 1861. The June 16, 1860 Census page for Hildale County, Michigan shows a James R. Hall at only age 13. If this were an accurate report, James Hall would have been no older than 15 at his 1861 enlistment and no older than 17 when he died of a battle wound at Gettysburg. However, this single Census report is not sufficient to decide the question.

89 **Soldier fighting under an alias**. Mrs. Ann Hastings' successful application for a widow's pension had required her to persuade the Pension Office that her husband Robert Hastings had been serving in the army under the truncated alias of "Hasty."

R4#9	PHILIP HILL **PHILLIP** HENRY HILL	28	5 Cav E	B 2/5/1835 England. R Armada, Macomb Co., MI. 1860 occ sawyer. E Aug 62 private. Promoted to corporal during service. C Jul 3: wounded through right lung. D Jul 4. Survivors (WC17447): W Clarissa 23 (M Jan 58); 2 chn: 1 ♀- Hannah 2 & 1 ♂- James 1.
R4#10	W A CROWELL (ALIAS) WILLIAM A CROEL[90] 5 Cav G			William Alanson Croel, under the alias of William A. Crowell, became a corporal in the 5th Cavalry Company G, but he was not a casualty at Gettysburg. Croel died in 1927 and was buried in the Tuttle Cemetery in Ionia, Ionia County, Michigan.
R4#11	MILES A WEBSTER[91] 5 Cav G			Miles Daniel Webster, a 5th Michigan Company G cavalryman, was a casualty at Gettysburg, but he survived the battle and war. He died in 1886 (age 44) and was buried in Sowle Cemetery in Saint Johns, Clinton County, Michigan.
R4#12	A S NORRIS ALBERT STARK NORRIS[92] 5 Cav G			Albert Stark Norris, a 5th Michigan Company G cavalryman, received a July 3rd left thigh wound at Gettysburg. He survived this wound. In August 1863, Norris was captured at Manassas and would die during imprisonment at Richmond on December 7, 1863 of diarrhea, pleurisy and pneumonia (age 24). He has gravestones at Gettysburg and at Merrihew Cemetery, Olve Township, Clinton County, PA. However, it is unclear whether his actual burial site is Richmond.
R4#13	JOHN NOTHING JAN NOTTING	21-22	5 Cav I	B ~1841 Holland. R Fillmore, Allegan Co., MI. 1860 occ farm laborer. E Aug 62 private. KIA Jul 3: wounded in the head.
R4#14	MOSES COLE[93] 5 Cav I			Moses Cole, a 5th Michigan Company I cavalryman, was wounded on July 3rd at Gettysburg. However, he survived the wound and left the army on a disability discharge in December. As of January 1, 1883, Cole was residing in Alpena, Michigan, while receiving a $5 monthly pension payment for a GSW of the left thigh.
R4#15	LIEUT G A DICKEY 24 Inf C			Duplicate gravestone. Likely misidentified soldier.

---

90 **Misidentified soldier in grave**. Here lies interred one of the several misidentified soldiers presumed to have been a member of the 5th Michigan Calvary. William A. Croel, fighting under an alias, survived the war and has a burial site in Michigan.

91 **Misidentified soldier in grave**. Here lies interred one of the several misidentified soldiers presumed to have been a member of the 5th Michigan Calvary. Miles Webster was wounded at Gettysburg but survived the war and has a burial site in Michigan.

92 **Misidentified soldier in grave**. Here lies interred one of the several misidentified soldiers presumed to have been a member of the 5th Michigan Calvary. Albert Norris was captured in October 1863 and died while imprisoned in Richmond in December 1863.

93 **Misidentified soldier in grave**. Here lies interred one of the several misidentified soldiers presumed to have been a member of the 5th Michigan Calvary. Cole was wounded at Gettysburg but survived the wound to leave the army on a disability discharge in December 1863. He retired to Michigan where he likely died and is buried.

R4#16	J MASON SILAS JAMES **M**ASON[94]	18	16 Inf D	B 3/21/1845 Camden twp, Hillsdale Co., MI. R same. E 1863 as substitute for 46 y/o father, James R Mason, drafted 2/10/63. Service stent would have been nine months. Silas joined regiment 3/18/63 at Falmouth, VA. KIA Jul 2.
R4#17	CORP J M WESTON JOHN MARTIN **NESTER**[95]	29	16 Inf A	B 6/18/1834 Germany. R Detroit, MI. E Jul 2 corporal. KIA Jul 2. Survivors (WC13121): W Elisa 21 (M Sep 62 | ReM | Mar 64); 1 ♀- Kasharina 3.
R4#18	EMERY TUTTLE	20	16 Inf B	B 6/22/1843 Portage, OH. R Ionia Co., MI. E Sep 61 private. KIA Jul 2.
R5#1	MASON PALMER (MN THOMAS)	22-23	24 Inf D	B 1840 England. R Dearborn, Wayne Co., MI. 1860 occ farm laborer. E Aug 62 private. C Jul 1: GSW fracturing right arm→amp. D Jul 14.
R5#2	LUTHER FRANKLIN	21	5 Inf C	B 11/9/1841 Seneca, Lenawee Co., MI. R Gratiot Co., MI. E Aug 61 private. C Jul 3: shot in left groin. D Jul 30.
R5#3	RICHARD AYLWARD	44-45	5 Inf E	B ~1818. R St. Clair Co., MI. E Sep 62 private. C Jul 2: GSW right arm→amp. D Jul 27. Survivor (WC131594): W Sarah 53 (M Feb 46), no chn.
R5#4	PETER E ROY (MN EUGENE)	~30	5 Inf C	B ~1833. R Detroit, MI. E Jan 63. KIA Jul 2.
R5#5	LIEUT J P THELAN JOHN P THELAN	~22	5 Inf A	B ~1841 Germany. 1860 occ: farm work on father's farm. E Jun 61 corporal. Promoted 6/1/62 to 1st sergeant. Commissioned 9/15/62 2nd lieutenant Promoted to 1st lieutenant on 11/17/62. KIA Jul 2.
R5#6	SERGT JAS HAZZARD **AMOS H MORRILL**[96]	~25?	5 Inf C	B ~1838? E Jun 61 corporal. Promoted to 1st sergeant. C Jul 2: shot in leg. D Jul 5. Survivors (WC98748): M Mrs. Lucinda Garcelon 57 in 1866 (2nd husband unable to do labor).
R5#7	D ZIMMERMAN **DIONIS** ZIMMERMAN	~26	4 Inf D	B ~1837. R Ann Arbor, Washtenaw Co., MI. E Jun 61 private. C Jul 2: GSW to the head. D Jul 9.

---

94 **Son substitutes for, then dies for drafted father**. On March 18, 1863, the eighteen-year-old Silas James Mason entered the service of the 16th Michigan Infantry, serving as a substitute for his 46-year-old father, James Mason, who had been summoned into service by the draft. Eighteen weeks later, Silas would be killed at Gettysburg.

95 **A German immigrant's month-long voyage to America**. The 20-year-old John Nester, accompanied by his 17-year-old brother Mathias, arrived in New York City Harbor on December 20, 1854, completing their emigration from Germany. It is noteworthy that during the approximately one-month voyage across the Atlantic Ocean aboard the Admiral, thirty-nine of the 388 passengers died during the journey.

96 **Fighting under an alias**. Mrs. Lucinda Garcelon's successful application for a dependent mother's pension had required her to submit testimony that her son, Amos Morill, had been employing the alias "James Hazzard" for some years prior to volunteering to enter the army. The suggestion in the testimony was that as Morill had for some time been using the alias "Hazzard," he evidently had felt no need to enlist under his real name.

R5#8	G W STEVENS GEORGE W STEVENS[97]	~30	16 Inf D	B ~1833 NY. Occ mechanic. Drafted 2/15/63 private. Joined regiment 3/18/63 in Falmouth, VA. C Jul 2: shot in chest. D Jul 10.
R5#9	SERGT E TRIP EDWIN G TRIPP	~21	4 Inf H	B ~1842 NY. R Mosherville, Hillsdale co., MI. 1860 occ farm laborer. E Jun 61 private. Promoted to sergeant on 1/1/63. C Jul 2: shot in both legs. D Jul 5.
R5#10	J GEINER JACOB GENNER	33-34	16 Inf G	B ~1829. E (Detroit, MI) Sep 61 private. C Jul 2: GSW to left chest. D Jul 10.
R5#11	G W ERVEY GEORGE WASHINGTON ERVAY[98]	18	16 Inf H	B 1845 NY. 1860: R Eaton County, MI, occ working on father's farm. E Aug 61 private. Aug 62: wounded at 2nd Bull Run. C Jul 2: GSW head. D Jul 6. Survivors (WC168590 not online) M Mrs. Eliza Ervay 51 in 1873 (widow of Daniel Ervay).
R5#12	SERGT H HOPKINS HIRAM HOPKINS	30	7 Inf I	B 12/23/1832 Monroe, Monroe Co. IL. R Marquette Co., MI. E Jul 61 corporal. Promoted to corporal. C Jul 2: shot in abdomen. D Jul 4. Survivor (WC109421): M Mrs. Maria Hopkins 64 in 1867 (widow of Samuel Hopkins).
R5#13	SERGT D C KIMBALL DUANE C KIMBALL	~20	4 Inf B	B ~1843, MI. R Adrian, Saginaw Co., MI. E Jun 61 private. Promoted to sergeant. C Jul 2: wounded in body & left leg→leg amp. D Jul 6. Survivors (WC142675 not online) M Mrs. Elizabeth Kimball ~42 (Charles Kimball unable to support wife).
R5#14	SERGT JOS MALLENBRE JOSEPH MUHLENBRIE or MALLENBREU	24	4 Inf B	B 5/29/1839 Germany. E (Ionia, Ionia Co., MI) Sep 61 corporal. Promoted to sergeant. Wounded 8/30/62 at 2nd Bull Run. C Jul 2: wounded left arm and left chest. D Jul 24.
R5#15	C H WILSON CHARLES H WILSON	~21	4 Inf H	B ~ 1842 MI. R Litchfield, Hillsdale Co., MI. 1860 occ: farm laborer. E Jun 61 private. C Jul 2: shot in left lung. D Jul 4 or 5.
R5#16	R MOODY ROBERT MOODIE	~24	4 Inf K	B ~1839 Scotland. R Wyandotte, Wayne Co., MI. 1860 occ: farm laborer. E Jul 61 private. C Jul 2. D Jul 15.
R5#17	SERGT FRED SHEETS FREDERICK SHEETS	~44	4 Inf D	B ~1819 MI. R Washtenaw Co., MI. 1860 occ tinsmith. E June 61 sergeant. C Jul 3: shot in right arm, left hand and leg. D Jul 25.

---

97 **Drafted soldier survives only 16 weeks in the army.** George Stevens was drafted on February 15, 1863 but would not join his 16th Michigan Infantry regiment until March 18, 1863. Fifteen weeks later, on July 2nd, he would be shot in the chest while fighting on Little Round Top. He would die the following week on July 10th.

98 **Minor at enlistment.** George Ervey's ages of 5 and 15 in the successive October 1850 and August 1860 U.S. Census reports attests to the likelihood that he was not 18, but likely 16 at his August 1861 enlistment. These dates also mean that George was likely 18 when he was killed in action likely on Little Round Top on July 2nd.

R5#18	J BAGS **JAMES P BOGART**	23-24	16 Inf I	B ~1839 NY. R Pinckney, Livingston Co., MI. 1860 occ farm laborer. E Dec 61 private. KIA Jul 2.	
R5#19	J HART JOHN A HART	30-31	16 Inf G	B 1832. E (Ann Arbor, Washtenaw Co., MI) Sep 61 corporal. KIA Jul 2.	
R5#20	EDWARD BURTON	~38	16 Inf K	B ~1825. R Sheridan, Montcalm Co., MI. Occ farmer. E Mar 62 private. KIA Jul 2. Survivors (WC30589): W Betsey 40 in 1864 (M Nov 1852); 2 chn: 1 ♂- Charles 9 & 1 ♀- Delia 8.	
R6#1	HENRY BUTLER	20-21	5 Cav I	B ~1842. R Howell, Livingston Co., MI. E Aug 61 private. C Jul 2: severely wounded in leg. D Jul 3.	
R6#2	SERGT C BALLARD CHARLES A BALLARD[99] 5 Cav E			Charles Alfonso Ballard, a 5th Michigan Company E cavalryman, was a casualty at Gettysburg, but he survived the battle and war. He died in 1929 and was buried in the Shultz Acre Cemetery in Spanaway, Pierce County, Washington.	
R6#3	CHRISTOPHER MILLER[100] 5 Cav E	20-21	5 Cav I	Christopher Miller, a 5th Michigan Company E cavalryman, received a wound to his right arm at Gettysburg, but he survived the wound and the war. He died in San Antonio, Texas in 1916 and he was likely buried in Texas.	
R6#4	EDWARD A WARNER[101] 5 Cav I			Edward A. Warner, a 5th Michigan Company I cavalryman, was not a casualty at Gettysburg and survived the war. He died in 1915 and was buried in the Greenwood Cemetery in York, York County, Nebraska.	
R6#5	SERGT H BICKER HENRY **BECKER**[102] 5 Cav F			Henry Becker rose from private to sergeant in Company F, 5th Michigan Calvary. On July 3rd at Gettysburg, Becker received a leg wound which required an amputation. This then led to a disability discharge from the army in December. He died in 1909 and was buried in the Clark Cemetery in Dayton township, Newaygo County, Michigan.	

---

99 **Misidentified soldier in grave**. Here lies interred one of the several misidentified soldiers presumed to have been a member of the 5th Michigan Calvary. Charles Ballard was wounded at Gettysburg but survived the war and has a burial site in Washington state.

100 **Misidentified soldier in grave**. Here lies interred one of the several misidentified soldiers presumed to have been a member of the 5th Michigan Calvary. Christopher Miller was wounded at Gettysburg but survived the war and has a likely burial site in Texas.

101 **Misidentified soldier in grave**. Here lies interred one of the several misidentified soldiers presumed to have been a member of the 5th Michigan Calvary. Edward Warner was not killed at Gettysburg and survived the war. He has a burial site in Nebraska.

102 **Misidentified soldier in grave**. Here lies interred one of the several misidentified soldiers presumed to have been a member of the 5th Michigan Calvary. Henry Becker was wounded at Gettysburg but survived the wound to leave the army on a disability discharge. He has a burial site in Michigan.

R6#6	JOHN S FOLKERTS JOHN GARRETT **FOLKERT**[103]	44-45	5 Inf K	B 1818 Netherlands. R Algonac, St. Clair Co., MI. Occ tailor. E Sep 62 private. C Jul 2. D Sep 5. Survivors (WC115295): W Jane 31 (M May 55): 4 chn: 2 ♂- John 7, Frederick 4 & 2 ♀- Clara 19 months, Martha 3 months (adopted).	
R6#7	HENRY RIOLO[104] 5th Cav Co F			Misidentified soldier in grave. A Henry Reed of 5th Michigan Cavalry Company F was wounded at Gettysburg on July 3rd, but he survived the wound and transferred out of the army six months later.	
R6#8	D M MEREFIELD DAVID MARKS **MERRIFIELD**[105] 5 Cav F			David Marks Merrifield, a 5th Michigan Company F cavalryman, on July 3rd at Gettysburg received a right arm wound, which required an amputation. This amputation led to a disability discharge in October. He died in 1999 and was buried in the Abilene Cemetery, Abilene, Kansas.	
R6#9	FRANCIS N KENT FRANCIS **P** KENT	20-21	5 Cav G	B ~1842 MI. R Fenton, Genesee Co., MI. 1860 occ: carriage maker apprentice. E Aug 62 private. KIA Jul 3.	
R6#10	J M SKINNER **IRWIN** M SKINNER	18-19	5 Cav G	B 1844 Essex, Clinton Co., MI. R same. E Sep 62 private. KIA Jul 3.	
R6#11	ARTEMUS CLARK **ARTIMUS** H CLARK[106] 5 Cav G			As pertains to the two Gettysburg Cemetery gravestones inscribed for Artimus Clark, the one here in Row 6 and the other in Row 1, Clark did not die during the Civil War. He died in 1904 (age 73) and was buried in the Byron Cemetery in Byron, Shiawassee County, Michigan.	
R6#12	CORP D HARRIS DELOS W HARRIS	22-23	5 Cav C	B ~1840 Virgil, Courtland Co., NY. 1860 R: Allen, Hillsdale Co., MI; occ: carpenter and joiner (same occupation as father, Francis Harris, whose home he shares). E Aug 61 private. Promoted to corporal during service. C Jul 3: wounded by a shell on the left side. D Jul 8.	
R6#13	JOHN M BROWN	~21	3 Cav K	B ~1842. R Newaygo Co., MI. E Jun 61 private. C Jul 3: shot in right knee→amp. D Jul 12.	

---

103 **Soldier's four young children must go to court-appointed guardian after their mother is institutionalized.** In a domestic tragedy, John Folkert's wife, Mrs. Jane Folkert, was judged insane in July 1866 and subsequently institutionalized. The care of their four pre-teen children was turned over to a court-appointed guardian. The ultimate fate of these children is not documented in the pension file.

104 **Misidentified soldier in grave**. Here lies interred one of the several misidentified soldiers presumed to have been a member of the 5th Michigan Calvary. If this misidentification is related to Henry Reed, Reed was wounded at Gettysburg on July 3rd, but he survived the wound and transferred out of the army six months later.

105 **Misidentified soldier in grave**. Here lies interred one of the several misidentified soldiers presumed to have been a member of the 5th Michigan Calvary. David Merrifield was wounded at Gettysburg but survived the wound to leave the army on a disability discharge in October 1863. He has a burial site in Kansas.

106 **Misidentified soldier in grave**. Artimus Clark is one of the fourteen 5th Michigan Calvary soldiers who was not killed at Gettysburg. Clark, who has a gravestone here in Row 6 and another gravestone in Row 1, was discharged from the army with a disability in 1864.

R6#14	CORP W A COLE WILLIAM A COLE	24-25	5 Inf G	R~1838. R Pontiac, Oakland Co., MI. E Aug 62 corporal. C Jul 2: GSW to left leg→ amp. D Jul 12. Survivor (WC38651) M Mrs. Frances Cole 56 in 1864 (Alonzo Cole deserted family in 1859).
R6#15	JAMES M PIERCE JAMES **NELSON** PIERCE[107]	26-27	3 Inf A	B ~1836 Washington Co., NY. Occ farmer. E Aug 62 private. C Jul 2: multiply wounded: head, neck, arm, wrist. D Jul 5 or 7. Survivors (WC73336): W Sarah 26 (M Dec 54 | ReM May 64); 3 chn: 1 ♂- James 7 & 2 ♀- Mary 3, Perley 17 months.
R6#16	GEORGE LAWRENCE	26-27	5 Inf C	B ~1836. R Saginaw Co., MI. E Aug 61 private. Wounded 5/31/62 at the Battle of Seven Pines, VA. C Jul 2: GSW to left leg→amp. D Jul 15.
R6#17	JOHN ROBERTS	23-24	5 Inf C	B ~1839 Ireland. R Detroit, MI. Occ laborer. E Sep 62 private. C Jul 2: GSW left lung and left forearm. D Jul 14.
R6#18	SERGT R B GODFREY RUSSELL B GODFREY	22-23	7 Inf B	B ~1840 MI. R Leslie, Ingham Co., MI. Occ farm hand. E Aug 61 corporal. Promoted to sergeant during service. KIA Jul 3.
R6#19	J K BEAGLE JOHN **R** BEAGLE	19-20	16 Inf G	B ~1843. R Detroit, MI. Occ printer. E Aug 61 private. KIA Jul 2. Survivors (WC55166): M Mrs. Elizabeth Mitchell 59 in 1865 (Jason Mitchell, 2nd husband, affirmed unable to labor due to age and infirmity).
R6#20	ISAAC H SCOTT[108]	17	16 Inf K	B 1846. E Jan 62 private. KIA Jul 2.
R6#21	SERGT H RAW HENRY **RAU**	21-22	16 Inf I	B ~1841 NY. R Detroit, MI. Occ shoemaker. E Dec 61 corporal. Promoted to sergeant during service. KIA Jul 2. Survivor (WC122644): F George Rau 64 in 1867 (affirmed disabled widower of Dorothea Rau).
R7#1	S BISONETTE SAMUEL BISONETTE	~24	4 Inf A	B ~1839 MI. R Monroe Co., MI. 1860 occ: farmer, working on father's farm. E Jun 61 private. KIA Jul 2.
R7#2	CORP C A TURNER CHARLES ALONZO TURNER	21-22	5 Inf B	B ~1841. R Macomb Co., MI. E Aug 61 private. No service record documentation that soldier received promotion to corporal. KIA Jul 2. Survivor (WC133800): M Mrs. Sarah Needham 53 in 1868 (Augustus Turner died in 1855 | divorced from 2nd husband, Samuel Needham, a "confirmed drunkard").

---

107 **Ninety-year-old widow applies for pension restitution after fourth husband's death.** In 1926, the former Mrs. Sarah Pierce, then Mrs. Sarah Anible and 90-years old, applied for a restitution of her 1863 widow's pension following the death of her fourth husband, Chauncey Anible, in October of that year. The intricacies of confirming Mrs. Anible's eligibility were such that the Pension Office had not made a final determination as of 1930. However, Mrs. Anible would die in 1932.

108 **Minor at death.** Isaac Scott's final service file card records his age as 17, which is at variance with the age of 18 he reported at enlistment. An Ancestry.com public member tree reports that an Isaac H. Scott was born in 1846 East Bloomfield, NY. Finally, in agreement with the 1846 birthyear reported in this public member tree, the June 27, 1860 U.S. Census for Shiawassee, Michigan shows him as being 14.

R7#3	EDWARD BRICKELL	18-19	7 Cav A	B ~1844 MI. R Niles, Cass Co., MI. 1860 occ: farm laborer on father's farm. E Dec 62 private. C Jul 3: severe wound to right arm→amp. D Jul 25.
R7#4	SERGT B CURCH BENJAMIN CHURCH	27-28	7 Cav C	B ~1835 NY. R East Saginaw, Saginaw Co., MI. 1860 occ: farmer, working on father's farm. E Nov 62 sergeant. KIA Jul 3.
R7#5	SERGT JOHN SHOLES JOHN C SHOLES	20-21	7 Cav G	B ~1841 Onondaga, Onondaga, NY. 1860: R Almont, Lapeer Co., MI; occ laborer. E Aug 61 corporal. Promotion to sergeant during service. Wounded on 6/30/62 at White Oak Swamp, VA. Wounded 12/11/62 at Fredericksburg, VA. KIA Jul 3.
R7#6	WILLIAM UNDERWOOD	33-34	7 Inf F	B ~1829. R Portage Lake, Onekama Twp, Manistee Co., MI. E Aug 61 private. KIA Jul 3.
R7#7	____ ALMAS WILLIAM ALMAS[109]	~23	7 Inf G	B 1840? Canada. 1860: R Attica, Lapeer Co., MI; occ laborer. E Aug 61 private. KIA Jul 3.
R7#8	SERGT F J DIVITT 5th Cav Co D			Identity of this soldier not found in military sources.
R7#9	JOHN LAVABY 5th Cav Co A			Identify of this soldier not found in military sources.
R7#10	JOHN ROBERTS	23-24	5 Inf C	B ~1839. R Detroit, MI. E Sep 62 private. C Jul 2: wounded in his lung and left forearm. D Jul 14 or 15 of tetanus complication.
R7#11	SERGT J MILFORNE JOHN L **MILBORN**	20-21	7 Cav D	B ~1842 OH. E Aug 62 corporal. No service record confirmation that soldier was ever promoted to sergeant, but rather reduced in rank to private. KIA Jul 3.
R7#12	SERGT S BUZZELL STEPHEN J BUZZELL 5 Cav A			Stephen Buzzell, a 5th Michigan Company A cavalryman, received a July 3rd wound at Gettysburg, but he survived the wound and the war. He died in 1875 and received a government-provided headstone at his burial site at the Twin Lake Cemetery in Twin Lake, Muskegon County, Michigan.
R7#13	AUSTIN WHITMAN	~26	1 Inf F	B ~1837. E Jul 61 private. KIA Jul 2. Survivor (WC70698): M Mrs. Catharine Whitman 72 in 1865 (widow of Samuel Whitman).

---

109 **Birthyear question**. The June 22, 1860 U.S. Census sheet in Attica, Michigan shows a William Alma at reported age 20, residing in a David Almas residence. If this is the Alma who is buried in this grave, his birthyear is around 1840.

R7#15	NELSON A ALLEN	19-20	5 Cav A	B ~1843 MI. R Plymouth, Wayne Co., MI. 1860: R Van Buren. Wayne Co, MI; occ: farmer on father's farm. E Aug 62 private. KIA Jul 3: wounded in brain.
R7#16	CHARLES MASTERS CHARLES S MASTERS 5 Cav D			Charles Masters, a 5th Michigan Company D cavalryman, received a July 3rd wound at Gettysburg, but he survived the wound and received a disability discharge from the army in September. He died in 1917 and was buried in the Wildwood Cemetery in Chesaning, Saginaw County, Michigan.
R7#17	CORP H BARSE HORACE SPRAGUE BARSE	18	5 Cav E	B 10/28/1844 Detroit, MI. R same. Occ clerk. E Aug 62 private. Promoted to corporal during service. C Jul 3: wound to head and left side. D Jul 14.
R7#18	JOHN DRENBERGER J **OWENBERGER** 5 Cav F			John Owenberger enlisted as a private into Company F 5th Michigan Cavalry and received a promotion to corporal during his service. He received a July 3rd wound to his left side but survived the wound. He was captured in June 1864 at Trevilian Station, Virginia, but returned from imprisonment and left the arm in July 1865. He likely died in 1907 and was buried in Michigan.
R7#19	SERGT CHAS FOX CHARLES W **COX**	21-22	6 Cav C	B ~1842 MI. R St. Clair, St. Clair Co., MI. E Sep 62 private. Promoted to 1st sergeant on 10/11/62. C Jul 2: wounded in cavalry battle at Hunterstown, PA. D Jul 3.
R7#20	SERGT C E MINER CHARLES ELBERT MINER	19	7 Cav F	B 6/4/1844 Madison, Dance Co., MI. R Palmyra, Lenawee Co., MI. Occ teacher. E Jan 63 sergeant. KIA Jul 3.
R7#21	L GIBBS LEVI GIBBS[110]	32-33	5 Cav C	B ~1830 NY. R Olive, Eaton Co., MI. Occ farmer. E Aug 62 private. C Jul 3: wounded in right thigh→amp. D Sep 18. Survivors (WC103005): W Mariah 36 (M Aug 52 | ReM 1866): 2 ♂- William Gibbs 8, George McClellan Gibbs 1.
R7#22	J FALKETTS 5 Cav H			No killed or serving Gettysburg soldier with this or similar name found in military sources.
R7#23	W B HUNT WILLIAM B HUNT[111]	17	16 Inf I	B ~1846 PA. 1860 R Hillsdale Co., MI. E Aug 61 private. KIA Jul 2.

---

[110] **Soldier has named his son after Union General, no not Meade.** Levi Gibbs gave the name George McClellan Gibbs to his son born July 31, 1862, before then enlisting in the 5th Michigan Calvary fifteen days later.

[111] **Minor at enlistment.** William B Hunt's reported ages of 6 and 16 in the successive August 1850 and July 1860 U.S. Censuses attest to the likelihood that William was not 18, but 17 at his August 1861 enlistment. This would mean that William was likely 19 when he was killed in action July 2nd on Little Round Top.

R8#1	JOHN DURRE JOHN **DEWYER**[112]	18	24 Inf D	B ~Jul 1845 Romulus, MI. R Dearborn, MI. Occ farmer. E Aug 62 private. KIA Jul 1.
R8#2	A JENKS AUGUSTUS JENKS	40-41	24 Inf A	B ~1822 NY. R Ash, Monroe Co., MI. Occ farmer. E Aug 62 private. KIA Jul 1. Survivors (WC11015): W Laura 35 (M May 44| ReM 1867); 6 chn: 4 ♀- Amelia 18, Frances 16, Emily 10, Evaline 10 weeks & 2 ♂- Charles 9, Edgar 6.
R8#3	CORP W H LUCE WILLIAM H LUCE	23-24	24 Inf G	B ~1839 Brighton, Monroe Co., NY. R Detroit, MI. Occ clerk. E Aug 62 corporal. KIA Jul 1.
R8#4	WILLIAM H COLE[113]	24-25	5 Inf G	B ~1838 MI. R Pontiac, Oakland Co., MI. E Aug 62 private. Promoted to corporal during service. C Jul 2: GSW to left leg→amp. D Jul 12.
R8#5	HERSON BLOOD **HIRAM** BLOOD	18-19	3 Inf I	B 1844 Grand Rapids, MI. R Walker, Kent Co., MI. 1860 occ: farm laborer on father's farm. E Aug 62 private. KIA Jul 2: head wound.
R8#6	E B BROWNING ELIAS B BROWNING	18-19	24 Inf G	B ~1844. R Detroit, MI. Occ painter. E Jul 62 initially as a musician, then rank change to private. KIA Jul 1.
R8#7	CORP J T FAILS JEROME TIMOTHY FAILS or FALES	20	24 Inf G	B 5/23/1843 Detroit, MI. R same. Occ farmer. E Jul 62 private. Promotion to corporal during service. KIA Jul 1.
R8#8	SERGT GEO KLINE GEORGE **CLINE**	29-30	24 Inf B	B ~1833 Germany. R Detroit, Mi. Occ cigar maker. E Jul 62 sergeant. KIA Jul 1: shot in abdomen. Survivors (WC93284): W Mary Ann 26 (M Jun 56| ReM 1866); 3 ♂- Stanley 6, William 4, George 2.
R8#9	SERGT J POWELL JOHN STUART POWELL	27	24 Inf H	B 4/29/1836 NY. R Detroit, MI. Occ painter. E Aug 62 private. Promoted to sergeant during service. KIA Jul 1: shot in abdomen.
R8#10	CORP N KING NORMAN L KING	27	4 Inf D	B 2/26/1836 Seneca, Ontario Co., NY. R Ann Arbor, MI. E Jun 61 private. May/Jun 62: promoted to corporal. KIA Jul 2.
R8#11	ELLIS COMSTOCK	~21	4 Inf D	B 1842 MI. R Salem, Washtenaw, MI. E Aug 62 private. KIA Jul 2.

---

112 **Accepted at seventeen for enlistment.** On August 8, 1862, John Dewyer was accepted into the 24th Michigan infantry, even though he admitted on his enlistment paper that he was underaged at 17 years and one month. He likely then had not yet turned 18 when he was killed in the July 1st fighting in McPherson's Woods.

113 **Soldier's two separate gravesites in Cemetery.** Corporal William A. Cole has both a gravestone here in Row 8 and another in Row 10. Because this gravestone correctly identifies Cole as a member of the 5th Michigan Infantry, not 5th Michigan Calvary (as is inscribed on the Row 1 stone), this Row 8 site is Cole's likelier actual burial site.

R8#12	A HOISINGTON ADDISON JOAB **HOISINGTON**	~21	4 Inf F	B ~1842 Walworth, Wayne Co., NY. R Hudson, Lenawee Co., MI. Occ farmer. E Jun 51 private. Wounded on 7/1/62 at Malvern Hill, VA. KIA Jul 2
R8#13	CORP C H LADD CHARLES H LADD	~25	4 Inf A	B ~1838. R Monroe Co., MI. E Jun 61 corporal. KIA Jul 2.
R8#14	H B FOUNTAIN HIRAM B FOUNTAIN	~22	4 Inf F	B 1841 MI. R Hudson, Lenawee Co., MI. 1860 occ: farm laborer on father's farm. E Jun 61 corporal. Whether missing vs captured 6/27/62 after Gaines' Mill is not clear in his army service record. KIA Jul 2.
R8#15	CORP J SHOOK JEROME SHOOK	18-19	5 Inf B	B 1844 Kinderhook, Columbia Co., NY. R Mount Clemens, MI. E Sep 61 private. Promoted to corporal on 3/1/63. KIA Jul 2.
R8#16	CORP A BENSON ADELBERT BENSON[114]	~17	4 Inf A	B ~1846 OH. R Monroe Co., MI. E June 61 private. Captured on 7/21/61 at 1st Bull Run. Confined at Richmond, not paroled until 1/3/62. Jan/Feb 62: absent on furlough. Nov/Dec 62 promoted to corporal. KIA Jul 2.
R8#17	ROBERT SLIGH or SLY	36	3 Inf K	B 6/24/1827 Scotland. R Kent Co., MI. E May 61 private. C Jul 2: severe wound to leg. D Jul 2 or 3.
R8#18	OLIVER N CULVER	~21	3 Inf K	B ~1842 NY. R Kent Co., MI. 1860 occ: painter apprentice. E May 61 private. KIA Jul 2.
R8#19	SERGT R POWER REUBEN **TOWER**	~27	3 Inf K	B 1836 Ionia, Ionia Co., MI. R same. 1860 occ teacher. E May 61 private. Promotion to sergeant during service. KIA Jul 2: GSW to brain.
R8#20	SERGT D A VODRIA DANIAL **VODRA**	~26	5 Inf A	B ~1837. R Wayne Co., MI. E Jun 61 corporal. Promoted to sergeant on 6/1/62. Promoted to 1st sergeant on 9/15/62. KIA Jul 2.
R8#21	THOMAS SHANAHAN THOMAS **SHANNAHAN**	22-23	1 Cav H	B ~1840. Occ horse trainer. E Aug 61 private. Court martial sentence on 9/25/62 to forfeit one-month's pay for an unrecorded infraction. Promoted to corporal on 1/1/63. C Jul 4: Wounded in cavalry battle at Fountain Dale, PA. D Aug 2.
R8#22	D C LAIRD DAVID C LAIRD	~21	4 Inf A	B ~1842 NY. E Jun 61 private. C Jul2: GSW to lumbar spine region, fracturing a lumbar vertebrae. D Sep 24.

---

114 **Minor at death**. Adelbert Benson's reported ages of 4 and 14 on the successive October 1850 and June 1860 U.S. Census reports is probative that Adelbert was not 18 at his June 1861 enlistment, but more likely 15. Accepting this timeline, Adelbert was likely only 17 when he was killed fighting in the Wheatfield on July 2nd.

R8#23	C PEASE CONSTANTINE PEASE[115]	~22	4 Inf C	B 1841 Clarkson, Monroe Co. NY. R St. Joseph Co., MI. 1860 occ: farmhand. E Jun 61 corporal. C Jul 2: GSW fracturing left hip joint. D Aug 7.
R9#1	GEORGE COLBURN	29-30	24 Inf G	B ~1833 MI. R Ash, Monroe Co., MI. 1860 occ: working on father's farm. E Aug 62 corporal. C Jul 1: shot in the head. D Jul 7.
R9#2	EDWARD B HARRISON[116]	20-21	24 Inf K	B ~1842. R Detroit, MI. E Aug 62 private. Placed under arrest 4/10/63 following being apprehended for a desertion. KIA Jul 1.
R9#3	ERSON H SMITH	~26	3 Inf A	B ~1837 Ingham, MI. R Kent Co., MI. 1860 occ: farmer working on father's farm. E Jun 61 private. C Jul 2: wounded in hip. D Sep 12.
R9#4	SILAS E THURSTON	~23	3 Inf G	B ~1840. R Ingham Co., MI. E Jun 61 private. KIA Jul 2.
R9#5	SERGT G PETTINGER GEORGE H PETTINGER	24-25	24 Inf G	B ~1835 NJ. R Detroit, MI. 1860 occ: carriage maker. E Aug 62 sergeant. KIA Jul 1. Survivors (WC111015): W Mary ~24 (M Feb 1856| ReM 1867); 3 chn: 2 ♂- George 6, James 1 & 1 ♀- Mary 4.
R9#6	CHARLES B BURGESS	~26	3 Inf A	B ~1837. E Jun 61 private. Sep/Oct→Nov/Dec 61: sick in hosp. Jan/Feb 62: detached extra duty as cook in hospital→4/10/63. C Jul 2: wounded in head. D Jul 2 or 3.
R9#7	LIEUT G A DICKEY GILBERT ARNOLD DICKEY[117]	20	24 Inf G	B 2/28/1843 Marshall, Calhoun Co., MI. R Detroit, MI. E Aug 62 private. Promoted sergeant on 12/2/62. Promoted to 1st sergeant 1/27/63. Commissioned 2nd lieutenant on 3/10/63. KIA Jul 1. Survivor (WC13071): W Rozetta 16 (M 7/1/62).
R9#8	JAMES O'NEIL JAMES HENRY O'NEIL	25	3 Inf H	B 1/25/1838 Ireland. R Muskegon Co., MI. E May 61 private. Mar/Apr 62: rank change to drummer/musician. C Jul 2: wound to right lung. D Jul 5.
R9#9	R K HORMAN K ROBERT **HERMANN**	45-46	24 Inf H	B ~1817 Germany. R Detroit, MI. E Aug 62 private. KIA Jul 1: shot in head.

---

115 **Soldier's Father a Baptist Minister**. Constantine Pease's father, Daniel Pease, was a Baptist minister.

116 **Final Statement $21.13 Charge for Lost Rifle**. Edward Harrison's service papers include a note that $21.13 would be withheld from any pay owed any dependents. The imperative to compensate the army for the lost gun of a killed soldier, especially if this loss occurred during the battle, appears difficult to understand.

117 **Soldier killed on first wedding anniversary**. The 24th Michigan Colonel Henry Morrow reacted to the loss of Gerald Dickey, referring to him as "an officer of great promise." Dickey, who had been one of the first enrollees of what today is Michigan State University, would die, leaving behind in Marshall, Michigan his 16-year-old wife Rozetta. As a sad addendum, Dickey's death happened to occur on the first anniversary of their wedding.

R9#10	CORP O SOUTHWORTH OTIS SOUTHWORTH[118]	28-29	24 Inf C	B ~1834 NY. R Wayne Co., MI. 1860 occ: farm laborer. E Aug 62 private. Promoted to corporal during service. KIA Jul 1. Survivor (WC12643): W Harriet 20 (M 7/4/60), no chn.
R9#11	CHARLES PHELPS	~23	4 Inf B	B ~1840 Amherst, Hillsborough Co., NH. R Washtenaw Co., MI. 1860 occ: painter apprentice. E May 61 private. KIA Jul 2.
R9#12	CORP F P WORDEN FREEMAN PENFIELD WORDEN	31	4 Inf C	B 9/30/1831 Rutland Center, Jefferson Co., NY. R St. Joseph Co., MI. E Jun 61 private. KIA Jul 2. Survivors (WC19856): Elijah Overshire (guardian as wife Margaret predeceased soldier in Apr 60); 2 chn: 1 ♀- Lorena 7 & 1 ♂- Charles 5.
R9#13	CORP W A PRYOR WILLIAM A PRYOR	~28	4 Inf D	B ~1835 England. R Ann Arbor, Washtenaw Co., MI. 1860 occ: painter. E Jun 61 private. Promoted to corporal during service. KIA Jul 2.
R9#14	CHARLES A ROUSE (MN AUGUSTUS)	~21	4 Inf D	B ~1842 NY. R Washtenaw Co., MI. 1860 occ: apprentice carpenter. E Jun 61 private. KIA Jul 2.
R9#15	CHARLES A THURLACH CHARLES **THURLACK**	~24	4 Inf A	B ~1839. R Monroe Co., MI. E Jun 61 private. KIA Jul 2.
R9#16	CHARLES W GREGORY (MN WAINWRIGHT)	20	4 Inf H	B 5/30/1843 Jonesville, Hillsdale Co., MI. R same. E Jun 61 private. KIA Jul 2.
R9#17	JAMES H PENDLETON (MN HALL)	20	4 Inf H	B 4/1/1843 Calhoun Co., MI. R Litchfield, Hillsdale Co., MI. E Jun 61 private. Captured at Fredericksburg 12/12/62. KIA Jul 2. Survivor (WC45049): M Mrs. Lydia Pendleton 55 in 1864 (widow of Lewis Pendleton).
R9#18	GEORGE PURDY[119]	19	4 Inf H	B 2/28/1844 Forbush Corner, Crawford Co., MI. Joined regiment in 1863 as substitute for 45 y/o father, Abram Purdy, who had been drafted on 2/11/63; private. KIA Jul 2.

---

118 **Seventy-three-year-old receives restitution of pension forty years after husband's death at Gettysburg**. Following the death at Gettysburg of Otis Southworth, Mrs. Harriet Southworth in 1868 would marry Otis's younger brother Seth. However, Seth Southworth would die prematurely in 1874. Some years later, Mrs. Southworth would marry a third time. This third marriage would last until this husband's death in 1900. As one example surely of the charity that could be exercised by the U.S. Pension with regards to Civil War widows, Mrs. Harriet White in 1903 and at the age of 73 applied for and again began receiving a widow's pension, earned by Otis Southworth's death forty years earlier.

119 **Son substitutes for, then dies for drafted father**. George Purdy, just short of his 19th birthday, would substitute for his 45-year-old father, Abram Purdy, who had been drafted February 11, 1863. On July 2, 1863, George would be killed in action while fighting with the 4th Michigan Infantry likely in the Wheatfield.

R9#19	JOSEPH BRINK[120]	~20	4 Inf H	B ~1843 Germany. R Wayne Co., MI. Occ farmer. Drafted 2/11/63 private. KIA Jul 2.
R9#20	SERGT N GOSHA NICHOLAS GOSHA	~23	7 Inf F	B ~1840. R Portage Lake, MI. E Aug 61 private. Promoted to corporal on 11/1/62. Promoted to sergeant on 5/1/63. KIA Jul 3.
R9#21	EDWIN BEEBE	20	7 Inf E	B Apr 1843 Attica, Lapeer Co., MI. R Tuscola Co., MI. 1860 occ: farm laborer on father's farm. E Aug 61 private. KIA Jul 3.
R9#22	WILLIAM DAFT 5 Cav A			No killed Gettysburg soldier with this name found in military sources. A William Theodore Dopp, born 1841 and serving in the 5th Michigan Cavalry Company A, was wounded Jul 3 at Gettysburg. He survived this wound and later obtained a certificate of disability for discharge from the army on 11/15/64.
R9#23	JAMES T BEDELL[121] (MN TRACY)	47-48	7 Cav F	B 1815 NH. R West Bloomfield twp, Oakland Co., MI. 1860 occ: farmer in Waterford, Oakland Co., MI. E Jan 63 private. C Jul 3: severe saber wound to the left side of the brain. D Aug 30.
R9#24	GEORGE W LUNDY	20-21	7 Cav H	B ~1842 Detroit, MI. R Litchfield, Hillsdale Co., MI. Occ gold pen maker. E Dec 62 private. C Jul 3: shot in head and right arm. D Jul 15.

---

120 **Drafted German immigrant in Cemetery**. Joseph Brink, a farmer immigrated from Germany, would be drafted into 4th Michigan Infantry on February 11, 1863. He would be killed in action July 2nd in the Wheatfield.

121 **Soldier overaged at enlistment**. U.S. Census records, in agreement with an Ancestry.com family tree, attest that James Bedell, at this January 1863 enlistment, was already at least two years beyond the 45-years upper-age acceptance into military service.

4TH MICHIGAN INF^TRY

4th Michigan Monument in the Wheatfield

★ ★ ★ ★ ★

Colonel Harrison Jeffords was the 4th Michigan commanding officer, who had only recently brought the regiment a new national flag, that he had been personally gifted and had pledged his guardianship of, during a recruiting trip back in Michigan. The monument cites its location as the spot, amidst the July 2nd fighting in the Wheatfield, where Colonel Jeffords received a mortal bayonet from a Confederate, as he fought in a melee to save that national flag from their capture. He would be taken for aid but would die the next morning. He is buried in the Forest Lawn Cemetery in Dexter, Michigan.

Minnesota

R1#1	EDWIN PARL EDWIN **PAUL**	22	1 Inf I	B 11/17/1840 MN. R Wasioja twp, Dodge Co., MN. 1860 occ: farm laborer in Macomb Co., MN. E May 61 private. C Jul2: severe leg wound→amp. D Jul 13. Survivor (WC104995): F James Paul 63 in 1867 (widower of Mrs. Elizabeth Paul, who died 1/12/62; widower is affirmed cripple who is unable to support himself).
R1#2	PHINEAS L DUNHAM (MN LEONARD)	22	1 Inf G	B 12/1/1840 Farmington, Hartford Co., CN. R Wells, 1860 C: Rice Co., MN. E Apr 61, private. Promotion to corporal during service. C Jul 2: GSW fracture of femur. D Jul 17. Survivor (WC45875): M Mrs. Sylvia Dunham 60 (widow of Albert Dunham).
R1#3	IRVINE LAWRENCE **IRVING** LAWRENCE	~23	1 Inf D	B ~1840. E Apr 61 private. C1: slightly wounded in side at Antietam on 9/17/62. Sent to hospital, then to a convalescent camp. Returned to regiment 12/18/62. C Jul 2: shot in head. D Jul 5.
R1#4	L J SQUIRES LEONARD J **SQUIRE**[122]	25	1 Inf F	B 8/15/1837 MI. E Apr 61 private. Oct 61: promoted to corporal. Assignment of his company F to skirmishing duties Jul 2nd on another part of the field absented him and his company from the Jul 2nd charge. C Jul 3: GSW to hip. D Jul 4 or 7.
R1#5	PETER WELM PETER **WELIN**	~32	1 Inf E	B ~1831 Sweden. E May 61 private. Served in pioneer corps. Wounded at 1st Bull Run on 7/21/61. C Jul 2: wounded in ankle→amp x 2. D Jul 26 or 29.
R1#6	HANS SIMONSON	~23	1 Inf A	B ~1840 Germany. E May 61 private. C Jul 2: wounded in thigh. D Aug 3.
R2#1	EDWARD HALE EDWARD P HALE	23-24	1 Inf I	B ~1839 NY. 1860: Whitewater, Winona Co., MN; occ day laborer. E Sep 61 private. C Jul 2: shot through left lung and fracture of left ankle→amp. D Sep 12.

---

122 **Soldiers debate: Is survival providential or just luck** In Sergeant James Wright's post-war memoir, he recalled an earnest conversation between Corporal. Squire and Sgt. Phil Hamlin in regards to the slight losses the 1st Minnesota had sustained in the successive Union bloodbaths of Fredericksburg and Chancellorsville. Hamlin, a greatly admired and devout officer in the regiment assured Squire that the men were being protected by "Providence." Squire demurred, preferring to explain for what had saved the regiment as "just luck."

R2#11	SERGT WADE LUFKIN[123]	26	1 Inf C	B 1/1/1837 Sedgwick, Hancock Co., MN. Occ lumberman. E May 61 private. Promoted to corporal on 8/1/61. Detachment of his Company C to provost guard duties Jul 2nd at division headquarters absented him from the famed charge from Cemetery Ridge. Promoted to sergeant on 6/1/62. KIA Jul 3.
R2#12	SERGT OSCAR WOODWARD OSCAR **WOODARD**	20	1 Inf I	B 1/1/1843 ME. 1860: R Elk River, Sherburne Co., MN. Occ lumberjack. E May 61 private. KIA Jul 2: killed instantly by a shell.
R3#4	SERGT FREDERICK DIEHR	~29	1 Inf H	B ~1834 Germany. 1860: R Mankato, Blue Earth Co., MN; occ clerk. E Jun 61 private. Feb 62: promoted to corporal. Promoted to sergeant on 7/3/62. KIA Jul 3: wound to right lung.
R3#5	JOHN ELLSWORTH JOHN E ELLSWORTH	22	1 Inf C	B 6/4/1841 Canada. 1860: R Florence, Carver Co., MN; occ farm laborer. E May 61 private. Wounded at Savage's Station 6/20/62. Detachment of his Company C to provost guard duties Jul 2nd at division headquarters absented him from the famed charge from Cemetery Ridge. C Jul 3: wounded in left leg→amp. D Jul 20. Survivors (WC143921): M Mrs. Mary Ellsworth 51 in 1864 (Thomas Ellsworth unable to perform any kind of manual labor).
R3#6	CLARK BRANDT **CLAUS** BRANDT	26	1 Inf A	B 2/19/1837 Germany. R Marine, Washington Co., MN. Occ farmer. E Apr 61 private. C Jul 2: shot in right knee→ amp. D Jul 21.
R3#7	TIMOTHY CRAWLEY	~28	1 Inf A	B ~1835 Ireland. R Minneapolis, MN. Occ blacksmith. E Apr 61 private. Wounded in leg on 6/29/62 in the Battle of Nelson's farm. Wounded in the left eye slightly on 9/17/62 at Antietam. Appointed corporal on 9/18/62. C Jul 2: wounded in leg →amp at thigh. D Jul 18.
R3#8	PETER MARKS	~31	1 Inf A	B ~1832 Germany. 1860: Woodberry, Washington Co., MN; occ blacksmith. E Apr 61 corporal. C Jul 2: severely wounded right ankle→amp. D Jul 23.
R3#9	CAPT JOSEPH PERIAM	32	1 Inf K	B 6/30/1831 NY. R Winona, Winona Co., MN. Occ hotel keeper. Apr 61: commissioned 2nd lieutenant. Promoted from 2nd lieutenant on 11/15/61. Jul 62: malarial flare. Promoted to captain during service. C Jul 2: GSW to head. D Jul 7.

---

123 **1st Minnesota Company C Detachment Saves Company from July 2nd Charge**. Two companies of the 1st Minnesota Infantry were absented from Cemetery Ridge when the sacrificial July 2nd charge took place. Company C had been detached to division headquarters for provost guard duties. Company F had been detailed to scrimmaging in an area near Little Round Top. Men from these two companies returning to their camp and finding so few survivors of the day's charge likely were seized by both a survivor's guilt and as well an appetite for revenge.

R3#10	CHARLES E BAKER[124]	~21	1 Inf D	B ~1842 NY. R Rosemont, Dakota Co., MN. 1860 occ: living on father's farm. E May 61 private. May/Jun 62 wounded, sent sick back to Minesota. Returned to ranks in Nov 62. Killed instantly Jul 2.
R3#11	BYRON WELCH BYRON WELCH **COBB**[125]	~25	1 Inf I	B ~1838. R Pepin, Wabasha Co., MN. E May 61 private. Rank change to wagoner. Becomes tentmate of Private John Churchill. KIA Jul 2: he charged with tentmate, although as a wagoner, he was exempt from battle action. Survivor (WC 107546): M Mrs. Mary Cobb 56 in 1867 (abandoned by Ariel Cobb in 1849).
R3#14	LIEUT WALDS FARRAR **WALDO** FARRAR	~27	1 Inf I	B 1836 Middlesex, Washington Co., VT. R Elgin, VT. Occ hotel manager/carpenter. E Apr 61 sergeant. Commissioned 2nd lieutenant on 9/17/62. Promoted to 1st lieutenant on 12/17/62. Jan 63: hospitalized for unspecified condition. Began 15-day leave-of-absence on 5/15/63 to attend to private business back in Vermont. KIA Jul 2.
R3#15	W MOORE (1 Inf)			No killed Minnesota soldier with this common surname found in military sources.
R3#16	HENRY NICKELS HENRY **NICKELL**	~24	1 Inf A	B ~1839 Germany. Occ shoemaker. E Apr 61 private. C Jul 2: wound of right thigh with fracture of femur. D Aug 10.
R3#17	JOHN McKENZIE	26	1 Inf E	B 1/1/1837 Scotland. 1860: R Sauk Rapids, Benton Co., MN; occ farm laborer. E May 61 corporal. C Jul 2: severe wound in left leg→amp. D Aug 4 or 7.
R4#1	JOSEPH V SISLER	33	1 Inf G	B 3/25/1830 Montgomery Co., PA. R Faribault, Rice Co., MN. Occ farmer. E Apr 61 private. KIA Jul 2 or 3. Survivor (WC145693): M Mrs. Frances Simpson 50 (widow of John Sisley and of 2nd husband Humphry Simpson).
R4#2	ALONZE C HAYDEN ALONZO HAYDEN	24	1 Inf D	B 10/6/38 Mayfield, Somerset Co., ME. 1860: R Champlin, Hennepin, MN; occ: farmer working on father's farm. E Apr 61 private. Hospitalized Jul 62→ 10/31/62. Hospitalized again in 1863 until return to regiment in Mar 63 (reason for these hospitalizations not specified in service record). C Jul 2. D Jul 3.
R4#3	GEORGE GRANDY	~21	1 Inf D	B ~1842 Germany. E Apr 61 private. Reenlist Nov 61 private, promoted to corporal. C Jul 2. D Jul 4.

---

124 **Soldier appears to have lost his life on his birthday.** A FindAGrave.com memorial gives Charles Baker's birthday occurred on a July 2nd. If this is an accurate report, Charles Baker was instantly killed at Gettysburg on his birthday. However, the 1840 birthyear given on the FindAGrave.com memorial does not appear accurate as both the 1850 and 1860 U.S. Censuses suggest a birthyear of 1842. Finally, consistent with a birthyear of 1842, Baker reported his age as 19 at his May 1861 army enlistment.

125 **Soldier fighting under an alias.** Mrs. Mary Cobb's successful application for a dependent mother's pension required her to persuade the U.S. Pension Office that her son, Byron Welch Cobb, had entered military service under an abbreviated alias of simply Byron Welch.

R4#4	CAPT N S MESSICK NATHAN S MESSICK[126]	~36	1 Inf G	B ~1827 NJ. 1860: R Faribault, Rice Co., MN; occ shoemaker. Commissioned 1st lieutenant on 4/29/61. Promoted to captain on 7/29/61. Absented 2/1-3/7/63 on doctor's recommendation for convalescing chronic hepatitis. Returned from directing action during the Jul 2nd charge to find himself the highest-ranking officer not killed or wounded and therefore in command of the regiment. KIA Jul 3: instantly killed by a shell fragment which penetrated his skull. Survivors (WC9549): W Amanda 32 (M Jul 49); 4 chn: 3 ♀- Mary 13, Euphenia 10, Lizzie 5 & 1 ♂- George 3.
R4#5	WILLIAM N PECK (MN NELSON)	23	1 Inf I	B 10/37/1839 Detroit, MI. 1860: R Minneola, Goodhue Co., MN; occ: farmer on father's farm. E May 61 private. C Jul 2: severe wound of right leg→Jul 3 amp. D Jul 27 of tetanus complication.
R4#6	CHARLES H GOVE	23	1 Inf B	B 6/29/1840 Grantham, Sullivan Co., NH. 1860: R Lakeland, Washington Co., MN; occ lumber mill hand. E Apr 61 private. C Jul 2: wound to spine and shoulder. D Jul 30. Survivor (WC32651): M Mrs. Mary Gove 65 (widow of Isaiah Gove).
R4#7	FREDER GLAVE FREDERICK GLAVE	~25	1 Inf A	B ~1838 Germany. R St. Paul, Ramsey Co., MN. E May 21 private. C Jul 2 severe wound to leg→amp. Aug 10.
R4#8	WILBER F WELLMAN (MN FISK)	20	1 Inf I	B 8/21/1842 Ravenna, Portage, OH. Occ farmer. E May 61 private. Promoted to corporal during service. C Jul 2: severe wound in left leg→amp. D Aug 2.
R4#9	ISRAEL DURR	22	1 Inf K	B 9/23/40 Buffalo, Erie Co., NY. E Jan 62 private. C Jul 2 shot in side and lung. D Jul 4 or 7. Survivors (WC61443 not online): W Phoebe 25 in 1864 (M Dec 59 | ReM 1869); 1 ♂- Alfred 10 months.
R4#10	SERGT PHILIP HAMLIN[127]	24	1 Inf F	B 5/24/1839 Warren Co., PA. 1860: R Fair Haven, Olmsted Co., NY; occ working on father's farm. E Apr 61 corporal. Promoted to sergeant on 11/1/62. Assignment of duties Jul 2nd on another part of the field absented him and his Company F to skirmishing absented him from the famed Cemetery Ridge. KIA Jul 3: instantly killed by four gunshot wounds to chest and leg. Providence had ceased to smile upon him. A man's man, widely admired and respected in the regiment, Hamlin was mournfully buried on the field after the battle by his comrades.

---

126 **Officer survives 1st Minnesota celebrated July 2nd charge, only to be killed July 3rd.** Captain Nathan Messick had been contending with the symptoms of chronic hepatitis in the winter of 1862-63 and had received a one-month home leave for convalescence that ended March 7th. Captain Messick participated in the famed 1st Minnesota charge down Cemetery Ridge on July 2nd. He returned from this charge to find himself the highest-ranking officer not killed or wounded in the charge. Manning the defenses the next day, he would be instantly killed by a shell during Longstreet's assault. His death would leave four young children without a father.

127 **On July 3rd, Providence ceased to favor Sergeant Phil Hamlin.** After fighting had ended July 3rd, a group of Hamlin's sorrowing comrades examined his body to note the multiple minié ball wounds. That evening his men decided to respectfully bury his body on the field.

R4#17   J H PRIME   ~24   1 Inf D   B ~1839 NY. R Minneapolis, MN. Occ painter. E May 61 private. KIA Jul 2.
        JOSEPH H PRIME

R4#18   JOHN W DAVIS   ~25   1 Inf E   B ~1838 NY. E Apr 61 private. Hospitalized 8/15/62→12/6/62 with unspecified
                                              condition. KIA Jul 2.

1st Minnesota Monument on Cemetery Ridge

★ ★ ★ ★ ★

Sacrificial Charge Ordered by BG Winfield Scott Hancock July 2nd of 200-Man Regiment off Cemetery Ridge Toward Cresting Confederate Brigade would lead to 80% casualties among these men.

76   Abraham Lincoln's Honored Dead at the Gettysburg National Cemetery

New Hampshire

R1#7	JOHN TAYLOR	39-40	12 Inf E	B ~1823 Centre Harbor, Belknap Co., NH. R New Hampton, Belknap Co., NH. Occ day laborer. E Aug 62 private. C Jul 2: wound to left thigh with femur fracture. D Aug 14. Survivors (WC62243): W Mary 23 (M Sep 54| ReM 1866); 1 ♂- George 5.
R1#8	KENDALL H COFREN KENDALL **W COFFRAN**[128] or COFRAN	~17	2 Inf B	B 1846 Weld, Franklin Co., ME. R Seabrook, Rockingham Co., NH. Occ farmer. E Nov 62 into 17th NH Infantry Company A. Transferred to 2nd Infantry Company B on 4/16/63. C Jul 2: shot in left shoulder. D Jul 30.
R1#9	JOSEPH BOND JR	28-29	5 Inf E	B ~1834 Gilford, Belknap Co., NH. R Laconia, Belknap Co., NH. Occ cook. E Oct 61 private. KIA Jul 2. Survivors (WC33506): M Mrs. Dorothy Bond 66 in 1864 1864 (Joseph Bond, Sr. with chronic rheumatism, heart palpitations, he is totally incapacitated).
R1#10	SERGT OSCAR D ALLEN	19-20	5 Inf E	B ~1843 Croydon, Sullivan Co., NH. R Groton, Sullivan Co., NH. E Oct 61 corporal. Wounded on 9/17/62 at Antietam→hospitalized to 4/10/63. Promoted to sergeant on 4/12/63. KIA Jul 2: wounded in head and shoulder. Survivor (WC40932) M Mrs. Matha Allen 49 (widow of Hiram Allen).
R1#13	CHARLES T KELLY CHARLES T **KELLEY**	34-35	12 H	B ~1828 Meredith, Belknap Co., NH. R Gilford, Belknap Co., NH. Occ mechanic. E Aug 62 private. Wounded at Chancellorsville, VA on 5/31/63. KIA Jul 2. Survivors (WC10887): W Priscilla 36 (M Sep 49| ReM 1871); 1 ♀- Lydia Ann 11.
R3#1	WILLIAM H SPRING (MN HENRY)	~21	2 Inf A	B ~1842 Grafton, Windham Co., VT. R Keene, Cheshire Co., NH. Occ farmer. E May 61 private. KIA Jul 2: head wound.
R3#2	CHARLES A MOORE	21	2 Inf C	B 3/4/1842 Chichester, Merrimack Co., NH. R Pembroke, Merrimack Co., NH. Occ: farmer. E Aug 62 private. KIA Jul 2: head wound.

---

128 **Minor at death.** The variability of U.S. Census reports in gaging birthyears is demonstrated with this underaged enlistee, Kendall Coffran. On the July 29, 1850 U.S. Census for Weld, Maine, he is reported 3 years old. On the June 19, 1860 U.S. Census for Milan, New Hampshire, he is reported 14 years old. It should not come as big surprise that 19th century parents, sometimes illiterate, being surveyed by Census takers might give inaccurate responses, or even that a young teenager might not accurately know his own age. In Kendall Coffran's case, even taking the later implied birthyear, he could not have been 18 at his November 1862 enlistment, but no older than 16. He was likely 17 when was mortally wounded near the Peach Orchard on July 2nd.

R3#3	E J PLUMMER EDWARD J PLUMMER[129]	19	2 Inf A	B 6/25/1844 Swanzey, Cheshire Co., NH. R same. Occ farmer. E Aug 61 private. C Jul 2: compound fracture of femur in thigh. D Aug 16. Survivors (WC39706): M Mrs. Eliza Plummer 46 in 1864 (Jones Plummer affirmed aged and feeble).
R3#4	STEPHEN H PALMER	~34	2 Inf I	B ~1829 Fryeburg, Oxford Co., ME. R Manchester, Hillsborough Co., NH. Occ machinist. E May 61 corporal. Jun 61: self-request to change rank to private. Jul/Aug 61→1/1/63: detailed as teamster. C Jul 2: GSW left ankle and fracturing ulnar bone in forearm→leg amp on Aug 10. D Aug 14.
R3#5	CHARLES V BUZZELL CHARLES **P** BUZZELL	22-23	12 Inf E	B ~1841 Ellsworth, Grafton Co., NH. R same. E Aug 62 private. D Jul 14 of typhoid. Survivor (WC124990 not online): M Mrs. Anna D. Buzzell ~60 in 1869 (widow of David Buzzell).
R3#6	ROLAND TAYLOR	34-35	5 Inf G	B ~1828 England. R Claremont, Sullivan Co., NH. E Sep 61 private. Captured on 10/2/62 at Bolivar Heights, VA. Paroled 10/6/62 at Winchester, VA. C Jul 2: GSW fracturing leg→amp. D Jul 11.
R3#7	S R GREEN SAMUEL R GREEN	45-46	5 Inf A	B ~1817 Pittsfield, Merrimack Co., NH. R same. Occ shoemaker. E Sep 61. Captured on 5/31/62 at the Battle of Seven Pines, VA. Parole on 9/13/62 at Aiken's Landing, VA. C Jul 2: shot in leg→amp. D Jul 29 or 30.
R3#8	JOHN HENDERSON (ALIAS) JOHN **HAURAHAN**[130]	~26	2 Inf F	B 6/24/1837 Ireland. Occ farmer. E Jun 61 private. C Jul 2: wound in right leg→amp. D Jul 8. Survivor (application 329543 not online and eventually abandoned) : F Patrick Haurahan 80 in 1885 (widower).
R3#9	SERGT G A JONES GEORGE A JONES[131]	~22	2 Inf E	B ~1841 Concord, Merrimack Co., NH. R same. Occ gunsmith. E May 61 corporal. Promoted to sergeant on 12/15/61. C Jul 2: wound to spine producing paralysis. D Jul 31. Survivor (WC219780 not online): M Mrs. Hannah Jones ~71 in 1884.

---

129 **Minor at enlistment**. An Ancestry.com public family tree gives Edward Plummer's birthdate as 6/23/1844. Assuming this to be accurate, Plummer would have enlisted at age 17, not 18 as claimed. This birthday also means he would have died of his battle wound six weeks after his 19th birthday.

130 **Soldier fighting under an alias**. An 1885 U.S. Pension Office application by the Patrick Haurahan, soldier's 80-year-old father, required that he provide affidavit support that John Henderson was an alias being used by his son in the army. Patrick Haurahan appealed for a government pension based on being an unsupported widower and living in extreme poverty. In an 1886 follow-up letter to the Pension Office, an advocate pressed the father's case: "Being in advanced years, if help is not quickly accorded, the father of John Haurahan of Co. F 2nd NH vols, who shed his life's blood at Battle of Gettysburg, fighting for the "Stars and Stripes," shall have to die in a workhouse, and sink unknown and unheeded into a pauper's grave." In the end, frustrated by the Pension Office's delay in acting on his appeals, Patrick Haurahan would return to Ireland for support, abandoning his application.

131 **Prior occupation a gun smith**. Reporting for enlistment with this surprisingly infrequent occupation for a new soldier, George Jones was a gun smith, as had been his father before him

R3#10	GEORGES VITTUM[132]	~36	2 Inf F	B ~1827 Sandwich, Carroll Co., NH. R same. Occ day laborer. E May 61 private. C Jul 2: shot in right thigh. D Jul 31. Survivors (WC94274): 2 chn: 1 ♂- Charles Jr. 9 & 1 ♀- Susan 6 (A Mr. Langdon Clark serving as court-certified guardian); M Margaret 28 (M Apr 53| abandoned family in Oct 60).
R3#11	LIEUT E DASCOMB EDMUND DASCOMB[133]	2 Inf G	~25	B ~1838 Hillsborough Co., NH. R Greenfield, Hillsborough, NH. Occ teacher, law student. E May 61 corporal. Dangerously wounded 5/5/62 at the Battle of Williamsburg, VA. Commissioned 2nd lieutenant on 9/1/62. C Jul 2: severely wounded in body. D Jul 13.
R3#12	CHARLES W TAYLOR 2 Inf D			No killed Gettysburg soldier from any New Hampshire regiment found in military sources. Sgt. Charles W Patch, with his last name misspelled, could be the 2nd Infantry soldier buried here, but this could only be true if Taylor's grave marker at the Harmony Cemetery in Portsmouth, New Hampshire, is a cenotaph.
R3#13	CORNELIUS CLEARY	36-37	2 Inf H	B ~1826 Ireland. R Keene, Cheshire Co., NH. Occ farmer. E Aug 61 private. C Jul 2: wounded in the thigh. D Jul 13. Survivors (WC23076): M Mary 34 (M Feb 51); 4 chn: 1 ♂- Willie 10 & 3 ♀- Katie 9, Mary 7, Hannah 5.

---

132 **Soldier's two young children, abandoned by their mother, must go to probate court for guardianship hearing**. The death of George Vittum at Gettysburg would mean that the guardianship of his two young children would have to be adjudicated in the Probate Court of Carroll County, New Hampshire. This became necessary as their mother, Mrs. Margaret Vittum, though still living, had in October 1860 walked out on her seven-year marriage and left town, abandoning the care of their children and even severing all contact with them. Immediately following George Vittum's death, Margaet Vittum would remarry. Whether she chose then to reinvolve herself in the lives of her still young children is not evident in the pension records.

133 **Poetic soldier**. Edmund Dascomb, the 25-year-old 2nd-lieutenant of the 2nd New Hampshire infantry, was mortally wounded July 2nd in the Peach Orchard. He had been a man of academic accomplishments, which extended to the writing of poems. Reportedly, his poem "The Dying Volunteer" was set to music and sung at his memorial service back in New Hampshire.

"I am dying, brother, dying.
'Mid the wounded and the slain,
And around me forms are lying
Which never strive again: Much I would but cannot tell thee,
Of a home I cherished dear,
  Of friends I've left behind me,
  Who will shed the silent tear.

I am dying, brother, dying,
See how fast my life blood flows,
 And I feel my soul is hieing
  Where in death 't will fine repose;
Farewell father, sister, mother.
Farewell all my friends so dear.
Farewell, world, I see another,
  Gasped the dying Volunteer."

R3#14	JAMES S HAWKINS[134]	21	12 C	B ~9/30/1841 East Springfield, Sullivan Co., NH. R Center Harbor, Belknap Co., NH. Occ laborer. E Aug 62 private. C Jul 2: wounded in the abdomen. D Jul 3.
R3#15	JOHN TOTTEN	~29	2 Inf A	B ~1844 Ireland. R Marlborough, Cheshire Co., NH. E April 61 into 1st NH infantry Company G; private. Mustered out 8/9/61 and reenlisted 8/24/61 into 2nd NH infantry. KIA Jul 2.
R3#16	JOSEPH M CHESLEY	~21	2 Inf E	B ~1842 Durham, Strafford Co., NH. R Pittsfield, Merrimack Co., NH. Occ shoemaker. E May 61 private. C Jul 2: canister wounds to the thigh. D Jul 22.

---

134 **Soldier had seen brother mortally wounded at the preceding Battle of Chancellorsville.** On August 14, 1863, James Hawkins and his older brother William together enlisted into the 12th New Hampshire infantry. In the regiment's disastrous May 3, 1863 charge at the Battle of Chancellorsville, the 12th New Hampshire infantry sustained 325 casualties of the 580 men engaged, counting William among the mortally wounded. Wounded in the thigh and knee, William Hawkins wound linger in a Union hospital before dying on June 15, 1863. A likely distraught James would continue on with the regiment until receiving an abdominal wound on July 2nd and dying the next day, or eighteen days after his brother's death.

5th New Hampshire Monument in the Rose Woods

★ ★ ★ ★ ★

This monument marks the spot where Colonel Edward Cross, commander of the 1st Brigade, 1st Division, 2nd Corps and former 5th New Hampshire regimental commander, was mortally wounded July 2nd by a Confederate sniper.

Cross is buried in the Wilder Cemetery in Lancaster, NH.

New Jersey

R1#6	WILLIAM H RAY 12 Inf F			Misidentified soldier. A William Ray did not enlist in the 33rd NJ infantry until 1865. Of the two 12th NJ infantry Co. K soldiers killed Jul 3rd, William H Johnson and William Henry Harrison Stratton, the latter is buried in Swedesboro, NJ.
R1#7	SERGT JAMES B RISTER **CORHAM RIGHTER**	24	11 Inf C	B 2/28/1839 Kenilworth, Union Co., NJ. E (Trenton, NJ) Aug 62 private. Promoted to corporal on 9/17/62. Promoted to sergeant on 4/1/63. KIA Jul 2.
R1#8	E BANER EDWARD BARBER[135]	25	11 Inf H	B 9/21/1837 Canada. 1860 R Pequannock, Morris Co., NJ; occ blacksmith. E Aug 62 private. KIA Jul 2. Survivors (WC147573- not online): M Mrs. Matilda Barber ~65 in 1871. Pension suspended 9/22/73 on grounds of non-dependence (Edward Barber, Sr., a teamster, was judged able to perform light work and support wife. However, reinstated 10 years later he proved more enfeebled after wife's death).
R1#11	J H McNULTY' McNULTY JEREMIAH **McANULTY**[136]	44-45	7 Inf F	B ~1818 Ireland. E Sep 61 private. April 63: absent sick. KIA Jul 2. Survivors (WC81075): Ms. Rose McAnulty 57 in 1864 (guardian); 1 ♀- Catharine 11 (W Catharine died 6/13/62).
R1#13	P WEENE PETER **WEAN**[137]	18-19	6 Inf H	B ~1844 Hunterdon Co., NJ. E Aug 61 private. C Jul 2: wounded in back. D Jul 11. Survivor (WC123160): M Mrs. Mary Wean 52 in 1868 (widow of Gershom Wean).
R1#14	CHARLES FIELDEN 11 Inf C			A killed Gettysburg soldier with this or similar name is not found in military sources Charles Perdun, a member of the 11th NJ Infantry Company C was taken prisoner on July 3 and would die in Andersonville Prison on May 13, 1864.
R2#1	W A E WILLIAM A EZEKIEL	24	7 Inf I	B 9/20/1838 Trenton, NJ. R same. Occ farm laborer. E Sep 61 private. Promoted to corporal on 5/22/62. Promoted to sergeant on 12/1/62. KIA Jul 2. Survivors (WC12623): W Susan 26 (M Jul 58): 3 chn: twins ♂- Edgar and ♀- Phebe 4 & William 17 months.

---

135 **Mother's pension is suspended for "non-dependence."** Edward Barber's dependent mother's pension was suspended two years after it was granted on "grounds of non-dependence."

136 **Soldier reportedly denied furlough request after receiving news of wife's death.** The guardian's pension application for Jeremiah McAnulty's daughter included a note from McAnulty's former corporal that stated that McAnulty inexplicably had been denied a furlough request after news had come to him in the regiment of his wife's death on 6/13/62.

137 **Minor-aged soldier loses father during his term in service.** An Ancestry.com family tree gives Peter Wean's birthyear as 1844. This birthyear cannot be confirmed in U.S. Census records where he is not found. If this report of a 1844 birthyear is accurate, Peter Wean's enlistment age in 1861 could have not been older than 17. During Peter's service, his father Gershom died on 5/12/62, possibly following an accidental gunshot wound during hunting.

R2#5	JOHN RYAN	23-24	5 Inf C	B ~1839. E Oct 61 private. KIA Jul 2. Survivor (WC15168): W Elizabeth 27 (M Aug 59); no chn.
R2#6	J F JAMES FLAVIGAR	~20	7 Inf A	B ~!843. E (Trenton, NJ) Aug 61 private. KIA Jul 2: killed while supporting Clark's Battery B, 1st NJ Light Artillery near the Peach Orchard.
R2#18	THOMAS FLANAGEN THOMAS **FLANIGAN**	20-21	7 Inf G	B ~1842. E Sep 61 private. Promoted to corporal on 2/17/63. KIA Jul 2.
R2#19	MARTIN V HOUTEN MARTIN VAN HOUTEN	21-22	7 Inv A	B ~1841 NY. 1850 R: Canandaigua, Ontario Co., NY. E (Trenton, NJ) Aug 62 drummer Elevated to private on 8/23/62. Promoted to corporal on 6/24/63. KIA Jul 2. Survivor (WC17826): M Mrs. Elizabeth Van Houten 53 (widow of Adrian Van Houton).
R2#20	GEORGE W BERRY	~22	7 Inf B	B ~1841 Washington, D.C. Occ laborer. E Feb 62 private. Admitted to a hospital at Alexandria, VA on 11/9/62 for rheumatism and deserted from the hospital a few days later. Returned from desertion on 3/17/63. KIA Jul 2.
R3#1	PATRICK RYAN	43-44	5 Inf A	B ~1819 Ireland. R Trenton, NJ. Occ laborer. E Aug 62 private. May 63: wounded slightly on the neck at Chancellorsville. C Jul 2: severe wound to one leg. D Jul 8. Survivors (WC28327): W Mary 29 (M Aug 52); 2 ♂- Patrick 10, Timothy 8.
R3#2	SERGT JOHN McIVER	25-26	5 Inf B	B ~1837. E Aug 61 private. Promoted to sergeant on 6/1/63. C Jul 2: wounded in back of shoulder. D Jul 16.
R3#3	THOMAS VAN CLEAF THOMAS VAN **CLEAVE**	28-29	8 Inf F	B ~1834 Rahway, Union Co., NJ. 1860: R Chatham, Morris Co., NJ; occ painter. E Aug 61 private. C Jul 1: shot in right knee. D Jul 17.
R3#4	B C JACKSON BENJAMIN F JACKSON	40-41	11 Inf B	B ~1822 NJ. 1860: R Newark, NJ; occ carriage maker. E Aug 62 private. C Jul 2. D Jul 7. Survivors (WC22604); W Isabella 40 (M Jul 47); 2 ♂- Lewis 7, Charles 4.
R3#5	JOHN RUE JOHN H RUE	29-30	11 Inf B	B ~1833. E Aug 62 private. C Jul 2: wound to left leg→amp. D Jul 19.
R3#6	JAMES FLETCHER[138]	~16	7 Inf G	B ~1847 Ireland. 1860 R: Paterson South Ward, Passaic Co., NJ. E Sep 61 private. C Jul 2: wounded in the back by a shell fragment. D Jul 8. Survivor (WC40955): M Mrs. Ellen Fletcher 50 (widow of Andrew Fletcher).

---

138 **Minor at death?** The 7/16/60 U.S. Census sheet for Paterson, NJ reports James Fletcher's age as 13. Unless this report is in error, James's age at his September 1961 was not 18, but no older than 15. This U.S. Census report, if accurate, would also mean that James was only 16 at death.

R3#7	MICHAEL GOFF	38-39	11 Inf G	B ~1824 NJ. 1860: R Plumsted, Ocean Co., NJ; occ sawyer. E Aug 62 private. Wounds involving bruising of cheeks and an arm on 5/3/63 at Chancellorsville. C Jul 2: GSW to left shoulder. D Jul 9. Survivors (WC12433): W Susan 34 (M Jan 49| ReM 1866); 2 ♂- Jacob 12, William 11.
R3#8	JOSEPH BURROUGHS JOSEPH SEAL BURROUGHS[139]	32-33	8 Inf B	B ~1830 Bethlehem, Hunterdon Co., NJ. R Paterson, Passaic Co., NJ. Occ farmer. E Oct 61 private. Detailed as ambulance driver 6/30/62→4/10/63. May/Jun 63: detailed as a teamster. C Jul 2. D Jul 16. Survivor (WC23153): W Arletta 31 (M Oct 56): 2 ♀- Eliza 6, Ella 4.
R3#9	HENRY ELBERSON HENRY **ELBERTSON**	32-33	11 Inf G	B ~ 1830 Burlington Co., NJ. R same. Occ farmer. E Aug 62 private. He began a furlough on 2/10/63, approved for seven days, but he overstayed leave due to illness. Returned to duty on 4/8/63. May 63: shoulders bruised by wounding at Chancellorsville. C Jul 2. D Jul 5.
R3#10	SERGT SAMUEL STOCKTON SAMUEL **SHACKLELTON**	~21	5 Inf K	B ~1842 Ireland. E Aug 61 private. Promoted to sergeant on 4/1/63. C Jul 2. D Jul 3.
R3#11	WILLIAM PRESER *(Egg Harbor City Cavalry)* WILLIAM **PREISER**	~23	27 PA Inf E	B ~1840. E May 61 private. Promoted to corporal on 11/2/61. Promoted to sergeant on 11/1/6MM 2. KIA Jul 1: GSW to head.
R3#12	HENRY DAMMIG **HEINRICH** DAMMIG	20	13 Inf G	B 3/1/1843 Germany. Occ silver plater. E Aug 62 private. May 63: wounded at Chancellorsville. KIA Jul 3. Survivor (WC223205 not online): M Mrs. Henriette Dammig 63 in 1881(widow of Augustus Dammig).
R3#13	CHARLES B YEARKES	22-23	6 Inf B	B ~1840 Brooklyn, NY. Occ farmer. E Aug 61 private. Jul/Aug 62: reported AWOL. Sep/Oct 62: to have pay deducted for cost of rifle stolen on 8/30/62 while owner was resting during a retreat movement. Promoted to corporal on 12/25/62. C Jul 2: severely wounded in one leg. D Aug 20.
R3#14	DANIEL SCHUH	~39	3 Inf H	B ~1824 PA. Occ gardener. E Jun 61 private. Nov/Dec 62: promotion to corporal. KIA Jul 5: killed in a cavalry skirmish near Fairfield, PA. Survivors (WC20885): W Phoebe 35 (M Feb 46); 4 chn: 3 ♀- Lydia 16, Maggie 15, Lizzie 10 & 1 ♂- Emmanuel.

---

139 **Soldier serves extended detail as an ambulance driver.** Private Joseph Burroughs was detailed nine months out of his total twenty-months' service as an ambulance driver. Concluding this extended detail in the Spring of 1863, he would be mortally wounded on July 2nd.

R3#15	J PARLIAMENT JAMES PARLIAMENT[140]	28	13 Inf C	B Sep 1834 Monroe Co., NY. Occ laborer. E Aug 62 private. Mar/Apr 63: court martial sentence for desertion on or about 1/13/63: to forfeit $5 of each month's pay for four consecutive months, commencing with his 2/26/63 pay. C Jul 2: severe wound to right arm→amp. D Jul 29.
R3#16	JOHN SMITH JOHN A SMITH[141]	17	6 Inf K	B ~1846 Camden, Camden Co., NJ. E Aug 61 private. C Jul 2: wounded in the right hand. Transferred to general hospital in Philadelphia on 7/13/63. D Nov 30.
R3#17	W T HAWKINS WILIAM S HARKER[142]	37	12 Inf H	B ~Oct 1825 Woodstown, Salem Co., NJ. R Richmond, Salem Co., NJ. Occ blacksmith. E Aug 62 private. KIA Jul 2 while regiment was taking a barn filled with Confederate sharpshooters. Survivors (WC7586): W Mary 38 (M Aug 47); 4 chn: 3 ♀- Emily 14, Hattie 12, Mattie 8 & 1 ♂- Charles 10.
R3#18	____ RILEY JAMES A RILEY	37-38	12 Inf E	B ~1825 Beverly, Burlington Co., NJ. R same. Occ cordwainer. E Aug 62 private. C Jul 2: shot in left lung. D Jul 4. Survivors (WC120267): 2nd W Mary 29 (M Mar 60| ReM 1868); 2 chn: 1 ♂- James 9 & 1 ♀- Permelia 6 (1st W Hannah died Feb 59).
R3#19	J B JAMES BENNETT	37-38	7 Inf F	B ~1825 Ireland. 1860 R: Jersey City, Hudson Co., NJ. Occ laborer. E Sep 61 private. May/Jun 62: absent sick in hospital. KIA Jul 2. Survivor (WC24840): M Mrs. Catharine Bennett 90 (widow of Mathew Bennett).

---

140 **Hard court martial sentence for desertion.** On March 4, 1863, private James Parliament faced a court martial proceeding for charge of desertion on or about January 13, 1863. Upon being found guilty, Parliament was sentenced to forfeit $5 of each month's pay for four consecutive months and to confined in the camp of his regiment on bread and water alone for two weeks.

141 **Minor-aged soldier experiences agonizing death in West Philadelphia hospital.** John A. Smith was received at a general hospital in West Philadelphia on July 24th. On July 2nd, a conical ball had struck his right hand at the middle finger joint at the knuckle and an amputation at this joint was performed. John had reported his age as 17 and this procedure should have led to a quick discharge. However, John was noted to be very anemic and to be showing signs of an acute alcohol withdrawal syndrome (likely sepsis mimicking alcohol withdrawal). John's condition steadily worsened in the hospital until he died on November 30th. A post-mortem examination revealed that he had died of severe peritonitis. A final hospital death record records that John's body was released to friends for burial, presumably eventually back for burial at Gettysburg.

142 **Soldier killed during charge to chase Confederate snipers sheltering in the Bliss Barn.** In one of the least well known, but still heroic actions on July 2nd, some 200 members of the 12th New Jersey Infantry charged the Bliss Barn to roust sheltering nests of Confederate snipers who had been harassing the Union line on Cemetery Ridge. William Harker was killed in this action. Harker has a burial marker in Woodstown, New Jersey, which is either a cenotaph or a reburial site.

R3#20	J H JOSEPH HALL[143]	41-42	7 Inf F	B ~1821. E Sep 61 private. Left 4/1/62 at Division hospital at Budd's Ferry, MD. May/Jun 62: remaining sick in hospital. Jul/Aug 62: following desertion attempt from the hospital, he is apprehended and sentenced to the forfeiture of $8.30 from his pay, representing the cost for his arrest and return transportation to the army. On 1/21/63, Hall again deserted during a hospitalization. He was again apprehended on 2/2/63. KIA Jul 2.
R3#21	H R HENRY ROURKE	36-37	7 Inf F	B ~1826 Ireland. Occ horse shoer. E (Trenton, NJ) Sep 61 private. Slightly wounded in the face on 5/3/63 at Chancellorsville, VA. KIA Jul 2.
R4#1	LIEUT R H TOWNSEND RICHARD HENRY TOWNSEND[144]	24	12 Inf C	B 6/13/1839 NJ. R Dennisville, Cape May Co., NJ. E Sep 61 1st sergeant. Mustered out 4/9/63. Continued service as commissioned 2nd lieutenant on 6/30/63. KIA Jul 3. Survivors (WC33314): W Mary 21 (M Jun 61| ReM 1872); 1 ♂- Edwin 19 months.
R4#2	SERGT T SUTPHIN THEODORE SUTPHIN	33-34	5 Inf E	B ~1829 Hunterdon Co., NJ. R Rocky Hill, Somerset Co., NJ. Occ millwright. E Aug 61 private. Promoted to corporal on 4/1/62. Promoted to sergeant on 8/1/62. Slightly wounded in one hand on 5/3/63 at Chancellorsville. KIA Jul 2. Survivors (WC8947): W Sarah 36 (M Jan 55); 1 ♂- Ryneer 7.
R4#3	I L T			A killed Gettysburg soldier with these initials not found not identified in military sources.
R4#4	L KREISEL LUDWIG KREISEL[145]	31-32	Batty A 1 NJ LA	B ~1831 (probably Germany). E Aug 61 private. KIA Jul 3.
R4#5	G CUTTER GEORGE **KUTTER**[146]	40-41	Batty A 1 NJ LA	B ~1822. E Aug 61 private. Apr→May/Jun 62: sick in general hospital at Fairfax, VA with an unspecified condition. KIA Jul 3.

---

143 **Determined deserter**. Joseph Hall'Ss service record documents his dubious distinction of having deserted during successive hospital stays, first in July 1862 and then again in January 1863. He was fairly promptly apprehended and returned to his regiment on both of these occasions. Private Hall's service record does not document what subsequent confinement or close monitoring might have followed these returns to his regiment. Hall's death on the battlefield July 2nd put an end to these concerns.

144 **Killed-in-action after only three days in the Army**. In the shortest term of service of any soldier who fought at Gettysburg, 2nd lieutenant Richard Townsend would be killed three days after joining the army as a new officer.

145 **Two Germans enlist together in an artillery unit**. On 8/12/61, Ludwig Kriesel and George Kutter, likely German immigrants who knew each other, presented in Hoboken, NJ to sign enlistment papers for New Jersey Light Artillery Battery A. Both these men would be killed in the July 3rd artillery duel. Today these two men are buried side-by-side in the cemetery.

146 **Two Germans enlist together in an artillery unit**. On 8/12/61, Ludwig Kriesel and George Kutter, likely German immigrants who knew each other, presented in Hoboken, NJ to sign enlistment papers for New Jersey Light Artillery Battery A. Both these men would be killed in the July 3rd artillery duel. Today these two men are buried side-by-side in the cemetery

R4#6	ISAAC H COPELAND (MN HENRY)	23-24	12 Inf E	B ~1839 Camden, NJ. R same. Occ painter. E Aug 62 private. Jan/Feb→Apr 63: detailed as wagon letterer. KIA Jul 3. Survivor (WC10285): W Harriet 25 (M Aug 1860); no chn.
R4#7	JOHN ALBRIGHT	34-35	12 Inf F	B ~1828 Germany. R Mullica Hill, Gloucester Co., NJ. Occ farmer. E Aug 62 private. Wounded slightly in the head in May 63 at Chancellorsville. KIA Jul 3. Survivors (WC12425): W Hannah 40 (M May 54 | ReM 1867); 1 ♂- Louis 7.
R4#8	JOSEPH SPACIOUS JOSEPH B **SPACHIUS**[147]	28-29	12 Inf B	B ~1834 Burlington Co., NJ. R same. Occ shoemaker. E Aug 62 private. Promoted to corporal on 1/1/63. KIA Jul 3. Survivors (no approved WC found in pension records): W Maria 27 (M? | ReM 1865); 1 ♂- Earl 4.
R4#9	GEORGE MARTIN GEORGE H MARTIN	20-21	12 Inf A	B ~1842 NJ. 1860: R Newark, NJ; occ silver plater. E Aug 62 private. D Jul 3 from wounds.
R4#10	O S PLATT SAMUEL PLATT	42-43	12 Inf B	B ~1820 Columbus, Burlington Co., NJ. Occ farmer. E Aug 62 private. KIA Jul 3. Survivor (WC20672 not online): W Martha 40 in 1864 (M ?); 2 chn: 1 ♂- Samuel 11 & 1 ♀- Mary 2
R4#12	DANIEL HIERMAN DANIEL **KIERNAN**[148]	37-38	12 Inf H	B ~1825 Ireland. R Asbury, Warren Co., NJ. Occ farmer. E Aug 62 private. KIA Jul 2. Survivors (WC22051): W Anna 25 (M Oct 52): 2 chn: 1 ♀- Sarah 10 & 1 ♂- Benjamin Franklin Kiernan 2.
R4#14	GEORGE W ADAMS[149]	19-20	12 Inf F	B ~1843 Beverly, Burlington Co., NJ. Occ farmer. E Aug 62 private. KIA Jul 3.
R4#15	WILLIAM REDROW THOMAS J **RUDROW**	21-22	12 Inf G	B ~1841 Salem Co., NJ. 1860 R: Camden, Camden Co., NJ. Occ machinist. E Jul 62 private. D Jul 3: killed instantly by a shell. Survivors (WC32441 not online): W Mary ~20 (M Oct 61 | ReM 1867); 1 ♂- Thomas J Rudrow 14 months
R4#16	WILLIAM SPENCER WILLIAM H SPENCER	~22	12 Inf B	B ~Jul 1841 Philadelphia, PA. 1860: R Bridgeton, Cumberland Co., NJ; occ glass blower. Occ farmer. E (Woodbury, Gloucester Co., NJ) Aug 62 private. KIA Jul 3.

---

147 **No widow's pension approval found in records.** There is no record of a successful pension application for Joseph Spachius's wife, Maria, nor his son, Earl, four-years-old at the time of his father's death.

148 **Soldier's widow dropped from pension rolls on charge of cohabitation.** In 1886, Anna Kiernan was dropped from the pension roll for non-dependence, after an investigation established that she was living with a man, by whom she has borne two children in previous twelve years of cohabitation. Mrs. Kiernan had sought to hold onto the pension by swearing that she had not married this man, that they slept separately in the house they shared, and that they had not had any sexual relations in the preceding two years. Not being able to make a case for immaculate conceptions, however, Mrs. Kiernan's attestations could not be accepted.

149 **Father brings in son for enlistment and presumably claims his enlistment bonus.** George Adams' father, Thomas Adams, was present at his enlistment and certified his son's age to be 19. With this enlistment, George Adams would have immediately earned the proffered $25 bonus plus a $2 premium add-on.

R4#19	JACOB SHEIK JACOB **SHEAK**	~21	4 OH Inf I	B ~1842. Occ farmer. E Jun 61 private. Apr 63: absent sick in corps hospital. KIA Jul 2: shell wound to the chest while serving on Brigade provost guard duty.
R4#20	SIMON W CREAMER[150] (MN WILSON)	23	12 Inf K	B 11/21/1839 Gloucester Co., NJ. Occ wheelwright. E (Bridgeton, Cumberland Co., NJ) Aug 62 private. Detailed to Arnold's Battery A of 1st RI Light Artillery on 3/6/63. KIA Jul 3: shot in the head. Survivor (WC306039): F Andrew Creamer 77 in 1890 (affirmed disabled).
R4#21	J W BUTTON WILLIAM J BUTTON[151]	22-23	5 Inf K	B ~1840. R Atlantic City, Monmouth Co., NJ. Occ farm laborer. E Aug 61 private. Mar/Apr 62: to forfeit $13.25 in pay for loss of his Austrian rifle. Wounded slightly 6/1/62 near Fair Oaks, VA. C Jul 2: GSW fracturing right knee. D Sep 24.
R4#22	R S PRICE RICHARD S PRICE[152]	24-25	Batty B 1 NJ LA	B ~1838 NJ. R Newark, NJ. E Sep 61 cannoneer. C Jul 3: Gunshot fractures of right lower leg and right forearm→amputations below knee and above elbow. D Aug 22. Survivor (WC360771): F Henry Price 79 in 1890.
R4#23	SWART PEREW **STEWART PARENT**	48	11 Inf G	B 11/27/1814 Upper Freehold, Monmouth Co., NJ. R same. Occ carpenter. E Jun 62 private. In convalescent camp from 11/26/62→Mar/Apr 63 for an unspecified condition. C Jul 2: shot in abdomen. D Jul 8. Survivors (WC24404): W Delilah 50 (M Jul 33); 10 chn: 7 ♂- (George 27, Joseph 26), Stewart 12, James 11, Lewis 8, Francis 2, Thomas 3 months (& 3 ♀- Helen 20, Josephine 19, Mary 17).

---

150 **Fateful detachment of an infantryman for service in an artillery unit.** On March 6, 1863, following nine months serving as an infantryman in the 12th New Jersey Infantry, Simon Creamer was detailed to Battery A of the 1st Rhode Island Light Artillery unit. Seventeen weeks later, Creamer would be shot in the head and killed during the July 3rd cresting Pettigrew-Trimble attack against the northern Cemetery Ridge Union line. Creamer's field burial must have been so marked such that his body would ultimately be taken to the New Jersey plot for burial. Creamer's artillery mate, John Zimmila, also shot in the head and killed during this attack, is buried in the Rhode Island plot in row 3, space 2.

151 **Soldier possibly refused an amputation for a minié ball wedged in knee.** Upon his July 30th acceptance into Camp Letterman Hospital, William Button still had the minié ball wedged in his right knee joint. His hospital progress notes do not document that an above-the-knee amputation was done. Possibly, William refused this surgery. His treatment log documents that he only received simple dressing changes and stimulants. William lingered into the hospital till he died with a hectic fever on September 24th. His hospital admittance paper reports his age as 21.

152 **Hospitalization complicated by development of large bedsore.** Richard Price had his hospitalization care transferred to Camp Letterman on August 3rd. His Medical Descriptive List reported that the double amputee's final nineteen days of life were complicated by "an exhausting diarrhea" and "a large bedsore on his sacrum."

Bas-relief on the 14th New Jersey Infantry Monument on Cemetery Ridge

★ ★ ★ ★ ★

Memorializing the regiment's assaults July 2nd and 3rd to roust Confederate snipers perched in the Bliss Barn and firing against Union soldiers entrenched at the northern Union positions on Cemetery Ridge. When the Bliss Barn was finally set ablaze on July 3rd, Union soldiers cheered.

New York

R1#1	LIEUT F F FREDERICK **FREILEWEH**	31	120 Inf E	B 12/20/1831 Germany. 1860: R Wawarsing, Ulster Co., NY; occ barber. Commissioned 2nd lieutenant Aug 62. KIA Jul 2: killed instantly near the Peach Orchard by shell fragment which struck his chest. Survivors (WC26263): W Bridget 27 (M Jan 53); 5 chn: 3 ♂- James 9, Oscar 5, Frederic 3 & 2 ♀- Catherine 7, Mary 7 months.
R1#5	DANIEL SMITH 120 Inf E			Misidentified soldier in grave. A Daniel Smith of this regiment was severely wounded at Gettysburg but returned to duty in Dec 63 and survived the war.
R1#7	CORP GILBERT MYER or GILBERT MYERS	19-20	120 Inf I	B ~1843 Ulster Co., NY. 1860: R Woodstock, Ulster Co., NY; occ apprentice blacksmith (working under master blacksmith Peter Myers, his father). E Aug 62 corporal. KIA Jul 2: instantly killed by shot through the heart. Survivors (WC221618 not online): M Mrs. Adaline Myers 58 in 1882 (Peter Myers unable to support wife).
R1#9	THEODORE VAN DEBORGERT THEODORE **BOGARD**	21-22	120 Inf I	B ~1841 Ulster Co., NY. 1860: R Brooklyn, NY; occ clerk. E Aug 62 private. KIA Jul 2
R1#10	R M W RUSH MERRILL WHITCOMB	20	120 Inf E	B 12/17/1842 Prattsville, Greene Co., NY. R Denning, Ulster Co., NY. Occ sawyer. E Aug 62 private. KIA Jul 2. Survivor (WC85300): M Mrs. Sally Whitcomb 51 in 1886 (widow of Isaac Whitcomb).
R1#22	W H ACKERMAN WILLIAM H ACKERMAN	~21	70 Inf I	B ~1842 Paterson, Passaic Co., NJ. Occ laborer. E (Paterson, NJ) Jun 61 private. KIA Jul 2.
R1#32	CORP LEWIS SOLOMON **LOUIS** SOLOMON[153]	~23	70 Inf B	B ~1840. E (NYC) May 61 private. Jun 62: reported AWOL. Nov/Dec 62: promotion to corporal. KIA Jul 2.
R1#35	SERGT P FARREL PETER **FAREWELL**	20	73 Inf D	B 2/27/1843 NYC (German parentage). R NYC. Occ spoon maker. E Oct 62 private. KIA Jul 2. Survivor (WC51862): M Mrs. Elizabeth Farewell 51 (widow of Joseph Farewell).

---

[153] **Jewish soldier in the Cemetery.** Louis Solomon, as identified by the Shapell Roster of Jewish Service in the American Civil War, was one of numerous Jewish soldiers serving in the Union Army and here a confirmed sacrifice at Gettysburg.

R1#36	RUFUS THOMPSON[154]	26-27	120 Inf C	B ~1836 Marbletown, Ulster Co., NY. 1860: R Rosendale, Ulster Co., NY. Occ cooper. E Aug 62 private. KIA Jul 2. Survivors (WC50109→WC216895 neither online): W Helen 28; 3 chn: 2 ♀- Mary 6, Elnora 2 & 1 ♂- Daniel 5.
R1#37	SETH HARPELL (MN WILLIAM)	44	74 Inf C	B Nov 1818 Nova Scotia, Canada. 1860: R Flushing, Queens, NY: occ stone mason, farmer. E Sep 62 private. KIA Jul 2. Survivors (WC130946): W Martha 43 (M Dec 41); 8 chn: 4 ♂- (John 19, George 18), David 15, Thomas 13 & 4 ♀- (Jeannette 20), Ann 8, Sarah 6, Arabella 8 months.
R1#38	HENRY WILSON HENRY W **WILLSON**	33-34	126 Inf E	B 1829 Canandaigua, Ontario Co., NY. R same. Occ farmer. E Aug 62 private. Captured 9/15/62 and paroled 9/16/62 at Harper's Ferry. KIA Jul 2.
R1#39	ALEXANDER GACON	~36	74 Inf B	B ~1827 Geneva, Switzerland. Occ soldier. E May 61 private. Promoted to corporal on 2/3/62. Promoted to sergeant on 6/1/62. KIA Jul 2.
R1#40	W H PIPER WILLIAM H **DIPER**	20-21	70 Inf H	B ~1842. E (Pittsburgh, PA) Sep 61 private. KIA Jul 2.
R1#41	SERGT BIE (1 NY A)			Not killed Gettysburg soldier with this name or partial name in this unit found in military sources.
R1#42	CHARLES GORMAN	~22	71 Inf E	B ~1841 NJ. R Orange, Essex Co., NJ. 1860 occ: hatter apprentice. E May 61 private. KIA Jul 2: shot in the head. Survivor (WC52345): M Mrs. Jane Gorman 44 in 1864 (widow of Phillip Gorman).
R1#43	SERGT W KNIGHT WASHINGTON KNIGHT	23	74 Inf C	B 4/24/1840 Queens, NY. 1860: Flushing, Queens, NY; occ blacksmith. E Jun 61 private. Promoted to corporal on 7/13/61. Promoted to sergeant on 9/1/62. KIA Jul 2. Survivor (WC73542): M Mrs. Nancy Knight 52 (widow of Henry Knight).
R1#44	GEORGE BUGGINS	~32	70 Inf I	B ~1831 Canada. 1860: R Pequannock Twp, Morris Co., NJ; occ laborer. E Jun 61 private. Captured 5/5/62 at Williamsburg, VA. KIA Jul 2. Survivors (WC37606): W Priscilla 27 (M Dec 53| ReM 1865); 4 chn: 3 ♀- Sarah 8, Mary 4, Ann 17 mos.

---

154 **Two brothers killed in Gettysburg battle**. In the same July 2nd action that would see Rufus Thompson killed in action, his younger brother, Isaac, a corporal in the same Company C, also received a mortal wound. Isaac was transported to Baltimore for hospital care there and he would die there on July 20.

R1#45	MICHAEL RILEY[155]	38-39	42 Inf G	B ~1824 Ireland. R NYC. Occ cartman. E Sep 61 private. KIA Jul 2. Survivors (WC71727): W Maria 35 (M Feb 50| died 9/21/1864); 3 chn: 2 ♀- Mary Ann 4, Christiana 2 & 1 ♂- Charles 3. (Mrs. Mary McManus, 60 in 1865, appointed guardian or orphaned children.)
R1#46	ELBERT BROWN[156]	17	111 Inf G	B ~1846 NY. 1860 R: Genoa, Cayuga Co., NY. E (Auburn, Cayuga Co., NY) private. KIA Jul 2: wound to intestines. Survivor (WC30255): M Mrs. Louisa Brown 62 (widow of Robert R Brown).
R1#47	JOHN CAREY JOHN **CASEY**	19-20	74 Inf H	B ~1843 NY. E (NYC) Nov 61 private. KIA Jul 2.
R1#56	O W HOTCHKISS ORIN W HOTCHKISS	20-21	120 Inf F	B 1843 Rome, Oneida Co., NY. R Catskill, Greene Co., NY. Occ tobacconist. E Aug 62 private. KIA Jul 2: struck by shell or cannonball. Survivor (WC41461): M Mrs. Susan Hotchkiss 53 (widow of Orin Hotchkiss).
R1#57	WILLIAM SHULEY WILLIAM **SHEELEY**	~23	120 Inf E	B ~1840 Tompkins or Ulster Co., NY. R Wawarsing, Ulster Co., NY. Occ farmer. E Aug 62 private. KIA Jul 2. Survivor (WC34183): W Louisa (M Aug 62| ReM 1868; no chn.
R1#60	JUSTUS WARNER JUSTUS WARNER, JR[157]	26-27	120 Inf I	B ~1836 Glasco, Ulster Co., NY. R Kingston, Ulster Co., NY. Occ ship carpenter. E Aug 62 private. KIA Jul 2. Survivor (WC36048): M Mrs. Sarah Warner 54 in 1864 (widow of Justus Warner, Sr).
R1#65	SERGT JOHN KNOX	21-22	74 Inf K	B ~1841. E (NYC) Oct 61 private. Promoted to corporal on 12/1/61. Captured on 8/29/62 at 2nd Bull Run. Paroled on 9/3/62 at Centreville, VA. Sep 62: held at Camp 62 Parole. Nov 62: sent to Alexandria. Promoted to sergeant 2/1/63. KIA Jul 2: GSW to head.
R1#66	JOHN NOLAN	~32	70 Inf K	B ~1831. E (Newark, NJ) Apr 61 private. Promoted to corporal on 7/25/61. Promoted to sergeant on 5/8/62. Reduction in rank on 6/8/63 for an unspecified offense. KIA Jul 2.

---

155 **Soldier's death July 2nd leaves behind three young children; then mother dies in September, leaving fate of couple's orphaned children to court proceeding.** Michael Riley's death at Gettysburg would be followed by the death of his wife in September 1864. On the July 2nd date that Riley, an Irish immigrant, was killed, he left behind children 4, 3 and 2 in age. The care of these children after their mother's death would go to a court-appointed guardian.

156 **Minor at death.** Elbert Brown's reported ages of 4 and 14 in the successive August 1850 and July 1860 U.S. Census reports attest to the likelihood that Elbert was 16, not 18 at his August 1862 army enlistment. A 1846 birthyear would also mean that Elbert was likely only 17 when he killed in action on July 2.

157 **Soldier's father dies five months after he musters into the army.** Justus's father, Justus Warner, Sr., died on January 5, 1863, less than five months after Justin had mustered into the army.

R1#67	SERGT J H MEAD			No killed Gettysburg soldier with this or similar name found in military sources. A sergeant James R Mead was in service in the 74th NY National Guard company I in July 1863. However, his was a 30-day enlistment and he survived the war.
R1#70	G W SPRAGUE GEORGE WASHINGTON SPRAGUE	47	82 Inf G	R ~1816 NYC. R same. Occ chair maker. E Jun 61 private. KIA Jul 2: killed by canister balls, one in the left side and another in the abdomen. Survivor (WC41846): W Susan 43 (M Apr 52); no claimed chn.
R1#71	SERGT L H LEE LYMAN HEZEKIAH LEE	22	82 Inf B	B 3/6/1841 Dover Plains, Dutchess, NY. R same. Occ fireman. E Apr 61 private. Hospitalized 9/1→12/11/61 with typhoid fever. Promoted to corporal on 12/11/61. Promoted to sergeant on 7/1/62. KIA Jul 2.
R1#72	CORP LUKE KELLY	~24	82 Inf F	B ~1839 Canada. R NYC. Occ sugar refiner. E (NYC) May 61 private. Jan/Feb 63: promotion to corporal. KIA Jul 3.
R1#73	THOMAS MURPHY	~27	82 Inf F	B ~1836. E (NYC) Jul 61 private. KIA Jul 2.
R1#74	HENRY IRVIN HENRY **IRVING**	~24	82 Inf F	B ~1839 England. Occ wire worker. E (NYC) 1/30/63 private. Placed under arrest on 4/9/63 for an unspecified infraction. KIA Jul 2
R1#75	HENRY DIEMER JOHN HENRY DIEMER	19-20	82 Inf F	B ~1843 Germany. Occ barber. E (NYC) Aug 62 private. Detailed to general hospital on 3/11/63 for an unspecified situation. KIA Jul 2.
R1#77	H THOMPSON HUDSON THOMPSON	32	111 Inf I	B 8/30/1830 Sempronius, Cayuga Co., NY. R same. Occ farmer. E Aug 62 private. C Jul 2. D Jul 2 or 3.
R1#78	ADAM C CADMUS **ABRAHAM** CADMUS	20-21	126 Inf I	B ~1842 Fayette, Seneca Co., NY. 1860: Bergen, Hudson Co., NJ. Occ clerk, farmer. E (Fayette, NY) Aug 62 private. Captured 9/15 and paroled 9/16/62 at Harper's Ferry. KIA Jul 3.
R1#79	JACOB FREY JACOB **FREI**	26-27	149 Inf B	B ~1836 Germany. 1860: R Syracuse, Onondaga Co., NY; occ tailor. E (Syracuse, Onondaga Co., NY) Aug 62 private. C Jul 3: wounded in back and lung. D Jul 5.
R1#80	M STOUT MARCENA STOUT[158]	18-19	136 Inf F	B ~1844. R Mount Morris, Livingston Co., NY. R same. Occ mason. E Aug 62 private. KIA Jul 3: reportedly struck by a cannonball. Survivors (WC118484): M Mrs. Fanny Stout 52 in 1868 (George Stout affirmed medically disabled).

---

158 **Mother in pension application reports two previous sons killed in service.** Mrs. Fanny Stout, in her dependent mother's pension application, lamented that Marsena had been only one of her only three sons, who had each joined the army and been killed. The service records and deaths in service for sons Henry and George Stout has not been verified.

R1#81	CYRUS W JONES[159]	23-24	9 Cav G	B ~1839 NY. 1860: R Syracuse, Onondaga Co., NY, residing at the home of his father, Vernan Jones, a police detective; occ: clerk. E Sep 61 private. Promoted to corporal on 10/2/62. Captured and imprisoned 1/6/63. KIA Jul 1. Survivors (WC15332): W Lucretia 24 (M Oct 57); 2 chn: 1 ♂- Charles 4 & 1 ♀- Mary 19 mos.
R1#82	SERGT JAS MELCHEN JAMES **MEEHAN**	21-22	82 Inf H	B ~1841 Ireland. R NYC. Occ laborer. E Sep 62 private. KIA Jul 2. Survivor (WC83447): M Mrs. Alice Meehan 50 in 1866 (widow of Paul Meehan).
R1#83	THOMAS HUNT	27	82 Inf H	B ~Oct 1835 Ireland. R Albany, NY. Occ carpenter. E Aug 62 private. C Jul 2: severely wounded in right leg→amp. D Jul 4.
R1#85	ROBERT LANING ROBERT **LANNING**	21	86 Inf K	B 8/10/1841 Steuben, Oneida Co., NY. Occ farmer. E (Elmira, Chemung Co., NY) Aug 62 private. KIA Jul 2.
R1#86	JOHN SLOAT (MN FRANCIS)	17	126 Inf E	B 11/4/1845 Springwater, Livingston Co., NY. 1860: R Gorham, Ontario Co., NY. Occ farmer. E Aug 62 corporal. Captured 9/15 and paroled 9/16/62 at Harper's Ferry. C Jul 3. D Jul 12.
R1#87	SERGT GEO BAKER GEORGE **BECKER**	26-27	40 Inf A	B ~1836 Germany. Occ hatter. E (Staten Island, NY) Aug 61 private in 55th NY. Promoted to corporal on 9/12/61. Promoted to sergeant on 10/1/62. Transferred to 38th NY on 12/23/62. Transferred to 40th NY on 6/3/63. C Jul 2: wounded in right thigh. D Aug 8.
R1#89	JOSHUA PURSEL (MN BLOOMER)	21	126 Inf C	B 2/18/1842 Romulus, Seneca Co., NY. R Ovid, Seneca Co., NY. Occ farmer. E Aug 62 private. Captured 9/15/62 and paroled 9/16/62 at Harper's Ferry. KIA Jul 3.
R1#90	DANIEL DAY	22-23	126 Inf B	B ~1840 Benton, Yates Co., NY. R same. Occ farmer. E Aug 62 private. Captured 9/15/62 and paroled 9/16/62 at Harper's Ferry. C Jul 3: wound to left thigh. D Jul 20.
R1#91	CHARLES T HARRIS	22-23	126 Inf C	B ~1840 Seneca Co., NY. 1860: R Ovid, Seneca Co., NY; occ: clerk in father's merchant store. E Aug 62 corporal. Captured 9/15 and paroled 9/16/62 at Harper's Ferry. Promoted to sergeant on 1/13/63. KIA Jul 2.

---

159 **First Union cavalryman killed at Gettysburg?** By virtue of his death in a cavalry skirmish preceding Confederate Gen. Ewell's forces approach of McPherson's Ridge, Corporal. Cyrus Jones is postulated to have been the first Union cavalryman killed in the Battle of Gettysburg. Interestingly, Cyrus Jones's father had been a police detective in Syracuse, NY.

R1#92	WM WOODRUFF WILLIAM WOODRUFF[160]	18	104 Inf A	B 11/1/1844 Almond, Allegany, NY. 1860: R Richmond, Ontario, NY. Occ farmer. E Dec 61 private. C Jul 1: wounded in stomach. D Jul 3. Survivor (WC57491 not online): M Mrs. Ann Woodruff 52 in 1865 (widow of Steptoe Woodruff).
R1#93	ROBERT MORRIS (CO C OF INSTRUCTION)			A killed soldier with this or a similar name is not found in military sources.
R1#94	ARTHUR McALPINE	17	111 Inf G	B 10/13/1845 Scotland. R Auburn, NY. 1860: attending school while living with a distiller named George Ashby. E Jul 62 private. C Jul 2: wounded through both thighs. D Jul 18. Survivor (WC11557): M Mrs. Ellen McAlpine 39 (widow of of Robert McAlpine).
R1#95	ELIHU JONES[161]	20	95 Inf G	B ~1843 NY. Occ harness maker. E Oct 61 private. Nov 62→Mar 63: serving as an officer's orderly. C Jul 1: shot through right lung. D Aug 16.
R1#96	LOUIS GUTTMAN 201 Inf F			B ~Aug 1873 Germany. E Jul 98 (following 4 years in a German army unit). Occ butcher. Hospitalized at Camp Meade, PA with typhoid fever from 9/16/98→ death at age 25 on 10/24/98. Remains subsequently moved to Gettysburg.
R1#107	SEBASTIAN SANDEL 94 Inf H			B ~1839. E Jul 64 private. Oct-Dec64: gained from desertion and awaiting court martial. Mustered out Jul 65. D 3/18/1901 in Ulster, NY almshouse (age 61).
R1#108	REV ENOCH K MILLER 108 Inf F			B 1/16/1840 London, England. R Rochester, Monroe Co., NY. Occ theology student. E Jul 62 corporal. Wounded 12/13/62 at Fredericksburg. C Jul 3 at Gettysburg: shot in chest. D/C June 64 to accept appointment as chaplain in Veterans Reserve Corps, 25th USCT. D 12/30/1903 (age 63).
R1#109	CAPT HARRISON FRANK	31-32	157 Inf G	B ~1831 NY. 1860: R Lenox, Madison Co., NY. Occ dealer in produce. Commissioned to 2nd lieutenant in Aug 62. Promoted to 1st lieutenant on 1/12/63. Promotion to captain 2/10/63. KIA Jul 1. Survivor (WC30986): M Mrs. Nancy Frank 51 in 1864 (widow of Andrew Frank).

---

160 **Soldier's mother must apply for pension support when husband dies five months after son is killed at Gettysburg.** Mr. & Mrs. Steptoe Woodruff were doubtless stunned by the news of their son's death at Gettysburg in July 1863. Just under five months later, Mrs. Ann Woodruff would be dealt a second loss with her husband's death on November 28, 1863.

161 **A soldier's hard six weeks in the hospital before dying.** As the minié ball had passed clean through Elihu Jones's right lung, there was little that the doctors at the Seminary Hospital at the time could do for him. Elihu Jones's hospital course was marked by pain, expectoration and difficulty breathing. As of August 13th, he was receiving one tablespoon of beef tea and a teaspoon of brandy every hour. On August 16th, a 7 a.m. progress note documented that Elihu was violently struggling for breath. The next note at 10:00 a.m. was that he had died.

R1#110	CAPT JASON K BACKUS	25-26	157 Inf E	B ~1837 Freetown, Courtland Co., NY. Occ student at law. Commissioned lieutenant in Aug 62. Promoted to captain on 3/25/63. KIA Jul 1: killed instantly during the retreat from the fields outside of Gettysburg and into the town.
R2#1	CORP JOS S CORBIN JOSEPH S CORBIN[162]	~32	80 Inf F	B 1831 Roxbury, Delaware Co., NY. R Rondout, Ulster Co., NY. Occ: public school principal. E Sep 61 as sergeant in the 20th NY State Militia. Sep 61: muster into 80th NY Infantry. Commissioned to Capt. KIA Jul 1: killed instantly by a shot through the forehead. Survivors (WC124886): W Sarah 32 (M Oct 51| ReM 1868); 3 chn: 2 ♂- Jason 10, Robert 6 & 1 ♀- Emma 4.
R2#2	CICERO TOLLS CICERO **TOLLES**	28	134 Inf A	B 2/9/1835 NY. R Schenectady Co., NY. Occ shoemaker. E Sep 62 private. KIA Jul 1. Survivors (WC138423 not online); M Mrs. Magdalene Tolles 69 in 1869 (Russell Tolles judged disabled and unable to support wife).
R2#3	A D TICE AKEXABDER D TUCE	21	80 Inf E	B 8/5/1841 Sullivan Co., NY. 1860: R Wawarsing, Ulster Co., NY; occ: farm laborer on father's farm. E Sep 61 private. KIA Jul 1.
R2#10	SERGT FRED DERBIN FREDERICK **DURBIN**	22-23	78 Inf I	B ~1840 England. Occ tailor. E Dec 61 sergeant. Nov 62: absent sick in hospital in Philadelphia. KIA Jul 2.
R2#11	THOMAS DAWSON	28-29	78 Inf A	B ~1834 Ireland. R Williamsburg, Kings Co., NY. Occ laborer. E Oct 61 private. KIA Jul 2: killed immediately by a ball to the head. Survivors (WC23332): W Frances 26 (M Nov 60| ReM 1865); 1 ♀- Sarah 1.
R2#12	ALFRED TRUDELL	22-23	78 Inf A	B ~1840 NYC. Occ farmer. E (NYC) Dec 61 private. Served detached service with Battery K of 1st NY Artillery 9/5/62→return to the regiment on 6/5/63. KIA Jul 2.
R2#13	FREDERIC HEI FREDERICK **HEINZEN**	~41	39 Inf A	B ~1822 Germany. R NYC. Occ farmer. E May 61 private. Captured and paroled at 9/15/62 at Harper's Ferry. Detached service on the brigade ambulance corps: 3/1→4/20/63. C Jul 3: wounded in the chest. D Jul 4.
R2#14	ELBERT TRAVER	22-23	44 Inf E	B ~1840 Clinton, NY. 1860: R Rhinebeck, Dutchess Co., NY. Occ teacher. E Aug 62 private. C Jul 2: wounded in back. D Jul 3.
R2#16	WILLIAM LACY	19-20	73 Inf D	B ~ 1843. E (Brooklyn, NY) Aug 62 163rd NY infantry Co D. Transferred 1/18/63 to 73rd NY Infantry Co D. KIA Jul 2. Survivor (WC18609): M Mrs. Ann Lacey 39 (widow of Philo Lacey).

---

[162] **Prior occupation a high school principal.** Joseph S. Corbin had been a high school principal in Ulster County, NY prior to enlisting into the army, eventually being commissioned a captain.

ID	Name	Age	Unit	Details
R2#17	J SIMOND JOHN **SALMON**	~25	73 Inf D	B ~1838 NY. 1860: R NYC; occ carman. E Jul 61 private. Promoted to sergeant on 1/1/63. KIA Jul 2.
R2#18	SERGT T LALLY THOMAS LALLY	~21	73 Inf K	B ~1842 NY. 1860: R Manhattanville, Manhattan, NY: occ operative. E Jul 61 private. Promoted to sergeant on 9/1/61. KIA Jul 2. Survivor (WC31568): M Mrs. Mary Lally 50 (widow of James Lally).
R2#25	DAVID HOLLAND	29-30	71 Inf F	B ~1833. R NYC. 1855 NY state census: occ laborer. E Aug 62 private. KIA Jul 2. Survivors (WC126351): W Bridget ~31 (M Dec 54); 3 chn: 1 ♂- Martin 7 & 2 ♀- Bridget 5, Mary 3.
R2#27	MICHAEL FLANEGAN 70 Inf B			Soldier with this name and specific regiment not found in military sources. Some have suggested this soldier might be Patrick Flanigan of the 73rd NY infantry Co B.
R2#28	SERGT P SULLIVAN PATRICK SULLIVAN	~41	73 Inf K	B ~1822. E Jul 61 private. Promoted to corporal on 9/1/61. Promoted to sergeant on 5/1/63. KIA Jul 2. Survivors (WC21746): W Margaret 26 (M Jan 54); 1 ♂- John 7.
R2#29	ROBERT H POOLE ROBERT HANNIBAL **POOL**	24	126 Inf A	B 7/271838 Canandaigua Co., Ontario Co., NY. Occ blacksmith. E Aug 62 private. Captured 9/15/62 and paroled 9/16/62 at Harper's Ferry. KIA Jul 2. Survivor (WC309223 not online) M Mrs. Mary Pool 79 in 1890 (Robert Pool died in 1889).
R2#30	CHARLES W GAYLORD	24-25	126 Inf B	B ~1838 Torrey, Yates Co., NY. 1860: Benton, Yates Co., NY; occ farmer. E Aug 62 private. Captured 9/15 and paroled 9/16/62 at Harper's Ferry. KIA Jul 2.
R2#34	CHARLES WELDEN CHARLES **WEEDEN**	30-31	111 Inf D	B ~1832 Germany. 1860: R Lyons, Wayne Co., NY; occ day laborer. E Aug 62 private. D Jul 2 of wounds.
R2#39	LIEUT A W ESTES ANDREW W ESTES	~28	71 Inf H	B ~1835 Sharon, Mercer Co., PA. 1860: R Hebron, Potter Co., PA.; occ: farm laborer on father's farm. E Jul 61 corporal. Promoted to sergeant on 1/14/62. Wounded 8/27/62 at Bristoe Station. Commissioned 2nd lieutenant on 12/20/62. KIA Jul 2.
R2#50	JOHN KAPP JOHN **RAPP** (anglicized) or JOHN RAAB (German)	37-38	70 Inf K	B ~1825 Germany. 1860: R Brooklyn, NY; occ laborer. E Jun 61 private. KIA Jul 2. Survivor (WC31904): W Maria 21 (M Jul 60); no chn.

R2#51	MICHAEL RYAN[163] 70 Inf C			Misidentified soldier in grave. Michael Ryan of 70th NY (1st Excelsior) Company C was transferred to the 2nd US Cavalry on 6/28/62 and later to the Veteran Corps in 1864.
R2#54	JOHN McKENNEY[164] 70 Inf C			Misidentified soldier in grave. A Charles McKenney of Co B of this regiment was wounded July 2 at Gettysburg but recovered to join the Veterans Corps 12/20/63.
R2#60	JAMES BRADY	~25	71 Inf A	B ~1838 Ireland. 1860: R Orange, Essex Co., NJ; occ hatter. E May 61 private. KIA Jul 2: instantly killed by a shell striking him in the chest. Survivors (WC144734): W Mary 23 (M Feb 59| ReM Oct 64); 2 chn: 1 ♂- James 3 & 1 ♀- Margaret 20 months.
R2#66	CHARLES GORMAN	~22	71 Inf E	B ~1841 NJ. 1860: R Orange, Essex Co., NJ; occ hatter. E May 61 private. KIA Jul 2. Survivor (WC52345): M Mrs. Jane Gorman 44 in 1864 (widow of Phillip Gorman).
R2#68	PATRICK OLVANY or OLVANEY	25	71 Inf A	B 4/29/1838 Ireland. E Jun 61 private. KIA Jul 2.
R2#69	ALONZO HENSTREAT ALONZO **HEMSTREAT**	20-21	105 PA Inf F	B ~1842 Albany Co., NY. 1855 R: Watervliet, Albany Co., NY. Occ apprentice. E (Pittsburgh, PA) Aug 61 private. Forfeited one month's pay 12/13/62 for straggling at the Battle of Fredericksburg. KIA Jul 2.
R2#71	GEORGE W DOUGLASS	18	70 Inf I	B 8/8/1844 Paterson, Passaic Co., NJ. 1860 R: same. E May 61 private. Promoted to corporal on 9/23/62. KIA Jul 2.
R2#88	JACOB JONES[165]			Misidentified soldier in gave. A Jacob Jones of the 19th IN Co K was killed Jul 1 at Gettysburg but is reported buried in Sparr Cemetery, Delaware Co., IN.
R2#93	AUGUSTUS McCLELLAN **WILLIAM McCLELLAND**	23-24	88 Inf	B ~1839 NY. 1860: R Jersey City, Hudson Co., NJ; occ printer. E Sep 61 private. Promoted to sergeant on 12/13/62. Commissioned 2nd lieutenant 2/5/63. Promoted to 1st lieutenant and adjuvant on 5/13/63. KIA Jul 3: wounded in head.
R2#95	P J HOPKINS PETER J HOPKINS	23-24	126 Inf H	B ~1839 Penfield, Monroe Co., NY. Occ laborer. E (Farmington, Ontario Co., NY) Aug 62. Captured and paroled on 9/15/62 at Harper's Ferry. C Jul 1: GSW to right leg. D Jul 11. Survivor (WC107048): M Mrs. Abigail Lemon 63 in 1867 (widow of John Hopkins and of 2nd husband James Lemon).

---

163 **Misidentified soldier in grave.** Michael Ryan was not killed at Gettysburg and transferred to the Veteran Corps in 1864.

164 **Misidentified soldier in grave.** Charles McKenney was wounded, but not killed at Gettysburg. He recovered sufficiently to transfer to the Veteran Corps in 1864.

165 **Misidentified soldier in grave.** Jacob Jones was killed at Gettysburg, but he is reported to have been reburied in Indiana.

R2#98	LIEUT R D LEWER RANDALL D **LOWER**	25	157 Inf I	B Mar 1838 Sullivan, Madison Co., NY. 1860: R Cicero, Onondaga Co., NY; Occ shoemaker. E Aug 62 private. Promoted to sergeant on 9/19/62. Commissioned 2nd lieutenant on 2/9/63. KIA Jul 1. Survivors (WC28873): W Annis 29 (M Mar 55); 2 ♀-Mabelle 5, Blanche 2.
R2#103	G M McCLEARY GEORGE **McGLEAR, JR**	~27	73 Inf F	B ~1836 NY. E (NYC) Mar 62 private. Jul/Aug 62: reported AWOL. Nov/Dec 62: absent sick. Promoted to sergeant on 6/1/63. KIA Jul 2. Survivor (WC118015): M Mrs. Eliza McGlear 55 in 1868 (widow of George McGlear, Sr).
R2#106	EDMUND HOLMES **EDWARD** HOLMES	~27	73 Inf F	B ~1836. E (NYC) Aug 61 private. Deserted from regiment 1/18/63. Jan/Feb 63: captured and returned to serve under arrest. KIA Jul 2.
R2#107	T TETWORTH **JAMES TITSWORTH**	~28	70 Inf D	B ~1835 NY. 1860: R Brooklyn, NY; occ printer. E June 61 private. KIA Jul 2.
R2#108	ADAM SHAW ADAM **SCHONDORF**	18-19	73 Inf D	B ~1844 Germany. E Sep 62 private in 163rd NY infantry Company D. Consolidated with 73rd NY infantry on 1/20/63. KIA Jul 2.
R2#111	WILLIAM H BELL WILLIAM HENRY BELL, JR[166]	~23	120 Inf F	B 1840 Catskill, Greene Co., NY. R same. Occ butcher. E Aug 62 private. KIA Jul 2. Survivors (WC20372→WC154693 neither online): W Mary 22 (M Dec 60| ReM 1868); 1 ♀- Sarah 2.
R2#112	JAMES M DELANEY JAMES MADISON **DELANOY**	28	120 Inf I	B 8/12/1834 Greene Co., NY. 1860: R Kingston, Ulster Co., NY. Occ cooper. E Aug 62 corporal. KIA Jul 2. Survivors (WC135400): W Martha 34 in 1869 (M Nov 55| ReM 1868); 3 chn: 2 ♂- David, Walter 3 & 1 ♀- Catharine 1 month.
R2#113	ANDREW DE WITT ANDREW M **DEWITT**	30-31	120 Inf H	B ~1832 Hurley, Ulster Co., NY. R Rosendale, Ulster Co., NY. Occ carpenter and farmer. E Aug 62 corporal. Jan→April 63: absent sick in hosp. KIA Jul 2: shot through the head. Survivors (WC91954): W Charlotte ~33 (M Aug 50| ReM 1866); 3 chn: 1 ♀- Mary & 2 ♂- James 4, William 18 months.
R2#115	THEODORE BOGARD or VAN DEBORGERT	21-22	120 Inf I	B ~1841 Ulster Co., NY. Occ farmer. E (Kingston, Ulster Co., NY) Aug 62 private. KIA Jul 2.
R3#1	JAMES GRAY	27-28	82 Inf C	B ~1835 Scotland. R NYC. Occ clerk. E Oct 62 private. C Jul 3. D Jul 3 or 4.

---

166 **Soldier's father was an Irish-born physician.** William Bell's father, William Henry Bell, Sr., was an Irish-born physician, who is reported to have returned to Ireland sometime in the 1860's and died there in 1867.

R3#5	NICHOLAS PAQUET NICHOLAS **BAQUET**	26-27	49 Inf E	B ~1836 Germany. R Buffalo, Erie Co., NY. Occ blacksmith. E Sep 61 private. Left sick 9/16/61 in Buffalo hospital with unspecified condition. Absent, sick from Oct 62. Returned from hospital on 3/17/63. C Jul 6: wound to right lung in skirmish at Fairfield, PA. D Jul 6.
R3#6	CHARLES ROOT[167]			Likely a misidentified soldier in this grave.
R3#7	JOHN P CONN	23-24	Batt L 1 LA	B ~1839 NY. 1860: R Rochester, Monroe Co., NY; occ printer. E Sep 61 private. C Jul 1. D Jul 8.
R3#8	FREDERICK BLACKSTEIN **FRIEDRICH** BLACKSTEIN[168]	~32	41 Inf A	B ~1831 Petersburg, Russia (German ethnicity). Occ mason. E Jun 61 corporal. Promoted to sergeant 6/8/62. Reduced in rank 3/7/63 for an unspecified infraction. C Jul 2: shell wound injuries to back, spine and liver. D Jul 18.
R3#10	A R TOWNSEND AMASA R TOWNSEND	19-20	60 Inf I	B 1843 Bombay, Franklin Co., NY. R Lawrence, St. Lawrence Co., NY. Occ farmer. E Sep 61 private. June 63: present as corporal. KIA Jul 2: wound through brain. Survivor (WC55407): M Mrs. Melissa Townsend 43 in 1864 (widow of Charles Townsend).
R3#10	CHARLES MANNING[169] (MN PLATT)	23	137 Inf C	B 2/18/1840 Owego, Tioga Co., NY. R same. 1860 occ: printer. E Aug 62 private. KIA Jul 3. Survivor (WC213415 not online): M Mrs. Eliza Manning 54 (widow of Robert Manning).
R3#11	H W NICHOLS HORACE W NICHOLS	30-31	137 Inf F	B 1832 Naugatuck, New Haven Co., CN. R Windsor, Broome Co., NY. Occ farmer. E Aug 62 private. KIA Jul 3. Survivors (WC20541): W Clarinda 27 (R Aug 56 | ReM 1888); 1 ♂- Adelbert 5.
R3#12	E VAN TASSEL EDWARD VAN **TASSELL** or VAN TASSILL	20	60 Inf C	B ~1843 NY. R Alexandria, Jefferson Co., NY. E (Ogsdensburg, St. Lawrence Co., NY) Sep 61 private. Detached 9/12/62 to Battery K 1st NY LA. KIA Jul 3: wounded through neck.

---

167 **Identity question.** Identification of this soldier is complicated by the numbers of soldiers with the name Charles Root in the army. Also unhelpful is the absence of any regimental information on the gravestone. A Charles Root, member of the 24th Michigan Infantry Company C was taken prisoner on July 1st at Gettysburg. It is certainly possible that some equipment with Root's name on it being found with an otherwise unidentified dead soldier could have led to a misidentification. In any case, the Charles Root of the 24th Michigan Infantry did not die at Gettysburg. He returned to duty in April 1865.

168 **Enlistment of an immigrant born in Russia.** Friedrich Blackstein was born in Petersburg, Russia, but he had been of German heritage.

169 **Soldier's July 3rd death at Gettysburg followed three days later by father's accidental death back home.** Three days after Charles Manning was killed at Gettysburg, his father, Robert Manning, was working as a carpenter when he fell from a building and was instantly killed. Robert Manning likely not yet received news of his son's death at Gettysburg. Charles Manning's mother, Eliza, would subsequently apply in October for a dependent mother's pension.

R3#13	P STEVENSON PHILO STEVENSON	24-25	60 Inf A	B ~1838 NY. 1860: R Canton, St. Lawrence Co., NY; occ carpenter. E (Hermon, St. Lawrence Co., NY) Sep 61 private. Dec 62: sick at Harper's Ferry. Promoted to corporal on 6/10/63. KIA Jul 2: wound to brain.
R3#14	P McDONALD PETER McDONALD	22-23	60 Inf I	B ~1840 NY. 1860: R Brasher, St. Lawrence Co., NY; occ farm hand. E Oct 61 private. Promoted to corporal during service. Detached 4/30/63 to Battery H 1st NY LA. Returned to regiment 6/30/63. KIA Jul 2: wounded through brain.
R3#15	CORP W W RAND WILLIAM W RAND[170]	~17	102 Inf E	B ~1846 VT. E (Burlington, Chittenden Co., VT) Oct 61 corporal. C Jul 2: wound to the head. D Jul 2 or 3.
R3#16	CORP L VINNING LUCIAN D **VINING**	21-22	137 Inf A	B 1841 Chenango Co., NY. 1860 R: Conklin, Broome Co., NY. E (Binghamton, Broome Co., NY) Aug 62 corporal. Occ farmer. C Jul 2: wounded in both lungs and hands. D Jul 4.
R3#17	SERGT CHAS F FOX CHARLES F FOX	21-22	137 Inf A	B ~1841 Herkimer, Herkimer Co., NY. R Lisle, Broome Co., NY. Occ farmer. E Aug 62 private. Promoted to corporal on 9/12/62. Promoted to sergeant on 3/1/63. C Jul 2: wounded in abdomen. D Jul 4 or 5.
R3#18	MAHLON J PARDEE **MALON** J PARDEE	21-22	137 Inf F	B ~1841 Kirkwood, Broome, Co., NY. 1860: R Broome Co., NY. Occ farmer. E Aug 62 private. KIA Jul 2.
R3#19	OLIVER ENGLISH (MN PERRY)	21-22	137 Inf A	B ~1841 Madison Co., NY. R Triangle, Broome Co., NY. Occ laborer. E Aug 62 private. KIA Jul 2.
R3#20	F A ARCHIBALD FREDERICK ARCHIBALD	28	137 Inf C	B 11/30/1834 Tioga Co., NY. R Oswego Co., NY. Occ farmer. E Aug 62 private. KIA Jul 3. Survivor (WC61334): W Helen 24 in 1864 (M Feb 1855); no chn.
R3#21	SERGT J W BROCKHAM JACOB W BROCKHAM[171] or BROUGHAM[172]	23-24	137 Inf C	B ~1839 Owego, Tioga Co., NY. R same. Occ clerk. E Aug 62 corporal. Promoted to sergeant 3/20/63. KIA Jul 3. Survivor (WC24611): M Mrs. Caroline Brockham 46 (widow of Albert Brockham, who died 4/17/63).
R3#22	WILLIAM W WHEELER	18-19	137 Inf F	B ~1844 Greenfield, Saratoga Co., NY. R Windsor, Broome Co., NY. Occ farmer. E (Windsor, Broome Co., NY) Aug 62 private. KIA Jul 2.

---

170 **Minor at death.** William Rand's reported ages of 4 and 14 on the successive August 1850 and September 1860 U.S. Census sheets attest to the likelihood that William was not 18, but no older than 16 at his October 1861 army enlistment. A birthyear of 1846 would also mean that William was likely 17 when he was killed at Gettysburg.

171 **Soldier's death follows eleven weeks after his father's death had just widowed mother.** In successive tragedies, Mrs. Caroline Brockham lost her husband Albert on April 17, 1863, then her son Jacob only eleven weeks later at Gettysburg.

172 **Accepted at seventeen for enlistment.** Alexander Stanton had admitted his actual age of 17 at enlistment.

R3#23	RICHARD W RUSH[173]	30-31	137 Inf A	B ~1832 Vestal, Broome Co., NY. R same. Occ farmer. E Aug 62 private. Attempted to desert from the regiment on 1/16/63, but he was apprehended by Provost Guard. Returned to company by Provost Marshal on 5/24/63. KIA Jul 2. Survivors (WC53069): W Emerette (Nov 60| ReM 1864); 1 ♀- Eldora 20 months.
R3#24	A STANTON ALEXANDER STANTON	17-18	137 Inf C	B ~1845 Nichols, Tioga Co., NY. R same. Occ farmer. E Aug 62 private. C Jul 2 or 3: wounded in abdomen. D Jul 3.
R3#25	PETER HILL	~28	137 Inf A	B 1835 Oxford, Chenango Co., NY. R Norwich, Chenango Co., NY. Occ boatman. E Jul 62 private. KIA Jul 2. (WC30483): W Catherine 28 (M Mar 58); no chn.
R3#26	DEAN SWIFT	~22	137 Inf A	B ~1841 Clarkson, Monroe Co., NY. Occ tinner. E (Little Falls, Herkimer Co., NY) Jul 62 private. Promotion to corporal during service. KIA Jul 2. Survivor (WC13486): M Mrs. Susan Swift 49 (widow of Jerome Swift).
R3#27	SERGT D CORBETT DANIEL CORBETT	28	60 Inf B	B March 1835 St. Lawrence Co., NY. 1860: R Macomb, St. Lawrence Co., NY: occ farmer. E Sep 61 corporal. Promoted to sergeant on 10/01/61. KIA Jul 3: GSW to the head. Survivors (WC16130): W Jane 28 (M Jan 53| ReM 1971); 3 chn: 2 ♂- John 8, Clark 5 & 1 ♀- Mary 2.
R3#28	SERGT HIRAM G HILTS (MN GEORGE)	27	122 Inf C	B 12/20/1835 DeWitt, Onondaga Co., NY. 1860 R: same. Occ laborer, teacher. E Aug 62 sergeant. Reduced from sergeant to private on 11/1/62 for an unspecified infraction. KIA Jul 3.
R3#29	P FANNING PATRICK FANNING	41-42	122 Inf C	B ~1821 Ireland. R Onondaga Co., NY. Occ farmer. E Aug 62 private. KIA Jul 3. Survivor (WC21963): W Catharine 40 (M Oct 54) no chn.
R3#30	W P HUNTINGTON WESLEY PERKINS HUNTINGTON	33	123 Inf C	B 12/5/1829 Fair Haven, Rutland Co., VT. R White Hall, Washington Co., NY. Occ farmer. E Aug 62 private. KIA Jul 3: shot through chest. Survivors (WC31252→WC177283 neither online): Luna 34 in 1966 (M Feb 51| ReM 1869); 3 chn: 2 ♂- John 10, Joseph 7 & 1 ♀- Cora 3.

---

173 **Stepfather's neglectful guardianship.** In 1901, Richard Rush's daughter Eldora submitted an affidavit to the Pension Office, charging that her stepfather had completely abandoned her support after he had been appointed guardian of her minor's pension. She charged that she had to turn to her deceased father's family for lodging and sustenance. Eldora Rush's experience unveils the reality that the various state Probate Courts could be unwieldy and ineffectual guarantors of war orphans' best interests.

R3#31	JAMES A WICKHAM[174]	37-38	122 Inf E	B ~1825 Manlius, Onondaga Co., NY. R Syracuse, Onondaga Co., NY. Occ laborer. E Aug 62 private. Nov 62→Feb 63: hospital attendant at regimental hospital. May 63: laborer at Division hospital. KIA Jul 3: shot through the brain. Survivors (WC71869): W Mary 29 (M Jul 48│ D 3/15/64); 2 chn: 1 ♂- Charles 13 & 1 ♀- Mary 10.
R3#32	J VANDYKE JOHN **VAN DYCK**[175]	23-24	107 Inf C	B ~1839 Covert, Seneca Co., NY. 1860 R: Windham, Greene Co., NY. Occ farmer. E (Canisteo, Steuben Co., NY) Aug 62 private. C Jul 3: severe wound shattering right arm→amp. D Sep 12.
R3#33	R GANDLEY RICHARD **GANLEY**[176] or GAULEY	19-20	44 Inf B	B ~1843 Ireland. R Norwich, Chenango Co., NY. Occ farmer. E Sep 62 private. C Jul 2: wound to right hip. D Aug 20. Survivor (WC23529): M Mrs. Margaret Ganley 66 (widow of John Ganley).
R3#34	G CHRISTANNA GEORGE **CHRISTANNA**	36	120 Inf A	B ~1827 Hurley, Ulster Co., NY. R same. Occ farmer. E Aug 62 private. C Jul 2: GSW Fracturing right ankle→amp Aug 10→2nd amp Sep 2. D Sep 26.
R3#35	DANIEL COOK			Killed Gettysburg soldier with this or similar name not found in military sources.
R3#36	SERGT F JELL FREDERICK **JELL**[177]	~34	95 Inf I	B ~1829 England. Occ machinist. Arrived US on passenger ship 1/14/62. Enrolled in regiment 2/8/62 as a private. Promoted to sergeant 5/1/63. C Jul 1: GSW to right knee→amp. D Sep 25.
R3#37	R T MYRES RUFUS **S MYERS**	19-20	111 Inf K	B ~1843 Aurora, Cayuga Co., NY. R same. Occ tinner. E Aug 62 private. Captured and paroled on 9/15/62 at Harper's Ferry. C Jul 3: severe wound to left leg→amp. D Aug 31.

---

174 **Soldier killed July 3rd, then soldier's widow dies eight months later, orphaning two children**. The tragedy for James Wickham's two children of his loss was compounded by the subsequent death of their mother only eight months later.

175 **Soldier's father a clergyman**. In 1860, the 20-year-old Van Dyck was living in the Greene Co, NY family home with his mother and two younger sisters and headed by his father, by profession a clergyman.

176 **Soldier dies of battle wound in August, then mother loses husband five weeks later**. Mrs. Margaret Ganley loss her son, Richard, to his battle wound on August 20. As a double tragedy, she then lost her husband John only five weeks later on September 28, 1863.

177 **Derisive autopsy note left by examining surgeon**. In his notes from the autopsy report of Private Frederick Jell, a surgeon uncharitably derided the soldier's "pitiable remnants of syphilitic disease." Jell, an Englishman, had arrived to the United States on January 14, 1862 and then enlisted into the 95th New York Infantry only 25 days later on February 8. 1862. Whatever were Jell's disease issues, he did well in the army, garnering a promotion to sergeant in May 1853.

R3#38	FELIX McCRAM FELIX **McGRANN**[178] or McGRAW	~30	42 Inf F	B ~1833. E Jun 61 private. C Jul 3: severely wounded in right leg→amp. D Jul 14. Survivors (WC148094): 2 ♀- Anne 14, Mary 11 (W Mary had died 9/9/1861); Ms. Sarah Woodside 38 in 1865 receives court-certified guardianship.
R3#39	JOSEPHUS GEE[179]	22-23	137 Inf G	B ~1840 Virgil, Courtland Co., NY. R Tioga Co., NY. Occ farmer. E Aug 62 private. Sent to a hospital in Baltimore 12/10/62 for an unspecified illness. Returned 1/16/63. C Jul 2: wounded in left thigh. D Jul 28. Survivor (WC552854 filed in 1901 not online): W Sarah ~56 in 1901 (M Aug 62| 18 at Gee's death); no chn.
R3#40	A J CHAFEE ANDREW JACKSON **CHAFFEE**	28	44 Inf E	B 1/7/1835 Onondaga Co., NY. R same. Occ mechanic. E Sep 62 private. C Jul 3: wounded in both legs→amp of right lower leg. D Aug 16.
R3#41	WILLIAM J SUTLIFF WILLIAM **T** SUTLIFF	45	137 Inf B	B 3/15/1818 New Hartford, Litchfield Co., CT. R Windsor, Broome Co., NY. Occ farmer. E Aug 62 private. C Jul 2: wounded in right shoulder→arm amp. D Jul 26. Survivors (WC26187→WC145193 neither online): W Harriet ~29 (M 1850| Remarried 1870 to William's younger brother Solomon); 3 chn: 1 ♂- George 12 & 2 ♀- Ava 9. Emma 3.
R3#42	JOHN JALOFF JOHN **JOLLOFF**	33-34	70 Inf F	B ~1829 England. R Susquehanna Co., PA. Occ farmer. E Aug 62 private. C Jul 2: wounded in left leg. D Aug 4. Survivors (WC110250): W Ann 33 in 1864 (M Jun 53| ReM Aug 64): 2 ♂- George 9, William 7.
R3#43	ELISHA LOOMIS	20	137 Inf C	B 3/19/1843 Owego, Tioga Co., NY. R same. Occ farmer. E Aug 62 private. C Jul 3: wounded in the abdomen. D Jul 26. Survivor (WC129676 not online): M Mrs. Rhoda Loomis ~54 in 1869 (Freeburn Loomis affirmed unable to care for wife).
R3#44	MICHAEL BURNS[180]	18-19	140 Inf C	B 1844 Buffalo, Eric Co., NY. Occ farmer. E (Rochester, Monroe Co., NY) Aug 62 private. C Jul 2: wounded in left thigh→amp. D Aug 4.

---

178 **Soldier's death orphans two motherless daughters.** Felix McGrann's wife, Mary, would die of some unspecified condition on September 9, 1861, a date occurring only eleven weeks after Felix had left home to muster into the army. McGrann's own subsequent death on July 14 would orphan his fourteen and eleven-year-old daughters. The two young girls would then have their guardianship determined through a court proceeding.

179 **Soldier's pleas to young wife back home: "Please rite soon and often and rite longer letters."** Josephus Gee's widow, the remarried Mrs. Sarah Roat in 1901 would submit a number of Gee's army letters to the U.S. Pension Office to support her application for a Civil War widow's pension. Josephus had married Sarah Ayers on August 20, 1862, or the day before he mustered into the army. The Josephus Gee letters submitted to the Pension Office are punctuated by his pleadings to Sarah to write to him more often. In a letter to Sarah penned April 12, 1863, or three months before he would die at Gettysburg, Josephus writes of "getting some tired of the war" and implores her to "please rite [sp]soon and often and rite longer letters." Following Josephus's death on July 27, 1863, his 18-year-old widow would marry Reuben Roat on November 8, 1863 and eventually bare him six children. At Roat's death in 1901, Mrs. Roat would apply for and receive the Civil War widow's pension earned by Josephus Gee's death 38 years before.

180 **Despondent soldier refuses treatment at Camp Letterman.** Upon July 28th acceptance into Camp Letterman Hospital, Michael Burns had become very despondent and refused both food and medicine. He was reported 20 years old. He died August 4th.

R3#45	JAMES GILES	~20	104 Inf F	B ~1843 NY. R Troy, Rensselaer Co., NY. Occ molder. E Mar 62 private. C Jul 1: wounded in left leg. D Jul 8.
R3#46	SERGT S LASAGE or LESAGE[181]	30	147 Inf A	B ~1833 Montreal, Canada. R Oswego Co., NY. Occ shoemaker. E Jul 62 private. C Jul 1: GSW fracturing left femur. D Oct 8.
R3#47	JOHN SLAVEN[182]	27-28	61 Inf I	B ~1835 Ireland. R NYC. Occ laborer. E Sep 62 1st sergeant. C Jul 2: GSW to right right thigh with compound fracture. D Aug 26. Survivor (WC98990): W Jane 30 (M Dec 61); no chn.
R3#48	HEINRICH DROEBER or DROBER	~26	119 Inf C	B ~1837 Germany. R NYC. Occ teamster. E Jul 62 private. Captured, placed in prisoner camp 12/31/62–4/10/63. Mar/Apr 63: hospitalized in Washington, D.C. C Jul 1: wound to right knee. D Aug 27. Survivor (WC25896): W Wilhelmine 20's (M Sep 62); no chn.
R3#49	JOHN RILEY JOHN **REILLY** or RIELLY[183]	17	145 Inf C	B ~1846. Occ picture framer. E Aug 62 fifer, drummer. C Jul 2: wound to the left thigh→amp. D Jul 29 of typhoid complication.
R3#50	H HAWKINSON HOMER **HAWKINSON**	~19	94 Inf I	B 1844 Orleans, Jefferson Co., NY. Occ farmer. E (NY) Mar 62 into 105th NY infantry as a private. Transferred 3/26/62 to 94th NY infantry. C Jul 1: wounded in abdomen. D Aug 7.
R3#51	JACOB DILBERT **GOTTLIEB DILPERT**	38	119 Inf C	B 5/30/1825 Germany. R NYC. Occ tailor. E Jul 62 private. C Jul 1: wounded in the right knee→amp. D Aug 13.

---

181 **Civil War wound care in the century before antibiotics.** Upon his September 2nd acceptance into Camp Letterman Hospital, Samuel Lesage appears not to have undergone an amputation for his left femur gunshot fracture. His wound was complicated by the development of several large abscesses above the wound on his upper thigh. He was treated with opiates and stimulants until he died on October 8th. Penicillin, used extensively for combat wounds during the second World War, would have likely saved this soldier's life.

182 **Horrific bedsore complicates Camp Letterman hospitalization.** Upon his August 8, 1863 acceptance into Camp Letterman Hospital, John Slavin had not undergone an amputation for his gunshot wound fracturing of his right femur. He was noted to have to a very large bedsore, covering the whole of his sacral region and extending down each hip. Sloughing of skin tissues down his right thigh followed. He further weakened and died on August 26th. His age had been reported as 22.

183 **Soldier admits at hospital that he is only 17.** John Reilly reported his age as 19 at his August 18, 1862 enlistment. However, at his July 23rd admission to the hospital, he gave his age as 17. Reilly had already undergone an amputation of his left lower leg and the stump was assessed as being nearly healed. However, Reilly's condition quickly deteriorated with his developing typhoid symptoms. He would die on July 29th.

R3#52	JOSEPH COTRELL **WILLIAM JOSEPH COTTRELL**[184]	30-31	43 Inf A	B ~1832 England. E (Albany, NY) Aug 61 private. C Jul 3: severe wound to right arm →amp at the shoulder joint. D Aug 13 following raging rheumatic complications in joints and heart and additionally sloughing of skin tissues. Survivors (WC58854→WC115758 not online): W Ellen ~24 (M 1854 in England | ReM 1865): 3 chn: 2 ♂- William 7, Joseph 5 & 1 ♀- Mary 3.
R3#53	ORIN SHEPHARD[185]	27-28	60 Inf A	B ~1835 Canada. R Canton, St. Lawrence Co., NY. Occ day laborer. E Oct 61 private. C Jul 1: GSW to right thigh. D Aug 1.
R3#54	LIEUT A WAGNER **ADOLPHUS WAGNER**	22	39 Inf F	B 1841 Germany. 1860: R Rochester, Monroe Co., NY. Occ shoemaker. E Sep 62 private (following 3-mo service in 1st Garibaldi Guards). May/Jun 62 sergeant. Detached to NYC for recruiting service: 5/1-8/31/62. Promoted to Sergeant Major on 11/12/62. Commissioned 2nd lieutenant on 12/17/62. C Jul 2: wounded in chest. D Aug 25.
R3#55	P NEWMAN **CHARLES** NEWMAN	~25	73 Inf F	B ~1838. E Jul 61 private. C Jul 2: wounded in right upper arm with fracture of humerus. D Aug 9.
R3#56	JOHN M NOSTRANT (MN MORRISON)	25	111 Inf G	B 5/8/1838 Seneca Falls, Seneca Co., NY. 1860: R Aurelius, Cayuga Co., NY; Occ ferryman. E Aug 62 private. C Jul 2. D Jul 5. Survivor (WC443659 not online): F John Widger Nostrant 81 in 1896.
R3#57	A S VAN VOLKENBURG AMBROSE S VAN **VALKENBURG**	19-20	111 Inf E	B ~1843 NY. R Arcadia, Wayne Co., NY. Occ machinist, student. E Aug 62 private. Captured and paroled on 9/15/62 at Harper's Ferry. Promoted 3/1/63 to corporal. KIA Jul 3.
R3#58	T JAY SNYDER **TYLER JAY SNYDER**	21-22	126 Inf G	B ~1841 Bethel, Sullivan Co., NY. R Waterloo, Seneca Co., NY. Occ farm laborer, teacher. E Aug 62 private. Captured and paroled on 9/15/62 at Harper's Ferry. Promoted to corporal 11/1/62. Promoted to sergeant on 3/4/63. C Jul 2. D Jul 3.
R3#60	HENDRICK HAYMAN **HEINRICH HOECHNER**	24-25	39 Inf A	B ~1838 Germany. R NYC. Occ cook. E May 61 private. Captured and paroled on 9/15/62 at Harper's Ferry. C Jul 2: wounded in pelvis. D Jul 3.

---

184 **Soldier is sole fatality in his regiment during the battle.** Joseph and Ellen Cottrell immigrated to the United States from England in 1857. The 43rd New York Infantry was a regiment which arrived on July 2nd with the rest of the 6th Corps 3rd Brigade. On July 3rd, the regiment deployed north of the Baltimore Pike to push back Confederate skirmishers. Of the four hundred soldiers the 43rd NY infantry would bring to Gettysburg, Joseph Cotrell would be the sole fatality in this battle. Upon his July 22nd acceptance into Camp Letterman Hospital, he reported his age as 32. He died August 18th.

185 **Soldier dies in hospital from sepsis complication.** Upon entering the hospital, Orrin Shepherd reported his age as 29. His July 23rd hospital admission note documented a muscular wound to the lateral right thigh. No bone fracture was noted and no amputation needed to be performed. The wound appeared to be healing. However, in the pre-antibiotic epoch of the 19th century, Shepherd would abruptly develop septic symptoms and die on August 1st. Penicillin, in use for war wounds during the second World War, would have likely saved this young man's life.

R3#61	J CLEGG JAMES CLEGG	~38	70 Inf I	B ~1825 NY. R Cohoes, Albany Co., NY. E May 61 private. KIA Jul 2. Survivors (WC15115): W Mary 40 (M Mar 46); 1 ♀- Elizabeth 13.
R3#62	CORP A RALPH ALFRED RALPH	39	62 Inf C	B 12/30/1823 England. R NYC. E May 61 private. Promoted to corporal on 7/15/61. Reduced to private 9/15/62 for an unspecified infraction. KIA Jul 3. Survivor (WC24222): W Mary 36 (M Jan 1861); no chn reported.
R3#63	J E BAILEY JOHN E BAILEY	30-31	111 Inf I	B ~1832 CT. R Sempronius, Cayuga Co., NY. Occ laborer. E Aug 62 private. KIA Jul 3: GSW to the head. Survivors (WC30191→WC110347): W Betsey 25 (M Jan 57| ReM 1867); 1 ♂- William 10 months.
R3#64	T SWENEY **FRANCIS** SWEENEY	~23	40 Inf D	B ~1840 Ireland. Occ laborer. E (Yonkers, Westchester Co., NY) Jun 61 private. Sick in hospital at Alexandria, VA: Sep 61→Jan 62. Captured 829/62 at 2nd Bull Run. Paroled 9/1/62. AWOL in Oct 62. KIA Jul 2.
R3#65	THOMAS SMITH	~40	70 Inf K	B ~1823. E (Boston, MA) Apr 61 private. KIA Jul 2.
R3#66	SERGT S VANDERPOOL SYLVESTER VANDERPOOL[186]	23-24	125 Inf I	B 1839 West Sand Lake, Rensselaer Co., NY. R Troy, Rensselaer Co., NY. Occ spinner. E Aug 62 private. Captured and paroled at 9/15/62 at Harper's Ferry. Promoted to corporal on 3/15/63. Promoted to sergeant on 4/12/63. KIA Jul 3. Survivor (WC22943): M Mrs. Sarah Vanderpool 66 (Peter Vanderpool affirmed as a "habitual drunkard.")
R3#69	LIEUT J ROSS HORNER JOHN ROSS HORNER[187] 80 Inf K			B 1/12/1837 Mount Joy Township, Adams Co., PA. Occ student. Commissioned 2nd lieutenant Sep 61 (Kingston, Ulster Co., NY). Promoted to 1st lieutenant on 12/21/61. KIA 8/30/62 at 2nd Bull Run (age 26).
R3#70	H BERMAN **RUDOLPH BEERMAN**	~32	41 Inf E	B ~1831 Germany. R NYC. E Jun 61 private. KIA Jul 3.
R3#72	H DELMONT HERMAN **DEHMEL**	~30	41 Inf E	B ~1833 Germany. R NYC. Occ carpenter. E Jun 61 private. Permitted leave for some period beginning 4/7/63. KIA Jul 2. Survivors (WC141314): W Auguste 30 (M Sep 56| ReM 1869); 2 chn: 1 ♂- August 6 & 1 ♀- Hermina 2.

---

186 **Widower determines to enter the army.** On March 17, 1862, Sylvester Vanderpool wound lose the wife, Laverna, whom he had married in April 1858. Her death, occurring five months before he would determine to enter the army, would mean that his survivor's pension would go to his mother, Sarah Vanderpool, whose indigent circumstances were the result of being married to Peter Vanderpool, a "habitual drunkard." Interestingly, Sylvester Vanderpool today has a grave tablet in the New Mount Ida Cemetery in Troy, New York, which is either a cenotaph or his actual relocated remains.

187 **Reburial of 2nd Bull Run soldier.** Lieut. Horner was killed at 2nd Bull Run and his remains subsequently reburied at Gettysburg.

R3#74	SOLOMON LESSER	~26	41 Inf E	B ~1837. E (NYC) Jun 61 private. May/Jun 62: absent sick in Winchester, VA hospital. C Jul 2: wounded severely. D Jul 3 (War Dept determination in 1903).
R3#75	CORP BOLLINGER GUSTAV BOLLINGER	25-26	41 Inf E	B ~1837. E (NYC) Nov 61 private. Promoted to corporal on 7/30/62. Wounded 5/3/63 at Chancellorsville: contusion of right leg by shell. KIA Jul 2.
R3#76	JOS KLEBENSPIES JOSEPH KLEBENSPIES	~38	41 Inf E	B ~1825. E (NYC) Jun 61 wagoner. Rank reduced from wagoner to private 9/1/61. KIA Jul 2.
R3#77	CORP CONRAD WAELDE	~43	41 Inf K	B ~1820 Germany. R NYC. Occ tailor, merchant. E Jun 61 private. Promoted to corporal as of 6/6/62. KIA Jul 2. Survivor (WC27591): W Rose 47 (M Jul 51); no chn.
R3#78	ALBERT SPITZ	~25	41 Inf H	B 1838 NY. E Jun 61 private. Performing extra duty in Quartermaster's Department in Jul/Aug 62 and Nov/Dec 62. KIA Jul 2.
R3#79	JOHN DIERSHAN JOHN **DERSHAW**	32-33	41 Inf B	B ~1830 Germany. Occ farmer. E Sep 62 private. KIA Jul 2.
R3#80	CORP F WOELL FREDERICK **WOEHL**	~36	41 Inf B	B ~1827. E (NYC) Jun 61 private. Promoted to corporal 1/16/63. KIA Jul 2.
R3#81	J SMITH **ISAIAH** SMITH	27-28	4 Indpt Batty NY LA	B ~1835. E Sep 61 private. KIA Jul 2. Survivors (WC19979): W Emma 31 (Dec 56| ReM 1869- WC146193); 2 ♀: Alice Cora 5, Lucy 3.
R3#82	C A CALDWELL CHESTER A **CADWELL**	23	64 Inf E	B ~1840 NY. 1860: R Ithaca, Tompkins Co., NY; occ tailor's apprentice. E (Tyrone, Schuyler Co., NY) Jan 63 private. KIA Jul 2.
R3#83	H C ROSEGRANT HENRY ROSEGRANT	19-20	Batty B 1 NY LA	B 1843 Bath, Steuben Co., NY. E (Baldwinsville, Onondaga Co., NY) Sep 61 private. KIA Jul 2.
R3#84	TIMOTHY KEARNS	~32	70 Inf A	B ~1831 England. R Brooklyn, NY. Occ currier. E May 61 private. Mar 63: detailed to the ambulance corps. Apr 63: assigned to Corps HQ. KIA Jul 2. Survivor (WC81089): W Mariah 33 (M May 54 in England); no chn.
R3#85	P OWENS[188] 61 Inf A			Misidentified soldier in grave. Patrick Owens, Co A of the 61st NY infantry, was discharged from the army as of 10/7/64.with expiration of his term of service.

---

[188] **Misidentified soldier in grave**. Patrick Owens was not killed at Gettysburg but was discharged from the army in 1864 at the expiration of his term of service.

R3#86	G W SECOSE GEORGE **SECOR**	21-22	73 Inf F	B ~1841 NY. 1960: R New Rochelle, Westchester Co., NY; occ clerk. E Aug 62 private. KIA Jul 2. Survivor (WC90656): W Mary ~23 (M Oct 60); no chn.
R3#88	P TRAINER PETER **TRAINOR** or TRANOR	23-24	73 Inf D	B ~1839 NYC. Occ farmer. E (NYC) Dec 62 private. KIA Jul 2.
R3#89	JOHN KENTON JOHN **RENTON**	23-24	73 Inf C	B ~1839. E Aug 61 private. KIA Jul 2.
R3#90	JOHN SMITH[189]	~50	57 Inf D	B ~1813 England. R Kirkland, Oneida Co., NY. Occ laborer. E Aug 62 private. KIA Jul 2.
R3#91	SERGT W H AMBLER WILLIAM HARVEY AMBLER	18	57 Inf D	B 9/8/1844 Pound Ridge, Westchester Co., NY. 1860: R Lewisboro, Westchester Co., NY.; occ shoemaker. E Sep 61 private. Promoted to corporal on 7/1/62. KIA Jul 2: killed instantly by a solid shot striking him at his right shoulder and passing through his body. Survivor (WC39788): M Mrs. Mary Ambler 37 (widow of Thomas V. Ambler).
R3#92	JOHN LANEGAR JOHN **LANIGER**	20-21	5 Cav D	B ~1842. E (Springfield, Otsego Co., NY) Sep 61 private. Captured at Front Royal, VA on 3/22/63 and paroled at 3/31/63 at City Point, VA. KIA Jun 30 at Hanover, PA.
R3#93	SERGT SELDEN D WALES	25	5 Cav A	B 12/9/1837 CT. E Aug 61 private. Promoted to corporal on 1/20/62. Promoted to sergeant on 5/4/62 and to 1st sergeant on 1/1/63. Captured 7/18/62 at Orange Court House, VA. Paroled 8/5/62. KIA Jun 30 at Hanover, PA. Survivor (WC134275): M Mrs. Polly Wales 61 in 1868 (widow of Norman Wales).
R3#94	ADJUVANT A GALL ALEXANDER GALL	38-39	5 Cav	B ~1824 Scotland. Occ painter. E Oct 62 private. Promoted to sergeant major on 10/11/61. Commissioned 1st lieutenant and adjutant on 1/1/63. KIA June 30: killed instantly at Hanover by bullet striking over right eye and piercing brain.
R3#95	J B COWELLS JOHN B **COWELL**	27	108 Inf E	B ~1836 Rochester, Monroe Co., NY. R same. Occ carpenter. E Jul 62 private. Absent sick 9/7/62 into Jan/Feb 63. Absent sick 6/20/63→died Aug 3 from this febrile illness. Survivors (WC59716): W- H Luetta 20 (M May 60); 1 ♀- Leslie 14 months.
R3#96	JOHN P WELLS	21	104 Inf E	B ~1842 Howard, Steuben Co., NY. R same. Occ farm laborer on father's farm. E Jan 62 private. C Jul1: GSW left arm. D Jul 20.

---

189 **Overaged at enlistment.** For his August 1862 enlistment, John Smith reported his age as 44. However, his reported ages of 36 and 47 in the successive 1850 and 1860 U.S. Censuses support that he was at least 49, or four years beyond the upper-age-limit for voluntary enlistment.

R3#97	WILLIAM FRANKLIN (MN GRISWOLD)	32	136 Inf H	B 8/14/1830 Fairfield, Herkimer Co., NY. R Wethersfield, Wyoming Co., NY. Occ: master carpenter. E Aug 62 private. C Jul 3: severely wounded in leg. D Jul 3. Survivors (WC36183): W Mary ~25; 1 ♂- William 7 & 1 ♀- Ella 5.
R3#98	A N POST ALBERT N POST[190]	22-23	43 Inf A	B ~1840. E Aug 61 private. KIA Jul 3: GSW chest. Survivor (WC920885 filed in 1917 and not online): W Ann 72 in 1917 (M Jul 62| ReM 9/17/63 and 1882).
R3#99	JOHN FERRY	19-20	88 Inf I	B ~1843. E (NYC) Dec 61 private. Nov/Dec 62: detailed as orderly to Gen. Meagher. Jan 63: serving as general orderly. KIA Jul 3.
R3#101	JAMES McBRIDE[191]	34-35	88 Inf A	B ~1829 Ireland. R NYC. Occ tinsmith. E Aug 62 private. KIA Jul 2. Survivors (WC27262): W Mary 28 (M Aug 51); 2 chn: 1 ♀- Mary 3 & 1 ♂- John 15 months.
R3#103	PATRICK KENNEY	36-37	63 Inf A	B ~1826. E (NYC) Aug 61 private. KIA Jul 2.
R3#104	CHARLES HOGAN	20-21	63 Inf A	B ~1842 NYC. Occ machinist, wheelwright. E Mar 62 private. KIA Jul 2.
R3#105	HENRY HITCHCOCK	19-20	1 Indpt NY LA	B ~1843 Auburn, Cayuga Co., NY. R same. Occ blacksmith. E Sep 61 private. C Jul 3: thigh wound by a shell. D Jul 4.
R3#106	GEORGE CLAXTON	45-46	111 Inf G	B ~1817 Ireland. R Skaneateles, Onondaga Co., NY. Occ farmer. E Aug 62 private. Captured and paroled on 9/15/62 at Harper's Ferry. May 63: company cook. C Jul 2: flesh wound to thigh. D Jul 25 of pyemia complication. Survivors (WC14447): W Mary 42 (M May 57); 2 ♂- Charles 5, Frank 2.
R3#107	AMOS OTIS HENRY AMOS OTIS	37	146 Inf K	B 3/13/1826 Fort Ann, Washington Co., NY. R Warsaw, Wyoming Co., NY. Occ teacher. E Aug 62 private. Dec 62: detailed as a hospital attendant. Absent sick at U.S. Hospital in Washington since 6/13/63. D Jul 1 of an unspecified illness.

---

190 **Thrice-widowed, seventy-one-year-old woman gains resumption of military pension she gave up fifty-two years before**. Mrs. Ann Post had only been married to Albert Post one year when he was killed on July 3, 1863. Being a war widow at only 17-years-old, she quickly married Benjamin French on September 17, 1863. Still only 33-years-old when Benjamin Franklin died in 1879, Mrs. Franklin now married the 24-year-old George McDaniels in 1882. This third marriage would last until McDaniels' death in 1915. Two years later, at now age 71, Mrs. McDaniels would apply for the resumption of her war widow's pension which would sustain her until her death at age 86.

191 **A daughter visits her father's grave 59 years after his death— with a purpose**? The widow's pension file for Mrs. Mary McBride includes a 1922 letter from the Mrs. Mary McBride Reilly, the daughter would have been only three years old when her father was killed at Gettysburg. Her letter speaks of her visiting her father's gravesite and of her being "delighted to find how wonderful the government had arranged everything for his last resting place." Before turning to these complementary comments, Mrs. Reilly's had alluded to her limited resources and so queried whether she, as the daughter of a Civil War soldier who had fell at Gettysburg, might be entitled to a pension. A polite reply letter from a U.S. Pension Commissioner informed Mrs. McBride that she was due no entitlement.

R3#108	SERGT SAMUEL FULLER[192]	24-25	105 Inf G	B ~1838 NY. R Rochester, Monroe Co., NY. Occ machinist. E Jan 62 sergeant. Sick at Alexandria on 7/12/62. Hospitalized at Mt. Pleasant Gen Hosp in D.C. Sep→Nov/Dec 62. Home on furlough 12/13/62. Jan/Feb 63: absent wounded at Fredericksburg. Deserted 3/18/63. Returned to regiment 5/8/63. Captured at Gettysburg Jul 1, he asked to attend to the sick and wounded and to aid in burying the dead. D Jul 18 from wounds received during this detail in a violent quarrel involving unspecified parties.
R3#110	E DEVELIN EDWARD **DEVLIN**	25-26	73 Inf A	B ~1837. E (NYC) Aug 61 private. Wounded in 6/25/62 action during Seven Days Battle. Jan/Feb 63: reported AWOL. KIA Jul 2.
R3#111	J RAETCHNER JOHN EDWARD **RICKLEY**	~23	70 Inf D	B 1840 Hanover Twp, Morris Co., NJ. E Jul 61 private. Feb→April 62: detailed as pioneer. KIA Jul 2.
R3#113	CORP RD SHERIDAN RICHARD SHERIDAN[193]	~24	82 Inf E	B ~1839 NY. Occ paper ruler. E Jun 61 private. Promoted to corporal on 1/1/63. KIA Jul 2. Survivor (WC117836): F John Sheridan 57 (disabled widower of Ellen Sheridan).
R3#114	D C CHARLES W DUBOIS[194]	19	120 Inf G	B 1844 Ulster Co., NY. Occ farmer. E Aug 62 private. Detached to hospital as a cook on 2/1/63. Initially thought to have deserted Jul 2 at Gettysburg. By end of war, he was administratively supposed him to have been killed at Gettysburg.
R4#1	FREDERICK D CLARK	~23	78 Inf K	B ~1840 LaGrange, LaGrange Co., IN. R York, Elkhart Co., IN. Occ farm laborer. E Feb 62 private. KIA Jul 2.
R4#3	WILLIAM C MARSH[195]	~22	78 Inf H	B ~1841 Buffalo, Orange Co., NY. R Monroe Co., NY. Occ farmer. E Mar 62 private. KIA Jul 2: killed while skirmishing with the enemy.

---

192 **Captured Sergeant Samuel Fuller asks to attend the wounded and help bury the dead.** Rather than choosing to huddle with the other captured soldiers, Sergeant requested to help attend to the wounded and in burying the dead. The record is mum but Fuller was involved in some violent quarrel, possibly with one of his Confederate captor, which ended in his being killed.

193 **A widower's totally dependence on support from his son in the army.** A person with knowledge of John Sheridan's circumstances gave testimony for John's pension application that affirmed he was disabled for work and wholly dependent on his only offspring, Richard, for financial support. Specifically, this testimony affirmed that even years before Richard had gone into the military, he had been paying his widower father's rent, buying his food, clothing and other necessary household expenses. In support of his dependent father's pension application, John Sheridan himself submitted several of his son's caring letters, which documented the regular sums of money being sent home from his army pay. There is no starker indicator of the destitute situation that his son's death left him in than that his application for a pension was submitted from a New York almshouse.

194 **Soldier never confirmed in his military record killed in action** Charles DuBois was never confirmed in his service record as killed-in-action on July 2nd, but certainly the presence of his grave at the National Cemetery is persuasive.

195 **Killed during skirmishing.** William Marsh was killed July 2nd while skirmishing for the 78th NY Infantry.

R4#4	LOREN EATON LOREN S EATON	26-27	149 Inf D	B 1836 Manlius, Onondaga Co., NY. R Onondaga Co., NY. Occ day laborer. E Aug 62 private. KIA Jul 2.
R4#5	FREDERICK PHELPS	18	137 Inf C	B 2/22/1845 Owego, Tioga Co., NY. 1860: R Candor, Tioga Co., NY. Occ laborer on father's farm. E Aug 62 private. Captured on 11/24/62 at Bolivar, VA. Paroled around 5/1/63. KIA Jul 2.
R4#6	WILLIAM MURPHY	21-22	60 Inf I	B ~1841 St. Lawrence Co, NY. R same. Occ farmer. E Sep 61 private. KIA Jul 2: wounded through brain.
R4#7	MICHAEL MOLOY MICHAEL **MOLLOY**	28-29	149 Inf C	B ~1834 Ireland. R Syracuse, Onondaga Co., NY. Occ laborer. E Aug 62 private. KIA Jul 2.
R4#8	E B ROBERTS ERASTUS BARTON ROBERTS	37-38	84 Inf B	B ~1825 Oneida Co., NY. R Brooklyn, NY. Occ miller. E Sep 62 private. C Jul 1. D Jul 4. Survivors (WC147648): W Josephine 47 (M Sep 50| died 6/26/66); 1 ♀- Josephine 12.
R4#11	SERGT J P CUSH JAMES P CUSH	~23	59 Inf B	B ~1840. E (Lowville, Lewis Co., NY) Jun 61 corporal. Promoted to sergeant on 2/1/62. Promoted to 1st sergeant on 2/27/63. KIA Jul 2.
R4#13	N SOUTHERD NELSON SOUTHARD	29-30	80 Inf K	B ~1833 NY. 1860: R Windham, Greene Co., NY. E (Kingston, Ulster Co., NY) Sep 61 private. KIA Jul 3: GSW to liver.
R4#14	JOHN TAPPER JOHN **CAPPER**	~27	83 Inf E	B ~1836 Ireland. Occ mason. E (NYC) Apr 61 private. Absent sick on furlough: 2/16→3/8/62. KIA Jul 2.
R4#15	PATRICK M MARRA PATRICK **McMORROW** or McMARA	~26	42 Inf E	B ~1837. E (Long Island, NY) Jun 61 private. Captured at Ball's Bluff on 10/21/61 at Leesburg, VA. Paroled 2/22/62. Held 8/15/62 at Camp Parole in Annapolis, MD. Returned to regiment on 10/31/62. KIA Jul 3: shell or fragment reportedly coursed from one side of the body through to the other side.
R4#16	FREDERICK TYBAL FREDERICK **TIBELL**	~27	42 Inf K	B ~1836. E (NYC) Jul 61 private. Nov/Dec 62: absent sick in general hospital with unspecified condition. KIA Jul 3: GSW through the heart.
R4#17	SERGT L DARVOE LOUIS D **DARVEAU**	23-24	Batty B 1 NY LA	B ~1839. E Aug 62 private with the Chicago Battery. Joined Battery B 1 NY LA on 11/12/61 transfer from dissolved Chicago Battery. Promoted to sergeant 3/3/62. KIA Jul 3.
R4#18	H WOOD HENRY WOOD	~22	111 Inf K	B ~1841 Courtland Co., NY. Occ farmer. E (Springport, Cayuga Co., NY) Jul 62 private. KIA Jul 3.

R4#21	JAMES H GRISWALD JAMES H **GRISWOLD**[196]	~17	111 Inf E	B ~1846 Galen, Wayne Co., NY. R Arcadia, Wayne Co., NY. Occ farmer. E Aug 62 private. Captured and paroled on 9/15/62 at Harper's Ferry. KIA Jul 3.
R4#22	J J BECK JOHN BECK	35-36	45 Inf D	B ~1827 Germany. Occ shoemaker. E (NYC) Sep 61. C Jul 1: wounded in right chest. D Jul 21.
R4#23	HENRY C DUNNELL[197]	~18	70 Inf D	B ~1845 NJ. R Troy, Rensselaer Co., NY. E Oct 61 private. Court martial sentence on 5/11/63 to forfeit one month's page for an unspecified infraction. C Jul 2: wounded in right thigh. D Aug 14.
R4#24	SERGT P FARRINGTON PATRICK FARRINGTON	19	82 Inf G	B 7/13/1843 Ireland. R NYC. 1860 occ: apprentice to brass molder. E May 61 private. Promoted to corporal on 10/1/62. Promoted to sergeant on 2/1/63. Promoted to 1st sergeant on 3/1/63. C Jul 2: wounded in leg→amp. D Jul 10. Survivors (WC112283): M Mrs. Bridget Farrington 55 in 1867 (husband sick with tuberculosis).
R4#25	CORP A H EDSON ALBERT EDSON	21	8 Cav A	B 3/26/1842 Point Lookout, Nassau Co., NY. R Rochester, Monroe Co., NY. 1860 occ: clerk. E Sep 61 corporal. KIA Jul 1.
R4#27	PATRICK McDONALD PATRICK **McDONNEL**	22-23	82 Inf H	B ~1840 Ireland. E Sep 61 private. Promoted to corporal on 1/1/63. C Jul 2: wounded in abdomen. D Jul 19.
R4#28	WILLIAM KREIS WILLIAM **KREISS**	41-42	52 Inf I	B ~1821. E (NYC) Oct 61 private, following previous service in 29th NY Light Artillery. C Jul 2: GSW to chest. D Jul 15.
R4#29	CASPER BONNELL CASPER **BONNET**	36-37	66 Inf C	B ~1826 Germany. R NYC. E Nov 61 private. Occ carpenter. Served as company cook Feb 62, Oct 62, Jan→Feb 63. C Jul 2: wounded in left knee→amp. D Jul 18.
R4#30	ELISHA ALLEN	25	59 Inf A	B 3/11/1838 Lorraine, Jefferson Co., NY. 1860: R Adams, Jefferson Co., NY; occ farm laborer. E Oct 61 private. Wounded on 9/17/62 at Antietam. C Jul 2: severe wound to right shoulder. D Jul 13.
R4#31	WESSEL WHITBECK WESSEL T WHITBECK	18-19	111 Inf E	B 1844 Arcadia, Wayne Co., NY. R Wayne Co., NY. 1860 occ: tinner apprentice. E Aug 62 private. C Jul 2: wounded in thigh→amp. D Jul 14.

---

196 **Minor at death**. An August 11, 1860 U.S. Census report for Arcadia, NY lists James Griswold's age as 14. If this age were correct, James was not 18, but likely 16 at his August 5, 1862 enlistment. The implied birthyear of 1844 would also mean that he was no older than 17 when he was killed at Gettysburg.

197 **Minor at enlistment**. The July 19, 1860 U.S. Census report for Troy, NY lists Henry Dunnell's age as 15. If this were accurate, his age as of his October 21, 1861 enlistment was not 18, but no older than 17. Given this implied birthyear of 1845, Dunnell was likely only 18 when he was killed at Gettysburg.

R4#32	SERGT E G AYLESWORTH EDWIN GRIFFIN **AYLSWORTH**	20	147 Inf G	B 12/3/1842 Oswego, NY. R same. E Aug 62 sergeant. Occ carpenter, farmer. C Jul 1: wounded in right thigh→amp. D Jul 10.
R4#34	GEORGE McCONNELL	~21	84 Inf I	B ~1842 Ireland. R Brooklyn, NY. Occ clerk. E Aug 61 private. Deserted 12/6/61. Returned to company on 3/29/63. C Jul 1: wounded in left arm→amp. D Jul 8. Survivor: M Mrs. Rebecca McConnell (widowed but no record of filed mother's pension application).
R4#35	FRANCIS CHAPMAN FRANCIS A CHAPMAN	25-26	76 Inf K	B ~1837 England. Occ blacksmith. E (Springfield, Otsego Co., NY) Sep 61 private. Wounded and captured on 8/28/62 at Gainesville, VA. Paroled 9/6/62→then held in the hospital/convalescent camp into Feb 63. Deserted some time in Feb 63, by one account fleeing to Canada. May/Jun 63: returned to regiment following an amnesty proclamation. C Jul 1. D Jul 8.
R4#36	SERGT JAMES HANIGAN	26-27	136 Inf E	B ~1836 Ireland. R Warsaw, Wyoming, NY. Occ mechanic. E Aug 62 private. Jan/Feb 63: promotion to corporal. Promoted to sergeant on 3/28/63. KIA Jul 2: GSW to head. Survivors (WC20063): W Margaret 28 (M Aug 56|ReM 1869); 4 chn: 1 ♀- Mary 3 & 3 ♂- John 4, James 3, George 16 months.
R4#37	THOMAS HURLEY	23-24	82 Inf G	B ~1839 Ireland. Occ clerk. E (NYC) Aug 62 private. Promoted to corporal on 4/15/63. C Jul 2. D Jul 4.
R4#38	DAVID R JOHNSTON	21-22	82 Inf C	B ~1841 Ireland. Occ clerk. E (NYC) Sep 62. Dec 62: Absent, sick at Convalescent Camp at Alexandria, VA. C Jul 2: GSW to both legs→amp of one leg. D Jul 31.
R4#39	PHILIP MARTYLER **LOUIS** METZLER	~21	39 Inf A	B ~1842 Nassau, Rensselaer Co., NY. R NYC. E May 61 private. C Jul 3: shell wounds to leg and back. D Jul 26. Survivor (WC34813): M Mrs. Wilhelmina Metzler 55 (widow of August Metzler).
R4#40	GEORGE SHUMDEKER GEORGE **SCHUMACHER**	23	39 Inf B	B ~1840. R NYC. E May 61 private. C Jul 1: severe wound to leg→amp. D Jul 25. Survivor (WC31638): M Mrs. Margaretha Schumacher 55 (widow of Phillip Schumacher).
R4#41	SERGT L STONE **CHISTOPHER** STONE	~21	42 Inf G	B ~1842 Ireland. 1860: R NYC; occ: apprentice rope maker. E Jun 61 private. Promoted to sergeant during service. KIA Jul 2. Survivor (WC23228): M Mrs. Julia Stone 42 (widow of John Stone).
R4#42	J W CESLER JOHN W KESSLER	~26	70 Inf D	B ~1837. E (Staten Island, NY) Jun 61 private. C Jul 2. D Jul 2 or 8.

R4#45	F PLATTE FRIERICH PLATTE or FREDERICK PLATTE	43	72 Inf E	B 10/29/1819 Germany. R Dunkirk, Chautauqua Co., NY. Occ saloon keeper. E Aug 62 private. C Jul 2: multiple bodily wounds, including most severely on left leg→amp. D Jul 8. Survivors (WC62980): W Sophia 34 (M Jun 60); 4 chn: 3 ♂- Christian 20, Frederick 17, John 15 & 1 ♀- Josephine 12.
R4#46	PATRICK LYNCH	~21	73 Inf D	B ~1842 Ireland. Occ butcher. E Oct 61 into the 70th NY infantry as a private. Transferred to 73rd NY infantry on 2/10/62. Jul 62: detailed as company waterman. Aug 62: detailed as company cook. C Jul 2: wounded in left knee→amp. D Jul 10.
R4#47	SERGT J MURPHY JOHN MURPHY	~24	73 Inf B	B ~1839 NYC. Occ machinist. E Jul 61 private. Promoted to sergeant on 9/1/62. Promoted to 1st sergeant on 5/1/63. C Jul 2: wounded in abdomen and back. D Jul 9.
R4#48	W M BROWN WILLIAM BROWN	21-22	73 Inf G	B ~1841 Brooklyn, NY. R same. Occ dairyman. E Aug 62 private. C Jul 2: wounded in thigh→amp. D Jul 9.
R4#49	CORP C LAMBERT **SAMUEL** LAMBERT	~27	70 Inf F	B ~1836 NJ. E Jun 61 private. Captured on 5/5/62 at Williamsburg, VA. Returned from missing 12/17/62. Promotion to corporal as of Apr 63. C Jul 2. D Jul 21.
R4#50	H ROSE HENRY ROSE[198] 111 Inf E			Misidentified soldier in grave. Henry Rose on July 3rd did sustain a gunshot compound fracture of the tibia in the right lower leg. He did not die of this wound, but on account of it, he would receive a disability discharge from the army on 1/15/64.
R4#51	JOSEPH BATTLE JOSEPH **BATTAILLE** or **BATTELLE**	~26	71 Inf A	B ~1837. E May 61 private. Promoted to corporal on 9/5/61. C Jul 2: wounds to foot, leg and shoulder. D Jul 15.
R4#52	JOSIAH D BARNES	21	120 Inf I	B 10/2/1841 Wawarsing, Ulster Co., NY. 1860: R same; occ: farm laborer on father's farm. E Aug 62 private. Promoted to corporal on 6/23/63. KIA Jul 2.
R4#53	N W WINSHIP NEHEMIAH WINSHIP	24-25	86 Inf K	B ~1838 Troupsburg, Steuben Co., NY. Occ school teacher., shoemaker. E Sep 61 private. Wounded 5/3/63 at Chancellorsville, VA. May/Jun 63: detailed on extra duty as clerk in Old Capitol Prison. KIA Jul 2.
R4#54	JABEZ FISK JABEZ BUTLER FISK	18	86 Inf K	B 7/14/1844 Paris, Oneida Co., NY. R Woodhull, Steuben Co., NY. Occ farmer. E Aug 62 private. Wounded in arms slightly on 12/13/62 at Fredericksburg, VA. KIA Jul 2.

---

198 **Misidentified soldier in grave**. Henry Rose was wounded at Gettysburg at July 3rd, but he did not die from the wound. The wound would be the basis for a disability discharge in 1864.

R4#55	MATTHEW BRYAN **MATHEW BYRNES**	~21	82 Inf C	B ~1842 NYC. R same. Occ machinist. E Apr 61 private. Detailed as teamster Oct 61→Apr 62. C Jul 2. D Jul 5.
R4#56	SERGT C FARNSBORTH CHARLES H **FARNSWORTH**	32-33	126 Inf G	B ~1830 Waterloo, Seneca Co., NY. R same. Occ shoemaker. E Aug 62 private. Captured and paroled on 9/15/62 at Harper's Ferry. Promoted to sergeant on 3/4/63. C Jul 3. D Jul 9. Survivors (WC81883): W Elizabeth 33 (M Dec 49); 3 chn: 2♂- George 13, Charles 9 & 1 ♀- Jane 7.
R4#57	WILLIAM McCORT	~29	39 Inf C	B ~1834. E May 61 private. Captured and paroled on 9/15/62 at Harper's Ferry. C Jul 2: wounded in chest. D Jul 10.
R4#58	E WHITMORE EMMETT WHITMORE	21	111 Inf E	B Jul 1842 NY. R Arcadia, Wayne Co., NY. E Jul 62 private. C Jul 3: wounded in the head. D Jul 11. Survivor (WC22027): M Mrs. Eliza Whitmore 53 (widow of Jacob Whitmore).
R4#59	WILLIAM DANICE **WILHELM DOENECKE**	~30	39 Inf B	B ~1833 Germany. Occ baker. E May 61 private. Captured and paroled on 9/15/62 At Harper's Ferry. C Jul 2. D Jul 6 or 15.
R4#60	JOHN FURGESON **JOHAN JUNGUNST** or JOHN YONKER	~32	39 Inf C	B ~1831. E (NYC) May 61 private. Captured and paroled on 9/15/62 at Harper's Ferry. May 63: served as company cook. C Jul 2. D Jul 6.
R4#61	SERGT C SANDERS CARLTON SANDERS	24-25	122 Inf H	B ~1838 NY. R Clarendon, Orleans Co., NY. R same. Occ carpenter. E Aug 62 private (no service record documentation of promotion to sergeant). C Jul 3. D Jul 6. Survivors (WC42835): W Margaret 22 in 1864 (M Aug 58); 1 ♀- Belle 3.
R4#62	JOHN CAIN	21-22	122 Inf K	B ~1841 Ireland. Occ laborer. E (Syracuse, Onondaga Co., NY) Aug 62 private. Apr/May 63: detached to pioneer corps. C Jul 3: shot through both cheeks. D Jul 10.
R4#63	C H CARPENTER CHARLES H CARPENTER[199]	~19	44 Inf I	B ~1844 NY. 1860: R Kinderhook, Columbia Co., NY; occ: farm laborer. E Sep 61 private. C Jul 2: shot in left chest. D Jul 22.
R4#66	H McDOWELL HENRY McDOWELL	33	60 Inf C	B 9/11/1829 Waddington, St. Lawrence Co., NY. Occ mechanic. E Sep 61 private. Promoted to corporal on 2/1/63. C Jul 2: wounded severely in face. D Jul 16. Survivor (WC25745): M Mrs. Sarah McDowell 61 (widow of William McDowell).

---

199 **Minor at enlistment**. Charles Carpenter's ages of 6 and 15 on the successive August 1850 and June 1860 U.S. Census reports suggests that he was not 18, but likely 17 at his September 1861 enlistment. He was likely 19 when he was mortally wounded on July 2nd.

R4#67	J WALTON JOSEPH WALTON	22-23	84 Inf H	B ~1840 England. R Brooklyn, NY. Occ shoemaker. E Sep 62 private. C Jul 1. D Jul 3.
R4#68	JAMES IVERS	~24	84 Inf A	B ~1839 Ireland. Occ laborer. E (Brooklyn, NY) Apr 61 private. Reported AWOL 11/14-22/61. Wounded 8/29/62 at 2nd Bull Run. Absent in hospital from 8/29/62 to 4/9/63. KIA Jul 1. Survivor (WC71874): M Mrs. Mary Ivers 51 (widow of Patrick Ivers).
R4#69	JACOB EISER JACOB **GEISSER**	30-31	134 Inf A	B ~1832 Germany. Occ laborer. E (Schoharie, Schoharie Co., NY) Aug 62 private. KIA Jul 1.
R4#70	DAVID HEYDEN DAVID **HADIN**	22-23	147 Inf B	B ~1840 Canada. Occ sailor. E (Oswego, Oswego Co., NY) Aug 62 private. Promotion to corporal during service. KIA Jul 1.
R4#71	J FINLIN JOHN **FENLON**[200]	27-28	15 Indpt Batty NY LA	B ~1835. E (NYC) Oct 61 private. Deserted 6/28/63 at Frederick, MD. Reported back for duty on Jul 1st. KIA Jul 2.
R4#75	SERGT CHARLES E CONKLIN	27	84 Inf K	B 6/19/1836 Long Island, NY. R Brooklyn, NY. Occ iceman. E Sep 61 private. Promoted to corporal on 3/10/62. Detached service at Division HQ Jul 62 to 2/23/63. Promoted to sergeant on 4/01/63. KIA Jul 1.
R4#79	ROBERT BLAIR	23-24	140 Inf D	B ~1839 Ireland. R Monroe Co., NY. Occ carpenter. E Aug 62 private. Promoted to corporal on 3/22/63. KIA Jul 2:
R4#81	DANIEL CASEY	20-21	44 Inf D	B ~1842 Ireland. R Saratoga Springs, Saratoga Co., NY. Occ cigar maker. E Aug 61 private. Wounded 7/1/62 at Malvern Hill, VA. KIA Jul 2: wounded in the neck and carotid artery.
R4#82	JOSEPHUS SIMMONS[201] 44 Inf E			Misidentified soldier in grave. Josephus Simmons of Company E 44th NY infantry was not a casualty at Gettysburg. His service continued to his 11/7/63 wounding at the Battle of Rappahannock Station, VA, a wound that caused him to take a disability discharge in April 1864.

---

200 **Soldier is killed the day after returning from a three-day desertion**. John Fenlon, a 20-month veteran of the 15th Independent New York Light Artillery, was reported to have deserted the battery unit at Frederick, Maryland on June 28, 1863. He returned for duty on July 1st, only to be killed in action the following day.

201 **Misidentified soldier in grave**. Josephus Simmons was not a casualty at Gettysburg. He would be wounded in a battle in November 1863, a wound that result in his leaving the army on a disability discharge in 1864.

R4#83	JOHN LOOK [JOHN overlying JAMES]	35-36	44 Inf A	B ~1827 Livingston, NY. Occ farmer. E (Pembroke, Genesee Co., NY) Sep 62 to 14th NY Infantry as a private. Transferred to 44th NY Infantry on 6/24/63. KIA Jul 2. Survivors (WC350884 not online): W Elizabeth 36 (M Feb 48| ReM Apr 64); 3 chn: 1 ♂- Harry 13 & 2 ♀- Nancy 9, Sarah 6.
R4#84	CHARLES SPEISBERGER CHARLES **SPIESBERGER**[202]	18-19	140 Inf D	B ~1844 Germany. R Gates, Monroe Co., NY. Occ machinist. E Aug 62 private. KIA Jul 2. Survivors (WC108221): M Mrs. Theresia Spiessberger 67 in 1868 (John Spiessberger affirmed disabled).
R4#85	PHILIP BECKNER PHILIP **BUCKNER** *or* BUCHNER	26-27	140 Inf D	B ~1836 Germany. Occ blacksmith. E (Rochester, Monroe Co., NY) Aug 62 private. KIA Jul 2.
R4#86	JUSTICE EISENBERG **JUSTUS EISENBERG**	~42	140 Inf D	B 1821 Germany. R Rochester, Monroe Co., NY. Occ farmer. E Aug 62 private. KIA Jul 2. Survivors (WC20803): W Christina 48 (M Jun 43); 3 chn: 2 ♂- John 14, Adam 9 & 1 ♀ Anna 4.
R4#87	DAVID NASH	22-23	44 Inf F	B ~1840 Ogdensburg, NY. Occ machinist. E (Albany, NY) Aug 61 private. KIA Jul 2: wounded in chest.
R4#88	GEORGE LERVY **FRANCIS GORX LEVOY**	24-25	44 Inf F	B ~1838 Canada. Occ mechanic, cooper. E Aug 62 private into the 14th NY Infantry. Transferred to 44th NY Infantry on 6/24/63. KIA Jul 2. Survivors: none claimed.
R4#89	SERGT S S SKINNER SIDNEY S SKINNER	30-31	44 Inf D	B ~1832 MA. Occ farm laborer. E (Albany, NY) Sep 61 private. Promoted to corporal on 7/15/62. Promoted to sergeant on 2/16/63. KIA Jul 2: shot through the heart. Survivors (WC17227): W Amelia 26 (M Jan 56); 2 ♀- Estella 4, Alice 2.
R4#90	JESSE WHITE	20-21	44 Inf G	B ~1842 New Scotland, Albany Co., NY. R Guilderland, Albany Co., NY. Occ carpenter. E Aug 61 private. Home 6/30/62→10/31/62 on extended furlough, which included Sep/Oct 62 in a recruitment effort. Promoted to corporal on 5/25/63. KIA Jul 2: wounded in neck and spine.
R4#91	CORP W C CRAFTS WILLIAM C CRAFTS	25-26	8 Cav E	B ~1837 Lawrence, Nassau Co., NY. Occ farmer. E (Albany, NY) Sep 61 private into 44th NY infantry Company C. Transferred 12/19/61 to 8th NY Cavalry. Commissioned 2nd lieutenant on 6/11/62. Promoted to 1st lieutenant on 12/23/62. D Aug 29 of disease in Weaversville, Fauquier Co., VA.

---

202 **Question as regards whether soldier left behind a widow and child.** An Ancestry.com public family tree identifies a Louis Spiesberger as the son of Charles Spiesberger, born October 30. 1863, or four months after Charles was killed at Gettysburg. The posting identifies a Philomena Salzman as the child's mother. However, Mrs. Theresia Spiessberger, in her dependent mother's pension application, denies that her son Charles was ever married or produced any offspring.

R4#92	GEORGE STROBRIDGE GEORGE L **STROWBRIDGE**	38-39	140 Inf E	B ~1824 Courtland Co., NY. R Yates, Monroe Co., NY. Occ boatman, farmer. E Aug 62 private. KIA Jul 2. Survivors (WC138525): Lucy 47 (M Nov 44); 1 ♀ Mary 16.
R4#93	ROSS THOMAS	21-22	140 Inf E	B ~1841 Harrisburg, Dauphin Co., PA. Occ boatman. E (Rochester, Monroe Co., NY) Aug 62. KIA Jul 2: GSW to side and to hip. Survivor (WC12807): M Mrs. Harriet Thomas 41 (widow of Braxton Thomas).
R4#94	CORP WM GOODMAN WILLIAM J GOODMAN	27-28	44 Inf H	B ~1835 Utica, Oneida Co., NY. Occ molder. E (Albany, NY) Sep 61 corporal. Hospitalization for wounding at David's Island in NY Harbor from 7/4/62 through Mar 63. Returned to duty by 4/10/63 special roster. KIA Jul 2.
R4#95	GEORGE WOLCOTT (MN BILSON)	22	44 Inf E	B 8/31/1840 Penn Yan, Yates Co., NY. R Milo, Yates Co., NY. Occ tinsmith. E Aug 62 private. C Jul 2: wound to the brain. D Jul 2 or 3.
R4#96	LEANDER T BURNHAM (MN TURNER)	21	44 Inf E	B 8/22/1841 Abington, Windham Co., CT. R Windham Co., CT. Occ manufacturer, thread finisher. Absent on furlough 4/6-4/20/63. KIA Jul 2: wounded in chest.
R4#97	R McELLIGOT RICHARD **McELLIGOTT**	22-23	44 Inf C	B ~1840 Ireland. Occ farmer. E (Penn Yan, Yates Co., NY) Aug 62 private. Mar/April 63: promotion to corporal. KIA Jul 2: GSW to abdomen.
R4#98	F GRISWALD FRANCIS M **GRISWOLD**[203]	18-19	44 Inf C	B ~1844 Italy, Yates Co, NY. R same. Occ farmer. E Aug 62 priv. KIA Jul 2: wounded in brain.
R4#99	PETER BEERS	20-21	44 Inf B	B ~1842 Stephentown, Rensselaer Co., NY. Occ farmer. E (Albany, NY) Sep 61 private. Detailed to Griffin's 5th US Artillery, Battery D 1/7/62→2/4/62. Hospitalizations for an unspecified condition 3/2/62→Oct/Nov 62. Taken prisoner on 11/8/62 while straggling at Snickers Gap, VA. Paroled on 11/22/62 at City Point, VA. Returned to duty on 2/26/63. KIA Jul 2.

---

203 **No widow's pension approval found in records.** An Ancestry.com public family tree places Francis Griswold's birth year as 1846, rather than the 1844 date implied by giving his age as 18 at his August 1862 enlistment. His age for the June 1860 U.S. Census sheet is reported as 15. The most liberal interpretation of these dates is that Francis is that he could have just turned 18 at this enlistment. Even allowing these dates, Francis would be killed when he was no older than 19. At the time of Francis's death, his mother, Mrs. Matilda Griswold had been widowed thirteen years. During the Civil War, the need to financially support a widowed mother at home was a driving force for young men entering the army. Mrs. Griswold then would have been anticipated to have filed for a dependent mother's pension after Francis's death. There is no record of her filing for a pension, perhaps as her ability to qualify may have been nullified by the fact of having of three older living sons, who presumably could provide her with amble support.

R4#100	JOHN M IRONS[204]	18-19	44 Inf E	B ~1844 Cooperstown, NY. R Utica, Oneida Co., NY. Occ farmer, cooper. E Jul 62 private in to 14th NY Co. B. Transferred with the 3-year-men to 44th NY on 6/25/63. KIA Jul 2.
R4#101	E STRONG **CORNELIUS STOREY**[205]	31-32	44 Inf K	B ~1831 Utica, Oneida Co., NY. R same. Occ farmer. E Oct 61 private into 14th NY Co. I. Transferred with the 3-year-men to 44th NY Infantry on 6/25/63. KIA Jul 2. Survivor (WC78264}: 1 ♂- William 7 (A Mr. Solomon Cooley 48 appointed guardian as mother, Mrs. Olive Cooley Storey had preceded her husband in death on 9/17/58).
R4#105	JOSEPH SCHNEIBACHER JOSEPH **SCHNEEBACKER**	43-44	146 Inf F	B ~1819 Germany. R Utica, Oneida Co., NY. Occ laborer. E Sep 62 private. KIA Jul 2. Survivors (WC10254): W Maria Anna 44 (M Feb 46); 3 chn: 2 ♀- Mary 14, Elizabeth 11 & 1 ♂- Anselm 9.
R4#109	MARTIN ROE	22-23	111 Inf K	B ~1840 Duchess Co., NY. R Poughkeepsie, Dutchess Co., NY. Occ farmer. E Aug 62 private. Captured and paroled on 9/15/62 at Harper's Ferry. D Jul 2 of wounds. Survivor (WC84518): M Mrs. Jane Roe 66 in 1866 (testimony of abandonment by William B. Roe about twenty years previous).
R4#110	HENRY C DETRICK	27-28	111 Inf K	B ~1835 Genoa, Cayuga Co., NY. R same. Occ farmer. E Aug 62 private. Captured and paroled on 9/15/62 at Harper's Ferry. Deserted on 9/17/62 at Frederck, MD. Voluntarily returned to duty on 3/12/63. KIA Jul 2: wound to the forehead causing instant death. Survivors (WC35292→WC164783 & WC210622 none of these online): W Nancy 28 (M Mar 60| ReM 1873): 1 ♂- Henry 1.
R4#111	J C K			Killed soldier with comparable initials in the absence of regimental clues could not be identified in military sources.
R4#112	CHARLES JOHNRID 5 Inf H			Killed soldier with this or similar name and belonging to this regiment and company not found in military sources.
R4#113	UNKNOWN CAV SERGT EDWIN ARNOLD M SLOCUM[206]	29	8 Cal A	B 6/5/1834 Perinton, Monroe Co., NY. Occ engineer. E Aug 61 sergeant. KIA Jul 1. Survivors (WC28303): W Mary 26 (M Aug 54| ReM 1867); 1 ♀- Mary 7.

---

204 **Death of a 14th New York Infantry "Three-Year Man."** In a situation identical to one impacting the 2nd Maine Infantry approaching the Gettysburg battle, the decommissioning 14th New York Infantry transferred to another New York regiment a contingent of men who had signed three-year papers. This extended service in the 44th New York Infantry would cost Private John Irons his life on Little Round Top.

205 **Death of a 14th New York Infantry "Three-Year Man."** In a situation identical to one impacting the 2nd Maine Infantry approaching the Gettysburg battle, the decommissioning 14th New York Infantry transferred to another New York regiment a contingent of men who had signed three-year papers. As with Private John Irons, this extended service in the 44th New York Infantry would cost Private Cornelius Storey his life on Little Round Top.

206 **Unknown calvary sergeant identified but not named on headstone.** Process of identification not known.

R4#118	W L BORT WILLIAM L BORT	40	157 Inf B	B Feb 1823 Onondaga Co., NY. 1860 R: Lenox, Madison Co., NY. Occ farmer. E Aug 62 private. C Jul 1: wounded in abdomen. D Jul 8. Survivors (WC17872): W Jane 36 (M Dec 43); 3 dependent chn: 2 ♂- William 11, Edgar 6 & 1 ♀- Mary 8.
R4#119	SIMEON IKINS[207] (MN DENNIS)	19-20	136 Inf K	B ~1843 England. Occ farmer. 1860 R: Elma, Erie Co., NY. E Aug 62 private. C Jul 3: shell wounding to left arm and head. D Aug 29.
R4#120	W W CLARK WILLIAM W CLARK[208]	24	60 Inf B	B ~1839 Morristown, St. Lawrence Co., NY. 1860 R: Brasher, St. Lawrence Co., NY. Occ farmer. E Sep 61 sergeant. Sent to Washington 8/31/62 by surgeon for undocumented complaint. Detailed as color sergeant in Oct 62. C Jul 3: GSW to right shoulder and right upper lung. D Aug 29.
R4#121	T MANLY TIMOTHY MANLEY	29-30	63 Inf A	B ~1833 Ireland. Occ tailor. E (NYC) Aug 61 private. C Jul 2: wounded in right leg causing compound fracture. Hospitalization was complicated by the development of a large bedsore. D Sep 8.
R4#122	D SMITH DAVID SMITH[209] or DAVIS SMITH	30	57 Inf I	B ~1833 Williamsburg, Brooklyn, NY. E Aug (NYC) 61 private. Served as company cook. Dec 61→May/Jun 62. C Jul 2: wound to left side of spine. D Sep 8. Survivors (WC64089→WC148125 neither online): W Eliza 26 in 1864 (M Feb 52 | died 10/8/69 of tuberculosis); 2 ♂- Samuel 7, Alexander 6.
R4#123	GEORGE S MOSS	27-28	125 Inf C	B ~1835 Lansingburgh, Troy, Rensselaer Co., NY. R same. Occ carpenter. E Aug 62 private. Captured 9/15/62 and paroled 9/16/62 at Harpers Ferry, VA. Promoted to sergeant on 10/6/62. C Jul 2: GSW to left thigh. D Aug 10.
R4#124	WILLIAM WYER WILLIAM **DWYER**[210]	17	119 Inf A	B ~1846 NY. R Brooklyn, NY. E Aug 62. C Jul 1: wounded in the head. D Aug 1.

---

[207] **After four years**, Marine Corp Lieutenant Colonel Chuck Ikins succeds in 2002 in convincing the Gettysburg National Military Park Service that it was his great-great-great-uncle, Private Simon Ikins, buried in this grave, not J. C. Kent. A July 13, 2003 Washington Post article details how Ikins, through battlefield hospital records, was able to document how "SIkins" became "JCKens" and finally "J.C. Kent."

[208] **Color Sergeant's death**. Death of Sergeant William Clark had been designated the color sergeant for the regiment in October 62. It is likely that he was still serving in this role when he was mortally wounded at Gettysburg.

[209] **Horrific posterior-entry gunshot wound**. In battle, civil war soldiers strained never to be wounded in the back, as such injuries could denote the cowardice of a soldier who has turned and attempted to run away from an engagement. When he was accepted into Camp Letterman Hospital on August 8, 1863, Davis Smith had a particularly injurious gunshot wound that had entered just to the left of the lower lumbar vertebral column and penetrated through the rectum and into the bladder. Nevertheless, Davis had been felt to be doing well until the morning of September 4th when he excreting considerable amounts of urine mixed with pus. He would then die on September 8th.

[210] **Minor at death.** An Ancestry.com public family tree places William Dwyer's birth year as 1846. This birthyear agrees with William's reported ages of 4 and 14 on the successive August 1850 and June 1860 U.S. Census sheets and attests to the likelihood that he was 16, not 18 at his August 1862 enlistment. This birthyear also means that William was only 17 when he would be would be mortally wounded in the head at Gettysburg.

ID	Name	Age	Unit	Details
R4#125	F M STOWELL FRANCIS STOWELL	~21	70 Inf D	B ~1842. E Jun 61 private. Promoted to sergeant on 5/26/63. C Jul 2: severe wound to left leg→amp. D Aug 3.
R4#126	H W DALE HORACE W DALE	20	3 ME Inf C	B 4/16/1843 Richmond, Sagadahoc Co., ME. R Gardiner, Kennebec Co., ME. Occ farm laborer. E Jun 61 private. D Jul 2 of wounds.
R5#9	LEVI RUST[211]	54-55	150 Inf A	B 1808 Standford, Dutchess Co., NY. R Dutchess Co., NY. Occ farm laborer. E Aug 62 private. KIA Jul 3. Survivor (WC11556): W Jane 53 (Oct 42); no chn.
R5#10	BARNARD C BURNETT[212]	53-54	150 Inf G	B 1809 La Grange, Dutchess Co., NY. R Fishkill, Dutchess Co., NY. Occ carpenter. E Sep 62 priv. Promotion to corporal during service. Reduction back to private 3/27/63 for an unspecified infraction. KIA Jul 3. Survivors (WC26902): W Maria 44 in 1864 (M Oct 39); 5 chn: 3 ♂- John 23, Orlando 15, James 14 & 2 ♀- Mary 21, Hannah 8 (only James and Hannah, both being under 16, earn their mother a supplemental $2 monthly addition to her pension).
R5#11	CHARLES HOWGATE	47	150 Inf A	B 3/3/16 England. R Poughkeepsie, Dutchess Co., NY. Occ painter. E Sep 62 private. KIA Jul 3. Survivor (WC13348): W Hannah 46 (M Sep 37); no live chn.
R5#12	GEORGE MABEE (MN WASHINGTON)	34-35	137 Inf D	B ~1828 Andes, Delaware Co., NY. R Van Etten, Chemung Co., NY. Occ carpenter. E Aug 62 private. KIA Jul 3. Survivors (WC12402): W Sarah 22 (M Nov 60); 2 ♂- Judd 2, George 16 weeks.
R5#14	A WALLACE ALONZO WALLACE	28-29	111 Inf A	B ~1834 NY. R Marion, Wayne Co., NY. E Jul 62 private. KIA Jul 62. Survivor (WC22947 not online): W Mary (age?| M?).
R5#15	W BROWN WILLIAM EDWARD BROWN[213]	21	111 Inf H	B 3/12/1842 Sterling, Cayuga Co., NY. R Cayuga Co., NY. Occ farmer. E Jul 62 private. Captured and paroled on 9/15/62 at Harper's Ferry, VA. KIA Jul 2: shot in the head. Survivor (WC13507): W Harriet 19 (M Jul 60| ReM 1865).

---

[211] **Overaged at enlistment**. At his August 30, 1862 enlistment, Levi Rust claimed he was 45 years old, the targeted upper-age limit for being accepted into the army. However, Levi Rust's reported ages of 42 and 52 in the successive 1850 and 1860 U.S. Censuses are in agreement with one family heritage source reporting a birthyear of 1808. At likely age 54 or 55, Levi was one of the oldest soldiers killed at Gettysburg. As an aside, a FindAGraave.com posting reports that Levi Rust was killed by the same minié ball that killed his company mate John Wing.

[212] **Overaged at enlistment**. At his September 22, 1862 enlistment, Barnard Burnett claimed that he was 40 years old. However, his reported age of 51 for the 1860 U.S. Census means that he was likely 53 or 54 when he was killed at Gettysburg.

[213] **Twice-widowed, sixty-four-year-old woman seeks restitution of military pension given up forty-five years in the past.** Mrs. Harriet Brown married Albert Mann in January 1865, or 18 months after William Brown had been killed at Gettysburg. In 1908 or four years after Albert Mann had died, Mrs. Harriet Mann, then 64-years-old, applied under the Pension Act of April 19, 1908 for be returned to the pension roll. Unfortunately, for Mrs. Mann, a stipulation of this Act had been that a war widow not have remarried prior to the passage of the Act. Hence her application was rejected.

R5#16	J MORGAN JOSEPH MORGAN[214]	21-22	111 Inf H	B ~1841 Cayuga Co., NY. E (Ira, Cayuga Co., NY) Jul 62 private. D Jul 2: GSW to head. Survivor (WC22947 not online): W Mary (age?| M?).
R5#17	JAMES CULLEN	~23	42 Inf F	B ~1840. E (NYC) Jul 61 private. Departed from camp 5/22/62 to report to the hospital and deemed a deserter when he did not return at the end of hospital muster 8/31/62. Returned to duty 10/23/62. KIA Jul 3.
R5#18	JOHN SMITH	~35	42 Inf D	B ~1828. E (Long Island, NY) Jun 61 private. July/Aug 62: absent, sick in hospital. KIA Jul 3.
R5#19	THOMAS BARREN	~35	42 Inf D	B ~1828. E (Long Island, NY) Jun 61 private. Wounded and captured on 9/17/62 at Antietam. Paroled on 9/18/62. KIA Jul 3: killed instantly by shell wound to the abdomen.
R5#20	JOHN ENOSENSE JOHN **ENOSENS**	22-23	59 Inf A	B ~1840 Germany. Occ farmer. E (NYC) Sep 61 private. KIA Jul 3.
R5#21	SERGT M DECKER **MINARD** DECKER[215]	38-39	80 Inf C	B ~1824 Berne, Albany Co., NY. R Shandaken, Ulster Co., NY. Occ farmer. E Sep 61 private. Wounded at 2nd Bull Run on 8/30/62. Nov 62: hospitalized in Washington, D. C. Promotion to corporal in Nov 62. Promoted to sergeant on 4/13/63. KIA Jul 3. Survivors (WC17004): W Catherine 37 (M Jan 51); 4 ♀- Mary 8, Alice 5, Lodema 3, Idella 1.
R5#22	SERGT L H DECKER[216] LUCIUS H DECKER	29-30	80 Inf K	B ~1833 Prattsville, Greene Co., NY. Occ farmer. E (Pine Hill, Ulster Co., NY) Sep 61 private. Promoted to sergeant on 9/17/61. KIA Jul 3.
R5#23	JAMES GALLAGHER[217]	34-35	82 Inf F	B ~1828 Ireland. Occ Tailor. E (NYC) Sep 62 private. KIA Jul 3. Survivors (WC119393): W Ann 35 (M Apr 49| D 10/19/64); 4 chn: 3 ♀-Margaret 8, Mary 6, Charlotte 21 months & 1 ♂- George 3.
R5#24	J L HALLECK JAMES LEANDER **HALLOCK**	20	80 Inf G	B 12/7/1842 Greenville, Greene Co., NY. R same. Occ farmer. E Sep 61 private. KIA Jul 3: GSW to the heart.

---

214 **Possible alias**. There is no genealogical footprint of this named individual, raising the possibility that this name was an alias.

215 **Purported brothers buried side-by-side**. A family genealogy posting postulates that Minard and Lucius Decker, buried next to each other, were brothers.

216 **Purported brothers buried side-by-Side**. A family genealogy posting postulates that Lucius and Minard Decker, buried next to each other, were brothers.

217 **Soldier killed-in-action July 3rd, then his widow dies fifteen month later, orphaning the couple's four young children.** Mrs. Ann Gallagher would die in October 1864 of tuberculosis, a very prevalent killer of adults and particularly young children in 19th century America.

R5#25	T D HAWKIN THOMAS D **HAWKINS**	33-34	111 Inf E	B ~1829. R Wayne Co., NY. R Macedon, Wayne Co., NY. E Aug 62 private. KIA Jul 3. Survivors (WC83111): W Elsia 28 (M Jan 56); 2 chn: 1 ♀- Sonia & 1 ♂- Alfred 2.
R5#26	H W ROBERTS HENRY W **ROBERTS**	18-19	111 Inf E	B ~1844 NY. 1860 R: Phelps, Ontario Co., NY. E Jul 62 private. KIA Jul 3.
R5#27	CORP GEO BLACHALL GEORGE **BLACKALL**	19-20	136 Inf G	B ~1843 Ireland. Occ student. E (Avon, Livingston Co., NY) Aug 62 corporal. KIA Jul 2.
R5#28	WILIAM WHITMORE[218]	~17	111 Inf E	B ~1846 NY. E Aug 62 private. KIA Jul 3.
R5#29	JOHN CRIPPS	28-29	111 Inf A	V ~1834 Albany, NY. Occ farmer. E (Arcadia, Wayne Co., NY) Aug 62. Captured and paroled on 9/15/62 at Harper's Ferry. KIA Jul 3.
R5#31	CORP A G McAFEE ARCHIBALD G **McAFEE**	28-29	111 Inf A	B ~1834 Canada. Occ farmer. E (Palmyra, Wayne Co., NY) Jul 62 private. Captured and paroled on 9/15/62 at Harper's Ferry. Jan/Feb 63: promotion to corporal during service. KIA Jul 3.
R5#32	D McGILL DAVID **McGILL**	23-24	10 Inf A	B ~1839 NYC. R same. Occ machinist. E Oct 61 private. Presumed MIA after Battle of Gaines' Mill on 6/27/62, but then confirmed hospitalized. Transferred to Germantown Hospital on 8/28/62. Present on Sep/Oct 62 muster with regiment. KIA Jul 3.
R5#33	WILLIAM H CROSS	34-35	61 Inf G	B ~1828 Ireland. Occ laborer. R NYC. E Oct 62 private. C Jul 2: wound to right leg →amp. D Jul 13. Survivor (WC36776): W Mary 35 in 1864 (M Jan 62); no chn.
R5#34	____ Conrad CONRAD **SCHMIDT**	~25	82 Inf C	B 1838 Germany. R NYC. Occ tailor. E Jan 63 private. C Jul 3. D Jul 10.
R5#35	LIEUT F K GARLAND FRANKLIN KELLOGG **GARLAND**	23	61 Inf A	B 4/19/1840 Sherburne, Chenango Co., NY. R same. Occ merchant. E Oct 62 sergeant. May/Jun 62: absent with typhoid symptoms, hospitalization→ 6/19/62 furlough. Promoted to sergeant major 11/1/62. Commissioned 2nd lieutenant on 4/5/63. C Jul 2: GSW through left lung. D Jul 4. Survivors (WC50541): M Mrs. Martha Garland 59 in 1864 (Erasmus Garland reported a "confirmed inebriate").

---

218 **Minor at death**. The August 4, 1860 U.S. Census report for Arcadia, NY shows William Whitmore at age 14. If this age report is accurate, William was 16, not 18 at his August 1862 enlistment in Arcadia. It would also mean that William was no older than 17 when he was killed in action on July 3rd. Interestingly, an Ancestry.com family tree gives William's birthdate as February 1847, which if accurate would mean William was 16 when he was killed.

R5#36	CORP AMOS COGSWELL (MN NATHANIEL)	25	76 Inf F	B 11/5/1837 Orwell, Oswego Co., NY. R same. Occ farmer. E Sep 61 into 24th NY Infantry, private. Transferred to 76th infantry on 5/13/63, corporal. C Jul 1: wounded in right lung. D Jul 13.
R5#37	JOHN H PHILIPS	20-21	95 Inf F	B ~1842 Haverstraw, Rockland Co., NY. R Rockland Co., NY. Occ shoemaker. E Oct 61 private. Hospitalized in Washington, D.C. Sep/Oct 62→Jan 63 for an unspecified condition. C Jul 1: shot through the head. D Jul 4.
R5#40	SERGT P RINBOLDT PETER **REINBOLD**	~34	39 Inf B	B ~1829 Germany. Occ baker. E (NYC) May 61 private. Promoted to corporal on 7/1/61. Captured and paroled on 8/15/62 at Harper's Ferry. Promoted to sergeant on 10/17/62. C Jul 2: shot in the thigh. D Aug 2.
R5#41	AUGUST ELLINBERGER CHARLES AUGUSTUS **ELLENBERGER**[219]	20	59 Inf H	B 5/19/1843 Dover, Tuscarawas Co., OH. E (Mansfield, Richland Co., OH) Sep 61 private. C Jul 3: friendly-fire wound to left elbow by soldier to his rear attempting to fire over his left shoulder. D Aug 1. Survivor (WC26177): M Mrs. Louisa Ellenberger 47 (widow of Christian Ellenberger).
R5#42	SERGT JOHN LARKINS JOHN **LARKIN**	~22	82 Inf E	B ~1841 NYC. Occ printer. E Apr (NYC) 61 private. Mar/Apr 62: promotion to corporal. Promoted to sergeant on 2/28/63. C Jul 3: GSW to chest. D Jul 31. Survivor (WC134723): F Michael Larkin F 59 in 1866 (affirmed infirmities).
R5#43	PETER WEST	23-24	42 Inf K	B ~1839. E (NYC) Aug 61 private. Captured on 10/21/61 at Ball's Bluff. Paroled 2/23/62 at Newport News, VA. Nov 62: sent for hospitalization in Alexandria, VA. C Jul 3: severely wounded in right leg→amp. D Jul 23 or 24.
R5#44	WILLIAM M STUART	29-30	82 Inf C	B ~1833 Scotland. E (NYC) Sep 61 private. C Jul 2: wounded in side. D Jul 8.
R5#45	JOHN BLACKMAN	19	86 Inf I	B 9/24/1843 Campbell, Steuben Co., NY. R same. 1860 occ: farm laborer on father's farm. E Sep 61 corporal. Reduced to private 10/9/61 for an unspecified infraction. C Jul 2: wounded in head. D Jul 5.
R5#46	JAMES PARTINGTON[220]	22	124 Inf I	B 12/10/1840 England. Occ laborer. E (Newburgh, Orange Co., NY) Aug 62 private. C Jul 2: wound to spine. D Jul 8. Survivor (WC14766): Mrs. Hannah McGraw (fraudulent applicant).

---

219 **Friendly fire death**. Charles Augustus Ellenberger was severely wounded in the left elbow by fire from a soldier in his rear who had been attempting to fire over Ellenberger's left shoulder. He was wounded July 3rd and would die August 1st.

220 **Caretaker's arrest for pension fraud**. On May 7, 1872, Mrs. Hannah McGraw was arrested on a charge of using the alias of Hannah Partington to fraudulently obtain a mother's pension in 1864. Mrs. McGraw offered the defense that she had taken charge of James after the death of his mother and when he was only a few weeks old, but that she had never sought to legally adopt him.

R5#47	JOHN CARRIGAN JOHN **CARREGIN**[221]	28-29	86 Inf I	B ~1834 NY. 1860: R Bethel, Sullivan Co., NY; occ laborer. E Oct 61 private. C Jul 2: wounded in left forearm causing a fracture. D Jul 15. Survivors (WC39938): W Cornelia 18 (M 6/19/60| Died 5 /17/64); 1 ♀- Orpha 21 months.
R5#48	IRA W ROSS	24-25	86 Inf B	B ~1838 Ontario Co., NY. Occ farmer. E (Elmira, Chemung Co., NY) Aug 62 private. C Jul 2: wounded in left lung. D Aug 1.
R5#49	WALTER GLOOBSON WALTER **GLADSEN**	27-28	40 Inf K	B ~1835 Delaware Co., NY. R same. Occ farmer. E Sep 61 into 101st NY infantry as private. May/Jun 62: absent, sick in Mt. Pleasant USA General Hospital in Washington, D.C. Detailed extra duty pay 6/21-22/62 as hospital nurse. Promoted to sergeant on 8/10/62. Transferred to 37th NY infantry on 12/24//62 with reduction of rank. Promotion back to sergeant on 5/24/63. Transferred to 40th NY infantry on 5/25/63. C Jul 2: severe wounds in arm and leg. D Aug 1.
R5#50	WILLIAM MORGAN	20	126 Inf K	B 11/28/1842 Wales. 1860 R: Seneca, Ontario Co., NY. Occ farmer. E Jul 62 private. Captured 9/15/62 and paroled 9/16/62 at Harper's Ferry. C Jul 2: wounded in arm →amp. D Jul 19. Survivor (WC140241); M Mrs. Ann Morgan 62 in 1869 (widow of Evan Morgan).
R5#51	G HUSKEY **GOTTLOB HERSCHE** or HIRSCHE	~22	72 Inf A	B ~1841 NY. E (NYC) Jun 61 private. Captured on 5/5/62 at Williamsburg, VA. Paroled on 5/11/62. Jul/Aug 62: $5 to be deducted from his pay as a reward offered and paid for his recovery as a deserter. C Jul 2: wounded in both feet. D Jul 26.
R5#52	WILSON M MOLLOY WILSON M **MALLOY**	22-23	73 Inf C	B ~1840 Troy, Rensselaer Co., NY. Occ clerk. E (NYC) Dec 62 private. C Jul 2: wounded in the left side. D Jul 2 or 6.
R5#53	LIEUT GEO DENNEN GEORGE PRATT **DENNAN**	25-26	73 Inf C	B ~1837 NYC. Occ stairs builder. E (NYC) Aug 61 sergeant. Promoted to 1st sergeant on 12/15/62. Commissioned 2nd lieutenant on 5/29/63. C Jul 2: wounded in left leg→amp. D Jul 11. Survivor (WC137229): F Thomas Dennan 63 in 1868 (dependent due to chronic rheumatism and old age).
R5#54	GEORGE ANDREWS GEORGE W **ANDERSON**	23	73 Inf B	B 4/13/1840 Staten Island, NY. E (Long Island, NY) Aug 61 private. Promoted to corporal on 5/5/62. C Jul 2: shell wound to thigh→amp. D Jul 5, 17 or 24.
R5#55	ALFRED G ARMES ALFRED G **ARMS**	19-20	71 Inf H	B ~1843 VT. 1860: R Clarksville, Allegany Co|, NY; occ: farm laborer on father's farm. E Jul 61 private. Present as corporal on 4/10/63 muster. KIA Jul 2.

---

221 **Soldier's death in July is followed by death of his widow ten months later, orphaning the couple's 3-year-old daughter.** The death of John Carregin's widow, Mrs. Jane Carregin, on May 17, 1864 meant that the couple's 3-year-old daughter, Orpha, have her guardianship determined through a court proceeding.

R5#56	SERGT G E SMITH GEORGE L SMITH	~22	120 Inf G	B ~1841 Chelsea, Orange Co., VT. Occ farmer. E (Kingston, Ulster Co., NY) Jul 62 private. Promoted to sergeant on 8/22/62. Promoted to 1st sergeant on 3/1/63. KIA Jul 2.
R5#57	DANIEL CAUTY DANIEL **CANTY**	~37	71 Inf C	B ~1826 Ireland. R NYC. Occ brick layer. E May 61 corporal. Reduced in rank to private on 6/30/61 due to "incompetency." Sep 62: reported AWOL. C Jul 2. D Jul 6. Survivor (WC70810): W May 46 (M Nov 53); no chn.
R5#58	CORP J A THOMPSON JOHN ALFORD THOMPSON[222]	28-29	4 Indpt Batty NY LA	B ~1834 NYC. R Brooklyn, NY. Occ showcase maker. E Sep 61 private. Promoted to corporal on 10/15/61. Detailed 8/9/62 on recruiting service. KIA Jul 2. Survivors (WC23232): W Emelia 27 (M May 56| ReM 1865): 3 chn: 1 ♂- William 3 & 1 ♀- Emma 8 and 6-months pregnant with ♀- Lilly (B 8/28/63).
R5#59	JAMES HIGGINS[223] 70 Inf I **JOHN** HIGGINS		→	James Higgins of 70th Infantry Company A was not killed at Gettysburg [B ~1839. E May 61 into 2nd NY Infantry Company H. Transferred to 70th NY Infantry Company G in May 63. KIA Jul 2 (age ~24)].
R5#60	JACOB RAISCH	38-39	125 Inf I	B ~1824 Germany. R Troy, Rensselaer Co., NY. 1860 occ: iron rolling mill worker. E Aug 62 private. Captured 9/15/62 and paroled 9/16/62 at Harper's Ferry. C Jul 2. D Jul 5. Survivors (WC14120): W Mary 40 (M Oct 48): 3 chn: 2 ♂- John 14, Jacob 12 & 1 ♀- Mary 4.
R5#61	J F McCORMICK JOHN **T** McCORMICK	20-21	10 Inf D	B ~1842 NYC. Occ clerk. E (NYC) Aug 62 private. C Jul 2: shot in abdomen. D Jul 3 or 4. Survivor (WC19590): M Mrs. Rosanna McCormick 50 (widow of Thomas McCormick).
R5#62	WILLIAM N NORRIS (MN NELSON)	27-28	44 Inf C	B ~1835 Yates Co., NY. R Barrington, Yates Co., NY. Occ farmer. E Sep 62 private. C Jul 2: wound to right knee→amp. D Jul 22.

---

222 **Soldier's widow bears couple's third child eight weeks after he is killed at Gettysburg.** Eight weeks after John Thompson was killed at Gettysburg, his wife Emelia back in Williamsburg neighborhood bore their 3rd child, Emelia.

223 **Identity conundrum.** James Higgins of the 70th NY Infantry Company A was not killed at Gettysburg but went on join the Veterans Volunteers Corps in December 1863. Both an Ancestry.com Civil War Soldier Records and Profiles page and a FindAGrave.com memorial page are among Internet sites that posit that John Higgins, who was a member of the 70th NY Company G and who was killed at Gettysburg, is in fact the soldier buried here. However, the fact that there was a James Higgins in the 70th NY Infantry, matching the inscription on this grave, must raise the possibility that this is simply a misidentified soldier who might have been found buried with some item carrying the name of James Higgins.

R5#64	JOSEPH LAROOST JOSEPH **LAROUCHE**	44-45	140 Inf H	B ~1818 Canada. R Rochester, Monroe Co., NY. Occ stone cutter. E Aug 62 into 13th NY Infantry as a private. Transferred to 140th NY on 6/26/63. C Jul 2: wounded in right side of the head and causing a paralysis of the left side of his body. D Jul 8. Survivors (WC21500): W Celia 44 (M Sep 43); 3 chn: (2 non-dependent ♀- Josephine ~20, Cecelia ~16) and 1 ♂- Joseph 7.
R5#65	EZRA HYDE	27	146 Inf B	B Nov 1835 Annsville, Oneida Co., NY. R same. Occ farmer. E Aug 62 private. C Jul 2: severely wounded in left shoulder or arm→amp. D Jul 24. Survivor (WC16086): M Mrs. Deborah 57 Hyde (widow of Asa Hyde).
R5#67	P TILLBURY PARLEY **TILBURY**	45-46	137 Inf B	B ~1817 Union, Broome Co., NY. R Vestal, Broome, Co., NY. Occ farmer. E Jul 62 private. C Jul 2: wounded in abdomen. D Jul 7 or 8. Survivors (WC34387): W Jane 49 (M May 40); 6 chn: 2 ♂- John 15, Edward 6 & 4 ♀- Alice 21, Catharine 20, Rebecca 12, Nancy 9.
R5#68	CAPT J N WARNER REMOVED			Removed to Woodhull Cemetery, Woodhull, Steuben Co., NY.
R5#69	CHARLES ROSEBILL CHARLES **ROSEBILLE**	18-19	119 Inf H	B ~1844 Queens Co., NY. Occ farmer. E (Hempstead, Nassau Co., NY) Aug 62 private. C Jul 1: wounded in the back. D Jul 12.
R5#70	JOHN PAUGH	42-43	154 Inf I	R ~1820 Montague, Sussex Co., NJ. R Hinsdale, Cattaraugus Co., NY. Occ farmer. E Sep 62 private. C Jul 1: wounded in right thigh. D Jul 16. Survivors (WC83676): W Almira 34 in 1865 (M Feb 51); 4 ♀- Catharine 12, Susan 9, Emma 8, Almira 6.
R5#71	HENRY MILLER HENRY **MULLER**	~21	141 Inf B	B ~1842 Germany. Occ cigar maker. E (NYC) Jun 61 private. C Jul 2: wounded in right hip. D Aug 4.
R5#72	M A CULVER MILES A CULVER	40	157 Inf C	B 2/9/1823 Pompey, Onondaga Co., NY. R Harford, Courtland Co., NY. Occ farmer. E Aug 62 private. C Jul 1: wounded in left lung. D Jul 15 or 16. Survivors (WC23530→WC179261 neither online): W Caroline ~38 (M Oct 47 | ReM 1877); 6 chn: 3 ♂- Millard 14, Charles 12, Lewis 5 & 3 ♀- Harriet 10, Laura 8, Caroline 4 months.
R5#73	PETER LINCK PETER **LINK**[224]	29-30	134 Inf K	B ~1833 Germany. R Schenectady, Schenectady Co., NY. Occ brickmaker, farmer. E Sep 62 private. C Jul 1: wounded in left hip. D Jul 10.

---

[224] **Brickmaker ironically killed in "Brickyard Fight."** There is tragic irony here in that Peter Link, a one-time brickmaker, would be mortally injured in the July 1st Gettysburg action referred to as the "Brickyard fight." The Brickyard fight occurred in John Kuhn's brickmaking lot northeast to the center of town. The fight entailed the catastrophic loss of the Union regiments that had been sent forward in a delaying action to allow retiring regiments from the morning July 1st action to move to Cemetery Hill. One celebrated casualty of the Brickyard fight was Sergeant Amos Humiston.

R5#74	GEORGE RODELOFF GEORGE **ROTHLAUF**	27-28	119 Inf E	B ~1835 Germany. Occ painter, tinner. E (NYC) Aug 62 private. 1863: promotion to corporal. C Jul 1: wounded in right leg. D Jul 9 or 10.
R5#75	J F CHACE JAMES FRANKLIN **CHASE**[225]	24	154 Inf D	B 11/5/1838 Franklin Co., VT. R Lyndon, Cattaraugus Co., NY. Occ farmer. E Sep 62 private. Jan→May 63: absent, sick in Washington, D.C. hospital for an unspecified condition. C Jul 1: injurious bullet wound entering just above the base of the penis and causing oozing excrement from this entrance wound and a posterior exit wound. D Jul 31. Survivors (WC46204): W Mariah 21 in 1864 (M Jan 60| ReM 1867); 1 ♀- Caroline 16 months.
R5#76	BENJAMIN BRICE BENJAMIN B **BICE**	23-24	134 Inf A	B ~1839 Middleburgh, Schoharie Co., NY. R Schenectady, Schenectady Co., NY. Occ shoemaker. E Aug 62 private. Promoted to 1st sergeant on 9/22/62. Absent in hospital with unspecified condition: Oct 62→Apr 63. Return to duty on 4/21/63. Reduction in rank to private on 3/1/63. C Jul 1: Wound to left shoulder. D Jul 31. Survivors (WC26368): W Mary 20 (M Dec 59| ReM 1867): 2 ♂- William 2, Benjamin 8 months.
R5#77	CORP P BEVER PETER **BEAVER** *or* **BEVER**	29-30	134 Inf K	B ~1833 Germany. R Schenectady, Schenectady Co., NY. Occ laborer (1860 occ: broom maker). E Aug 62 private. Promoted to corporal on 3/24/63. C Jul 1: wounded in the small of back. D Jul 10 or 11.
R5#78	SERGT A WILLMAN (ALIAS) **CARL FRIEDRICH WILLMANN**[226]	37-38	54 Inf F	B ~1825 Germany. R NYC. Occ iron worker. E Dec 61 private. Promoted to corporal on 7/20/62. Oct 62: wounded, sick in the hospital. Promoted to 1st sergeant on 10/30/62. C Jul 1: wounded in left thigh. D Jul 10. Survivors (WC71406): W Adolfine 37 (M Dec 54); 1 ♂- William 9.
R5#79	THOMAS HALEY	23-24	157 Inf E	B ~1839 Ireland. Occ cooper. E (Cortlandville, Cortland Co., NY) Aug 62 private. Nov/Dec 62: hospitalized at Fairfax Courthouse, VA. C Jul 1: wounded in thigh→ amp. D Jul 12 or 15.
R5#80	GEORGE CONNER GEORGE W CONNER	18-19	157 Inf D	B ~1844 Courtland Co., NY. 1860: R Scott, Courtland Co., NY. Occ farmer. E Aug 62 private. C Jul 1: wounded in hip. D Jul 20.
R5#81	BROUGHTON HOUGH	25-26	157 Inf K	B ~1837 Chautauqua Co., NY. Occ farmer. E (Marathon, Cortland Co., NY) Aug 62 private. C Jul 1: wounded in left hip. D Jul 13.

---

225 **Father arrives at Gettysburg to find his son already dead.** James Chase, James F Chace's father, came to Gettysburg to see his son in the hospital camp. Sadly, he arrived just the day after his son had died from a torturing wound and been buried. As the family oral history recalls, the father was left to experience his grieving at the site of his son's fresh grave.

226 **Soldier fighting under an alias.** Carl Willmann's widow reported in her pension application that her husband never informed her that he was joining the army until he had already been mustered into his regiment, furthermore employing alias of Henry Willmann.

R5#82	GEORGE HALBRING GEORGE **HALBING**	26-27	119 Inf G	B ~1836 Germany. R NYC. Occ stone cutter. E Aug 62 private. Mar/Apr 63: duty as company cook. C Jul 1. D Jul 5.
R5#83	HENRY LIMERICK	35-36	136 Inf F	B ~1827 Ireland. R Mount Morris, Livingston Co., NY. Occ tailor. E Aug 62 private. C Jul 2. D Jul 5 or 8.
R5#84	CORP J JOHNSOTN JERRY **JOHNSON**	~25	157 Inf C	B ~1838 Cincinnatus, Cortland Co., NY. R same. Occ shoemaker. E Jul 62 corporal. C Jul 1. D Jul 1 or 6.
R5#85	J B CHURCH JONATHAN B CHURCH	40-41	147 Inf F	B ~1822 Onondaga Co., NY. R Palermo, Oswego Co., NY. Occ farmer. E Aug 62 private. C Jul 1: shot hitting and fracturing hip. D Jul 27. Survivors (WC21035): W Caroline 30 (M Oct 58); 3 ♂- George 14, Frederick 2, Charles 5 months.
R5#86	C E DAY CHARLES E DAY[227]	22-23	94 Inf D	B ~1840 NY. R Lancaster, Erie Co., NY. Occ coal dealer. E Oct 62 private. Absent beyond the 10-day furlough which began 4/25/63. Captured Jul 1, he asked to attend to the sick and wounded and to aid in burying the dead. D Jul 12 of typhoid fever. Survivors (WC28276); W Angeline 20 (M Dec 60); 1 ♂- Abner ~4 months old at his father's death and would die at one year old.
R5#87	SERGT A W SWART ABRAHAM W SWART	20-21	80 Inf I	B ~1842 Ulster Co., NY. R same. Occ farm laborer. E Sep 61 corporal. Rank of sergeant at his death is not confirmed. C Jul 1: wound to right thigh→amp. D Jul 25. Survivor (WC47513): M Mrs. Sarah Bemis 55 in 1864 (widow of Abram Swart; abandoned by 2nd husband Lewis Bemis around 1858).
R5#88	J GLAIR, JR JOHN **GLAIRE**, JR	18-19	94 Inf D	B ~1844. R Elma, Erie Co., NY. E (Amherst, Erie Co., NY) Nov 62 private. C Jul 1. D Jul 2 or 3.
R5#89	JOHN GLAIR 101 Inf B JOHN **GLANZ**	27-28	124 Inf B	B ~1835 Germany. Occ laborer. E Aug 62 private. C Jul 2: wounded hand. Death at Gettysburg not confirmed in personal service record.
R5#90	HORACE BURGESS	29-30	104 Inf D	B ~1833 Genesee, Allegany Co., NY. R Springwater, Livingston Co., NY. Occ farmer. E Oct 61 private. C Jul 1: GSW to left shoulder and exiting the breast. D Jul 4 or 6. Survivors (WC88960): W Helen 26 (M Jul 56| ReM 1866): 2 ♂- Eugene 6, Joseph 3.

---

227 **Soldier overstays his home furlough on visit to see his first-born son.** Charles Day would overstay a 10-day furlough granted him in April 63. Likely, this furlough had been requested so that he could visit his first child, Abner, born in March 1863. Returning to the army, Charles Day would be captured by Confederates on Jul 1st. Likely his conscientiousness led him to request of his captors that he be allowed to tend to the sick and wounded and to aid in burying the unburied Union dead. Carrying out these tasks, Charles Day would contract typhoid fever and die on July 12. Meanwhile, back in his home in Lancaster, New York, his newborn, Abner Day, would die before he reached the age of one year.

R5#91	SERGT F E MUNSEN FREDERICK **MUNSON**	27-28	97 Inf D	B ~1835 Salisbury, Herkimer Co., NY. Occ farmer. E (Salisbury, NY) Sep 61 corporal. Promoted to sergeant on 10/16/61. Wounded 8/30/62 at 2nd Bull Run. Returned to duty in Oct 62. KIA Jul 1.
R5#92	JAMES MAHONEY	39-40	147 Inf B	B ~1823 Ireland. R Oswego, Oswego Co., NY. Occ shoemaker. E Aug 62 private. KIA Jul 1. Survivors (WC86606): W Johanna 30 (M Nov 52| ReM 1866); 2 ♀- Mary 8, Margaret 6.
R5#93	SERGT H SANDERS HENRY SANDERS	25-26	94 Inf C	B ~1837 Claremont, Sullivan Co., NH. R Watertown, Jefferson Co., NY. Occ farmer, mechanic. E Oct 61 private. Promoted to corporal on 3/8/62. Promoted to sergeant on 2/27/63. Absent on furlough 4/10→4/17/63. C Jul 1: wounded in abdomen. D Jul 3. Survivors (WC76065): M Mrs. Esther Finney 58 (widow of Parley Sanders and 2nd husband Earl Finney affirmed disabled).
R5#94	J M BOUREN JOEL MORSE **BOUGHTON**	~24	154 Inf C	B ~1839 Greene, Chenango Co., NY. Occ painter. E (Olean, Cattaraugus Co., NY) Jul 62 corporal. KIA Jul 1.
R5#100	C W RADEU CHARLES W **RADUE**	23-24	Batty B 1 NY LA	B ~1839. E (Chicago, IL) Sep 62 private with the Chicago Battery. Joined Battery B 1st NY LA on 11/12/61 transfer from dissolved Chicago Battery. KIA Jul 3.
R5#102	JOHN FITZNER or JOHANN FITZNER	27-28	108 Inf F	B ~1835 Germany. R Greece, Monroe Co., NY. Occ farmer. E Aug 62 private. KIA Jul 3. Survivors (WC20531) W Elizabeth 22 (M Feb 61| ReM 1865); 2 ♀- Florinda 2, Mary 5 months.
R5#103	HENRY J DAVIS	23-24	125 Inf B	B ~1839 Troy, Rensselaer Co., NY. R same. Occ carpenter, Yankee Notions. E Aug 62 private. Captured 9/15 and paroled 9/16/62 at Harper's Ferry. C Jul 2. D Jul 2 or 3.
R5#104	EDWARD BEREN EDWARD **BEREAN**	35-36	125 Inf I	B ~1827 Catskill, Greene Co., NY. R Troy, Rensselaer Co., NY. Occ laborer. E Aug 62 private. Captured 9/15 and paroled 9/16/62 at Harper's Ferry. KIA Jul 3. Survivor (WC17000): W Abygail 41 (M Apr 49); no living children
R5#105	J O'BRIEN JOHN O'BRIEN	~44	82 Inf H	B ~1819 NYC. R NYC. Occ porter. E Jun 61 private. Wounded in Dec 62 at Fredericksburg. Promoted to corporal on 1/1/63. KIA Jul 2.
R5#106	D HAMMOND DEWITT CLINTON **HAMLIN**	18	80 Inf A	B 7/19/1844 Watertown, Jefferson Co., NY. R same. Occ: bell boy, clerk. E Sep 62 into 35th NY infantry a private. Transferred to 80th NY infantry on 5/18/63. May/Jun 63: on detached service at HQ and telegraph office. KIA Jul 1.

R5#107	LAFAYETTE BURNS	23-24	65 Inf D	B ~1839 Tiffin, Seneca Co., OH. 1860: R Big Spring, Seneca Co., OH; occ: school teacher. E Feb 62 into 65th NY Infantry (1st US Chasseurs) as private. For muster, he was forwarded from Cincinnati, OH. KIA Jul 3. Survivor: W Mary 28 (M Dec 53 | died 11/9/63); no chn.
R5#109	CORP D CASEY DANIEL CASEY[228]	~16	122 Inf G	B ~1847 Ireland. R Elbridge, Onondaga Co., NY. Occ farmer. E Aug 62 private (enlistment as minor certified by James Lynch, stepfather). Promoted to corporal 8/15/62. May 63: absent on fatigue duty at Potomac Creek Hospital. KIA Jul 3.
R5#110	WILLIAM RAYMOND	21-22	126 Inf B	B ~1841 Palmyra, Wayne Co., NY. Occ farmer. E (Milo, Yates Co., NY) Aug 62 private. Captured 9/15 and paroled 9/16/62 at Harper's Ferry. Feb→Mar 63: served as company cook. C Jul 2. D Jul 13.
R5#111	ASA PETTINGILL ASA **PETTENGILL**[229]	20-21	147 Inf F	B ~1842 Parish, Oswego Co., NY. R same. Occ farmer. E Aug 62 private. C Jul 1. D Jul 5. Survivors (WC38616): W Matilda 22 (M Aug 62); 9-week-old twin children- 1 ♀- Alza & 1 ♂- Aza.
R5#112	J STOWTENGER JOSEPH **STOUGHTENGER**	19	147 Inf G	B 7/13/1844 Oswego, Oswego Co., NY. R same. Occ farmer. E Sep 62 private. C Jul 1: severely wounded in leg→amp. D Jul 16.
R5#113	JAMES PFEIFFER 145 Inf E			Killed soldier with this name in this or any other regiments not found in military sources.
R5#116	JAMES GREY JAMES A **GRAY**	20-21	1 NY Indpt Batt LA	B ~1842 Ireland. Occ laborer. E (Auburn, Cayuga Co., NY) Nov 61 private. KIA Jul 3: wounded in head.
R5#117	EDWARD PETO	29-30	1 NY Indpt Batt LA	B ~1833 England. R Ledyard, Cayuga Co., NY. Occ laborer. E Oct 61 private. KIA Jul 3: reported nearly cut in two by shell or shell fragment hitting abdomen. Survivor (WC35453): W Jemima 27 in 1864 (M Sep 56| ReM 1868); no chn.
R5#118	R ELLOT PHILIP **ELLIOTT**	36-37	82 Inf D	B ~1826 Ireland. Occ hackman. E Sep 62 private. KIA Jul 3.

---

228 **Minor at death**. A Mr. James Lynch, representing himself as Daniel Casey's stepfather, accompanied Daniel at his August 7, 1862 army enlistment. Lynch likely thought he needed to be present to certify that Daniel was 18, particularly if the youthful appearance of his stepson tended to give the impression that he was considerably underaged. And in fact, the June 27, 1860 U.S. Census report for Onondaga County, New York gave Daniel's age as 13. Taking this Census age to be accurate, Daniel was probably 15, but no older than 16 when his stepfather accompanied him to the enlistment center. He would have been likely 16, but no older than 17 when he was killed in action on July 3rd. What remorse Daniel's stepfather might have felt we cannot know. However, he likely pocketed the entirety of Daniel's $100 enlistment bonus.

229 **Eleven-months-married soldier leaves behind twin nine-week-old infants**. On August 20, 1862, Asa Pettingill married Matilda Allen. One month later, on September 22, 1862, Pettingill left home to muster into the 147th New York Infantry. His death on July 5, 1863 would leave his wife of less than one year the care of their twin 9-week-old girl and boy. Asa Pettingill likely never saw his twins.

R5#119	SERGT T DEVINE THOMAS DEVINE	~34	82 Inf A	B ~1829 Ireland. Occ clerk. R West Hoboken, Hudson Co., NJ. Occ clerk. E (NYC) May 61 corporal. Promoted to 1st sergeant on 9/1/61. KIA Jul 3: struck by a solid shot. Survivors (WC47987): 2 chn: 1 ♂- William 10 & 1 ♀- Helen 8 (Mrs. Eliza Munson appointed guardian as mother Ann Devine had died 7/18/62).
R5#123	R E CLAFLIN			No killed Gettysburg soldier with this or similar name found in military sources.
R5#129	E F KRAUSE 19 Inf K			No killed Gettysburg soldier with this or similar name found in military sources.
R6#1	WILLIAM CRANSTON WILLIAM H CRANSTON (MN HENRY)	25-26	76 Inf A	B ~1837 NYC. 1860 R: Cohoes, Albany Co., NY. Occ mason. E (Watervliet, Albany Co., NY) Sep 62 into 30th NY infantry as a private. Transferred to 76th NY on 5/25/63. KIA Jul 1. Survivor (WC219475 not online) M Mrs. Catherine Cranston ~65 in 1880.
R6#6	SERGT CAREY 9 Inf F			No killed Gettysburg soldier with this name in this rank not found in military sources.
R6#8	AMASA TOFFING AMASA C **TOPPING**	32-33	157 Inf D	B ~1830 NY. R Preble, Courtland Co., NY. Occ farmer. E Aug 62 private. KIA Jul 1. Survivors (WC30385): W Francis 34 (M Feb 50); 1 ♂- Daniel 6.
R6#12	CORP P STONE PHILANDER STONE	34-35	157 Inf H	B ~1828 Tully, Onondaga Co., NY. R Truxton, Courtland Co., NY. Occ farmer. E Aug 62 private. Promoted to corporal on 1/3/63. Sick, sent in division hospital on 4/25/63. KIA Jul 1. Survivors (WC18335): W Lovina 29 (M Mar 51| ReM 1868); 3 chn: 2♀- Lucy 10, Frances 8 & 1 ♂- Charles 5.
R6#14	SERGT A HUMISTON AMOS HUMISTON[230]	33	154 Inf C	B 4/26/1830 Owego, Tioga Co., NY. R Portville, Cattaraugus Co., NY. Occ: former whaler, harness maker. E Jul 62 corporal. Promoted to sergeant on 1/25/63. D Jul 1 of wounds. Survivors (WC74921): W Philinda 33 in 1864 (M Jul 54| ReM 1869); 3 chn: 2 ♂- Franklin 8, Fred 4 & 1 ♀- Alice 4.

---

230 **Gettysburg Cemetery's most celebrated soldier**. The story of an unknown soldier choosing to view an ambrotype of his three young children as he lay mortally wounded would make Amos Humiston the most celebrated soldier buried in the National Cemetery. Contrary to what may commonly be believed, his identification was not accomplished by publishing copies of the ambrotype along with the unknown soldier's story in newspapers. Rather, newspapers, beginning first in Philadelphia and later picked up by other Northern newspapers, reported the story along accompanied by a description of the poses, dress, and presumed ages of the two boys and one girl. One of these newspaper accounts eventually made its way to a woman who knew Mrs. Philinda Humiston living in Portville, New York, knew that she had a husband in the army, and knew that the descriptions of the children could be hers. Shown this newspaper account, Mrs. Humiston confronted the likelihood that she was a widow. In the course of time, as news of the identification of Gettysburg's unknown soldier spread through Eastern newspapers, tremendous support poured forth for Mrs. Humiston. In 1866, Mrs. Humiston and her three children were relocated to Gettysburg at the opening of a new orphanage and widow's home. Three years later, Mrs. Humiston would marry a Methodist minister who had visited the orphanage and relocate with her children to his home in Massachusetts.

R6#15	_____ CHAMBURG JESSE P **CHAMBERLIN**[231]	40-41	134 Inf	B ~1822 NY. R Duanesburg, Schenectady Co., NY. E Aug 62 private. KIA Jul 1. Survivors (WC51002): W Huldah (M May 55 | died 11/28/63); 3 chn: twin ♂- Arthur and Oscar 7 & 1 ♀- Cornelia 5 (A Mr. Jacob White appointed guardian as their mother Huldah had died five months after their father).
R6#17	EDWARD VAN DYCK[232]	14	134 Inf C	B 9/21/1848 (he was **not** 18 as he was reported at enlistment, but one month short of turning 14) Prattsville, Greene Co., NY. Occ student. E Aug 62 private. KIA Jul 1.
R6#18	LEVI CARPENTER	21	64 Inf D	B 12/16/1841 Farmersville, Cattaraugus Co., NY. 1860 R: same. Occ farmer. E Oct 61 private. GSW to the arm on 6/1/62 at Fair Oaks, VA. Jun 62: absent in hospital. KIA Jul 2.
R6#19	HARRIS HUSEHELL HARRIS **HENSHEL**	20-21	40 Inf E	B ~1842 Germany. R Staten Island, NY. Occ cap maker. E Aug 61 into 55th NY infantry as a private. Transferred to the 38th NY infantry. Transferred into 40th NY infantry on 6/3/63. KIA Jul 2.
R6#20	CORP JOHN VAN ALSTYNE	35	150 Inf A	B 2/19/1828 Chatham, Columbia Co., NY. 1860 R: Chatham, Columbia Co., NY. Occ mechanic. E Sep 62 private. Promoted to corporal on 6/1/63. KIA Jul 3: instantly killed by GSW to the head. Survivors not known.
R6#21	JOHN P WING[233]	19-20	150 Inf A	B ~1843 Sharon, Litchfield Co., CT. R Amenia, Dutchess Co., NY. Occ farmer. E Aug 62 private. KIA Jul 3: shot in the chest.
R6#22	G ULMER GILBERT ULMER **JOHANN GOTTLIEB** ULMER	19	149 Inf B	B 8/11/1843 Germany. Occ cooper. E (Syracuse, Onondaga Co., NY) Aug 62 private. C Jul 3: wound to the head. D Jul 4.
R6#23	CORP W FOSTER WALLACE FOSTER	23	137 Inf C	B 6/27/1840 Oswego, Tioga Co., NY. R same. Occ farmer. E Aug 62 private. Promoted to corporal on 3/5/63. D Jul 3 of wounds.

---

231 **Soldier's death July 1st, followed by his widow's death five months later sends their three orphan children into a court-supervised guardianship proceeding.** Following the death of her husband, Jesse Chamberlin, Mrs. Hulda Chamberlin appears not to have completed the application process for her widow with dependent children's pensions before she herself died on November 28, 1863. By the next year, the 65-year-old Jacob H. White, also of Duanesburg, New York, had secured legal guardianship of the three Chamberlin children, in addition to entitlement to Chamberlin's $8 monthly service pension.

232 **Youngest identified soldier killed at Gettysburg— aged 14.** Edward Van Dyke's reported ages of 1 and 11 for the successive August 1850 and July 1860 U.S. Censuses are in agreement with his Dutch Reformed Church baptismal record citing a birthday of September 21, 1848. Hence, rather than being 18 when he enlisted as a private into the 134th NY regiment, Edward was actually just under 14. Whether Edward actually enlisted as a private or a drummer-musician, he remains the youngest documented soldier buried in the National Cemetery at age 14 years, 10 months and 20 days.

233 **Single minié ball kills two soldiers.** A FindAGrave.com memorial reports that John P. Wing was killed by the same minié ball that killed his company mate Levi Rust.

R6#24	SERGT C GRAY CHARLES GREY	~32	60 Inf I	B ~1831. E (Ogdensburg, St. Lawrence Co., NY) Jan 61 corporal. Promoted to sergeant during service. KIA Jul 3.
R6#25	P AYRES PHILETUS **AYERS**	20-21	60 Inf H	B ~1842 Chazy, Clinton Co., NY. Occ farmer. E (Ogdensburg, St. Lawrence Co., NY) Sep 61 private. Sent to hospital on 8/21/62. Returned to duty on 12/9/62. C Jul 2: wounds to brain and chest. D Jul 2 or 3.
R6#26	JAMES H MULLIN JAMES **MULLEN**	18-19	137 Inf B	B ~1844 Union Vale, Dutchess Co., NY. Occ laborer. E (Binghamton, Broome Co., NY) Sep 62 private. KIA Jul 2.
R6#27	JOHN CARNINE JOHN **CARMINE**[234]	45-46	137 Inf E	B ~1817 Montgomery Co., NY. R Union, Broome Co., NY. Occ farmer. E Aug 62 private. KIA Jul 2. Survivors (WC59957): W Lucinda 58 (M Feb 31); 1 dependent child under16- ♀- Harriet 13 and 4 older siblings- 1 ♀- Agnes 24 & 3 ♂- Edgar 21, Silas 19, Morris 17.
R6#28	BENJAMIN CLARK	18-19	137 Inf E	B ~1844 Danby, Tompkins Co., NY. 1860: R same; occ farm laborer on father's farm. E Aug 62 private. KIA Jul 2.
R6#29	SERGT H JOHNSON HENRY JOHNSON	22-23	137 Inf E	B ~1840 Lisle, Broome Co., NY. 1860 R: Warren, Herkimer Co., NY. Occ farmer. E Aug 62 private. Promoted to sergeant on 12/24/62. KIA Jul 2.
R6#30	HANNIBAL DORSET HANNIBAL **DOWNS**	31	60 Inf F	B 11/5/1831 Edwards, St. Lawrence Co., NY. R same. Occ farmer. E Sep 61 private. Oct 62: hospitalized at Washington, D.C. with an unspecified condition. Nov 62: detailed as guard at Harper's Ferry ordinance department. KIA Jul 3. Survivors (WC92113): W Lucretia 33 in 1864 (M Sep 57| ReM 1866): 2 ♀- Frances 6, Letta 2.
R6#31	HUGH MURPHY	~34	42 Inf G	B ~1829. E (Long Island, NY) Jun 61 private. Feb→Apr 63: working in regimental bakery. KIA Jul 2: ball to the left chest.
R6#32	PETER BRENTZEL PETER **BRENTZER**	~24	42 Inf I	B ~1839. E (NYC) Jun 61 private. Wounded on 6/30/62 towards end of the Seven Days' Battles at Glendale, VA. Mar/Apr 63: present on muster as corporal. KIA Jul 2: wounded in right temple.
R6#34	LIEUT R P HOLMES RUFUS P HOLMES	31	126 Inf G	B 3/13/1832 Lyons, Wayne Co., NY. Occ painter. E (Seneca, Ontario Co., NY) Jul 62 sergeant. Captured on 9/15/62 and paroled on 9/16/62 at Harper's Ferry. Promoted to 1st sergeant on 1/6/63. Commissioned 2nd lieutenant on 3/4/63. C Jul 2 or 3. D Jul 3 or 4.

---

[234] **Overaged at enlistment.** John Carmine's reported ages of 35 and 45 on the successive October 1850 and October 1860 U.S. Census sheets constitute good evidence that he was beyond the 45-year age-limit for voluntary enlistment.

R6#36	A McGILLORA ALEXANDER McGILLORA	40	111 Inf G	B 1/4/1823 Argyle, Washington Co., NY. Occ cooper. E (Auburn, Cayuga Co., NY) Aug 62 private. Captured and paroled on 9/15/62 at Harper's Ferry. KIA Jul 3: wounded in chest.
R6#37	G BEMIS GEORGE **BEMIS**[235]	25-26	111 Inf K	B ~1837 NY. Occ baker. E (Chicago, IL) Nov 62 private. Detailed as brigade teamster 2/15/63→3/12/63. KIA Jul 3: shell wound to head. Survivor (WC108806): M Mrs. Clarissa Bemis 52 in 1867 (widow of Timothy Bemis).
R6#38	ALBERT BRUNER ALBERT **BRUNNER**	27-28	1 NY Indpt Batt LA	B ~1835 Germany. Occ baker. E (NYC) Sep 62 into 2nd NY Independent Light Artillery as a private. Transferred to Company C 1st NY Independent Light Artillery on 6/6/63. C Jul 2: wound to right foot. D Aug 2.
R6#39	FRANKLIN COLE	27-28	61 Inf G	B ~1835 NY. Occ farmer. E (NYC) Oct 61 Private. Jan/Feb→Jun 62: sick with smallpox in Washington, D.C. hospital. C Jul 2: severe wound to left leg→amp. D Jul 13.
R6#40	JOHN F FANSSEN JOHN **TENNISON**	34-35	82 Inf K	B ~1828 Ireland. R NYC. Occ carpenter. E Jan 63 private. C Jul 3: wound to left leg. D Jul 19. Survivor (WC60579): W Mary 26 (M Aug 59); no surviving chn.
R6#42	DANIEL MAHONEY	22-23	69 Inf B	B ~1840 Ireland. R NYC. Occ blacksmith. E Sep 61 private. Wounded 5/31/62 at the Battle of Fair Oaks, VA. Rejoined company from hospital on 8/7/62. C Jul 2. D Jul 2 or 4. Survivor (WC24171): M Mrs. Johanna Mahoney 60 (widow of Thomas Mahoney).
R6#43	JOHN BURNS	44-45	59 Inf A	B ~1818 Ireland. Occ carpenter. E (NYC) Aug 61 private. Sep/Oct 61: sick in city hospital in NY. Jan/Feb 63→April 63: detailed to Brigade HQ. C Jul 2: skull fractured by artillery shell. D Jul 13.
R6#44	WILLIAM M STEWART WILLIAM **STUART**	29-30	82 Inf C	B ~1833 Scotland. Occ carpenter. E (NYC) Sep 61 private. C Jul 2: wounded in side. D Jul 4 or 8.
R6#45	DANIEL L CONFER	22-23	136 Inf I	B ~1840 West Sparta, Livingston Co., NY. Occ farmer. E (Nunda, Livingston Co., NY) Aug 62 private. KIA Jul 2 or 3. Survivor (WC121100): F Michael Confer 78 in 1868 (affirmed totally disabled widower of Elizabeth Confer).
R6#46	JOHN STOWELL (MN PRYOR)	18	136 Inf H	B 8/16/1844 Cuba, Allegany Co., NY. R same. Occ farmer. D Aug 62 private. C Jul 2. D Jul 4.

---

[235] **Soldier substituting for drafted soldier is killed.** George Bemis is recorded as joining the 111th NY infantry as a substitute for a Charles Gould.

R6#47	C C ELWELL CHARLES CHANDLER ELWELL	28-29	136 Inf H		B ~1834 Granville, Washington Co., NY. R Wethersfield, Wyoming Co., NY. Occ farmer. E Aug 62 private. KIA Jul 3. Survivors (WC17003): W Lucinda 24 (M Sep 56); 2 chn: 1 ♀- Emma 2 & 1 ♂- Charles 5 weeks.
R6#48	JAMES DORAN	24-25	136 Inf E		B ~1838 Ireland. R Covington, Wyoming Co. NY. Occ farmer. E Aug 62 private. KIA Jul 2 or 3. Survivor (WC36196): M Mrs. Mary Doran 65 IN 1864 (widow of John Doran).
R6#49	SERGT W HOOVER WILLIAM HOOVER[236]	25-26	136 Inf G		B ~1837 Avon, Livingston Co., NY. R same. Occ porter. E Aug 62 corporal. Promoted to sergeant on 1/11/63. May 63: absent from 5/22/63 on 10-day furlough. KIA Jul 3. Survivors (WC61624): W Bridget 27 in 1864 (M Jul 56); 3 ♂- William 5, John 2, James 7 weeks (born 5/12/63).
R6#50	DAVID REED DAVID **READ**	24-25	59 Inf A		B ~1838 Westchester Co., NY. E (NYC) Nov 61 private. Captured 9/17/62 at Antietam. Paroled not noted. C Jul 2: wounded in right arm. D Jul 5 or 6.
R6#51	WILLLIAM BRYAN WILLIAM F **BYRNE**	25	42 Inf K		B ~ 1838 Ireland. R NYC. E Jun 61 private. Captured on 10/21/61 at Battle of Ball's Bluff. Paroled 2/19/62. Deserted following parole. Nov/Dec 62: forfeited $5 to be paid to soldier credited with apprehending him while he was a deserter. C Jul 3: severely wounded in right leg→amp. D Jul 23 or 24. Survivors (WC23676): W Amelia 36 (M Jul 55); 2 chn: 1 ♀- Eliza 11 & 1 ♂- Hugh 11 (Hugh was same age but younger by 9 months).
R6#52	SERGT S WEBB SIEGMUND **WEIL**	22	7 Inf F		B 8/19/1840 Germany. Occ soldier. E (NYC) Aug 62 private. Promoted to corporal on 2/28/63. Temporarily transferred to 52nd NY infantry on 4/23/63. No service record documentation of promotion to sergeant. C Jul 2 or 3. D Jul 4.
R6#53	THOMAS J BOYD (MN JEFFERSON)	~37	82 Inf H		B ~1826 NY. R NYC. Occ cooper. E May 61 private. KIA Jul 3. Survivors (WC112918): W Eliza 30 in 1864 (M May 59); 5 chn: 4 ♀- Mary 15, Eleanor 8, Catherine 3, Sarah 6 & 1 ♂- William 10.
R6#54	JOHN KING	41-42	82 Inf K		B ~1821 Ireland. R Brooklyn, Kings Co., NY. Occ laborer. E Sep 62 private. KIA Jul 2. Survivor (WC68150): M Mrs. Mary King 88 in 1864 (widow of John King).
R6#55	J B MOORE JAMES B MOORE	30-31	124 Inf E		B ~1832 New Windsor, Orange Co., NY. R Newburgh, Orange Co., NY. Occ printer (1860 occ: grocer). E Aug 62 private. C Jul 2: wounded in thigh. D Jul 8.

---

236 **Soldier killed one month after returning from home visit to see family, in particular, his new two-week-old son**. Sergeant Hoover departed from his regiment on May 22, 1863 for a 10-day furlough, which was likely granted to allow him to visit his wife and 3 boys, in particular the youngest, James, who had just been born on May 12, 1863. Returning to his regiment around the first of June, William's death would follow one month after this home visit.

R6#56	T HARRINGTON TIMOTHY **HORRIGAN**	~28	40 Inf F	B ~1835 Ireland. R NYC. Occ carpenter. E Jun 61 private. C Jul 2: wounded in left thigh. D Jul 10 or 12. Survivor (WC71051): W Bridget 33 in 1864 (M Nov 57); no chn.
R6#57	TIMOTHY KELLY	21-22	40 Inf E	B ~1841 Boston, MA. Occ glassblower. E (NYC) Sep 61 private. Transferred to the 40th NY infantry on 9/1/62. Captured on 12/13/62 at Battle of Fredericksburg. Paroled on 1/9/63 at City Point, VA. Received at Camp Parole on 1/11/63. Returned to regiment on 5/15/63. C Jul 2: wounded in the head. D Jul 2, 3 or 10.
R6#58	BENJAMIN F ATKINS	35-36	40 Inf F	B ~1827 NY. R Poughkeepsie, Dutchess Co., NY. Occ carpenter. E Oct 61 into 87th NY infantry as a private. Promoted to sergeant on 3/1/62. Transferred to 40th NY Infantry on 9/26/62. Detached on recruiting service on 10/20/62. Rejoined regiment on 2/4/63. C Jul2. D Jul 9. Survivors (WC14903): W Mary 25 (M Dec 56); 3 chn: 2 ♂- Ervin 4, Charles 11 months & 1 ♀- Henrietta 2.
R6#59	WILLIAM PEISDALE WILLIAM **TEESDALE**	40	68 PA Inf C	B 11/25/1822 Scotland. R Philadelphia, PA. Occ miller. E Aug 62 private. C Jul 2: wounded in the back, neck and left lung. D Jul 10. Survivors (WC17908): W Margaret 39 (M Jan 46); 2 chn: 1 ♂- Robert 14 (and 1 ♀- Margaret ~17).
R6#60	SIMON FREER	29	40 Inf F	B 9/28/1833 New Paltz, Ulster Co., NY. 1860: R same; occ laborer. E Sep 61 into 87th NY infantry. Transferred to 40th NY infantry on 9/6/62. C Jul 2: wounded in the hip. D Jul 31.
R6#61	FRANK STALEY FRANZ **STHALE**[237]	22-23	40 Inf A	B ~1840 Germany. R NYC. Occ carver. E Sep 61 into 55th NY Infantry as a private. Transfer from the 55th NY Infantry to the 38th Infantry on 12/23/62. Promoted to corporal on 3/26/63. Transfer from the 38th NY Infantry to the 40th NY Infantry on 6/3/63. C Jul 2: wounded in head and leg→amp. D Jul 22. Survivor (WC31641): W Charlotte 21 (M May 61); no chn.
R6#62	W M McABOY JAMES **McAVOY**	21-22	73 Inf G	B ~1841 Brooklyn, NY. R same. Occ clerk. E Sep 62 into 163rd NY infantry as a private. Captured 7/2/62 at Malvern Hill, VA. Transferred into 73rd NY infantry on 1/18/63. C Jul 2. D Jul 7.
R6#63	J GALLIGER MICHAEL **GALLAGHER**	19-20	73 Inf G	B ~1843 Williamsburg, Brooklyn, NY. R same. Occ peddler. E Sep 62 into 163rd NY infantry as a private. Transferred into 73rd NY infantry. Wounded slightly in hand at Chancellorsville on 5/3/63. C Jul 3: severely wounded in left leg→amp. D Jul 8 or 18.

---

237 **Death during an amputation surgery**. On July 22, 1863, as Franz Sthale was preparing to undergo the leg amputation that the doctors said was the only chance to save his life, he asked a ward nurse to write to his wife, should anything happen to him. The ward nurse unexpectantly would have to write the wife that same day that Franz did die during the amputation.

R6#64	J J CONNIFF JOHN **CONIFF**	~21	73 Inf K	B ~1842. E (Staten Island, NY) Jul 61 private. Promoted to corporal on 12/31/61. Promoted to sergeant on 10/31/62. C Jul 2: wounded in thigh. D Jul 14.
R6#65	DAVID MAYWOOD	26-27	74 Inf E	B ~1836 Philadelphia, PA. E (NYC) Aug 61 private. Jul/Aug 62: court martial sentence of stoppage of five days' pay for AWOL. C Jul 2: severe wound to left leg →amp. D Jul 15.
R6#66	SERGT THOS KING THOMAS KING	~24	71 Inf E	B ~1839. E (NYC) May 61 sergeant. Wounded at Chancellorsville on 5/3/63. C Jul 2: severe wound to left leg→amp. D Jul 16. Survivors (WC115667): M Mrs. Catherine King 60 in 1868 (John King affirmed unable to perform any labor).
R6#67	SERGT IRA PENOYAR (MN TOBIAS)	28	111 Inf D	B 11/3/1834 Lyons, Wayne Co., NY. R Rose, Wayne Co., Occ farmer. E Aug 62 private. Captured and paroled on 9/15/62 at Harper's Ferry. C Jul 3: wounded in the head. D Jul 10. Survivors (WC74615): W Lavina 27 (M Mar 59| died 2/7/66); 1 ♂- Herbert 3.
R6#68	JOHN J DUNNING	19	111 Inf D	B 4/7/1844 Holland. E (Williamson, Wayne Co., NY) Jul 62 private. Captured at Harper's Ferry on 9/15/63 and held until prisoner exchange in Nov 62. Subsequent hospitalization at Annapolis, MD until return to regiment 3/4/63. Jul 2: wounded in head. D Jul 7 or 10.
R6#69	J K SAULSPAUGH JOHN **HENRY** SULPAUGH	22-23	126 Inf E	B ~1840 Phelps, Ontario Co., NY. Occ printer. E (Geneva, Ontario Co., NY) Aug 62 private. Captured 9/15/62 and paroled 9/16/62 at Harper's Ferry. Jan/Feb 63: company cook. C Jul 3. D Jul 4. Survivors (WC605142 not online): W Mary (M May 60| ReM 1865); 1 ♀- Julia 6 months.
R6#70	P DEVOS PETER DEVOS	21-22	111 Inf D	B ~1841 Holland. R Sodus, Wayne Co., NY. Occ farmer. E Aug 62 private. Captured 9/15 and paroled 9/16/62 at Harper's Ferry. C Jul 2: severe wound to leg→amp. D Jul 8. Survivors (WC41747): W Magdeline 31 (M Jul 57); no chn.
R6#71	B CONRAD BARTHOLOMEW **CARMODY**	18-19	125 Inf A	B ~1844 Ireland. R Hoosick, Rensselaer Co., NY. Occ farmer. E Aug 62 private. Captured 9/15 and paroled 9/16/62 at Harper's Ferry. KIA Jul 3. Survivor (WC143783): M Mrs. Mary Carmody 51 in 1864 (Patrick Carmody disabled by virtue of an arm amputation).
R6#72	AMBROSE PAINE	~30	42 Inf F	B ~1833 NY. E (Long Island, NY) May 61 private. C Jul 3: wounded in both legs. D Jul 23.
R6#73	GEORGE NICHOLSON	40-41	126 Inf K	B ~1822 NY. Occ laborer. E (Manchester, Ontario Co., NY) Aug 62 private. Captured 9/15 and paroled 9/16/62 at Harper's Ferry. C Jul 3: severe wound to right leg→ amp. D Jul 15.

R6#74	DENNIS McCARTHY	18-19	122 Inf K	B ~1844 Ireland. Occ farmer. E (DeWitt, Onondaga Co, NY) Jul 62 private. C Jul 3: wounded in arm→amp. D Jul 6.
R6#75	JOHN NORTON	22-23	60 Inf C	B ~1840 Hammond, St. Lawrence Co., NY. R same. Occ farmer. E Oct 61 private. Jan/Feb 63: Performing extra duty since 2/11/63 at work upon fortifications. C Jul 2: wounded severely near right eye. D Jul 11.
R6#76	WILLIAM MARKS	28-29	140 Inf E	B ~1834 Ireland. R Rochester, Ulster Co., NY. Occ stone cutter. E Aug 62 private. Promoted to corporal on 4/10/63. C Jul 2: GSW fracturing left foot. D Jul 26. Survivors (WC36130): W Elizabeth 26 (M Jun 56): 4 chn: 2 ♂- Francis, James 6 months & 2 ♀- Margaret 4, Mary 2.
R6#81	LIEUT M STANLEY MYRON STANLEY	24-25	60 Inf E	B~ 1838 Morristown, Lamoille Co., VT. R Franklin, Franklin Co., NY. Occ shoemaker. E Sep 61 sergeant. Commissioned 1st lieutenant on 3/11/63. C Jul 2. D Jul 7.
R6#82	TALMADGE WOOD	48-49	155 Inf C	B ~1814 Otsego Co., NY. R Stanford, Dutchess Co., NY. Occ farmer. E Sep 62 private. C Jul 3. D Jul 14. Survivor (WC10842): W Lydia 55 (M Dec 39); no chn.
R6#83	W H KEYES WILLIAM HARRISON KEYES	22-23	78 Inf G	B ~1840 NY. R Centreville, Allegany Co., NY. R same. E Oct 61 private. Deserted from regiment 9/1/62 and musters surreptitiously into 154th NY infantry on 9/24/62. Arrested 4/01/63 and returned to 78th NY infantry. C Jul 3: wounded in lungs. D Jul 15.
R6#84	J KOUGH JAMES M **KEOUGH**	35-36	102 Inf G	B ~1827 NYC. R same. Occ machinist. E Aug 62 private. C Jul 3: shot in right hip. D Jul 22. Survivors (WC35182): W Sarah 33 (M Jun 47| ReM 1871); 5 chn: 3 ♂- Charles 15, James 13, Alfred 1 & 2 ♀- Mary 11, Sarah 9.
R6#85	SERGT S A SMITH SAMUEL A SMITH	29-30	137 Inf B	B ~1833 Grafton, Worcester Co., MA. R Binghamton, Broome Co., NY. Occ shoemaker. E Jul 62 sergeant. C Jul 3: wounded in head. D Jul 6. Survivors (WC20545): W Juliette 29 (M Jun 54| ReM 1868); 1 ♂- DeWitt 8.
R6#86	W JOHNSON WILLIAM JOHNSON	22	60 Inf B	B August, 1840 Macomb, St. Lawrence Co., NY. R Ogdensburg, St. Lawrence Co., NY. Occ farmer. E Sep 61 private. C Jul 3: wounded in chest and left wrist. D Jul 8.

R6#87	G W STRONG GEORGE WASHINGTON STRONG[238]	23-24	137 Inf G	B ~1839 Geneva, Ontario Co., NY. R Caroline, Tompkins Co., NY. Occ farmer. E Aug 62 private. C Jul 2: GSW to left arm. D Jul 8. Survivors (WC22032): W Ellen ~29 (M Jun 60); 2 ♀- Louisa 2, Georgia 9 months.
R6#88	J BOWIE JAMES BOWIE	21-22	102 Inf I	B ~1841 Scotland. R Sharon, Schoharie Co., NY. Occ farmer. E Oct 61 private. Detailed as a sharpshooter 6/26→7/22/62. Detailed as a Provost Guard 11/4→12/9/62. C Jul 3: wounded in right leg→amp. D Jul 6.
R6#89	JAMES E HOMAN	22-23	124 Inf H	B ~1840 Orange Co., NY. R same. Occ carpenter. E Aug 62 private. C Jul 2: wounded in breast. D Jul 3.
R6#90	BERNARD GERMANN **BERNHARD** GERMANN	~23	119 Inf D	B ~1840 Germany. R NYC. Occ sailor, boilermaker. E Jun 62 private. Jan/Feb 63: performing extra duty as a teamster. C Jul 1. D Jul 1 or 10.
R6#91	DANIEL V HULL	19-20	136 Inf G	B ~1843 Springville, Erie Co., NY. R York, Livingston Co., NY. Occ farmer. E Aug 62 private. Hospitalization at Fort Schuyler 12/10/62→3/26/63 from an unspecified condition. C Jul 3: wounded in right thigh. D Jul 12.
R6#92	ALBERT HATCH	21-22	157 Inf I	B ~1841 Sullivan, Madison Co., NY. R same. Occ farmer. E Aug 62 private. C Jul 1: wounded in the head. D Jul 10 or 12.
R6#93	WILLIAM SCHUMNE **JOHANN** SCHERER	19-20	54 Inf D	B ~1842 Germany. Occ baker. E (Hudson City→Jersey City, Hudson Co., NJ) Sep 61 private. KIA Jul 1.
R6#94	J E JOYNER JAMES E JOYNER	18-19	157 Inf E	B ~1844 Taylor, Cortland Co., NY. Occ farmer. E (Cortlandville, Cortland Co., NY) Jul 62 private. Promoted to corporal on 3/15/63. C Jul 1. D. Jul 14.
R6#95	SERGT J C WEISENSAL **JOHANN** WEISENSEL	29-30	45 Inf E	B ~1833 Germany. R NYC. Occ cabinet maker. E Sep 61 private. Promoted to corporal on 3/1/63. C Jul 2: shell fragment wound while performing duty as Provost Guard. D Jul 31. Survivors (WC50548→WC174589 neither online): W Emeline ~27 (M Apr 57| ReM 1865); 1 ♀- Catherine 3.

---

238 **Widow dropped from pension rolls for "open and notorious adulterous cohabitation."** In 1884, after twenty years as war-widow pension recipient, Mrs. Ellen Strong was dropped from the pension based on a finding of "open and notorious adulterous cohabitation" with a Mr. Ed Johnson. In the special examiner investigation leading to this action, Ed Johnson, under oath, had been evasive when asked if he had ever had sexual relations with Mrs. Strong. Mrs. Strong in her sworn testimony acknowledged that on and off over the past several years Ed Johnson had resided in her home, but importantly in a separate upstairs bedroom. She vehemently denied ever having had sexual relations with him. The investigation may have stalled here. However, creditable witnesses, including a physician who had been consulted, gave testimony that in 1872 Mrs. Strong likely underwent an abortion to terminate a pregnancy from Ed Johnson. After being dropped from the pension rolls, she undertook efforts to have it reinstated, but none of her reinstatement efforts proved successful.

R6#96	G M REAGLES GEORGE M REGELE	22-23	134 Inf H	B ~1844 Germany. Occ farmer. E (Duanesburg, Schenectady Co., NY) Aug 62. Sick with unspecified condition in Washington, D.C. hospital: 9/22/62→Mar/Apr 63. C Jul 1: wounds to the back and hip. D Jul 19.
R6#97	LIEUT L DIETRICK **FRANZ** LOUIS **DIETRICH**	34-35	58 Inf	B ~1828 Germany. R Brooklyn, NY. E Sep 61 NY US. Rifles as sergeant major. Transferred 11/23/61 to 58th NY infantry. Commissioned 2nd lieutenant 5/15/62. May 63: promoted to 1st lieutenant and adjutant 5/1/63. KIA Jul 2. Survivors (WC93477): W Marie 33 (M Mar 54); 2 ♂- Gustav 8, Louis 7.
R6#98	JOHN CASSIDY	24-25	108 Inf D	B ~1838 Rochester, Monroe Co., NY. R same. Occ molder. E Jul 62 corporal. KIA Jul 3: shot in the chest.
R6#99	MORGAN L ALLEN MORGAN LABAN ALLEN, SR[239]	43-44	147 Inf C	B ~1819 Williamstown, Oswego Co., NY. R same. Occ carpenter. E Aug 62 private. Company cook in Dec 62 & Feb 63. Jan 63: absent guarding supplies. C Jul 1: wounded in left thigh. D Jul 21. Survivors (WC24493): W Nancy 50 (M Feb 31); 3 chn: twins Julian ♂ and Julia ♀ being 12 & ♀- Laura 10.
R6#100	H F MORTON HENRY FREDERICK MORTON	24-25	147 Inf F	B ~1838 Mexico, Oswego Co., NY. R same. Occ cooper. E Aug 62 private. Had initially enlisted for 110th NY infantry but sent to the 147th to muster into service. C Jul 1: minié ball through the body and wounding left hand→amp. D Jul 25. Survivors (WC85977→WC864894 neither online): W Kate 20 (M Oct 59 | ReM Nov 64); 1 ♂- Frederick 2.
R6#101	GEORGE W LAMPHEART GEORGE W **LAMPHERE**	19-20	76 Inf E	B ~1843 Fairfield, CT. Occ boatman. E (Albany, NY) Aug 61 into 30th NY infantry as a private. Transferred to 76th NY on 5/25/63. C Jul 1: wounded in right lung. D Jul 22.
R6#102	CORP E A NORRIS ELIAS A NORRIS	22-23	126 Inf B	B ~1840 Barrington, Yates Co., NY. Occ farmer. E (Starkey, Yates Co., NY) Aug 62 private. Captured 9/15 and paroled 9/16/62 at Harper's Ferry. Promoted to corporal on 3/15/63. KIA Jul 2.
R6#103	FRANCIS CHAPMAN	27-28	76 Inf K	B ~1835 England. Occ blacksmith. E (Springfield, Otsego Co., NY) Sep 61 private. Wounded 8/28/62 at Gainesville, VA. Paroled 9/6/62 and left wounded→sent to D.C. hospital. Feb 63: deserted convalescent camp and reportedly went to Canada. May 63: apprehended and sent back to regiment 5/31/63. C Jul 1: severe wound to right arm→amp. D Jul 8.

---

239 **Father and son enlist the same day into the 147th New York Infantry.** On August 28, 1862, Morgan Laban Allen, Jr. would accompany his father, Allen, Sr., to enlist into the 147th New York Infantry regiment. The father and son were both assigned to Company C. Morgan Laban Allen, Sr. would be mortally wounded on July 1 and would die on July 12. The son would continue active in service after Gettysburg. However, in October 1863, he would be captured by Confederates near Haymarket, Virginia and subsequently die at Andersonville in March 1864.

R6#104	CORP W McKENDRY WILLIAM **McKENDREY**	~33	94 Inf G	B ~1830 Ireland. Occ teamster. E (Sackets Harbor, Jefferson Co., NY) Jan 62 private. Promoted to corporal on 3/8/62. Wounded at 2nd Bull Run on 8/30/62 and sent to Washington, D.C. Promoted to sergeant on 1/19/63. Court martial sentence of reduction back to the rank of private for unspecified offense. C Jul 1. D Jul 3.
R6#105	D LYNES DAVID LYNES	19-20	76 Inf I	B ~1843 Middleburgh, Schoharie Co., NY. R same. Occ clerk. E Oct 61 private. Nov/Dec 62: on guard duty at Brigade HQ. KIA Jul 1.
R6#106	SERGT J STRATTON JOHN STRATTON[240]	38-39	76 Inf A	B ~ 1824 England. R Henderson, Jefferson Co., NY. Occ laborer. E Oct 61 private. Muster as hospital nurse 11/14/61→1/10/62. Promoted 6/25/62 from corporal to sergeant. KIA Jul 1: wounded in head. Survivors (WC70139→WC218482 neither online): W Mary 36; 8 chn: 4 ♂- William 11, Job 7, Benjamin 5, Henry 3 & 4 ♀- Mila 9, Sarah 4, Rose 2 & 3-months pregnant with Ann (born 1/15/64).
R6#107	JOHN KURK JOHN **KAUTT**	29-30	97 Inf H	B ~1833 Germany. Occ farmer, laborer. E (Utica, Oneida Co., NY) Nov 61 corporal. C Jul 1: wounded in left side and hand. D Jul 2.
R6#108	CHARLES A HYDE (MN ADDISON)	22	76 Inf B	B 7/27/1840 Pitcher, Chenango Co., NY. R same. Occ farmer. E Sep 61 private. C Jul 1. D Jul 4.
R6#109	P SHUTTS PETER SHUTTS	32	147 Inf G	B 11/9/1830 Montgomery Co., NY. R Oswego, NY. Occ laborer. E Aug 62 sergeant. KIA Jul 1. Survivors (WC132789): 2nd wife Mary 22 (M Oct 61⎮ dies 9/1/67); 1 ♂- Byron 7 (1st wife Hannah's child⎮ M Aug 54→Died 3/6/59).
R6#110	S W VEAZEY STRONG WARNER **VEASEY**	19-20	104 Inf F	B ~1843 Centerville, Allegany Co., NY. 1860 R: same. Occ farmer. E oct 61 private. C Jul 1: wounded in leg→amp. D Jul 4.
R6#116	WILLIS CHAMBERLAIN[241] 150 Inf A	38-39	150 Inf A	Misidentified soldier in grave.
R6#117	D_____NGTON RICHARD TITTERINGTON	35-36	82 Inf G	B ~1827 Ireland. R NYC. Occ shoemaker. E Sep 62 private. KIA Jul 2. Survivors (WC34167): W Isabella 29 in 1864 (M Apr 50); 3 chn: 2 ♂- Richard 6, Joseph 4 & 1 ♀- Annie 3.

---

[240] **Soldier's death leaves widow three-months pregnant with their eighth child.** Sergeant John Stratton's death left his wife seven children aged eleven to two and three-month pregnant with their ninth child.

[241] **Misidentified soldier in grave.** As Willis Chamberlain was killed August 23, 1864 in action near Atlanta, the presence of his remains in this grave, saving the unlikely circumstance of a reburial, would appear doubtful.

R6#118	FRANK DEICENROTH FRANK **DEISENROTH**	18-19	108 Inf A	B ~1844 Germany. R Monroe Co., NY. Occ farmer. E Jul 62 private. KIA Jul 3.
R6#119	JOHN HOFER **JOHANN** ULRICH HOFER[242]	48	108 Inf A	B 5/8/1815 Switzerland. Occ farmer. E (Rochester, Monroe Co., NY) Jul 62 private. KIA Jul 3: shot through the chest. Survivors (WC73450): W Mary 50 (M Mar 42); 2 ♂- Jacob 23, Frederick 20.
R6#120	JOHN CLARK[243]	33-34	65 Inf B	B ~1829 Ireland. E (NYC) Aug 61 private. Sep/Oct 62: promotion to corporal. Jan/Feb 63: serving as brigade guard. KIA Jul 3. Survivors (WC50400): W Mary 40 (M Dec 48); 4 chn: 2 ♂- Michael 9, John 7 & 2 ♀- Catherine 9, May 3.
R6#121	PATRICK BURNS	~23	83 Inf H	B ~1840. E (NYC) May 61 private. Jun 61: detailed to training in Camp Cameron in Washington, D.C. Oct 61: company cook. Nov 61: detailed as teamster. Feb 62: reported AWOL. Sep/Oct 62: detached to ambulance corps. Return detachment to ambulance service 4/10→5/1/63. KIA Jul 1.
R6#122	N A THAYER NELSON ANDERSON THAYER[244]	21	123 Inf K	B 8/24/1841 Day, Saratoga Co., NY. 1860: R Middle Granville, Washington Co., NY. occ: farm laborer. E Aug 62 private. KIA Jul 2: shot through the head. Survivor (WC56541): M Mrs. Hannah Thayer Woodward 54 (widow of David Thayer and of 2nd husband Orison Woodward).
R6#123	SERGT M BUCKINGHAM MAURICE BUCKINGHAM	27	104 Inf C	B 11/1/1835 England. Occ mechanic. E (Geneseo, Livingston Co., NY) Feb 62 private. Promoted to sergeant on 1/1/63. C Jul 1: wounds to shoulder and right thigh→amp. D Jul 20.
R6#124	SAMUEL G SPENCER	33-34	76 Inf D	B ~1829 Summerhill, Cayuga Co., NY. R Cayuga Co., NY. Occ farmer. E Sep 61 private. Captured near 2nd Bull Run on 8/29/62. and paroled 9/1/62. Jan/Feb 63: present at Camp Parole. C Jul 1: severe wound in leg→amp. D Jul 8. Survivors (WC125006): W Lucinda 25 (M Oct 54| Dies 11/22/66); 2 chn:1 ♂- Charles 7 & 1 ♀- Mary 6. (MGF Andrew Smith appointed guardian).
R6#125	JOHN M DAWSON	36-37	76 Inf H	B ~1826. E (Breakabeen, Fulton, Schoharie Co., NY) Oct 61 private. May 63: company cook. C Jul 1: wounded in side and left arm. D Jul 7.

---

242 **Overaged in enlistment**. A marriage certificate submitted with Mary Hofer's widows' pension application revealed that John Hofer was 47 and not 38 as he claimed at his army enlistment. Frederick, the younger of John Hofer's two sons, had enlisted in the same regiment and company, as had his father. one month earlier. Continuing in service after his father was killed July 3rd, Frederick would himself be killed 10 months later at Spotsylvania.

243 **A "Dear Madam letter" recounts husband's thunderclap wounding and death**. In a "Dear Madam" letter to John Clark's wife, a sergeant in his company gave the following account of her husband's death. "Your husband was laying on his back calmly talking of the 'Union' when a fragment of a shell struck him nearly taking both legs off."

244 **Friendly fire death**. A FindAGrave.com memorial offers that Nelson Thayer was shot through the head and killed in a "friendly fire" incident.

R6#128	JAMES MONTGOMERY	~22	70 Inf E	B ~1841 PA. E (Pittsburgh, PA) May 61 private. Wounded on 5/5/62 at Williamsburg, VA. KIA Jul 2.
R6#129	DENNIS BRADY	25-26	15 Indpt Battery NY LA	B ~1837. E (NYC) Sep 61 private. Promoted to corporal op 9/18/61. Promoted to sergeant on 12/21/61. Reduced to private on 1/20/62 by battalion order for an unspecified infraction. KIA Jul 2.
R6#131	ROBERT SHIELDS	23-24	140 Inf C	B ~1839 Ireland. 1860: R Rochester, Monroe Co. NY; occ cooper. Occ carriage trimmer. E Aug 62 private. KIA Jul 2. Survivors (WC85298): F Robert Shields 56 pensioned for care of soldier's sister Mary 13 & two 2 half-sisters-Martha 6 and Fanny 3.
R6#132	JOHN ALLEN	18-19	140 Inf C	B ~ 1844 Rochester, Monroe Co., NY. R same. Occ shoemaker. E Aug 62 private. KIA Jul 2. WC111341 M Mrs. Ellen Mulqueen 52 in 1866 (widow of William Allen and 2nd husband Michael Mulqueen affirmed unable to support her).
R6#134	JOHN ZUBBER JOHN **ZUBLER**[245]	25-26	140 Inf B	B ~1837 Germany. R Buffalo, NY. Occ butcher. E Aug 62 private. KIA Jul 2. Survivors (WC78268): W Johana 22 (M Jul 59| ReM 1865): 2 chn: 1 ♀- Mary 2 & 1 ♂ John 9 months.
R6#135	SANFORD WEBB	21-22	140 Inf G	B ~1841 Richmond, Ontario Co., NY. 1860: R Pittsford, Monroe Co., Ny; occ farmer on widow mother's farm. Occ farmer. E Aug 62 private. Absent sick in Carver Hospital, Washington, D.C. with an unspecified illness: 9/23/62→1/17/63. KIA Jul 2. Survivor (WC26193): M Mrs. Lydia Webb 55 (widow of Stephen Webb).
R6#138	LIEUT CHARLES CLARK CHARLES A CLARK[246]	25	83 Inf G	B 5/12/1838. R NYC. Occ clerk. E May 61 private. Jun 61: promoted to sergeant. Wounded 9/17/62 at Antietam and hospitalized at Frederick, MD. Promotion to captain on 11/27/62. Commissioned 1st lieutenant on 12/17/62. C Jul 1: wounded in the abdomen. D Jul 2.
R7#1	L VANGORDER LEONARD **VAN GORDER**	19-20	80 Inf E	B ~1843 Ellenville, Ulster Co., NY. Occ laborer. E (Wawarsing, Ulster Co., NY) Sep 61 private. KIA Jul 1. Survivor (WC264187 not online): M Mrs. Ann Van Gorder 56 in 1879 (widow of Hiram Van Gorder).
R7#2	G H BABCOCK GEORGE H BABCOCK	20-21	80 Inf E	B ~1842 Salisbury, Litchfield CO., CT. Occ axe polisher. E (Wawarsing, Ulster Co., NY) Sep 61 private. Jul 62→Jan 63: detached butcher to Brigade HQ. Feb 63: hospitalized for an unspecified condition. KIA Jul 1.

---

245 **Soldier musters into service one day before his son is born at home**. John Zubler appears to have enlisted into the army when his wife was about eight-months pregnant. He then embarked to muster into the regiment the day before his son John was born.

246 **Lieutenant mortally wounded gallantly leading a charge**. A FindAGrave.com memorial reports that Lieutenant Charles Clark was mortally wounded in the abdomen July 1 while in the act of "gallantly leading his company in a charge."

R7#3	_____ EASTER **LUDWIG ISLER**	~21	84 Inf K	B ~1842. E (NYC) Jul 61 private. KIA Jul 1.
R7#4	E B MILLER FREDERICK MILLER	21-22	146 Inf D	B ~1841 NYC. Occ clerk. E Aug 62 into 5th NY infantry as a private. Transferred to 146th NY on 5/9/63. C Jul 2: wound fracturing lower leg. D Oct 30.
R7#5	WILLIAM MILLARD WILLIAM S MILLARD	~21	84 Inf I	B ~1842. E (Brooklyn, NY) Nov 62 corporal. Reduced from corporal to private for an unspecified infraction. AWOL 1/23/62→2/6/62. KIA Jul 1.
R7#14	GEORGE A ATKIN GEORGE A **ATKINS**	21-22	84 Inf D	B ~1841 England. Occ stone cutter. E (Brooklyn, NY) Aug 62 private. KIA Jul 1.
R7#20	JOHN WOOD	29-30	76 Inf B	B ~1833 England. R Cohoes, Albany Co., NY. Occ spinner, factory worker. E Sep 62 into 30th NY infantry as a private. Transferred to 76th NY on 5/25/63. C Jul 1. D Jul 1 or 2. Survivors (WC33150): W Rhoda 37 (M Jun 48); 4 chn: 2 ♀- Frances 13, Mary 8 & 2 ♂- Charles 6, George 1.
R7#21	SERGT L HENNESSY LAWRENCE HENNESSY	~31	94 Inf F	B ~1832 Ireland. E (Batavia, Genessee Co., NY) Jan 62 into 105th NY infantry as a private. Promoted to 1st sergeant on 10/15/62. Wounded severely in leg on 12/13/62 at Fredericksburg, VA. Consolidation transfer with the 94th NY with reduction in rank to private on 3/10/63. KIA Jul 1.
R7#25	HENRY KELLOG HENRY **KELLOGG**[247] 157 Inf G			Misidentified soldier in grave. B ~1825 Oneida Co., ME. Occ farmer. E Aug 62 private. Absent in hospital since Dec 63. Jul 65: mustered out.
R7#26	JOSEPH PHARETT JOSEPH **McDARGH**[248] 157 Inf G			Likely a misidentified soldier in grave. B ~ 1840 Champaign Co., OH. Occ farmer. E (Harford, Cortland Co., NY) Aug 62 private. Absent, wounded in action on July 1st at Gettysburg, but not noted killed. Administratively, thereafter, this soldier is carried with the regiment until a muster-out year of 1865. Also tending to disprove that he was killed at Gettysburg, his service record includes a notation that he was serving as a captain's waiter in February 1865.
R7#31	J A CASAD JACOB A CASAD or CASARD	20-21	137 Inf I	B ~1842 Sussex County, NJ. R Ulysses, Tompkins Co., NY. Occ farmer. E Aug 62 private. KIA Jul 2 or 3.

---

[247] **Misidentified soldier in grave.** Henry Kellogg was not killed at Gettysburg. He mustered out of the army in July 1865.

[248] **Likely a misidentified soldier in grave.** Joseph McDargh's service record reports that he was wounded in action on July 1st. Following this report, there is no notation of McDargh's return to service, save for a queer notation that he was serving as a captain's waiter in 1865. What could be this soldier is a Joseph McDargh appearing on the 1900 U.S. Census for Cortland, NY and at age 59 years.

R7#33	VENERABLE WESLEY[249]	30	137 Inf B	B 3/20/1833 Elmira, Chemung Co., NY. R Ithaca, Tompkins Co., NY. Occ cigar maker. E Aug 62 private. KIA Jul 2. Survivors (WC72319): W Elizabeth 26 (M Apr 54 | ReM 1865); 2 ♂- James 6, John 4.
R7#34	IRA MARTIN IRA G MARTIN, JR	19	137 Inf K	B 6/30/1844 Danby, Tompkins Co., NY. R same. Occ farmer. E Aug 62 private. KIA Jul 2.
R7#35	JOHN NICKELS JOHN **NICHOLS**	22-23	149 Inf B	B ~1840 NYC. Occ finisher. E (Syracuse, Onondaga Co., NY) Aug 62 private. KIA Jul 3.
R7#36	WILLIAM BESIMER WILLIAM **BEISIMER**[250] *or* BESEMER	17	137 Inf D	B 1846 Caroline, Tompkins Co., NY. Occ farmer. E (Ithaca, Tompkins Co., NY) Aug 62 private. KIA Jul 2.
R7#37	CORP W MILLER WILLIAM MILLER	20-21	60 Inf G	B ~1842 Ireland (1860 U.S. Census reports birth in Canada from immigrant Irish parents). R Fine, St. Lawrence, NY. Occ mechanic. E Sep 61 corporal. Appointed to serve on color guard 12/12/62. Absent sick 1/18/63→2/27/63. KIA Jul 2: wounded in brain. Survivors (WC141699): M Mrs. Elizabeth Miller 53 in 1867 (William Miller affirmed unable to provide support due to rheumatism).
R7#39	JOHN BARRY	~26	Batty B 1 NY LA	B ~1837. Occ chair maker. E (Baldwinsville, Onondaga Co., NY) Oct 61 private. KIA Jul 3.
R7#40	SERGT B F ELLIOTT	~28	82 Inf F	B ~1835 NYC. Occ cigar maker. E (NYC) Apr 61 private. Promoted to corporal on 8/31/61. Promoted to sergeant on 1/1/63. KIA Jul 2.
R7#41	L W McCLELLAND LUTHER W McCLELLAND[251]	22	80 Inf D	B 1/21/1841 Olive, Ulster Co., NY. E (Kingston, Ulster Co., NY) Aug 61 corporal. Promoted to sergeant on 12/30/62. KIA Jul 3: GSW to chest.
R7#42	THOMAS JAMES	~25	42 Inf A	B ~1838. E (Long Island, NY) Jun 61 private. Captured on 10/21/61 at the Battle of Ball's Bluff. Paroled in Feb 62. Returned for duty with regiment on 3/19/62. KIA Jul 3.

---

249 **Killed during skirmishing.** Venerable Wesley's service record includes the rare commendation that he "was a willing soldier doing his duty well, when killed was out as one of the skirmishers in front of the breastworks."

250 **Minor at death.** The NY Town Clerks' Register of Men who served during the Civil War gives William Beasmer's birthyear as 1846. An Ancestry.com public member story further relates that William Besemer had run away from home at age 17 to enlist into the army.

251 **Soldier's father and oldest brother were physicians.** Luther McClelland had two physicians in his immediate family. Dr. Gordon McClelland, his oldest brother, died prematurely in 1859. Their father, Dr. Barnett McClelland, died in March 1862, or seven months after Luther had enlisted into the army.

ID	Name	Age	Unit	Details
R7#43	I HEIMBACHER IGNATZ **HEIMBUCHER**	~38	39 Inf B	B ~1825 Germany. Occ baker. E (NYC) May 61 private. Captured and paroled on 9/15/62 at Harper's Ferry. March 63: reported AWOL. KIA Jul 3.
R7#44	R SNYDER ROBERT SNYDER	37	125 Inf E	B 5/10/1826 North Greenbush, Rensselaer Co., NY. R same. Occ laborer. E Aug 62 private. Captured at Harper's Ferry on 9/15 and paroled 9/16/62. KIA Jul 3. Survivors (WC14706): W Maria 33 (M Nov 45); 3 ♀- Sarah 7, Ellen 4, Anne 2.
R7#45	JOHN R PHILIPS JOHN MILLISON **PHILLIPS**	28	126 Inf F	B 5/3/1835 Gorham, Ontario, NY. Occ farmer. E (Seneca, Ontario Co., NY) Aug 62 private. Captured and paroled on 9/15/62 at Harper's Ferry. Mar/Apr 63: stoppage of pay for 43 days of AWOL. KIA Jul 3. Survivors (WC64472→WC194836 not online): W Millison 25 (M ~1859| ReM ~1870): 2 ♀- Rhoda 3, Anna 1.
R7#46	MARX ENGLERT	26-27	108 Inf I	B ~1836 Germany. R Rochester, Monroe Co., NY. Occ: brick tucker, mason. E Aug 62 private. Promoted to corporal on 9/18/62. Promoted to sergeant on 12/01/63. KIA Jul 3. Survivors (WC13601): W Frances 23 (M Mar 59| ReM Oct 64); 2 ♀- Barbara 2, Joanna 16 months.
R7#48	H BURCH HIRAM BURCH	~22	111 Inf K	B 1841 Portland, Chautauqua Co., NY. E (Genoa, Cayuga Co., NY) Jul 62 private. KIA Jul 2: wound to head.
R7#50	EDMUND STONE EDMUND STONE, JR	21	64 Inf D	B 10/23/1841 Lyndon, Cattaraugus Co., NY. R Rushford, Allegany Co., NY. E Oct 61 private. Wounded on 12/13/62 at Fredericksburg, VA. Promoted to corporal 3/15/63. KIA Jul 2 (may have served as color bearer at Gettysburg).
R7#51	FRANCIS W HOWARD	22-23	64 Inf D	B 1840 Farmersville, Cattaraugus Co., NY. R same. Occ farmer. E Aug 62 private. KIA Jul 2.
R7#52	LIEUT J FERRETZY JULIUS **FRIEDERICI**	29	119 Inf D	B ~Jan 1834 Germany. Occ clerk. E (NYC) Jun 62 sergeant. Ten-day furlough from 12/2/62. Hospitalization on 5/4/63 for right arm wound at Chancellorsville, VA. Furlough for some period beginning 6/8/63. C Jul 1: penetrating wound to back. D Jul 15.
R7#53	CHESTER SMITH	20	44 Inf A	B 6/5/1843 North Collins, Erie Co., NY. R same. Occ farmer. E Sep 62 private. KIA Jul 2.
R7#54	ROWLA'D L ORMSBY ROWLAND LAMPHUR ORMSBY	22	66 Inf B	B 12/14/1840 Alfred, Allegany Co., NY. 1860 R: Ward, Allegany Co., NY. Occ farmer. E Sep 61 private. C Jul 2: wound to right leg→amp. D Jul 16.
R7#55	JAMES F JOLOPH	22-23	66 Inf G	B ~1840 England. Occ tinsmith. E (NYC) Sep 61 private. Flesh wound to arm on 9/17/62 at Antietam. C Jul 2: wound to right hip. D Jul 10 or 17.

ID	Name	Age	Unit	Details
R7#56	RICHARD CORCORAN **MICHAEL** CORCORAN	~39	82 Inf G	B ~1824 Ireland. 1860 R: North Collins, Erie Co., NY. Occ carman. E Jan 62 private. Wounded slightly on 5/3/63 at Chancellorsville, VA. C Jul 2. D Jul 17 or 18.
R7#57	FREDERICK REMPMIR FREDERICK **RAMPMEIER**	23-24	52 Inf B	B ~1839 Germany. Occ cigar maker. E Aug (NYC) 61 private. Appointed corporal, later reduced back. Detached to Brickell's 30th Independent NY Light Artillery 7/1→10/31/62. Returns to 52nd NY on 6/9/62. C Jul 2: wounded in hip. D Jul 18.
R7#58	PATRICK MARTIN	35-36	61 Inf H	B ~1827 Ireland. Occ varnisher. E Sep 61 private. D Jul 2 of wounds.
R7#59	JOHN O BRIEN JOHN **O'BRIEN**	`23	63 Inf A	B ~1840 Ireland. Occ clerk. E (NYC) Jan 62 private. C Jul 2. D Jul 2 or 4.
R7#60	CORP G DALGLEISH GEORGE DALGLEISH	~42	82 Inf K	B ~1821 Scotland. Occ soap maker. E (NYC) Jun 61 private. Captured 9/4/62 at Centerville, VA. Paroled and sent to Washington, D.C.9/26/62 for hospitalization. Rejoined regiment on 10/12/62. Promoted to corporal on 12/31/62. C Jul 3: wounded in thigh. D Jul 10.
R7#61	CORP PETER JUNK	21-22	119 Inf E	B ~1841 Germany. 1860: R Brooklyn, NY. Occ baker. E Aug 62 private. Corporal as of 4/10/63. Jun 63: assigned duty on color guard. C Jul 1. D Aug 1.
R7#62	L A GODFREY LURENDUS A GODFREY	22-23	9 Cav G	B ~1840 PA. 1860: R Elk Creek, Erie Co., PA; occ laborer. E Oct 61 private. Promoted to corporal on 19/12/61. KIA Jul 1: shot in the head. Survivor (WC143303): M Mrs. Betsey Godfrey 70 in 1869 (widow of Irad Godfrey).
R7#63	W A G WILLIAM ANDREW CALLAN	27-28	125 Inf A	B ~1835 Galway, Saratoga Co., NY. R Hoosick Rensselaer Co., NY. Occ mechanic. E Aug 62 sergeant. Captured on 9/15 and paroled 9/16/62 at Harper's Ferry. KIA Jul 3. Survivors (WC16997): W Sarah 27 (M May 56); 3 chn: 2 ♂- Andrew 6, Charles 3 & 1 ♀- Anna 9 weeks.
R7#64	Z E WIGGINS ZELOTUS **CARDOVIC** WIGGINS	18	136 Inf D	B 12/20/1844 Warsaw, Wyoming Co., NY. R same. Occ farmer. E Aug 62 private. Nov/Dec 62→Jan/Feb 63; absent sick. KIA Jul 3.

R7#65	ELIAS GAGE ELIAS OAKLEY GAGE, JR[252]	28	136 Inf B	B 4/4/1835 Danbury, Fairfield Co., CT. R Allegany Co., NY. Occ farmer. E Aug 62 private. KIA Jul 2 or 3. Survivors (WC28988): W Lodorsca 23 in 1864 (M Jun 60); Chn: 2 ♀- Suan 2, Mary 5 months.
R7#66	ARZY WEST	29-30	136 Inf H	B ~1833 Middlebury, Wyoming Co., NY. R Bennington, Wyoming Co., NY. Occ farmer. E Sep 62 private. KIA Jul 3.
R7#67	JOHN SALSBURY	22-23	64 Inf E	B ~1840. E (Ithaca, Tompkins Co., NY) Oct 61 private. Aug 62: hospitalization→ convalescent camp. C Jul 2. D Jul 5 or 6.
R7#68	SERGT PLATT LEGRAND PLATT	20-21	86 Inf B	B ~1842 NY. R: Thurston, Steuben Co., NY: occ: farmer on his father's farm. E Aug 61 into the 86th NY Infantry as a 61 private. May 63: assignment to 10th NY Battery. KIA Jul 2.
R7#69	MICHAEL CADDY COLOR SERGT MICHAEL CUDDY[253]	~24	42 Inf	B ~1839.Ireland. E (Long Island, NY) Jun 61: private. Promoted to sergeant on 1/1/63. May/Jun 63→Jul 63: serving as regimental color sergeant. C Jul 3: wounds to right lung and arm. D Jul 5.
R7#70	LIEUT COL M A THOMAN MAXMILLIAN THOMAN[254]	~33	59 Inf	B ~1830 Germany. 1860: R NYC; occ restaurant operator. Jul 61: commissioned captain. Wounded 9/17/62 at Antietam with shell wound over his left scapula. Received medical letter 9/29/62 certifying unfitness for duty for 20+ days. Promoted to major on 11/17/62, dating back to 9/17/62. Promoted to lieutenant colonel on 1/9/63. C Jul 2: artillery shell wound to right shoulder with fracture of right arm. D Jul 11.

---

252 **Brothers enlist together into the 136th NY Infantry.** There is some uncertainty as to what state Elias Gage, Jr. was born in. In his regimental muster, he gave his birthplace as Dutchess County, New York. For the 1850 U.S. Census, he is reported as born in New York state, the only one of Elias Gage, Sr.'s seven children not reported born in Connecticut. For the 1860 U.S. Census, Gage reports that he was born in Connecticut. In any case, Elias and his older brother Joshua together mustered into the 136th New York Infantry, Company B on the same September 25, 1862 date. While Elias would be killed in action at Gettysburg, Joshua would die shortly after him on July 23, 1863 at a Washington, D.C. hospital of typhoid.

253 **Color Sergeant's death.** Michael Coddy, identified as the regimental color bearer on his burial stone, was said to have raised himself back up after falling mortally wounded and then to have begun vigorously waving his colors in the face of advancing Confederates.

254 **"Bury me, boys, with our men."** Lieutenant Colonel Maxmillian Thoman, in the realization that he would not survive his battle wounds, requested that he be buried with the other killed soldier from his 59th New York infantry. This would not have been a request to be buried in a national military cemetery, as the decision to establish such a cemetery on this battleground would not have been made by the time he was about to die. Today, Lieutenant Colonel Thomas and Lieutenant Colonel George Stevens of the 2nd Wisconsin Infantry are the two highest ranking Gettysburg soldiers buried in the National Cemetery.

R7#71	CORP G S SMITH GEORGE SIMEON SMITH[255]	17	64 Inf G	B 1/20/1846 Germany. R Allegany, Cattaraugus Co., NY. Occ laborer. E Sep 61 private. Promoted corporal during service. Jan/Feb 62: sick with unspecified condition in Washington, D.C. hospital. Mar/Apr 62: sick with unspecified condition at Philadelphia hospital. Detailed to extra duty 5/1/62 as hospital nurse until relieved 11/10/62. C Jul 2. D Jul 27.
R7#72	MYRON H VAN WINKLE	26-27	111 Inf E	B ~1836 Williamstown, Oswego Co., NY. Occ farmer. E (NYC) Aug 62 private. Captured and paroled 9/15/62 at Harper's Ferry. April 63: detailed as wood chopper. D Jul 3: severely wounded in left leg→amp. D Jul 29. Survivors (WC109202): W Rhonda 28 (M Mar 57| ReM 1867); 2 chn: 1 ♂- Phillip 4 & 1 ♀- Emma 11 months.
R7#73	H WILLIAMS HENRY WILLIAMS	~32	82 Inf F	B ~1831 Germany. Occ glassblower. E (NYC) Jan 63 private. C Jul 3: wounded in the neck. D Jul 4 or 5.
R7#74	SERGT J B WILSON JOHN B WILSON	~34	82 Inf C	B ~1829 Scotland. Occ clerk. E (NYC) Jun 61 private. Sep/Oct 62: present as corporal. Jan/Feb 63: promotion to sergeant. KIA Jul 3.
R7#75	SERGT J M MARTIN JAMES M MARTIN	33-34	59 Inf H	B ~1829. E (Bellville, Richland Co., OH) Sep 61 private. Promoted to corporal during service. Promoted to sergeant on 10/31/62. C Jul 3: wounded in head. D Jul 4.
R7#76	GEORGE SHAFFER GEORGE **SHAEFER**	23-24	39 Inf A	B ~1839 Germany. 1860 R: NYC. Occ shoemaker. E Jul 62 private. Captured and paroled on 9/15/62 at Harper's Ferry. C Jul 3: wounded in knee. D Jul 24.
R7#77	J D SLATTERY JEREMIAH SLATTERY	~26	40 Inf K	B ~1837 Ireland. E (NYC) Jun 61 wagoner. Promoted to corporal on 12/01/62. Wounded 12/13/62 at Fredericksburg, VA. C Jul 2: shot through left lung. D Jul 15. Survivor (WC24052): M Mrs. Margaret Slattery 44 (widow of Daniel Slattery).
R7#78	E A POTTER ENOS POTTER[256]	17	40 Inf I	B ~1846 NY. E (Syracuse, Onondaga Co, NY) Nov 61 into 101st NY. Transferred by a regimental consolidation order to the 40th NY on 5/29/63. C Jul 2. D Jul 15 of typhoid fever complication. Survivor (WC92969): F Noel Potter 45 in 1866 (widower of Lucy Potter and unable to support himself, having lost his right arm being in poor health).

---

255 **Minor at death**. A family history web posting gives George Smith's birthday as January 20, 1846, a date which is in agreement with his age of 14, given for the June 22, 1860 U.S. Census report. Accordingly, George Smith was not 18 at his September 2, 1861 enlistment, but rather 15. This birthdate also means that he was only 17 when he died from his battle wound at Gettysburg.

256 **Minor at death**. Enos Potter's reported ages of 4 and 14 for the successive August 1850 and August 1860 U.S. Census reports attest to the likelihood that he was not 18, but no older than 16 at his November 1861 enlistment. These Census ages constitute strong evidence that Enos was only 17 when he was killed at Gettysburg.

ID	Name	Age	Unit	Details
R7#79	A KRAPPMAN ANDREW KRAPPMAN	37-38	40 Inf A	B ~1825 Germany. Occ varnisher. E (NYC) May 61 into 55th NY Infantry as a private. Transferred from 55th NY infantry to 38th NY Infantry on 12/21/62. Transferred to 40th NY Infantry on 6/3/63. C Jul 2: severe wound to right ankle. D Jul 16.
R7#80	THOMAS SEBRING	24-25	126 Inf I	B ~1838 Romulus, Seneca Co., NY. Occ farmer. E (Fayette, Seneca Co., NY) Aug 62 private. Captured 9/15 and paroled 9/16/62 at Harper's Ferry. C Jul 2. D Jul 8.
R7#81	LIEUT T C PAUSCH CARL THEODORE PAUSCH or BAUSCH	~30	39 Inf H	B ~1833 Germany. R NYC. E May 61 sergeant. Promoted to sergeant major on 6/8/62. Nov/Dec 62: commissioned 2nd lieutenant. Promoted to 1st lieutenant on 2/3/63. C Jul 3: shot in abdomen. D Jul 9.
R7#82	CONRAD SCHULER	~21	71 Inf D	B ~1842 Newark, NJ. R same. Occ silver smith. E Jul 61 private. Promoted to corporal on 9/1/62. C Jul 2: severely wounded in right leg→amp. D Jul 21.
R7#83	JACOB VAN PELK	27-28	11 NJ Inf B	B ~1835 Richmond Co., Staten Island, NY. R: Elizabeth, Union Co., NY. Occ oysterman. E Jul 62 private. C Jul 2: wound to both knees→leg amp. D Jul 9. Survivors (WC30051): W Joanna age? (2nd wife M Mar 61); 1 ♂- John 8 months; 1st wife Mary's 3 chn:-1 ♀- Anna 9 & 2 ♂- David 7, Joseph 3.
R7#84	LIEUT C A FOSS CHARLES A FOSS	~24	72 Inf C	B ~1839 NH. R Dunkirk, Chautauqua Co., NY. Occ blacksmith. E May 61 corporal. Promoted to sergeant on 6/20/61. Commissioned 2nd lieutenant on 5/5/63. C Jul 2: severe wound to leg→amp. D Jul 7.
R7#85	JOHN C CURREN	~20	73 Inf E	B ~1843. E Staten Island, NY Jul 61 private. Wounded on 5/3/62 at Williamsburg, VA. Absent wounded to 7/29/62. Detached as hospital during service. Deserted on 12/13/62. Returned to duty in Mar 63. C Jul 2. D Jul 18. Survivor (WC43959): M Mrs. Catharine Curren 35 (widow of John Curren).
R7#86	EDWIN A HESS	~21	74 Inf F	B ~1842 Warren Co., PA. 1860: R Spring Creek, Warren Co., PA. E Jul 61 private. Reported AWOL beginning 8/27/62. Sep/Oct 62: returned to duty. C Jul 2: shot in the chest. D Jul 13.
R7#87	CORP HENRY BURK	~22	74 Inf B	B ~1841. E (NYC) May 61 private. Promoted to corporal on 12/1/62. C Jul 2: wounded in abdomen. D Jul 13.
R7#88	ELDRIDGE G THOMPSON **ELBRIDGE E** THOMPSON	22-23	86 Inf G	B ~1840 Deerfield, Tioga Co., PA. Occ farmer, teamster. E (Elmira, Chemung Co., NY) Sep 61 private. Sep/Oct→Dec 62: hospitalized in Washington, D.C. with an unspecified condition. C Jul 2. D Jul 3.

R7#89	DANIEL O'HARA[257]	22	40 Inf G	B 4/18/1841 Ireland. R Whitehall, Washington Co., NY. Occ farmer. E Oct 61 into 87th NY infantry, private. Transferred to 40th NY on 9/5/62. Detached service with Provost Guard Oct→Nov/Dec 62. C Jul 2: wounded by shell fragment hitting his right side. D Jul 8.
R7#90	C J CRANDELL CHAUNCEY J **CRANDALL**	18-19	125 Inf K	B ~1844 Schaghticoke, Rensselaer Co., NY. R same. Occ farmer. E Aug 62 private. Captured 9/15 and paroled 9/16/62 at Harper's Ferry. C Jul 3: wounded in the chest. D Jul 9. Survivors (WC132551): M Mrs. Amanda Crandall, 60 in 1868 (Albert Crandall affirmed disabled due to heart disease).
R7#91	A B USHER ALLURING BLOOMFIELD USHER	21-22	125 Inf D	B `1841 Waterford, Saratoga Co., NY. Occ molder. E (Troy, Rensselaer Co., NY) Aug 62 private. Captured 9/15 and paroled 9/16/62 at Harper's Ferry. C Jul 3. D Jul 9.
R7#92	STEPHEN BLAKE	21	122 Inf B	B 5/16/1842 England. Occ farmer. E (Syracuse, Onondaga Co., NY) Aug 62 private. C Jul 3. D Jul 16.
R7#93	SERGT J L DECKER ISAAC L DECKER	25	70 Inf F	B 9/11/1837. 1860: R Wawayanda, Orange Co., NY. Occ farmer. E Apr 61 sergeant. C Jul 2. D Jul 3.
R7#94	PHILIP BANSELL PHILIP **BENTZELL**	20-21	10 Cav E	B ~1842 Germany. 1860: R Buffalo, Erie Co., NY; occ grocer's clerk. E Nov 61 private. KIA Jul 2
R7#95	DAVID KNAPP[258]	~20	111 Inf I	B ~1843 Venice, Cayuga Co., NY. R same. Occ farmer. E Jul 62 private. Wounded in left lung on 9/15/62 at Harper's Ferry. Dec 62→5/9/63: absent receiving care following wounding. May 63: serving as company cook. C Jul 2: wounded in abdomen. D Jul 14.

---

[257] **"I Die for our Flag."** The FindAGrave.com memorial for Daniel O'Hara, the 22-year-old Irish immigrant turned soldier, excerpts a heartrending and stirringly patriotic letter he penned after being told by a doctor his July 2nd wound was mortal. O'Hara wrote: "Do not weep for me though I may no longer be with you in this world I shall watch over you until we meet again. I Die for our flag and the union I have learned to love so much that even death cannot quell it in my heart. Farewell from your ever-loving son Daniel."

[258] **Soldier survives Harper's Ferry severe wounding only to be killed at Gettysburg.** David Knapp was one of the rare woundings during the September 15, 1862 Confederate capture of Harper's Ferry. He received a gunshot wound to the left lung. He only returned to his regiment May 9, 1863, following over six months of wound care. He would then be mortally wounded seven weeks later at Gettysburg.

R7#97	JOHN BIGGS JOHN C **BEGG**[259]	39-40	5 Indpt Battery NY LA	B ~1823 Scotland. R Greenpoint, Brooklyn, NU. Occ manufacturer. E Nov 62 private. C Jul 2: Burns sustained from accidental explosion of caisson. D Jul 7. Survivors (WC36770): W Mary 39 (M Apr 49); 6 chn: 5 ♀- Christina 13, May 11, Emma 9, Alice 7, Nellie 3 & 1 ♂- Alonzo 1.
R7#99	FREDERICK FEIGHT or FEITH	18-19	140 Inf F	B ~1844 Germany. Occ stone mounter. E (Rochester, Monroe Co. NY) Aug 62 private. C Jul 2: wounded in head. D Jul 6 or 8.
R7#100	E BRYANT ELIJAH **RYANT**	40-41	137 Inf K	B ~1822 NY. R Danby, Tompkins Co., NY. Occ farmer. E Aug 62 private. C Jul 2: wounded in the hip. D Jul 17. Survivors (WC18586): W Elizabeth 46 (M Dec 49); 4 chn: 3 ♀- Helen 12, Adaline 8, Augusta 6 & 1 ♂- Grandison 3.
R7#102	J DORE JAMES DORE	35-36	137 Inf B	B ~1827 Ireland. R Binghamton, Broome Co., NY. Occ railroad hand, laborer. E Aug 62 private. C Jul 3: wound to abdomen. D Jul 8. Survivors (WC98207): W Hester 26 (M Oct 54| ReM 1866); 3 ♂- William 8, James 4, Charles 2.
R7#103	H MOORE HENRY MOORE[260]	39-40	149 Inf H	B ~1823 DeWitt, Onondaga Co., NY. R Cicero, Onondaga Co., NY. Occ farmer. E Sep 62 private. C Jul 2: wounded in right lung. D Jul 3. Survivors (WC21914): W Charlotte 37 (M Mar 44); 5 ♂- John 17, Jewett 14, William 12, Freeman 10, Charles 8.
R7#104	THOMAS GANNON	26-27	6 Cav D	B ~1836 Ireland. Occ laborer. E (Ballston Spa, Saratoga Co., NY) Dec 62 private. C Jul 2: wounded in leg. D Jul 2 or 5.
R7#105	SAMUEL STILLS SAMUEL **STELTZ** or STELLS	~22	40 Inf F	B ~1841. E (Yonkers, Westchester Co, NY) Jun 61 private. Promoted to corporal on 3/1/63. KIA Jul 2.
R7#106	FREDERICK WENTZ **FRIEDRICH** WENTZ	~39	41 Inf I	B ~1824 Germany. Occ shoemaker. E (NYC) Jun 61 private. May/Jun 62: hospitalization near Clarysville, Allegany Co., MD for an unspecified condition. C Jul 2: severe wound in right arm→amp. D Jul 12.
R7#107	CORP A MIRACLE ALBERT **MERICLE**	19-20	154 Inf H	B ~1843 Greene Co., NY. R Randolph, Cattaraugus Co., NY. Occ farmer. E Aug 62 corporal. C Jul 1: wounded in abdomen and right leg (may have been continuing in his Jun 63 position as a color guard corporal). D Jul 10. Survivors (WC90581): M Mrs. Betsey Mericle 52 in 1886 (Cornelius Mericle, injured in threshing machine accident eleven years earlier, affirmed disabled).

---

259 **A Captain's compassion for a dead comrade's widow and six fatherless children**. John Begg's death was caused by an accidental explosion of a caisson limber, which was being advanced toward the battlefield. Begg's death would widow his wife, Mrs. Mary Begg, and leave her the care of six children under fourteen years of age, all but the one-year-old being girls. Such was the esteem for John Begg that, Elijah Taft, a captain in the battery, collected $77 from the officers and men in the battery and tendered this sum to Mrs. Begg just before Christmas 1863.

260 **Empty grave**? Henry Moore's service records include a post-mortem note that his body was removed from Gettysburg and taken to be buried at his home. No confirmation of this removal and reburial has been found.

R7#108	HENRY RHOADES	18-19	108 Inf B	B ~1844 Monroe Co., NY. 1860: R Greece, Monroe Co., NY. Occ farmer. E Jul 62 private. Wound on 9/17/62 at Antietam. C Jul 3: wound to left side. D Aug 2.
R7#109	SERGT L BISHOP LEWIS BISHOP[261]	25-26	154 Inf C	B ~1837 Lancaster, Eric Co., NY. Occ farmer. E (Olean, Cattaraugus Co., NY) Aug 62 corporal. Promoted to sergeant on 4/4/63. On duty as the color bearer since 9/28/62, including continuing as Color Sergeant at Gettysburg. Absent 4/10/63 for a 10-day furlough. C Jul 1: wound to left knee→amp. D Jul 31. Survivor (WC16290): W Lucy 25 (M 4/12/63).; no chn.
R7#110	JEREMIAH BARRY[262]	18	134 Inf E	B 4/20/1845 Schoharie Co., NY. 1860: R Summit, Schoharie Co., NY. Occ farmer. E Aug 62 private. C Jul 3: wounded in leg. D Jul 31. Survivor (WC80779): M Mrs. Margaret Barry, 60 in 1866 (widow of John Barry).
R7#111	WILLIAM WEIGHT 84 Inf K			No killed Gettysburg soldier with this name from this or any other regiment found in military sources. A William Weightman of the 134th NY Infantry would have been present at Gettysburg but he was not a reported casualty.
R7#112	HORACE ANGUISH	22-23	157 Inf I	B 1840 Sullivan Co., NY. R same. Occ farmer. E Aug 62 private. Jan/Feb 63: hospitalized for an unspecified at Dumfries, VA. Promoted to corporal on 3/15/63. C Jul 1: severe wound in right arm→resection of head of humerus. D Jul 31.
R7#113	CORP J B THOMAS JOHN B THOMAS	18-19	134 Inf E	B 1844 Jefferson, Schoharie Co., NY. 1860: R same. Occ farm laborer. E Aug 62 private. Mar/Apr 63: promotion to corporal. C Jul 3: wounds to the right hip, elbow and arm. D Jul 19.
R7#114	THURSTON THOMAS	17	134 Inf D	B 8/29/1845 Schoharie Co., NY. 1860: R Middleburgh, Schoharie Co., NY. Occ laborer. E Aug 62 private. C Jul 3: wounded in leg. D Jul 20 or 21.
R7#115	SAMUEL HAGUE	42-43	119 Inf B	B ~1820 Ireland. R NYC. Occ brush maker. E Aug 62 private. C Jul 1: wounded in the ankle. D Jul 16. Survivor (WC33517): W Sarah 38 (M Sep 44); no chn.
R7#116	PHILIP DANEY PHILIP W **DANA**	19-20	134 Inf E	B ~1843. Seward, Schoharie Co., NY. Occ farmer. E (Jefferson, Schoharie Co., NY) Aug 62 private. C Jul 1: wound to right hip. D Jul 12.

---

261 **Color Sergeant's death**. On April 4, 1863, Lewis Bishop received promotion to the prestigious but extremely hazardous post of color sergeant for the 154th NY Infantry. Bishop then left the regiment on April 10th for a ten-day furlough, the main purpose appears to have been to marry Miss Lucy Hall on April 12th. Fifteen weeks following this wedding, Mrs. Lucy Bishop would be a new widow.

262 **Enlisting into the army for monies to support a widowed mother**. Mrs. Margaret Barry's application for a mother's pension contains testimony which suggests that Jeremiah's wish to financially support his widowed mother was a strong motivation for surreptitiously entering the army at age 17. Likely thousands of young men enlisted into the army for excitement and for regimentation. However, that many thousands of young men joined the army to secure income to support a widowed mother back home is clearly established by this motivation frequently being attested to in these dependent mother applications from the Gettysburg dead.

R7#117	P C WILBER PHILIP C WILBUR	27	134 Inf E	B 3/30/1836 Conesville, Schoharie Co., NY. 1860: R Gilboa, Schoharie Co., NY: occ: farmer on father's farm. E Aug 62 private. C Jul 1: wound to leg. D Jul 7.
R7#118	THADDEUS L REYNOLDS	18-19	154 Inf I	B ~1844 Cattaraugus Co., NY. Aug 62. 1860: Olean, Cattaraugus Co., NY; occ: painter, as is his father in their household. E Aug 62 drummer→Oct 62: rank change to private. C Jul 1: wounded in hip and left hand. D Jul 12. Survivors (WC130397 not online): M Mrs. Elizabeth Reynolds ~41 (David Reynolds affirmed disabled).
R7#119	LEWIS FRENTO LEWIS **TERANGO** or **TERONGO**	43-44	76 Inf G	B ~1819 Canada. Occ laborer. E (Watervliet, Albany Co., NY) Sep 62 into the 30th NY infantry as a private. Transferred to the 76th NY Infantry on 5/25/63. C Jul 1: C Jul 1: GSW fracture of left femur. D Sep 3.
R7#120	CHARLES F WEBBER	37	84 Inf A	B 12/23/1825 Germany. R NYC. Occ shoemaker. E Apr 61 private. Reported absent, sick 9/9/62. Reported AWOL 9/21→10/1/61. Nov 62: reported sick. Jan/Feb 63: returned to duty. C Jul 1: wound to hand→amp. D Jul 19 from post-wound infection. Survivor (WC48374): W Matilda 35 (M May 45); no chn.
R7#121	HENRY MILLER	18-19	147 Inf B	B ~1844 Eaton, Madison Co., NY. Occ farmer. E (Oswego, Oswego Co., NY) Aug 62 private. Jul 1: wounded in right thigh→amp. D Aug 3. Survivors (WC134732): M Mrs. Ruth Maxwell ~56 (1st husband, William Miller, died in 1851; 2nd husband, Hamilton Maxwell, married Apr 58, affirmed disabled by a hernia).
R7#122	GEORGE A DOUGLASS	~20	84 Inf F	B ~1843 Brooklyn, NY. R same. Occ clerk. E Apr 61 private. Absent sick in Washington, D.C. 9/9/62→Dec 62. Jul 1: GSW to left lung. D Jul 31. Survivor Survivor (WC88687): M Mrs. Caroline Douglas 50 in 1865 (widow of Robert A. Douglas).
R7#123	SERGT F LEAFFLED **JOSEPH LEAFFLETH**[263]	27-28	104 Inf D	B ~1835 Germany. R Rochester, Monroe Co., NY. Occ gardener. E Dec 61 private. Promoted to corporal on 2/20/62. Promoted to sergeant on 9/20/62. Furloughed 2/23-2/28/63. C Jul 1: severe wound in left leg→amp. D Sep 6. Survivors (proposed by one Ancestry.com public family tree) W Hannah 24; 2 chn: 1 ♂ Charles 4 & 1 ♀ Anna 1 (No approved WC found in pension records).
R7#124	ALBERT D WILSON	20-21	157 Inf E	B ~1842 Courtland, Westchester Co., NY. Occ harness maker. E Jul 62 private. C Jul 1. D Aug 6.
R7#125	SERGT W SHEA WILLIAM H SHEA	~22	104 Inf I	B ~1841 Ireland. R same. Occ blacksmith. E Feb 62 private. Promoted to sergeant on 12/13/62. C Jul 1: wounded in right leg. D Sep 8.

---

263 **No widow's pension approval found in records.** An Ancestry.com public family tree reports that joseph Leaffleth had both a wife and two young children when he died at Gettysburg. However, there is no record of an approved pension application for this reported family.

R7#126	J LOHRUSS JOHN **LODWICK**	~27	104 Inf B	B ~1836 Germany. Occ farmer. E (Geneseo, Livingston Co., NY) Jan 62 private. Aug/Sep 62: reported AWOL. KIA Jul 1.
R7#127	MORTIMER GARRISON	19-20	126 Inf B	B ~1843 Rochester, Monroe Co., NY. Occ carpenter. E (Milo, Yates, NY) Aug 62 private. Captured and paroled on 9/15/62 at Harper's Ferry. C Jul 2: wounded in right leg→amp. D Jul 18.
R7#128	CORP G W FORRESTER GEORGE W FORRESTER	~20	84 Inf C	B ~1843 NYC. Occ clerk. E (Brooklyn, NY) Apr 61 private. Sick in Washington, D.C.: 4/18/62→Jun 62. Promoted to corporal on 11/1/62. C Jul 1. D Jul 2. .
R7#133	P LAPPEN PATRICK **LAPPIN**	~23	82 Inf H	B ~1840 Ireland. R NYC. Occ varnisher. E May 61 private. Wounded slightly on 7/21/61 at 1st Bull Run. Promoted to corporal on 8/15/61. Promoted to sergeant on 10/01/62. Reported overstaying Apr 63 furlough. KIA Jul 2. Survivor Survivor (WC23337): M Mrs. Sarah Lappin 51 in 1864 (widow of Patrick Lappin).
R7#134	SERGT M E HISCOX MARSHALL EBERLE HISCOX[264]	22	125 Inf D	B 12/7/1840 Petersburgh, Rensselaer Co., NY. R Rensselaer Co., NY. Occ clerk. E Aug 62 sergeant. Captured 9/15 and paroled 9/16/62 at Harper's Ferry. KIA Jul 3.
R7#135	JOHN BELL	18-19	123 Inf E	B ~1844 Ireland. R Hartford, Washington Co., NY. Occ farmer. E Aug 62 private. KIA Jul 3.
R7#136	W W SCOTT WILLIAM WINFIELD SCOTT	19-20	145 Inf C	B ~1843 Westchester Co., NY. Occ butcher. E (NYC) Sep 62 private. Promoted to corporal 4/10/63. Left sick in Baltimore 12/10/62 with an unspecified condition. Returned to regiment 5/28/62. Reduction in rank on 6/1/63 (possibly related to prolonged absences from regiment). KIA Jul 3. Survivor (WC31158): M Mrs. Harriet Bolton 53 (widow of John Scott and of 2nd husband Robert Bolton).
R7#137	D WELCH DAVID WELCH[265] *or* WALCH	43	147 Inf E	B ~1820 Washington Co., NY. R Sandy Creek, Oswego Co., NY. Occ farmer. E Aug 62 private. C Jul 1. D Jul 15. Survivors (WC29769→WC530797 neither online): W Rebecca 31 (M Oct 50| ReM 1892); 6 chn: 3 ♂- James 10, Clark 2, Walty 5 months & 3 ♀- Clarissa 9, Mary 6, Emma 5.
R7#138	W POOKE WILLIAM LLEWELLYN **POOLER**	21-22	76 Inf G	B ~1841 Cortland, Cortland Co. NY. R DeRuyter, Madison Co., NY. Occ farmer. E Oct 61 private. C Jul 1: GSW to leg. D Jul 13 or 15.

264 **Soldier's father a physician**. The 1860 U.S. Census reports that Marshall's father was Dr. David Hiscox, a physician.

265 **Overaged at enlistment**. David Welch's reported age of 46 for the July 28, 1860 U.S. Census would have already placed him beyond the upper age-limit for voluntary enlistment, which was 45. However, Welch at his August 1862 enlistment gave his age as 42. If instead Welch gave his correct age for the 1860 Census, then he would have been 48 or 49 at his enlistment and similarly been killed at 49. Whatever his true age at his death, Welch left behind his 31-year-old wife Rebecca and six children, aged 10 to 5 months.

R7#139	SERGT T J CURTIS THOMAS J CURTIS[266]	24-25	104 Inf A	B ~1838 Hume, Allegany Co., NY. Occ farmer. E (Geneseo, Livingston Co, NY) Oct 61 private. Promoted to corporal on 11/4/61. Promoted to sergeant on 2/4/62. Wounded 9/17/62 at Antietam. Hospitalized 9/17/62→Jan/Feb 63. Promoted to 1st sergeant on 1/19/63. KIA Jul 1. Survivor (WC129894): F Joseph Curtis 57 in 1868 (widower of Mrs. Adaline Curtis, who himself has been disabled for 25 years due to rheumatism and blindness).
R7#140	SERGT H ROBERTS **JOHN ERASTUS** ROBERTS	22	104 Inf C	B 2/18/1841 Springport, Cayuga Co., NY. R Livingston Co., NY. Occ blacksmith. E Oct 61 corporal. Promoted to sergeant on 2/1/63. C Jul 1: wounded in thigh. D Jul 16.
R7#141	CHAUNCEY SNELL (MN CHANNEY)	18-19	147 Inf F	B ~1844 New Haven, Oswego Co., NY. R same. Occ farmer. E Aug 62 private. KIA Jul 1.
R7#142	ELIAS HANNIS ELIAS **HANNESS**	43-44	147 Inf C	B ~1819 Paris, Schoharie Co., NY. R Richland, Oswego Co., NY. Occ laborer. E Aug 62 private. C Jul 1. D Jul 15. Survivors (WC104442): W Ann 38 (M May 42| ReM 1867); 4 chn: 2 ♂- DeGrasse 20, Oscar 14 & 2 ♀- Sophronia 17, Esther 8
R7#144	LIEUT THEO BLUME FREEDRICH JOHANN THEODORE BLUME	~21	2nd Indpt Batty NY LA	B ~1842 Berlin, Germany. 1860: R Brooklyn, NY; occ: clerk with father Louis Blohm, a grocer. Commissioned 2nd lieutenant 12/4/61. Promoted to 1st lieutenant on 2/13/63. Detached to recruiting serve in NY 4/10→5/01/63. KIA Jul 1: shot while serving as top engineer on field staff of Col. Leopold von Gilsa.

---

266 **Father's patriotic naming of his twin boys.** The ardent patriotism of Joseph Curtis shown through in the naming of his twin boys Thomas Jefferson Curtis and George Washington Curtis. George Washington Curtis had enlisted in the 1st NY Dragoons two months prior to his brother and mustered out of service in 1865. Surviving to 1904, George in 1866 named his second son Thomas Jefferson Curtis in memory of his killed twin brother.

Ambrotype of Sergeant Amos Humiston's Three Children

★ ★ ★ ★ ★

The finding of an ambrotype of a soldier's three children with his dead body led to a series of newspapers running articles describing the children in the ambrotype in an effort to identify the children's father. Only in November would an article be brought Mrs. Philinda Humiston in Portville, NY, which would explain why she had no communication from her husband since Gettysburg. Three years later, Mrs. Humiston, Franklin, Frederick, and Alice would relocate to Gettysburg as residents of a new National Homestead for Orphaned War Children.

Ohio

R1#1	SERGT JASPER C BRIGGS	22	73 Inf G	B 7/4/1840 Fayette Co., OH. 1860: R Perry, Fayette Co., OH. Occ farmer. E Nov 61 corporal. Promoted to sergeant on 9/23/62. KIA Jul 2.
R1#2	JOHN C KISSKA JOHN CHARLES **KIPKA**[267]	~31	8 Inf A	B ~1832. E Apr 61 corporal. Promoted to sergeant on 4/26/61. C Jul 3: wounded in abdomen. D Jul 4.
R1#3	ANDREW J DILDINE	~27	8 Inf A	B ~1836 Clinton, OH. R same. Occ farm laborer. E Jun 61 private. C Jul 3. D Jul 4. Survivor (WC18978): 1 ♂- William 4 (Grandfather Andrew Dildine granted guardianship after 10/25/62 divorce & abandonment by mother Augusta Dildine).
R1#4	JACOB J RANCH JOHN JACOB **RAUCH**[268]	~22	8 Inf A	B ~1841. 1860: R Paris, Stark Co., OH. E May 61 private. KIA Jul 3. Survivors (WC84852): M Mrs. Catharine Rauch 63 in 1864 (Martin Rauch affirmed disabled).
R1#5	JOSIAH D JOHNSON	25-26	29 Inf F	B ~1837 OH. 1860: R Linn, Woodford Co., OH; occ: farm laborer on father's farm. E Oct 61 private. KIA Jul 3.
R1#6	SERGT ISAAC WILLIS	20-21	73 Inf G	B ~1842 OH. 1860: R Jackson, Jackson Co., OH; occ farmer on father's farm. E Sep 61 corporal. Promoted to sergeant on 6/1/63. KIA Jul 2.
R1#7	DANIEL PALMER DANIEL W PARKER	25-26	107 Inf D	B ~1837 OH. 1860: R Monroe, Allen Co., OH; occ: laborer on father's farm. E Aug 62 private. C Jul 2. D Jul 3.
R1#8	JAMES RAY	48	73 Inf G	B 1/12/1815 Jackson, Jackson Co., OH. 1860: R same. Occ farmer. E Nov 61 private. Captured at 8/30/62 at 2nd Bull Run. Parole date not-noted. KIA Jul 2. Survivors (WC142080): W Nancy 52 (M Aug 39); 4 chn: 2 ♂- David 22, Simon 12 & 2 ♀- Emzey 17, Emily 9.
R1#11	NICHOLAS FARRELL Hosp Corps Btn 9			B ?; African-American. E ? private. D Nov 28, 1893.

---

267 **A prior burial site in the Evergreen Cemetery** Sergeant John C. Kipka also has a headstone in the Evergreen Cemetery. Presumably the National Cemetery site is a reburial. Kipka died of his July 3rd abdominal wound at a 2nd Corps field hospital and presumably have been buried near this site. Of course, a pregnant Elizabeth Thorn with some aid from her father buried many soldier in the Evergreen Cemetery, if somehow this could be the explanation.

268 **Younger brother's grave at the Antietam National Cemetery.** Jacob Rauch and his 17-year-old brother Charles both enlisted into the 8th Ohio Infantry on May 28, 1861. Charles would contract an illness and subsequently die of it on October 10, 1861. Today Charles Rauch has a gravestone at the Antietam National Cemetery. Jacob would fight on with the 8th Ohio until he was killed in action on July 3.

R1#12	EMMET MARTIN Co A Btn 9			B ~1868 Rockingham, Richmond Co., NC (African-American). R Springfield, Clark Co., OH. Occ laborer. E Apr 1898 private (previous service: two years in the Ohio National Guard). Sep/Oct 1898: absent, sick in hospital. Admitted 10/25/1998 to St. Joseph Hospital, Lancaster, PA. Died of typhoid fever on 11/3/1898 (aged 30).
R1#13	CLIFFORD HENDERSON Co A Btn 9			B ~1878 Springfield, Clark Co., OH (African-American). R same. Occ laborer. E Apr 1898 private. Detailed to Division Headquarters 4/26→8/13/1898. Died at Camp Meade 2nd Corps hospital of typhoid fever on Sep 8, 1898 (aged 20).
R2#1	THOMAS DURM THOMAS **DUNN**	25	25 Inf K	B ~1838 England. Occ sailor. E Jun 61 private. May/Jun 63: present as corporal. KIA Jul 1.
R2#2	B F PONTIOUS BENJAMIN FRANKLIN PONTIOUS	23	29 Inf D	B 3/14/1840 Coventry, Summit Co., OH. 1860: R Washington, Elkhart Co., IN; Occ: farm laborer. E Sep 61 private. KIA Jul 3.
R2#3	GEORGE H THOMPSON	~28	5 Inf G	B ~1835. E Apr 61 private (3 months). ReE (Cincinnati, OH) Jun 61. Promotion to corporal during service. KIA Jul 3.
R2#4	B F SHERMAN[269]	~19	61 Inf G	B ~1844. E Feb 62 private. KIA Jul 2.
R2#5	JOHN DEBOLT (MN MARION)	26	4 Inf B	B 4/8/1837 Knox Co., OH. 1860: R Washington, Adams Co., OH; occ farmer. E Jun 61 private. Promoted to corporal on 5/3/63. D Jul 2 or 3. Survivors: (no approved WC found in pension records) W Hannah ~21 (M Oct 59| ReM ~1870); 1 ♀- Eva (B 2/25/64 or 8 months after father's death).
R2#6	HASKELL FARR (MN EMORY)	18	55 Inf G	B 1/4/1845 Ravenna, Portage Co., OH. 1860: R Scipio, Seneca Co., OH; occ: farm laborer. E Dec 61 Private. C Jul 2: wounded in right thigh. D Oct 3.
R2#7	WILLIAM MYERS	~20	8 Inf A	B ~1843 OH. 1860: R Tiffin, Seneca Co., OH; occ: hotel clerk. E May 61 private. Promoted to corporal on 1/17/63. Jul 3: wounded in right arm and chest. D Aug 22.
R2#8	J LAVEDEN JONATHAN **LARABA** or LARIBE, LARABEE	19-20	75 Inf E	B ~1843 OH. 1860: R Scipio, Meigs Co., OH. E Nov 61 private. C Jul 1: severe wound in left leg→amp. D Aug 20.

---

269 **B. F. Sherman first and middle names a mystery**. Private B. F. Sherman's service file does not report what these first and middle-name initials stood for. Possibly, the use of these initials reflected the young enlistee's discomfort at being named after a Founding Father, in this case Benjamin Franklin. However, Sherman's service record does not confirm the names his first two initials stood for.

R2#9	PERRY TAYLOR	35-36	75 Inf G	B ~1837 OH. 1860: R Yellow Springs, Greene Co., OH. E Oct 61 private. C Jul I: severe wound fracturing left leg. D Oct 15. Survivor (WC40130): M Mrs. Ruth Taylor 60 (widow of David Taylor).
R2#10	T McCAIN TALLIS E McCAIN[270]	~16	29 Inf G	B ~1847 OH. E Sep 61 private. C Jul 3: severe wound with compound fracture of the left femur. D Aug 8.
R2#11	GEORGE CASE[271]	~17	5 Inf C	B ~1846 OH. 1860 R: Mecca, Trumbull Co., OH; occ: attending school while residing on father's farm. E Jun 61 private. C Jul 2: shot in spine. D Aug 2.
R2#12	ISAAC JOHNSON	20-21	Batty K 1 OH LA	B ~1842 Wetzel Co., VA. 1860: R Marietta, Washington Co., OH. Occ farmer. E Sep 61 private. Jul/Aug 62: absent in hospital in Washington, D.C. with an unspecified condition. Promotion to corporal ~11/1/62. Nov 62: sick, ordered absent by surgeon. C Jul 1: compound fracture wound of left femur→amp. D Oct 19.
R2#13	ASA O DAVIS (MN OTIS)	21	4 Inf G	B 12/3/1841 Adams, Washington Co., OH. 1860 R: Washington, Francklin Co., OH. E Apr 61 private. C Jul 2: wounded in left side. D Jul 4.
R2#14	WILLIAM OVERHOLT[272]	~17	73 Inf I	B ~1846 Ross Co., OH. 1860 R: Buckskin, Ross Co., OH. Occ farmer. E (Lyndon, Ross Co., OH) Dec 61 private. KIA Jul 2. .
R2#15	LEWIS DAVIS (MN SAMUEL)	19	75 Inf D	B 10/7/1843 Athens Co., OH. 1860: R Starr, Hocking Co., OH; occ: attending school while residing on father's farm. E Oct 61 private. May/Jun→Jul 62: absences, hospitalizations for illnesses. KIA Jul 2.
R2#16	SERGT JOHN W PIERCE (MN WILLIAM)	21	25 Inf C	B 5/8/1842 Lebanon, Monroe Co., OH. R Morgan, Scioto Co., OH. Occ laborer. E Jun 61 private. Promoted to corporal on 11/19/61. Promoted to sergeant on 1/1/63. D Jul 2 or 3 of wounds.
R2#17	HIRAM HUGHES[273]	~24	25 Inf H	B ~1839 Morgan Co., OH. R same. Occ farmer, laborer. E Jun 61 private. C Jul 1. D Jul 1 or 2.

---

270 **Minor at death**. Tallis McCain's reported age of 4 and 13 in the successive September 1850 and July 1860 U.S. Censuses, if accurate, suggest that he may have had his birthday sometime between July and September. Referencing his September 1850 U.S. Census age, Tallis should have been about age 14, not 18 at his September 1861 enlistment. And again, using this 1860 Census age, he was likely 16 when he died of a Gettysburg battle wound on August 2, 1863.

271 **Minor at death**. George Case's reported ages of 4 and 14 in the successive September 1850 and July 1860 U.S. Censuses attest to the likelihood that he was 15, not 18 at his June 1861 enlistment. Assuming a 1846 birthyear, George was likely only 17 when he was killed at Gettysburg.

272 **Minor at death**. William Overholt's age is reported as 14 on the July 11, 1860 U.S. Census sheet for Buckskin, Ross County, Ohio. These reports attest to the likelihood that William was not 18, but no older 16 at his December 1861 enlistment. Assuming a 1846 birthyear, William was likely only 17 when he was killed at Gettysburg.

273 **Burial next to maternal uncle**. The FindAGrave.com memorial for Hiram Hughes reports that buried to his left is his maternal uncle, Wesley Raikes.

R2#18	WESLEY RAIKES[274]	39-40	75 Inf G	B 1823 Lancaster, Lancaster Co., PA. 1860: R Somers, Preble Co., OH; occ butcher. E Nov 61 private. KIA Jul 2. Survivors (WC20422→WC154997 neither online): W Sarah 38 (M Jan 52| ReM 1882): 3 chn: 2 ♀- Amanda 9, Barbara 8 & 1 ♂- George 4.
R2#19	SAMUEL P BAUGHMAN	36-37	75 Inf C	B ~1826 Lancaster Co., PA. 1860: R Preble Co., OH; occ wagon maker. E Oct 61 private. KIA Jul 2. Survivors (WC15623): W Mary 43 (M Mar 47); 3 chn: 2 ♀- Eliza 11, Rhoda 9 & 1 ♂- Charles 5.
R2#20	JOSEPH JUCHEM	20-21	107 Inf G	B ~1842 Germany. Occ shoemaker. E (Camp Cleveland, OH) Oct 62 private. KIA Jul 2.
R2#21	JACOB BISE[275]	45-46	107 Inf K	B ~1817 Germany. R Tiffin, Seneca Co., OH. Occ bookbinder. E Aug 62 private. KIA Jul 1. Survivor (WC22494): W Frances 48 (M Mar 60); no chn.
R2#22	H SCHRAM HENRY SCHRAM	22-23	Batty H 1 OH LA	B ~1840 Norway. R Belpre, Washington Co., OH. Occ farmer. E (Marietta, Washington Co., OH) Oct 61 private. KIA Jul 2.
R3#1	SERGT CHARLES LADD	25-26	25 Inf E	B ~1837 NY. 1860: R Beekmantown, Clinton Co., OH; occ: farmer on mother's farm. E Jun 61 sergeant. Wounded and captured on 8/30/62 at 2nd Bull Run. Paroled on 9/1/62 at Gainesville, VA. Filed as a deserter on 10/20/62 following failure to return from furlough. Filed AWOL since 11/15/62. New furlough granted 12/27/62→1/27/63 "on account of ill health and important business." Reported back to camp on 1/31/63. C Jul 1: wound to left leg→amp. D Jul 14.
R3#2	CASPAR BOHRER	23-24	107 Inf G	B ~1839 Germany. 1850 R: Cleveland, OH. Occ chair maker. E (Ridgeville, OH) Aug 62 private. C Jul 1: wounded in right leg and side. D Jul 16.
R3#3	JACOB HOFF[276]	~25	28 Cav C	Probable reburial of soldier killed at Chancellorsville. B ~1838. E Jul 61 private. Wounded on 9/17/62 at Antietam. Promoted to corporal on 3/2/63. KIA 5/2/63.
R3#4	JOSEPH W CUNNINGHAM	~23	25 Inf I	B ~1840 Guernsey Co., OH. 1860: R Elk, Noble Co., OH. Occ farmer. E Jun 61 corporal. Jul 1: GSW to left knee. D Jul 28.

---

274 **Burial next to nephew**. The FindAGrave.com memorial for Wesley Raikes reports that buried to his right is his nephew, Hiram Hughes.

275 **Overaged at enlistment**. Jacob Bise's reported age of 47 in a July 1860 Census report raises the possibility that he had misrepresented his age at enlistment and may have been 50 when killed.

276 **Chancellorsville reburial?** Cavalryman Jacob Hoff was killed-in-action at Chancellorsville on May 2, 1863. Either Jacob Hoff's grave here is a reburial or the soldier buried here has been misidentified.

R3#5	JOHN AEIGLE	38-39	107 Inf K	B ~1824 Germany. R Tiffin, Seneca Co., OH. E Aug 62 private. Captured at Chancellorsville on 5/3/63. Paroled 5/15/63 and admitted to Corps hospital. C Jul 1 or 2: head and flesh wound to the left side. D Jul 18. Survivor (WC56757): W Susannah 25 (M Sep 56); no chn.
R3#6	BALTS BEVERLY **BALTES BENERLE**	34-35	107 Inf C	B ~1828. R Wooster, Wayne Co., OH. E Aug 62 private. C Jul 1: wounded in shoulder region. D Jul 14 or 15. Survivors (WC74970): W Frederika 37 (M Aug 53│ ReM 1866); 4 chn: 3 ♂- Frederick 9, Louis 4, John 2 & 1 ♀- Elizabeth 6.
R3#7	GEORGE RICHARDS	23-24	75 Inf D	B April 1839 Athens Co., OH. R same. Occ farmer. E Dec 61 private. Nov/Dec 62→Jan/Feb 63: absent, sick in hospitals. C Jul 1. D Jul 12.
R3#8	SERGT P SHIPLIN	22-23	75 Inf F	B ~1840 Germany. 1860 R: Van Buren, Montgomery Co., OH. Occ shoemaker. E Sep 62 private. Promoted to sergeant on 12/14/61. C Jul 1. D Jul 12.
R3#9	SAMUEL L CONNER	19-20	82 Inf E	B ~1843 Hardin Co., OH. E 1860 R: Marion, Hardin Co., OH. Occ farm laborer. Dec 61 private. Nov/Dec 62→Jan/Feb 63: absent, sick in hospitals. C Jul 1: GSW to right thigh. D Jul 16
R3#10	JOSEPH GASLER JOSEPH **GESSLER, JR**	18-19	107 Inf K	B ~1844 OH. 1860: R Tiffin, Seneca Co., OH; occ laborer, attending school at age 15. E Aug 62 private. C Jul 2. D Jul 3. Survivor (WC27222: M Mrs. Frances Gessler 52 (widow of Joseph Gessler, Sr.).
R3#11	WILLIAM McVEY WILLIAM DAVISON **McVAY**	18	73 Inf H	B 9/28/44 Athens, Athens Co., OH. R Waterloo, Athens Co., OH. E Oct 61 private. C Jul 3: wounded in the right chest. D Jul 7.
R3#12	ASA HINES	20-21	82 Inf K	B ~1842 OH. 1860: R Mifflin, Ashland Co., OH; occ: boot and shoe maker apprentice. E Oct 62 private. KIA Jul 1.
R3#13	SERGT W NORTON WILLIAMS WILLIAM NORTON WILLIAMS	~24	8 Inf C	B ~1839 OH. 1860: R Bucyrus, Crawford Co., OH; occ farmer on father's farm. E Jun 61 corporal. Sep 62: absent, wounded in hospital. Promoted to sergeant on 1/5/63. KIA Jul 2 or 3.
R3#14	DAVID W COLLINS (MN WASHINGTON)	27	4 Inf G	B 9/9/1835 PA. 1860: R Cessna, Hardin Co., OH; occ schoolteacher. E Jun 61 private. Apr→May/Jun 62: detached service as hospital nurse. Aug 62: hospitalization for an unspecified condition. Feb→May 63: absent, sick in hospital for unspecified condition. KIA Jul 2.

R3#15	WILLIAM BAIN	~28	4 Inf G	B ~1835 Delaware Co., OH. Occ laborer. E (Camp Dennison near Cincinnati, OH) Aug 61 private. Hospitalization since 9/28/62 & 11/14/62→Feb 63 for unknown condition. KIA 2. Survivor (WC39355): M Mrs. Mary Bain 62 in 1864 (widow of Findley Bain).
R3#16	LIEUT ADDISON EDGAR	~24	4 Inf	B ~1839 Allegheny County, OH. 1860: R Washington, Hardin Co., OH. Occ schoolteacher. E Jun 61 private. Promoted to sergeant on 6/6/61. Promoted to 1st sergeant on 1/9/02. Commissioned 2nd lieutenant on 3/29/63. C Jul 1: wounded in left shoulder. D Jul 2.
R3#17	ANDREW MYERS or MYRES	~24	4 Inf G	B ~1839 Germany. 1860: R Pleasant, Hardin Co., OH. Occ laborer. E (Kenton, Hardin Co., OH) Jun 61 private. Aug 62: absent, sick shipped onboard transport at Harrison's Landing, VA. Sep/Oct 62: present with regiment. KIA Jul 2.
R3#18	LIEUT GEORGE HAYWARD	23-24	29 Inf E	B ~1839 OH. Occ clerk. E (Conneaut, Ashtabula Co., OH) Sep 61 2nd sergeant. Oct/Nov 62: absent, assigned guard duties at hospital in Frederick City, MD. Promoted to 1st sergeant on 1/2/63. Commissioned 1st lieutenant on 5/25/63 (not mustered). KIA Jul 3. Survivor (WC31016): M Mrs. Betsey Hayward 60 (widow of Samuel Hayward).
R3#19	JEREMIAH MYERS 74 Inf G			No killed Gettysburg soldier with this or similar name in any Ohio regiment found in military sources.
R3#20	JOHN OWENS	19-20	75 Inf G	B ~1843 Preble Co., OH. Occ farmer. E (Camden, Preble Co., OH) Oct 61 private. Absent, sick with unspecified condition in Union Hospital, Georgetown, D.C: 4/30→8/31/62. KIA Jul 1: wounded in both thighs.
R3#21	IRA L BRIGHAM	~36	8 Inf H	B ~1827 VT. R Medina, Medina Co., OH. Occ blacksmith. E Jun 61 private. C Jul 2. D Jul 2 or 4.
R3#22	G WALKER GEORGE WASHINGTON WART[277]	31-32	82 Inf F	B ~1831 Northampton, Northampton Co., PA. 1860 R: Madison, Hancock Co., OH. Occ cooper. Drafted Oct 62 private. KIA Jul 1: GSW to the head. Survivors (WC85995): W Elizabeth (M Nov 55| ReM 1865): 2 ♂- Michael 6, George 4.
R3#23	JOHN GLOUCHLEN 25 Inf H			No killed Gettysburg soldier with this or similar name in any regiment found in military sources.

---

277 **Drafted soldier's death leaves wife and two young children**. George Wart was drafted in October 1862 and would leave his wife and two sons, aged 4 and 3, to head off to war.

R4#1	ANTHONY MERVALE ANTOINE **MERVILLEE** or MERVALD	28	5 Inf G	B 6/23/1835 Belgium. Occ farmer. E (Camp Dennison near Cincinnati, OH) May 61 private. May/Jun 62: reported AWOL. C Jul 3: wound to right arm→amp. D Jul 14 or 17.
R4#2	J SENARD GEORGE **LANEHART**	~30	5 Inf D	B ~1833 Germany. R Cincinnati, OH. Occ laborer. E Jun 61 private. Wounded on 6/9/62 at the Battle of Port Republic in Rockingham Co., VA. May/Jun 62: sent to the hospital in Washington, D.C., then absence on furlough. C Jul 3: GSW to right thigh. D Jul 16.
R4#3	CHARLES REINHARDT CHARLES **RHINEHARDT** or REINHARDT	39-40	Batty I 1 OH LA	B ~1823 Germany. E (Cincinnati, OH) Sep 61 private. Nov 62→Mar 63: absent, sick in the hospital with an unspecified condition. C Jul 1: wounded in both thighs. D Jul 1 or 2
R4#4	GEORGE NIXON[278]	41-42	73 Inf f	B 1821. Canton, Washington Co., PA. R Vinton Co., OH. Occ farmer. E 61 private. C Jul 2: wound in the right hip and side incurred during scrimmaging. D Jul 10. Survivors (WC84443): W Margaret 37 (M Jan 43| D 1865); 3 chn: 1 ♀- Sarah 11 & 2 ♂- Boston 7, Hiram 5.
R4#5	AUGUST RABER	20-21	107 Inf F	B ~1842 Germany. E (Sandusky Co., OH) Aug 62 private. Detached to ambulance service: 12/22/62→May 63. C Jul 1: wounded in left forearm. D Aug 2.
R4#6	ELISHA L LEAKE (MN LYMAN)	34-35	73 Inf G	B ~1828 OH. R Jackson Co., OH. Occ farmer. E Nov 61 private. C Jul 2: wounded in jaw and right eye. D Jul 8. Survivors (WC79491): W Margaret 24 (M Mar 55| ReM 1864); 3 chn: 2 ♀- Christiana 7, Harriet 5 & 1 ♂- Cyrus 2.
R4#7	LUCAS STRUBLE LUCAS **STROBEL**	19-20	107 Inf A	B ~1843 Germany. E Aug 62 private. 1860: R Sandy, Tuscarawas Co., OH. Occ: attending school while residing on father's farm. C Jul 2: wounded in right thigh. D Jul 25.
R4#8	JOHN DAVIS	36-37	75 Inf K	B ~1826 OH. R Vernon, Scioto Co., OH. Occ furnace laborer. E Oct 61 wagoner→private. C Jul 1: wounded in both thighs→amp at left thigh. D Jul 10. Survivor (WC27850): W Elizabeth 50 (M Feb 1855); no chn.

---

278 **Brave rescue of a future U.S. President's great grandfather.** Richard Enderlin, then a musician with the 73rd OH, would earn a Congressional Medal of Honor 34 years later for crawling out between opposing lines to bring in the wounded and wailing George Nixon, great-grandfather of the future 37th President of the United States. Upon returning safely to the Union line tugging Nixon, Captain Thomas Higgins extolled to Enderlin: "Dick, you are a brave boy and I now make you a sergeant." Notwithstanding Enderlin's highly meritorious rescue, George Nixon would die on July 10.

R4#9	THOMAS GILLERAN[279]	43-44	61 Inf K	B ~1819 Ireland. E Sep 61 private. KIA Jul 3. Survivor (WC162221 not online): W Honora 56 (M May 40); no chn.
R4#10	CORP G B GREINER GEORGE B GREINER	30	73 Inf G	B Jul 1833 Staunton, Augusta Co., VA. R Wayne, Fayette Co., OH. Occ: farm laborer. E Aug 62 private. KIA Jul 2. Survivors (WC21635); W Sarah 26 (M Sep 54| ReM 1865); 3 ♂- William 8, Emit 6, Columbus 5.
R4#11	JACOB SWACKHAMER JACOB **SWACKHAMMER**	25-26	73 Inf G	B ~1837 OH. R Vinton Co., OH. Occ day laborer. E Dec 61 private. C Jul 2: wound fracturing right femur. D Jul 20.
R4#12	J J SPARRY ISAAC J SPERRY	37	73 Inf G	B 7/9/1825 Ross, Butler Co., OH. R Good Hope, Fayette Co., OH. Occ merchant. E Dec 61 private. C Jul 2: wounded in right chest. D Jul 5. Survivors (WC19739): W Huldah 32 (M Mar 50); 2 ♀- Ada 12, Alice 7.
R4#13	JACOB MITCHELL[280]	24-25	55 Inf C	B ~1838 NY. 1860: R Southport, Chemung Co., NY; occ farm laborer. E Nov 61 private. C Jul 3: wounded in left leg and right arm. D Jul 30. Survivor (WC41272): M Mrs. Elizabeth Mitchell 49 (widow of William Mitchell).
R4#14	CHAUNCEY HASKELL	27-28	82 Inf F	B ~1835 VT. Occ laborer. E Dec 61 private. C Jul 1: severe wound in right leg→amp. D Jul 25.
R4#15	WM E POLLOCK WILLIAM E POLLOCK	30-31	55 Inf C	B ~1832 NY. R Huron Co., OH. Occ machinist. E Nov 61 private. C Jul 2: wounds caused by premature explosion of a shell from a Union battery. D Jul 5. Survivor (WC10266): W Sarah 24 (M Oct 55| ReM Jul 1864); 1 ♀- Ida 6.
R4#16	BENJAMIN F HARTLEY (MN FRANKLIN)	25-26	75 Inf E	B ~1837 VA. R Athens, Dover Co., OH. Occ coal miner. E Aug 62 private. C Jul 1: compound fracture wound of the right femur caused by a double canister ball. D Jul 17. Survivors (WC103659): W Margaret 21 (M Feb 59| ReM 1865); 2 chn: 1 ♂- William 3 & 1 ♀- Sedalia 15 months.
R4#17	SERGT THOMAS H RICE	37-38	73 Inf B	B ~1825 Gallia Co., OH. R Waterloo twp, Athens Co., OH. Occ carpenter. E Aug 62 private. Promoted to sergeant on 11/7/62. C Jul 3: wounded in the head. D Jul 16. Survivors (WC28750): W Mary 30 (M Jun 54); 5 chn: 3 ♀- Charlotte 8, Huldah 6, Elizabeth 7 months & 2 ♂- Henry 4, Thomas 2.

---

279 **Incongruous death**. Honora Gilleran's widow's pension application included a note from a company captain. The note that her husband had been killed improbably as he was performing the chore of carrying emptied coffee kettles from the men back to the cooks.

280 **Soldier's death prompts brother to enlist**. Eleven months after Jacob had enlisted into the army, his father William died at 55 years of age. Jacob had been the main support of his enfeebled father and mother. Four months after Jacob's death, his brother George would enlist into the army and in 1864 sustain a disabling wound at Petersburg.

R4#18	JOSEPH BARRETT	29-30	73 Inf G	B ~1833 Jefferson Co., OH. R Ross Co., OH. Occ day laborer. E Sep 62 private. C Jul 2: wound to right knee→amp. D Jul 18. Survivor (WC17164): W Mary 29 (M Mar 56); no chn.
R4#19	ANDREW SAMILLER ANDREW **LAHMILLER**	28-29	107 Inf A	B ~1834 Stark Co., OH. R same. Occ carpenter. E Aug 62 private. C Jul 1. D Jul 20.
R4#20	WM R CALL WILLIAM R CALL	25	73 Inf B	B 10/01/1837 OH. R Portsmouth, Scioto, OH. Occ laborer. E Nov 61 private. C Jul 2. D Jul 16. Survivors (WC40914): W America 27 in 1864 (M Oct 57); 3 chn: 2 ♀- Effie 4, Elizabeth (born 10/19/63 or 15 weeks after father's death) & 1 ♂- William 2.
R4#21	ISAAC RICHARDS	28-29	82 Inf A	B ~1834 Champaign Co., OH. R Hardin Co., OH. Occ farmer. E Nov 61 private. C Jul 1.
R4#22	ADAM SCHNEIDER[281] ADAM **SNYDER**	~17	107 Inf H	B ~1846 Stark Co., OH. R Stark Co., OH. E Aug 62 musician. Oct 62: present as a private. C Jul 1. D Jul 1 or later.
R4#23	CORP J R GOODSPEED JAMES **H** GOODSPEED	19-20	75 Inf D	B ~1843 OH. 1860: R Athens, Athens Co., OH; occ: farmer residing on father's farm. E Oct 61 private. Promoted to corporal on 10/6/62. C Jul 2: wounded in right hip. D Jul 19.
R4#24	WM MILLER WILLIAM MILLER	~21	25 Inf G	B ~1842 Muskingum Co., OH. Occ farmer. E Jun 61 private. C Jul 1: wound to left knee. D Jul 22 due to complicating typhoid pneumonia.
R4#25	NATHAN HEALD[282]	19	73 Inf h	B 1/23/1844 OH. 1860 R: Rome, Athens Co., OH. E Nov 61 private. C Jul 2: wounded in the arm and chest. D Jul 3.
R5#1	E T LEVETT EDWARD T **LOVETT**	~21	25 Inf I	B ~1842 OH. 1860: R Elk, Noble Co., OH; occ farmer. E Jun 61 corporal. KIA Jul 1.

---

281 **Minor at death.** In Louisville, Ohio, Adam Snyder enlisted into the 107th Ohio infantry as a musician, giving his age, as of August 1862, as 18, or the minimal qualifying age for entrance into the army. A July 11, 1860 U.S. Census identifies a 14-year-old Adam Snyder residing in Nimishillen, Stark County, Ohio, less than four miles from Louisville. If this is the same Adam Snyder who enlisted into the army in 1862, then he was likely only 16 at this enlistment. Interestingly, an Ancestry.com family tree gives Snyder's birthyear as 1847, which would translate to an enlistment age of 15 or 16 and an age at death of 16 or 17.

282 **Minor at enlistment.** Nathan Heald's birthdate is given as January 23, 1844 on both an Ancestry.com and a FindAGrave.com web posting. Taking this birthdate to be accurate, Nathan was 17, not 18 at his enlistment and 19 when he was killed at Gettysburg.

R5#2	WM WILLIAMS WILLIAM WILLIAMS	26	73 Inf I	B ~Jan 1837 Saratoga Co., NY. Occ boatman. E (Camp Dennison near Cincinnati, OH) Nov 61 private. Discharged from service due to disability of a pre-existing, large inguinal hernia (Discharging surgeon commented that "man should never have been accepted"). Nevertheless, soldier re-enlisted (surreptitiously?) on 8/31/62. KIA Jul 3.
R5#3	HENRY OPHIR HENRY **OPHER**	24-25	55 Inf E	B ~1838 Germany. E (Vermilion, Erie Co., OH) Nov 61 private. KIA Jul 3.
R5#4	WM ACKERMAN WILLIAM ACKERMAN[283]	35-36	73 Inf D	B ~1827 Germany. 1860: R Milton, Jackson Co., OH; occ butcher, farmer. E Oct 61 private. Aug→Nov 62: on duty as teamster. D Jul 4: killed by an accidental discharge of a musket.
R5#5	J MYERS JOHN R **MYER**	19-20	55 Inf C	B ~1843 Switzerland. R Milan, Erie Co., PA. Occ farmer. E Sep 61 private. KIA Jul 3.
R5#6	SERGT CALEB DEWEES	26	73 Inf F	B 9/24/1836 Morgan, Morgan Co., OH. R Marion twp, Morgan Co., OH. Occ carpenter. E Oct 61 corporal. Promoted to sergeant on 9/1/62. KIA Jul 3. Survivors (WC19799): W Rachel 27 (M Dec 58); 1♂- Charles 3.
R5#7	A J MADDOX **A I** MADDOX	~21	73 Inf C	B ~1842 OH. 1860 R: Washington, Jackson Co., OH. E Sep 62 private. KIA Jul 3. Survivors (WC123230): M Mrs. Rebecca Maddox 57 in 1866 (Jesse Maddox affirmed disabled due to breast cancer condition).
R5#8	O C FORD OZIAS C FORD	32	55 Inf A	B 8/18/1830 Newfield, Tompkins Co., NY. 1850: R Huron Co., OH; occ farmer. E Jul 62. D Jul 2 of wounds.
R5#9	WM WHITBY WILLIAM WHITBY	18-19	73 Inf H	B ~1844 OH. 1860 R: Liberty, Ross Co., OH. E Jul 62 private. KIA Jul 3.
R5#10	J R BLAKE JOSEPH R BLAKE	18-19	73 Inf I	B ~1844 Ross Co., OH. 1860 R same. Occ farmer. E (Greenfield twp, Fairfield Co., OH) Oct 62 private. Mar/Apr→May/Jun 62: hospitalizations for an unspecified condition. Nov/Dec 62: fined $0.50 in a court martial for an evidently minor, but unspecified infraction. KIA Jul 2.
R5#11	A MILLER ANDREW MILLER	20-21	73 Inf I	B ~1842 Ross Co., OH. 1860 R: Greenfield twp, Fairfield, OH. Occ laborer. E Nov 61 private. March/Apr 62: absent, sick. Aug 62: AWOL as of 8/25/62. Nov/Dec 62: fined $2 in a court martial sentence for an unspecified infraction, possibly the AWOL. KIA Jul 3.

---

283 **Accidental shooting**. On July 4th, William Ackerman was purportedly killed by an accidental discharge of a musket.

R5#12	WM McCLUE WILLIAM **McCLUEN**	45-46	73 Inf B	B ~1817 Ireland. Occ laborer. E (Waverly, Pike Co., OH) Nov 61 private. Detached to the 12th Independent Battery OH Light Artillery on 5/1/62. Aug/Sep 62: absent sick. Transferred back to 73rd OH infantry on 1/7/63. KIA Jul 2.
R5#13	CORP JAMES H LEE	26	73 Inf H	B 12/01/1836 Collinsville, Butler Co., OH. E (Albany Co., OH) Oct 61 private. Appointed 1st corporal 12/23/61. Mar/Apr 62: absent, sick. AWOL 12/15/62→4/5/63. KIA Jul 3.
R5#14	WM C HANES WILLIAM **E HAYNES**	29-30	73 Inf B	B ~1833 OH. R Huntington, Ross Co., OH. Occ farmer. E Oct 61 private. KIA Jul 3: shot though both thighs and died on the field. Survivors (WC20989): W Mary 26 (M Nov 54); 4 chn: 3 ♀- Ann 7, Mary 6, Nancy 4 & 1 ♂- Abraham 2.
R5#15	ALLEN YAPLES ALLEN **YAPLE**	35	73 Inf A	B 12/16/1827 Ross Co., OH. R Colerain, Ross Co., OH. Occ school teacher. E Aug 62 private. Dec 62: promoted to corporal. KIA Jul 3: shot in the head.
R5#16	A M CAMPBELL ANDREW **McKINNEY CAMPBELL**	20-21	105 PA Inf E	B ~1842. R Westmoreland Co., PA. E Sep 61 private. Absent, hospitalization: Jul/Aug 62 and 10/31/62→3/1/63 for unspecified conditions. C Jul 2: wounded in head. D Jul 8.
R5#17	HENRY C STARK	21	4 Inf I	B 3/8/1842 Kingston, Delaware Co., OH. R same. Occ farmer. E Jun 61 private. C Jul 2: wounded by a shell. D Jul 11.
R5#18	J W HARL JAMES W HARL	~22	4 Inf A	B ~1841 Mt Vernon, Knox Co., OH. Occ laborer. E Jun 61 private. Absent sick: 10/25/61→Nov 61. Absent in hospital: 8/28/62→Nov 62. Jun 63: company cook. C Jul 2. D Jul 5, 7 or 9.
R5#19	BERNARD McGUIRE	~27	8 Inf B	B ~1836. E Jun 61 private. Promoted to corporal on 10/31/62. C Jul 3. D Jul 10.
R5#20	JOHN McKELLIPS JOHN **McCILLIP**	~33	8 Inf C	B ~1830 PA. 1860: R Champion, Trumbell Co., OH; occ blacksmith. E Jun 61 private. C Jul 2: wounded in the hip while fighting on an advanced skirmish line. D Jul 10.
R5#21	G MARTIN GEORGE H MARTIN	~23	4 Inf G	B ~1840 Beaver Co., PA. Occ laborer. E Apr 61 private. Aug 62: absent (AWOL vs sick?). Attached to Washington, DC since 9/28/62 where employed as a cook. Nov 62: on extra duty as a nurse. Jan 63: absent, sick at Washington, D.C. C Jul 2: GSW to abdomen. D Jul 6.
R5#22	SERGT P F TRACEY PHILIP **TRACY**	~26	8 Inf G	B ~1837 OH. 1860 R: Silvercreek twp, Greene Co., OH. E Apr 61 corporal. Promoted to sergeant on 6/5/61. C Jul 3: wound to shoulder. D Jul 5. Survivors (WC34370): 1 ♂- William 6; Maternal GM Mrs. Catharine Atherton 51 in 1864. M Susannah (M Feb 56; died 2/11/57).

R5#23	COLOR CORP WM WELCH[284] WILLIAM WELCH	19-20	8 Inf I	B ~1843 Sheffield, Berkshire Co., MA. R Lorain Co., OH. E Aug 61 private. Promotion to corporal during service. C Jul 3. D Jul 12.
R5#24	SAMUEL MOWERY SAMUEL **MAURER**	18-19	107 Inf A	B ~1844 Switzerland. E Aug 62 private. C Jul 2: wounded in right leg. D Jul 15. Survivors (WC95280): M Mrs. Annie Maurer 50 in 1865 (Jacob Maurer affirmed unable to perform labor).
R5#25	E K RANNY EDWARD **GEORGE RANNEY**	19	61 Inf D	B 12/21/1843 Peninsula, Summit Co., OH. 1860 R: Northfield, Summit Co., OH. E Mar 62 corporal. C Jul 2: wounded in right shoulder and lung. D Jul 6.
R6#1	E M DETTY ENOCH MILTON DETTY[285]	22-23	73 Inf G	B ~1840 OH. 1860: R Liberty, Ross Co., OH; occ: farm laborer. E Jan 62 private. D Oct 26 of chronic diarrhea.
R6#2	2 LIEUT GEORGE McCARY GEORGE W **McCREARY**	31	82 Inf C	B 7/15/1831 Davisville, Jackson Co., OH. E Nov 61 sergeant. Wounded 5/2/63 at Chancellorsville. Commissioned 2nd lieutenant during service. KIA Jul 2: wound to head by a shell fragment.
R6#3	WILLIAM FOLK[286] 82 Inf D			Misidentified soldier in grave. Military sources affirm that William Folk was captured Jul 1 at Gettysburg and would die at Andersonville one year later.
R6#4	M JACOBS MARTIN JACOBS	23-24	82 Inf D	B 5/4/1839 Germany. 1860 R: Pleasant, Marion Co., OH. E Nov 61 private. KIA Jul 1.
R6#5	JOHN WISER JOHN **WEISER**[287] 82 Inf D			Misidentified soldier in grave. A John Weiser would be wounded at Gettysburg, but he would be exchanged and continue in service until leaving the army under a disability discharge in July 1864.

---

284   **Eighth Ohio Infantry Color Corporal is mortally wounded in audacious July 3rd charge.** A company card included in William Welch's National Archives service file gives his age at enlistment as 16, not the age 18 he affirmed on this enlistment paper. A post-enlistment discovery within his company that he was actually 16 might have led to this notation on the company card.   However, this age would have been at variance with the successive 1850 and 1860 U.S. Censuses where William's ages were given respectively as 7 and 17. At the cresting moments of the July 3rd Confederate approach on the Union center, William Welch was a member of the 8th Ohio color guard, as the 220-odd men of the regiment rose from an embankment section of the upper Emmitsburg Road to audaciously perform a left wheel maneuver and pour a disrupting, flanking fire into the passing leftmost columns of the Longstreet-Pickett-Pettigrew assault.

285   **First burial in National Cemetery.** A FindAGrave.com memorial identifies Enoch Detty was the first soldier to have been reburied into the National Cemetery.

286   **Misidentified soldier in grave.** William Folk was captured at Gettysburg on July 1st and would die in Andersonville one year later.

287   **Misidentified soldier in grave.** John Weiser was captured at Gettysburg on July 1st, but he would be exchanged and would leave the army with a disability discharge in July 1864. Dying in Ohio the next year, he is buried in a cemetery in Ashley, Delaware County, Ohio.

ID	Name	Age	Unit	Details
R6#6	R BROILLER RICHARD BROLLIER[288] 82 Inf D			Misidentified soldier in grave. A Richard Brollier, or Braller, did enlist into the 82nd Ohio infantry Company D. However, this soldier's service record shows that he mustered out of the unit in Dec 63 before reenlisting with the Veteran Volunteers Corps in Jan 64.
R6#7	E A HAIN ELI ALBERT HAIN	20	82 Inf H	B 2/6/1843 Marion Co., OH. 1860 R: Pleasant, Marion Co., OH. Drafted in Oct 62 as a private. KIA Jul 1.
R6#8	WM H BUSK WILLIAM H **BUSH**	24-25	82 Inf F	B ~1838 NJ. 1860: R Hanover, Ashland Co., OH. E Nov 61 private. Occ farmer. KIA Jul 1.
R6#9	J WARNER JACOB WARNER	22-23	82 Inf H	B ~1840. 1860: R Richland, Marion Co., OH; occ farmer. Drafted Aug 62 as a private for a one-year term. KIA Jul 1.
R6#10	ELMER LEROY ROSS	20	82 Inf C	B 9/12/1842 Auburn, Crawford Co., OH. R Mifflin twp, Wyandot Co., OH. E Nov 61 private. KIA Jul 1. Survivor (WC11499): Alzina 23 (M Aug 61| ReM 1870); no chn.
R6#11	FRANCIS H BLOUGH	20-21	82 Inf C	B ~1842 Belpre, Washington Co., OH. 1850 R same. Occ farmer. E (Patterson, Hardin Co., OH) Nov 61 private. Jan/Feb 63: detailed as wood chopper. Mar 63: detailed as HQ teamster. KIA Jul 1
R6#15	JOHN McCLEARY JOHN **McCLARY**	23-24	66 Inf D	B ~1839 Bath Co., VA. 1860 R: Jefferson, Franklin Co., OH. Occ saddler. E (Quincy, Logan Co., OH) Oct 61 private. Jun/Jul 62: AWOL since Jun 8. Sep/Oct 62: confirmed held in Confederate confinement. Paroled at Aiken's Landing on 9/13/62. Sent to Washington, D.C. on 9/26/62. Feb/Mar 63: assigned fatigue duty at Provost Marshall's HQ since 2/27/63. KIA Jul 3.
R6#16	GEORGE K WILSON GEORGE **R** WILSON[289]	~24	8 Inf B	B ~1839. E (Cleveland, OH) Jun 61 private. KIA Jul 3.
R6#17	O A WARREN ORVILLE A WARREN	~25	8 Inf K	B ~1838. E May 61 private. Jull/Aug 62→Dec 62; absent, sick at Alexandria. Jan/Feb 63: absent in convalescent camp. KIA Jul 3.
R6#18	OZRO MOORE	~43	8 Inf I	B ~Jul 1820 Avon, Lorain Co., OH. 1850 R same. E Aug 61 private. KIA Jul 3.

---

288 **Misidentified soldier in grave**. Richard Brollier was not killed at Gettysburg. In December 1863, he mustered out of the 82nd Ohio Infantry to reenlist in the Veteran Volunteers Corps the next year.

289 **Empty grave**? George Wilson's remains were likely disinterred and taken back to his home state of Ohio. An 1864 burial registration card identifies a George Wilson, belonging to this same 8th Ohio Company B unit and citing the identical enlistment and killed-in-action dates, buried in the GAR section of the Greenwood Cemetery in Hamilton, Ohio.

R6#19	WILLIAM BROWN	~20	8 Inf B	B ~1843 Blackman, MI. E Jun 61 private. Jun 62: hospitalized at Williamsport, MD. Jul 62: absent, sick in Winchester, VA. Sep 62: hospitalized in Strasburg, VA. Oct 62: absent, wounded in Frederick, MD. Nov 62→Feb/Mar 63: AWOL. Apr/May 63: absent, sick in Cleveland hospital. Jun 63: charged with straggling on return from Cleveland hospital. KIA 3.
R6#20	SERGT J K BARCLAY **JOHN KENDALL** BARCLAY	~22	8 Inf C	B ~1841 PA. E (Camp Dennison near Cincinnati, OH) Jun 61 private. Promoted to sergeant on 6/24/63. KIA Jul 2. Survivor (WC78588): M Mrs. Martha Barclay 58 in 1866 (widow of George Barclay).
R6#21	T SHAFFER **FRANK** SHAFFER or SCHAFER	~34	8 Inf D	B ~1829 Richland Co., OH. Occ harness maker. E Bellevue, OH. Jun 61 private. Aug/Sep 62: on duty as captain's cook. Jan/Feb 63: promotion to corporal. KIA Jul 3.
R6#22	DAUFORD PARKER **DANFORD** PARKER	36-37	8 Inf K	B ~Oct 1825 Canada. R Harrisville, Medina Co., OH. Occ wagon maker, farmer. E Aug 62 private. Survivors (WC18913): W Sophronia 34 (M Aug 47 | ReM 1865): 3 ♂- William 13, Henry 9, Austin 5.
R6#23	PERRY CRUBAUGH **JEREMIAH** BLACKFORTH CRUBAUGH	19	75 Inf C	B Oct or Dec, 1843 OH. 1860: R Van Buren, Montgomery Co., OH; Occ farm hand. E Nov 61 private. C Jul 2. D Jul 3.
R6#24	JOHN EDMUNDS JOHN N **EDMONDS**[290]	24-25	Batty H 1 OH LA	B ~1838 OH. 1860 R: Lucas Co., OH; occ teacher? E Oct 61 private. C Jul 2: shell wound causing compound fracture of left ankle→amputation→gangrene onset →2nd amputation. D Jul 16. Survivor (WC203217 not on line) M Mrs. Emeline Vanfleet 61 (widow of Tyler Edmonds, 2nd husband Mathias Van Fleet).
R6#25	JAMES MYER **JOHN FREDERICK HUMELMEYER**	37-38	Batty I 1 OH LA	B ~1825 Germany. R Cincinnati, OH. Occ drayman (wagon driver). E Nov 61 private. C Jul 2: wounded in the head and left hand by shell. D Jul 6. Survivors (WC82459): W Mrs. Antoinette Humelmeyer 44 (M Apr 49); 4 chn: 2 ♂- Ferdinand 13, John 4 & 2 ♀- Mary 10, Eliza 8.
R6#26	A HOUCK ANDREW W HOUCK	36-37	82 Inf F	B ~1826 Baltimore Co., MD. 1860 R: Jackson, Hancock Co., OH. Occ carpenter. Drafted in Oct 62 as a private. Wounded 5/2/63 at Chancellorsville, VA. KIA Jul 1.
R6#27	JOSEPH KLINEFETTER JOSEPH **KLINEFELTER** or CLINEFELTER	39-40	55 Inf F	B ~1823 York Co., PA. Occ mechanic. R Jackson twp, Sandusky Co., OH. E Oct 61 private. KIA Jul 3: GSW causing instant death. Survivors (WC19244): W Mrs. Sarah Clinefelter 29 in 1864 (M Aug 52); 4 chn: 2 ♀- Amanda 8, Lovina 6 & 2 ♂- John 4, Charles 10 months.

---

290 **Dying declaration.** On July 15, 1863, a hospital attendant wrote to Mrs. Emma Van Fleet, John Edmonds' mother, to relay to her son's thoughts that he did not expect to see her again but that he was "happy because I trust in God and died to help save my country." Before sending off the letter the following day, the hospital attendant would add the postscript that Edmonds had died that day.

74th Pennsylvania Infantry Monument on Howard Avenue

★ ★ ★ ★ ★

Model of Color Sergeant George Eckert, cited for bravery at Chancellorsville and wounded at Gettysburg, as statement of regiment's resistance before being overwhelmed as part of the 11th Corps rout on the first day's battlefield.

Pennsylvania

R1#1	SERGT SAMUEL JAMES SAMUEL T JAMES	21-22	106 Inf B	B ~1841 Philadelphia. R same. E Aug 61 sergeant. C Jul 2: wounded in neck. D Jul 2 or 4.
R1#2	A F STROCK ANDREW F STROCK	25-26	72 Inf D	B ~1837 Bucks Co., PA. Occ ship joiner. E (Philadelphia, PA) Aug 61 private. Promoted to corporal on 3/14/62. Promoted to sergeant on 1/1/63. KIA Jul 3.
R1#6	CHARLES HAVERMEHEL 87 Inf I			B ~1817. E Sep 61 private. D 3/13/1874 (age ~66-67).
R1#9	LOUIS HEITZMAN **LEWIS** HEITZMAN 11 Inf E			B ~1829. E Sep 64 private. D/C date? D 2/16/1877 (age ~47-48).
R1#10	EBENEZER H JAMES	~23	121 Inf A	B ~1840. E Jul 62 private. C Jul 1: wounded in arm. D Jul 15 or 16. Survivor (WC193220 not online): M Mrs. R. D. McElvay.
R1#11	SERGT S C GIFFIN PVT SAMUEL C GIFFIN[291] 15 Cav A			B 5/3/1816 Gettysburg, PA. Present at Gettysburg with the 41st PA Infantry Company C. ReE Jan 64 with the 15th PA Calvary Company E. D/C Jul 65. D 7/11/1881 (age 65).
R1#13	ADAM McELROY 101 Inf K			B ~1818. R Gettysburg, Adams Co., PA. Occ painter. E Nov 61 private. Discharged with disability certificate 12/16/63. D 9/10/1884 (age 65-66)
R1#16	LT CLARENCE M CAMP (MN MORTIMER) Battery B Indpt PA LA			B 1/23/1841. R Butler twp, Adams Co., PA. E Aug 61 private. D/C 10/12/65. D 3/8/1888 (age 47).
R1#17	THOMAS C HARDY US Ship Savannah			B 1837. E Marine Corps private. D 11/8/1888 (age ~51)

---

291 **Post Civil War burials.** As reburials into the state lots of the Gettysburg cemetery were begun from their back rows, Pennsylvania found itself with the opportunity to complete the nearly-empty first row with ceremonial burials of local Civil War soldiers, including later some who served during other wars. Samuel Giffin was one such soldier, who was born in Gettysburg, who was present during the battle, who survived it and who went on to serve two more years in the army. A FindAGrave.com memorial explains his posthumous honoring as "sergeant," as owing to the fact that local townspeople referred to him as "Color Sergeant." He had earned this sobriquet by faithfully presenting to carry the American flag at every memorial celebration until the year he died.

R1#18	CHARLES H WEAVER 15 Cav M			B 6/24/1837 Adams Co., PA. 1860: R Gettysburg, PA; occ: livery keeper. E Aug 62 private. D 11/21/1888 (age 51).
R1#19	GOTTLIEB MILTENBERGER 74 Inf B			B Germany. Purportedly reported MIA at Gettysburg. D 9/17/1889 from accidental severe head injury at a GAR encampment.
R1#20	FREDERICK REITINGER AND WIFE		87 Inf I	B ~1836 Germany. 1860: R Oxford twp, Adams Co., PA; occ laborer. E Oct 61 private. D 5/6/1890 (age ~53-54); Sarah Reitinger (M Jul 1857| died 12/21/1907.
R1#21	JOHN H HOFFMAN (MN HENRY) 21 Cav B			B ~1842. 1860 R: Adams Co., PA. E June 63. private. D/C Feb 64. D 7/10/1890 (age 47-48).
R1#22	W J ROBINSON WILLIAM J ROBINSON 138 Inf E			B ~1840. E Aug 62 private. Wounded on 5/5/64 at the Wilderness. D/C May 64. D 10/8/1891 (age ~51).
R1#23	CORP HERBERT S BOYD 21 Cav H			B ~1829. E Feb 64. corporal. D/C Jul 65. D 10/28/1894 (age ~65).
R1#24	ELIJAH LEECH 1 PRC K			B ~Aug 1842. E Sep 61 private. D/C May 64. D 4/15/1895 (age 52).
R1#25	HENRY RICHTER 48 Inf E			B ~ 1833. E Aug 63 corporal. D/C Dec 64. D 11/10/1896. (age ~63).
R1#26	SERGT JAMES P McLAUGHLIN 1 PRC H			B 4/27/1837 Gettysburg, PA. 1860: R same; occ brickmaker. E Sep 61 private. D/C Jul 97. D 7/13/1897 (age 60).
R1#27	PETER G HOAGLAND	22-23	Batty B 1 Res LA	B 1840 NJ. R Lawrence Co., PA. 1860 occ: apprentice shoemaker. E Aug 61 private. C Jul 2. D Jul 2 or 4.
R1#28	GEO W KING GEORGE W KING 3 Art C			B ~1838. E Oct 62 private. D 12/29/1902 (age ~64).
R1#29	JOHN A ARENTZ 165 Inf C			B ~1838. Drafted Oct 62 private. D/C date? D/C date? D 4/27/1906 (age 67-68).

R1#30	G W FLEMMING GEORGE WASHINGTON FLEMMING 87 Inf I		B Sept 1836. E Oct 61 private. D 11/7/1906 (age 70).
R1#31	WILLIAM TINSLEY ANNIE, HIS WIFE	5 S Cav F	B ~10/13/1840. E Aug 61 private. D 7/11/1908 (age 67). Annie (M Sep 92	died 3/23/1931.
R1#32	ISAAC ROOF 165 Inf A		B ~1838. Drafted Oct 62 private. D 11/16/1908 (age ~70).
R1#33	LEO P NACE 2 H Art D		B 3/31/1835 Adams Co., PA. E Feb 64 private. D/C Jan 66. D/C Jan 66. D 11/25/1910 (age 75).
R1#34	SAMUEL LITTLE SAMUEL A LITTLE, JR. 205 Inf I		B 1/12/1835 Adams Co., PA. E Aug 64 private. D/C Jun 65. D/C Jun 65. D 2/10/1911 (age 76).
R1#35	THEO CULLISON THEODORE CULLISON 188 Inf F		B 3/21/1837. E Jan 64. private. D/C Dec 65. D 9/23/1911 (age 74).
R1#36	ELIAS STEINOUR 99 Inf F		B ~1842. E Mar 65. private. D/C Jul 65. D 2/14/1912 (age ~69-70).
R1#37	DAVID BROWNELL 16 Cav F		B ~1841. E Sep 62. private. D/C Aug 65. D 6/7/1912 (age ~70-71).
R1#38	JAS BINGAMAN JAMES ANDREW BINGAMAN 101 Inf K		B ~1835 Gettysburg, PA. E Apr 61 private. D/C date? D/C date? D 8/31/1912 (age 76-77).
R1#39	JEFF CASSATT JEFFERSON THOMAS CASSATT 87 Inf F		B 4/29/1835. E Jan 64 private. MO Apr 64 on disability discharge. D 2/16/1913 (age 77).
R1#40	GEORGE W STOVER 98 Inf C		B 4/29/1839. E Mar 65 private. D/C Jun 65. D 12/23/1913 (age 74).

R1#41	WILLIAM H EPLEY (MN HENRY) 138 Inf B	B 2/9/1839 Gettysburg, PA. E Aug 62 private. MO Jun 65. D 9/9/1915 (age 76).
R1#42	CORP GEORGE F BLACK 1 Cav H	B 10/9/1843. E Feb 64 corporal. MO Jun 65 to transfer to the 1st Provisional Cavalry. D 5/2/1916 (age 72).
R1#43	JOHN T WEIKERT (MN THOMAS) 138 Inf B	B 2/23/1838. E Aug 62 private. MO Jul 65. D 7/29/1916 (age 78).
R1#44	HENRY F SLONAKER (MN FRANCIS) Warren's Indpt Cav	B ~1835. E Jul 64 private. MO Nov 64 (100 days). D 8/2/1917 (age ~82).
R1#45	THOMAS FLAHARTY 21 Cav B	B ~1847 private. E Feb 1865. Mo Jul 65. D 11/17/1917 (age ~70).
R1#46	SAMUEL C WADDLE 126 Inf C	B ~1840. E Aug 62 private. MO Sept 62. D 5/17/1921 (age 80-81).
R1#47	ADAM SNYDER (MN JOHN) 21 Inf D	B 3/13/1843. E Jun 63 private. MO Jul 65. D 6/30/1921 (age 78).
R1#48	GEO W STAPE GEORGE W STAPE 107 Inf E	B 11/29/1845 Lancaster Co., PA. Occ laborer. E Jan 62 private. Feb 63: detailed from ranks to serve as captain's cook. C Jul 1: slight wound in the arm at Gettysburg. Desertion from hospital for an undocumented period. Transfer to Invalid Corp 2/11/64, then returned to company 6/6/64. Captured Aug 64 at Weldon RR. Parole date not found. MO June 65. D 11/20/1921 (age 75).
R1#49	PETER M LOWE (MN MORSE) 188 Inf B	B 9/5/1846. E Oct 62 into 3rd PA HA Co C as a private. Transferred to 188th PA Infantry on 4/1/ 64. Wounded in the cheek in Jun 64 at Cold Harbor. D 1/18/1922 (age 75).
R1#50	FRANK X WEIRICK War with Spain 5 Inf M	B Feb 1863. E Jul 1898 private. D 9/7/1902, reportedly of "heart and lung trouble," contracted while in the service during the Spanish American War (age ~39).

R2#5	_____ BARR JOHN BARR[292]	21-22	140 Inf G	B ~1841. E Aug 62 private. KIA Jul 2.
R2#13	_____ OXFORD			No killed Gettysburg soldier with this name found in military sources.
R2#17	WILLIAM McGREW	23-24	70 Inf K	B ~1839 PA, native of Mummasburg, Franklin twp, Adams Co., PA. R Adams Co, PA. Occ shoemaker. E Sep 62 private. C Jul 2. D Jul 26. Survivor (WC39486): M Mrs. Jane McGrew 55 in 1864 (widow of Alexander McGrew).
R2#19	CHARLES MARTIN	32	107 Inf C	B ~Mar 1831. R Sullivan Co., PA. Occ botanist. E Aug 62 private. KIA Jul 1. Survivors (WC59543): W Abigail 35 in 1865 (M May 61 | ReM 1866); 1 ♂- Luther 21 months.
R2#21	A K COOLBAUGH ABSALOM **RUNYON** COOLBAUGH	31-32	141 Inf C	B ~1831 PA. R Asylum, Bradford Co., PA. Occ farm laborer. E Aug 62 private. KIA Jul 2: immediate death caused by shot in the head. Survivors (WC11968): W Emily 30 (M Mar 1852); 3 ♀- Margaret 9, Anna 6, Carrie 21 months.
R2#22	JOSHUA M HIDER	24-25	106 Inf I	B ~1838 PA. E Aug 61 private. D Jul 3 of wounds. Survivor (WC11082): M Mrs. Elizabeth Hider 59 (widow of John Hider).
R2#24	MATTHEW JOHNSTON **MATHEW JOHNSON**	21-22	11 Inf H	B ~1841. E (Mauch Chunk, Carbon Co., PA) Oct 61 private. Sick, sent to the hospital Oct 62. May/Jun 63: returned to regiment. C Jul 1. D Jul 2.
R2#26	G M S GEORGE M STEFFEY	19-20	148 Inf F	B ~1843 Huntingdon Co., PA. E Aug 62 private. KIA Jul 2. The exact matching of the initials "G M S" with those of the killed Pennsylvanian soldier George M. Steffey is highly confirmatory. Also tending to confirm this identification is the fact that Joseph Carver buried on the left is also a soldier of the 148th PA infantry. Survivors (WC174556 not online): M Mrs. Elizabeth Steffey 60 in 1873 (George Steffey unable to provide support to old age and rheumatism).
R2#27	JOSEPH CARVER JOSEPH CARVER, JR	25-26	148 Inf C	B ~1837. R Centre Co., PA. Occ laborer. E Aug 62 private. KIA Jul 2. Survivor (WC72634): M Mrs. Mary Carver 50 in 1865 (widow of Joseph Carver, Sr.).
R2#28	JOHN McNUTT	~18	140 Inf G	B ~1845 PA. 1860 R: Chartiers, Washington Co., PA (on father's farm). E (Pittsburgh, PA) Aug 62 private. D Jul 2 of wounds.

---

292 **Identity question**. Private John Barr of the 140th PA infantry is proposed as the likely soldier interred in this grave, even though the headstone indicates that the "Barr" was a soldier in 195th PA. In actuality, the 195th PA infantry was not even organized until July 1864.

R2#29	FRANCIS A OSBORNE (MN ALBERT)[293]	18-19	16 Cav E	B 1844 Rockland, Venango Co., OH. E (Franklin, Venango Co., PA) Sep 62 private. KIA Jul 3.
R2#32	GEORGE COGSWELL	~25	26 Inf A	B 1838. R Philadelphia, PA. E May 61 private. Promoted to corporal during service. KIA Jul 2.
R2#33	JOHN BUNN JOHN **BURNS**	20-21	26 Inf C	B ~1842. R Philadelphia, PA. E May 61 private. Slightly wounded 5/5/62 at Williamsburg, VA. KIA Jul 2.
R2#34	WILLIAM KELLEY WILLIAM H KELLEY	~24	121 Inf A	B ~1839. E (Franklin, Venango Co., PA) Aug 62 private. KIA Jul 1.
R2#37	S BROOKMEYER **DANIEL WILLINGMEYRE**	30	26 Inf A	B ~ March 1833 Philadelphia, PA. R same. Occ boot fitter. E Sep 62 private. KIA Jul 2.
R2#38	J LITTLE JOHN LITTLE	~35	26 Inf B	B ~1828. E (Philadelphia, PA) May 61 private. KIA Jul 2.
R2#41	PETER McMAHON	~42	26 Inf E	B ~1821. R Philadelphia, PA. E May 61 private. Promotion to corporal during service. KIA Jul 2. Survivors (WC11917): W Mary 42 (M Nov 41); 2 chn: 1 ♀- Emma 14 & 1 ♂- William 2.
R2#42	CHARLES KELLY			Scant information beyond the common name on this grave stone prevents identifying this buried soldier.
R2#43	E B BROWN **ELKIHAN** BROWN or ELIAKIM BROWN	~27	26 Inf K	B ~1836. E (Philadelphia, PA) Jun 61 private. Promotion to corporal during service. KIA Jul 2. Survivor (WC32496): 1 ♀- Mary 11; Mrs. Mary Sweeney 33 (sister of Elkihan Brown, whose guardianship is established in lieu of the death of the mother, Mrs. Mary Brown, on 1/18/58 due to tuberculosis).
R2#46	JON ZONWELL			No killed Gettysburg soldier with this or similar name in any regiment found in military sources.
R2#48	WILLIAM NEIL WILLIAM **NEILL**	~37	26 Inf I	B ~1826 PA. R Philadelphia Co., PA. Occ tailor. E May 61 private. KIA Jul 2. Survivors (WC36529): W Margaret 35 (M Jan 52); 2 chn: 1 ♀- Margaret 4 & 1 ♂- William 3.

---

293 **Minor at enlistment?** Osborne may have been underaged at enlistment. Francis and his family are not found in the 1860 U.S. Census. Francis Osborne is found in the 1850 Census and reported 3 years old. However, a birthyear of 1847 is not elsewhere confirmed.

R2#51	SAMUEL FITZINGER	21-22	106 Inf B	B ~1841 PA. R Philadelphia, PA. E Aug 61 private. Promoted to corporal on 7/5/62. C Jul 2: wound to groin. KIA Jul 2. Survivor (WC17280): M Mrs. Margaret Fritzinger 42 (widow of John Fritzinger).
R2#53	H C TAFEL HENRY C TAFEL	~21	62 Inf I	B ~1842 PA. R Birmingham, Allegheny Co., PA. 1860 R: same. Occ sailor. E Jul 61 sergeant. Court martial sentence on 1/1/62 of reduction of rank back to private and forfeit of one month's pay on account of unspecified offense. KIA Jul 2.
R2#55	DAVID W BOYD	23-24	140 Inf G	B ~1839 PA. 1860 R: Somerset, Washington Co., PA; residing on father's farm. E (Canonsburg, Washington Co., PA) Aug 62 private. KIA Jul 2.
R2#61	HARRY EVANS HENRY EVANS[294]	26-27	88 Inf B	B ~1836. E (Philadelphia) Sep 61 sergeant. KIA Jul 1. Survivors (WC15646→ WC840382 neither online): W Emma 27 (M Apr 54│ Dropped 1883); 3 ♀- Mary 8, Clara 6, Ella 4.
R2#66	G MICKLE GEORGE MICKLE	~19	72 Inf C	B 1844 Philadelphia, PA. Occ laborer. E (Philadelphia) Aug 62 private. KIA Jul 3.
R2#75	S B STEWART SAMUEL BERNARD STEWART[295]	~26	2 PRC F (31 Inf)	B 1837 Huntingdon Co., PA. R Blair Co., PA. E Aug 62 private. Oct 62: court martial sentence of $3 to be forfeited from one month's pay for an unspecified infraction. D Jul 3 of wounds. Survivors (WC86011): W Sarah 25 (M Oct 56); 3 ♂- James 6, John 4, Samuel 2.
R2#76	_____ WELSH			Scant information beyond the simple last name on this grave stone prevents identifying this buried soldier.
R2#78	WALTER S BRIGGS Adjutant	26	27 Inf	B Sep 1836 Weymouth, Atlantic Co., NJ. 1860: R Camden, NJ; occ clerk. E Sep 61 private. Appointed corporal 10/1/61. Commissioned 2nd lieutenant 1/18/62. Promoted to 1st lieutenant/adjutant 9/25/62. C Jul 2. D Jul 2 or 3.
R2#79	W D MILLARD WESTON D MILLARD	19	149 Inf F	B 10/6/1843 Luzerne Co., PA. 1860 R: Huntington Mills, Luzerne Co., PA. E Aug 62 private. KIA Jul 1.
R2#80	ANDREW R McKINNEY			Killed Gettysburg soldier with this name not found in military sources.

---

294 **Widow dropped from pension rolls for "adulterous cohabitation."** Following up on a fraud allegation, a special examiner for the U.S. Pension Office in October 1883 advised dropping Mrs. Emma Evans from the pension rolls on account of "adulterous cohabitation." The same month, Mrs. Evans married David L. Evans (not Henry's brother, but a Civil War veteran of the 205th Pennsylvania Infantry), to whom she bore five children, the first in 1867f. At David Evans' death in 1916, the 80-year-old Mrs. Evans applied for and received approval of a widow's pension based on this second husband's service.

295 **Separate gravesite in the Evergreen Cemetery.** Samuel Stewart also has a headstone in the Evergreen Cemetery. Presumably the National Cemetery site is a reburial.

R3#1	REUBEN MILLER	~27	71 Inf K	B ~1836 Philadelphia, PA. R Philadelphia, PA. E Jun 61 private. Jul/Aug→ Sep/Oct 62: sick in hospital at Sharpsburg, MD. KIA Jul 3.
R3#2	JACOB CHRIST or JACOB CRIST	~36	56 Inf D	B ~1827 PA. R Coal, Northumberland Co., PA. Occ miner. E 1861? or MI Mar 62? KIA Jul 1: GSW into the forehead. Survivors (WC111518): W Barbara ~36 (M Dec 48); 2 chn: 1 ♀- Eva 9 & 1 ♂- Samuel 7.
R3#3	ROBERT JOHNSTON	~23	28 Inf G	B ~1840. E (Sewickley, Allegheny Co., PA) Jul 61 private. Wounded 9/17/62 near Sharpsburg, MD. KIA Jul 3.
R3#4	AUTON FRANK **ANTON FRANZ FRANK**	~29	74 Inf H	B ~1834 Germany. E (Pittsburgh, PA) Aug 62 private. KIA Jul 3.
R3#5	JOHN W BUCHANAN (MN WESLEY)	~21	1 PRC A (30 Inf)	B ~1842 Honey Brook, Chester Co., PA. 1860: R same: occ blacksmith apprentice. E Jul 61 private. KIA Jul 3.
R3#6	N TOWNSEND **CHARLES** TOWNSEND	31-32	1 PRC C (30 Inf)	B ~1831 Austin, TX. Occ seaman. E (West Chester, Chester Co., PA) Jul 61 private. Wounded and captured on 8/30/62 at 2nd Bull Run. Nov 62: paroled and sent to Alexandria. KIA Jul 3.
R3#7	W H BURREL WILLIAM H H **BURRELL**	22-23	148 Inf F	B ~1840 Potter, Centre Co., PA. R Spring, Mills Co., PA. Occ carpenter. E Aug 62 private. Promoted to corporal on 1/12/63. KIA Jul 2. Survivors (WC61760): W Anne 23 (M Feb 61); 1 ♂- James 14 months.
R3#8	WILLIAM ORR[296]	~25	62 Inf I	B ~1838 Ireland. R Jefferson Co., PA. E Jul 61 private. KIA Jul 2.
R3#9	SERGT R DOTY ROBERT DOTY	26	105 Inf F	B 7/07/1836 Grant township, Indiana Co., PA. E Sep 61 sergeant. Killed Jul 2: headwound inflicted by a stray ball striking him while company not engaged in battle.
R3#10	DAVID WINNING DAVID WALLACE **WINANS**	21	18 Cav D	B 12/2/1841 Crawford Co., PA. E Oct 62 private. KIA Jun 29 in skirmish in Hanover, York Co., PA.
R3#11	JACOB HARVEY	21-22	18 Cav M	B ~1841. E (Philadelphia, PA) Oct 62 private. Promotion to corporal during service. KIA Jun 30 in Hanover, York Co., PA.

---

[296] **One of the thousands of Irish immigrants to fight in the Civil War.** William Orr, accompanying his older brother Joseph, arrived in Philadelphia from Ireland in October, 1854. Irish immigrant enlistees were present in large numbers in both Union and Confederate armies.

R3#12	WILLIAM CRAWFORD	~48	18 Cav C	B ~1815. R Richhill, Greene Co., PA. Occ: farmer and stone cutter. E Sep 62 private. KIA Jun 30: body found lying in the street in Hanover, having been killed with a saber wound. Survivor (WC31824): W Barbara 52 (M Jul 45); 3 grown chn:2 ♂- Alpheus 23, Solomon 21 & 1 ♀- Mary 20.
R3#13	W N WILLIAMS	30-31	143 Inf K	B ~1832 Wayne Co., PA. 1860 R: Hartford, Susquehanna Co., PA. Occ carpenter. E Aug 62 corporal. C Jul 3. D Jul 6.
R3#14	JACOB ZIMMERMAN	44-45	151 Inf I	B ~1818 PA. R Richmond, Berks Co., PA. Occ laborer. E Sep 62 private. Detached to artillery corps 2/28/63. C Jul 1. D Jul 14. Survivors (WC16716): W Mary 38 (M Jan 45); 3 chn: 1 ♂- Nathan 16 & 2 ♀- Mary 13, Susannah 11.
R3#15	A R FISH ALVA **H** FISH	19-20	150 Inf I	B ~1843 Broome Co., NY. 1860: R Oil Creek, Crawford Co., PA; occ farm laborer on father's farm. E Aug 62 private. C Jul 1. D Jul 30.
R3#16	A LEES ALFRED LEES	19-20	150 Inf A	B ~1843 England. 1860: R Philadelphia, PA; occ carpet weaver. E Aug 62 private. C Jul 3. D Jul 12.
R3#17	WILSON MILLER	29	90 Inf G	B ~Apr 1834 Ireland. R Philadelphia, PA. Occ gardener. E Aug 62 private. C Jul 3: mortal wound to the bowels incurred while skirmishing. D Jul 5. Survivors (WC41143): W Eliza 29 (M Mar 62); 1 ♂- Francis 4 months.
R3#18	J STROBLE JACOB **STRUBLE**	21-22	11 Inf D	B 1841 PA. 1860: R Hempfield, Westmoreland CO., PA; attending school. E Sep 61 private. Wounded 9/17/62 at Antietam. C Jul 1. D Jul 5.
R3#19	C B LING CHRISTIAN B LING	20-21	56 Inf B	B ~1842 PA. R Indiana Co., PA. Occ farmer. E (Blairsville, Indiana Co. PA) Sep 61 private. C Jul 1: wound to right ankle→amp. D Jul 18.
R3#20	WENDLE DORN[297] **WENDELL DORNBECKER**	21-22	139 Inf I	B ~1841. R Allegheny, Allegheny Co., PA. E (Pittsburgh, PA) Aug 62 private. D Jul 3 of wounds. Survivor (WC42204): W Mary 19 (M Aug 62); no chn.
R3#22	SAMUEL DEARMOTT	~23	62 Inf C	B ~1840. R Clarion Co., PA. Occ farmer. E Jul 61 private. C Jul 2. D Jul 2 or 3.

---

[297] **Fighting under an alias.** In her pursuit of a widow's pension, Mary Dornbecker was required to explain her husband's use of the alias "Dorn" in enlisting into the army. Mrs. Dornbecker offered that her husband had always disliked the name Dornbecker and that he had begun using the beyond the abbreviated "Dorn" prior to entering the army.

R3#23	JOHN STOTTARD JOHN STODART[298]	19	110 Inf A	B 4/30/1844 Canada. E (Tyrone, Blair Co., PA) Aug 61 private. Captured 8/29/62 at 2nd Bull Run. Paroled 9/5/62 at Gainesville, VA. Nov 62: Camp Parole, then sent to Alexandria, VA. KIA Jul 2. Survivor (WC85731):M Mrs. Joanna Stodart 44 in 1865 (widow of Robert Stodart).
R3#24	FRANCIS M HANSEL (MN MERRIAN)	19-20	140 Inf E	B ~1843 Fayette Co., PA. E (Pittsburgh, PA) Aug 62 private. KIA Jul 2.
R3#25	SERGT JOSEPH HCORE or CARE	30-31	110 Inf A	B ~1832. R Blair Co., PA. E oct 61 sergeant. KIA Jul 2: GSW to the head.
R3#26	J D CAMPBELL JAMES D CAMPBELL	29-30	140 Inf C	B ~1833 PA. R Washington Co., PA. Occ shoe merchant. E Aug 62 private. KIA Jul 2. Survivor (WC217777) M Mrs. Elizabeth Miller 80 in 1884 (presumed widow of John Campbell, who deserted wife and was never heard from again).
R3#27	T J CARPENTER THOMAS J **CARTER**	23-24	140 Inf K	B ~1839 PA. R Washington Co., PA. E Sep 62 private. KIA Jul 2.
R3#28	TOBIAS JONES[299]	19	153 Inf B	B 9/1/1843. 1860: R Bethlehem, Northampton Co., PA; attending school. E Sep 62 private. KIA Jul 1.
R3#30	JESSE COBURN SAMUEL JESSE **COLBURN**	30-31	142 Inf C	B ~1832 PA. R Venango Co., PA. E Aug 62 private. C Jul 1. D Jul 6 or 10. Survivor (WC87947): W Catherine 21 (M Jun 60); no chn.
R3#31	JOHN W McKINNEY[300] (MN WESLEY)	19	1 PRC K (30 Inf C)	B ~Aug 1843 PA. R Mount Joo, Adams Co., PA. E Aug 61 private. Jan/Feb 63: sick in general hospital at Alexandria. D Feb 24 of typhoid fever. Survivor (WC49747): M Mrs. Eliza McKinney 42 (widow of Robert McKinney).
R3#32	SERGT H McCARTY HENRY McCARTY	32-33	114 Inf K	B ~1830 NY. R Philadelphia, PA. Occ bookbinder. E Aug 61 private. Nov/Dec 62: promotion to sergeant. KIA Jul 1. Survivor (WC25722): M Mrs. Mary McCarty 56 (widow of Patrick McCarty).

---

298 **Brothers enlist the same date into 110th Pennsylvania Infantry.** On August 23, 1861, John Stodart and his older brother, James, together signed enlistment papers to join the 110th Pennsylvania Infantry, both being assigned to Company A. Less than six months later, James would lie dead in a Hagerstown hospital.

299 **Empty grave.** The 1865 Report of the Select Committee Relative to the Soldiers' National Cemetery, in its listings of all of the named soldiers buried there, notes that Tobias Jones's remains were removed. This notation, however, does not appear on his Gettysburg gravestone. Nevertheless, Tobias Jones does have another gravestone in the Nisky Hill Cemetery in Bethlehem, Pennsylvania. Likely this is where today his remains are interred.

300 **Misidentified soldier in grave?** John McKinney's death in an Alexandria hospital four months before the Gettysburg battle poses the question of whether the soldier here is a reburial or a misidentification.

R3#39	JOHN WALKER JOHN W WALKER	27-28	110 Inf C	B ~1835. R Blair Co., PA. E Nov 61 private. Dec 62: detached to serve in Pioneer Corps. Apr 62: absent sick in Division hospital. KIA Jul 2.
R3#41	WILLIAM CROWL XXX	21-22	141 Inf K	B ~1841 PA. R Sullivan Co., PA. Occ stone mason. E Aug 62 private. C Jul 2. D Jul 8.
R3#42	ROBERT ROBINSON ROBERT **ROBISON**	33-34	4 Cav L	B ~1829. E Sep 61 private. Nov 62→Jan 63: detailed as a teamster. KIA Jul 3 or 5.
R3#43	GUY SOUTHWICK	20	16 Cav L	B 1/6/1843 Crawford Co., PA. R same. Occ miner. E Oct 62 private. C Jul 3: accidentally shot by a member of his own regiment. D Jul 7.
R3#44	JOHN G COYLE (MN GRIFFIN)	43	150 Inf C	B 7/13/1819 Rome, Crawford Co., PA. R Meadville, Crawford Co., PA. Occ farmer. E Aug 62 private. KIA Jul 1.
R3#45	F HUBBARD[301] 150 Inf B			Misidentified soldier in grave. One internet source has suggested that private Stephen Hubbard of the 150th PA infantry Company B is buried here. However, Hubbard was captured at Gettysburg on July 1st, not killed. He would return to Union service and he would remain active until transferred out in July 1865.
R3#47	WILLIAM VOSBURG 2nd Division Buford's Cav			No killed Gettysburg soldier with this name found in military sources.
R3#49	G WM **GERSHAM WILLIAMS**[302]	~23	CONFED GA 3 Inf A	B ~1840 Richmond Co., GA. 1860; occ attending school. E Apr 61 private. Hospitalized in Richmond, VA 7/4→7/29/62 with typhoid fever. Granted 30-day furlough following release. Hospitalized again in Richmond, VA 2/22→3/6/63 with typhoid fever. C Jul 2. D Jul 9.
R3#51	SERGT GEORGE O FELL (MN OGDEN)	19	143 Inf B	B 7/12/1843 PA. R Luzerne Co., PA. Occ farmer. E Aug 62 private. Promoted to corporal on 2/1/63. C Jul 3: wounded in one hip. D Jul 5.
R3#81	LIEUT JOHN F COX	30-31	57 Inf I	B ~1832 New Castle. Lawrence Co., PA. R Mercer Co., PA. Occ cabinet maker. E Sep 61 sergeant. Commissioned 2nd lieutenant on 8/11/61. KIA Jul 2. Survivors (WC92116): W Harriet 26 in 1866 (M Apr 57): 2 ♀- Jennie 4, Eula 2.

---

[301] **Misidentified soldier in grave**. Stephen Hubbard was captured on July 1st at Gettysburg, not killed. He ultimately would be returned to Union service and only transfer out of service in 1865.

[302] **Confederate in the Cemetery**. Gersham Williams is the soldier generally accepted interred here beneath the headstone "G Wm." Gersham Williams was a member of the 3rd Georgia Infantry, Company A and is one of the nine known Confederates mistakenly buried in the National Cemetery.

R4#3	CALVIN POTTER	21-22	149 Inf H	B ~1841 NJ. Occ farmer. E (Strattanville, Clarion Co., PA) Aug 62 private. KIA Jul 1.
R4#6	SAMUEL M CALDWELL	~19	118 Inf D	B ~1844 Philadelphia, PA. R same. Occ clerk. E Aug 62 corporal. KIA Jul 2: shot in the head.
R4#7	FREDERICK SHONER	23-24	72 Inf E	B ~1839 PA. R Philadelphia, PA. 1860 occ: apprentice to scale maker. E Aug 61 private. KIA Jul 3.
R4#8	JEREMIAH BOYLE	28-29	69 Inf H	B ~1834 Ireland. R Philadelphia, PA. E Sep 61 sergeant. KIA Jul 3: instant death being caused by being struck by a shell. Survivors (WC12283): W Mary 27 (M Oct 55); 4 chn: 2 ♂- William 6, John & 2 ♀- Catharine 3, Mary 1.
R4#9	GEORGE HERPICH	27-28	71 Inf H	B ~1835 Philadelphia, PA. E Aug 61 corporal. Resigned rank→becomes private on 10/2/61. KIA Jul 3.
R4#10	JAMES McMANUS JAMES **McCANN**	24-25	69 Inf D	B ~1838. R Philadelphia, PA. E (Philadelphia) Aug 61 corporal. KIA Jul 3.
R4#11	JAMES GALLAGHER	30-31	71 Inf H	B ~1832 Philadelphia, PA. R same. E Aug 61 private. KIA Jul 3.
R4#12	SERGT J GALLAGHER JEREMIAH GALLAGHER	30-31	69 Inf D	B ~1832 Ireland. R Philadelphia, PA. E Aug 61 sergeant. KIA Jul 3: "riddled with gunshot." Survivor (WC42712): 1 ♀- Abagail 2| W Sarah (M Dec 59| D 12/5/62).
R4#13	S S ODARE SAMUEL SYLVESTER **O'DARE**	24	71 Inf I	B 1/6/1839 Philadelphia, PA. E May 61 private. C Jul 3. D Jul 5.
R4#14	WILLIAM SHULTZ WILLIAM CORSON SHULTZ[303] or SCHOLTZ	~23	71 Inf I	B ~1840 PA. R Philadelphia, PA. E Jun 61 corporal. C Jul 2: wound through right thigh and into left thigh. D Sep 29.
R4#15	WILLIAM SIMPSON	26-27	145 Inf D	B ~1836. R Eric Co., PA. E Aug 62 private. C Jul 2: GSW fracture of femur. D Jul 16.

---

[303] **Pain management of dying soldier.** Following his August 6th acceptance into Camp Letterman Hospital, William Schultz appeared to be improving. However, beginning September 1st, William began experiencing very severe cramping pains in the lower part of his abdomen. Chloroform and all forms of opiates were found to only temporarily relieve these pains. William would go on to die on September 29th. William had had a young brother, Henry, who has a member of the 51st Pennsylvania Infantry had been killed in action at Antietam.

R4#16	ANTHONY STARK ANTHONY **STARR**	30-31	106 Inf G	B 1832 PA. R Moreland, Lycoming Co., PA. Occ laborer. E Apr 62 private. C Jul 2: wounded in leg→below-knee amp→above-knee amp. D Jul 15. Survivors (WC61204): W Lucinda 29 (M Jun 54); 3 chn: 2 ♂- Alfred 8, Anthony 14 months & 1 ♀- Selecta 3.
R4#17	CHARLES TRISKET CHARLES PORTER **TRISCUT**	19-20	145 Inf E	B ~1843 Freehold, Warren Co., PA. 1860: R Wayne, Eric Co., PA; occ laborer. E Aug 62 private. C Jul 2: shot in the face and hip. D Jul 15.
R4#18	CHARLES F SOBY (MN FINNEY)	30	118 Inf I	B 3/13/1833 Philadelphia, PA. 1860: R Suffield, Hartford Co., CT; occ cigar maker. E Apr 61 20th PA inf; MI Aug 61, then E Aug 62 118th private. C Jul 2. D Jul 3.
R4#24	G H ALLEN GEORGE HARVEY ALLEN	21	57 Inf C	B 4/4/1842 PA. R Middlesex, Butler Co., PA. Occ farmer. E Nov 61 private. Promoted to corporal during service. C Jul 3: wound from solid shot. D Jul 5.
R4#25	CHARLES McCONNEL or McCONNELL	20-21	11 Inf K	B ~1842 PA. 1860: Loyalhanna, Westmoreland Co., PA; occ laborer. E (Youngstown, Westmoreland Co., PA) Sep 61 corporal. Wounded on 12/13/62 at Fredericksburg. C Jul 3. D Jul 4.
R4#26	JOHN AKER JAMES L AKERS[304]	~18	CONFED MS 2 Inf K	B ~1845 MS. 1860: Tishomingo Co., MS; occ farm laborer. E Jul 1862 private. C Jul 1. D Jul 1 or 3.
R4#28	JACOB KEIRSH	22-23	Indpt Battery F PA LA	B ~1840 Alleghany Co., PA. Occ blacksmith. E (Pittsburg, PA) Oct 61 private. May 63: detailed to Norton's Battery H, 1st OH Light Artillery and posted on Cemetery Hill Jul 1-2. C Jul 2: leg severed by a shell during battle. D Jul 2 or 4.
R4#30	J GRAVES THOMAS JEFFERSON GRAVES	34	CONFED GA 21 Inf I	B 6/29/1829 GA. R Stewart Co., GA. E Jul 61 private. Promoted to sergeant during service. KIA Jul 2
R4#36	GEORGE MOYER or MYERS	~25	2 PRC F (31 Inf)	B ~1838. E/ReE Aug 61 private. Court martial on 10/27/62 with sentence of forfeit of one month's pay for an unspecified offense. C Jul 2. D Jul 26.
R4#37	CORDILLO COLLINS **CORDELLO H** COLLINS	33	13 PRC D (42 Inf)	B ~1840 NY. 1860: R Kinzua, Warren Co., PA; occ blacksmith. E May 61 private. C Jul 3: wounds to right thigh and left hand. D Jul 30.

---

[304] **Confederate in the Cemetery.** James Akers, one of the nine known Confederates mistakenly buried in the National Cemetery, had entered the 2nd Mississippi infantry as a substitute for his older brother John, who had been drafted.

R4#38	ANDREW J PETTIGREW[305]	~21	11 PRC C (40 Inf C)	B ~1842 PA. R Butler Co., PA. Occ day laborer. E Jun 61 private. C Jul 3: wound to right thigh→amp. D Jul 13. Survivor (WC21840): W Mary 21 (M 3/27/63); no chn.
R4#39	MILTON CAMPBELL	~21	11 PRC C (40 Inf C)	B ~1842 PA. E Jun 61 private. C Jul 1 or 2: GSW fracturing left femur→amp. D Aug 1.
R4#40	SAMUEL ZACHMAN SAMUEL **SECHMAN**	~24	6 PRC E (35 Inf E)	B ~1839 Limestone, Union Co., PA. Occ laborer. E (Danville, Montour Co., PA) May 61 private. C Jul 2: mortal bayonet wound. D Jul 15.
R4#41	A S DAVIS ABRAHAM S DAVIS	~26	1 PRC G (42 Inf)	B ~1837 Canada. R Penfield, Clearfield Co., PA. Occ lumberman. E May 61 private. C Jul 2 or 3: wounded in left shoulder. D Jul 24.
R4#42	GEORGE STEWART	38-39	2 PRC E (31 Inf E)	B ~1834. R Philadelphia, PA. E Aug 61 private. Jan/Feb 63: forfeit of one month's pay for an unspecified infraction. Promotion to corporal on 5/9/63. C Jul 3: wound to left ankle. D Jul 26. Survivors (WC22559): W Caroline 33 (M Nov 46); 8 chn: 5 ♂- Thomas 16, William 13, George 6, twins Abram and John 18 months & 3 ♀- Catharine 11, Ann 8, and Caroline 3.
R4#43	ROBERT LEUZENMYER ROBERT **LINSENMEYER**	24-25	2 PRC E (31 Inf E)	B ~1838 PA. 1860: R Pittsburgh, PA; occ blacksmith. E Aug 61 private. Promoted to corporal on 9/20/62. C Jul 2. D Jul 25.
R4#44	F SMITH FRANCIS SMITH	~20	26 Inf I	B ~1843. R Philadelphia, PA. E May 61 private. KIA Jul 2. Survivor (WC24811): M Mrs. Mary Catharine Smith 59 in 1864 (widow of Francis Smith).
R4#46	JAMES BINKER	~19	106 Inf B	B ~1844 Philadelphia, PA. R Philadelphia, PA. E Aug 61 private. C Jul 2: wounded in the abdomen. D Jul 4. Survivors (WC21309): M Mrs. Hester Binker 45 (Thomas Binker affirmed crippled and unable to support wife).
R4#47	HENRY W BEEGEL HENRY W **BEEGLE**	20-21	110 Inf H	B ~1842 PA. R Blair Co., PA. Occ farmer. E Aug 62 private. C Jul 3: wounds to the jaw, neck and shoulder. D Jul 9.
R4#48	JAMES L PURYNE (MN LESTER)	25	Batty F 1 Res LA	B 12/11/1837 PA. R Wayne Co., PA. Occ farmer. E Jul 61 private. C Jul 3: severely wounded in right leg. D Jul 20.

---

305 **Soldier killed fifteen weeks after marriage.** On March 27, 1863 in Butler County, Pennsylvania, Mary Wiles married private Andrew Pettigrew of the 11th Pennsylvania Reserves Infantry. With Pettigrew's death July 10th from a July 3rd battle wound, the new Mrs. Pettigrew would be a widow after only fifteen weeks of marriage.

R4#49	O S CAMPBELL ORLANDO S CAMPBELL	25-26	111 Inf K	B ~1837 PA. 1860: R Fox, Elk Co., PA; occ day laborer. E Dec 61 private. KIA Jul 3: GSW to head. Survivors (WC126093): W Martha 42 in 1867 (M Aug 59| ReM 1/31/64); 1 ♀- Irene 1.
R4#50	J WATSON JOHN WATSON	~46	29 Inf I	B ~1817 PA. 1850: occ clerk. E (Philadelphia, PA) Jul 61 private. Sep/Oct 61: hospitalized in Baltimore for unspecified condition. Nov/Dec 61: continuing in the Baltimore hospital for four months first for convalescence and then retained as a nurse. Taken prisoner 5/18/62 near New Market, VA. Paroled 9/13/62 at Aiken's Landing, VA. KIA Jul 3.
R4#51	THOMAS ACTON[306]	32	29 Inf B	B ~1831 Boston, MA. R Philadelphia, PA. Occ seaman. E Jun 63 private. Joined regiment on the march 6/27/63 while in Frederick, MD. KIA Jul 2.
R4#52	JAMES MORROW	~29	29 Inf I	B ~1844. E (Philadelphia) Jun 61 private. KIA Jul 2.
R4#53	JAMES D BUTCHER	~23	28 Inf D	B ~1840 Camden, Camden, NJ. R Philadelphia, PA. 1860: occ coachmaker apprentice. E Jan 62 private. Promoted to corporal on 12/1/62. C Jul 2 or 3. D Jul 3.
R4#54	JOHN RICHARDSON	18	111 Inf B	B 11/15/1844 Deerfield, Warren Co., PA. R Warren Co., PA. Occ laborer. E Dec 61 private. Nov/Dec 62: absent, wounded on 9/17/62 at Antietam. KIA Jul 3: shot through the head.
R4#55	CHARLES MILLER	20-21	111 Inf B	B ~1842. Occ laborer. E (Warren County, PA) Dec 61 private. KIA Jul 3: shot through the head.
R4#56	G B WINEMAN GEORGE B WINEMAN	~22	107 Inf E	B ~1841 Metal township, Franklin Co., PA. R Franklin Co., PA. Occ farmer. E Feb 62 private. KIA Jul 3.
R4#57	JOHN S POMEROY	33	2nd BN 17 US Inf B	B 6/17/1830 Lawrence Co., PA. R New Castle, Lawrence Co., PA. E May 62 corporal. KIA Jul 2. Survivors (WC14967): W Susan 30 (M Jun 53); 1 ♀- Sally 16 months.
R4#58	T MILLER THEODORE MILLER	~27	Batty G 1st PA Res LA	B ~1836. R Philadelphia, PA. Occ weaver. E Jul 61 private. KIA Jul 1.

---

306 **Soldier killed-in-action six days after uniting with regiment.** On June 27, 1863, new recruit Thomas Acton joined the 29th Pennsylvania infantry on its march in pursuit of the Confederate army into Pennsylvania. He would be killed in action six days later at Gettysburg.

R4#59	S D CAMPBELL SAMUEL D CAMPBELL	18	142 Inf A	B 10/23/1844 PA. 1860: R Fairview, Mercer Co., PA; occ farm laborer. E Aug 62 private. C Jul 1: wound to right hip. D Aug 17.
R4#60	JOHN METZ[307]	25-26	68 Inf A	B ~1837 Philadelphia, PA. R same. Occ laborer. E Aug 62 private. C Jul 2. D Aug 18. Survivor (WC20708): W Eliza 25 (M Aug 62); 1 ♀- Hannah 11 months.
R4#61	E T GREEN ELI T GREEN[308]	~24	CONFED VA 14 Inf E	B ~1839 VA. Occ saddler. E May 61 private. C Jul 3: GSW fracturing forearm bones just below elbow→amp. Admitted to Camp Letterman hospital on Aug 7. D Aug 15.
R4#62	S N WAMER STEPHEN NATHAN **WARNER**	20-21	83 Inf H	B ~1842 Syracuse, Onondaga Co., NY. R Conneautville, Crawford Co., PA. Occ laborer. E Aug 61 private. Captured on 6/27/62 at Gaines' Mill, VA. Paroled 8/15/62 at Aiken's Landing VA. C Jul 2: GSW through left knee joint→amp. D Aug 14.
R4#63	A P McCLAREY ANDREW **McCLEARY**	23-24	63 Inf B	B ~1839 PA. E (Pittsburgh, PA) Aug 61 corporal. Rank change after 10/31/62 to private. Mar/Apr 63: approved 30-day furlough to begin 4/15/73. C Jul 2: GSW fracturing right ankle and nearly severing foot→amp. D Sep 1.
R4#64	N P GOVAN NATHANIEL P **GOWEN**[309]	26	150 Inf C	B ~1837 Allegheny Co., PA. 1860 R: Rockdale, Crawford Co., PA. Occ farmer. E Aug 62 musician. Jan/Feb 63: rank status changed to private. C Jul 1: GSW to right knee→amp. D Sep 25.
R4#65	ELISHA BOND **ALEXANDER** BOND	~39	27 Inf K	B ~1824 Ireland. R Philadelphia, PA. Occ laborer. E May 61 private. C Jul 1: wound to lower left leg→amp. D Oct 1.
R4#66	J BEIDER **ISAIAH BUDD** Proposed	~25	1 PRC F (30 Inf)	B ~1838 Gloucester Co., NJ. R Media, Delaware Co., PA. Occ operative. E May 61 private. Slightly wounded 6/30/62 in the Seven Days Battles. C Jul 2: wounded in left ankle. D Aug 1 or 3.

---

    307 **Widow dropped from pension rolls for misrepresentations**. Mrs. Eliza Metz's qualification for a supplemental dependent-child payment was reversed when an investigation revealed that that false birthdates for the child had been submitted with her pension application. The fact was that Eliza's child been born out-of-wedlock some months before her marriage to John Metz and was not certain to have been his child. Furthermore, testimony revealed that the child had always lived with Eliza's mother because Eliza "liked to drink." Subsequently, Eliza qualification for a widow's pension would also be reversed when it was revealed that following John Metz's death, she had been and was continuing to live with a man to whom she was not married.

    308 **Confederate in the Cemetery**. Eli T. Green is one of nine identified Confederates mistakenly buried in the National Cemetery. The 1850 Census shows that his father was then employed as an overseer. It does not appear that the family owned any slaves.

    309 **Tormenting last three weeks at Camp Letterman**. Following his July 24th acceptance in Camp Letterman Hospital, Nathaniel Govan's amputated thigh stump had continued to heal. However, beginning September 2nd, attacks of diarrhea and vomiting began to torment him until he finally died on September 25th.

R4#67	N McWITKIN NELSON **McMICKEN**	24	151 Inf A	B ~1839 PA. R Susquehanna Co., PA. Occ farm laborer. E Sep 62 private. C Jul 1: GSW into right knee→amp on 8/1. D Aug 12.
R4#68	HUGH FARLEY	30-31	57 Inf H	B ~1832 Bradford Co., PA. E (Litchfield, Hillsdale Co., MI) Sep 61 private. Promotion to corporal as of 12/31/61. Promoted to sergeant 11/01/62. C Jul 2: GSW to right knee. D Aug 28.
R4#69	H H HAYS HARRISON H HAYS	27-28	145 Inf A	B ~1835. R Girard, Erie Co., PA. Occ farmer. E Aug 62 private. Died Sep 15 of lung disease manifesting with hemoptysis (coughing up blood), subsequently filed as condition contracted during U.S. service. Survivors (WC62390): W Martha 26 (M Feb 59) 1 ♀- Esther 16 months.
R4#70	MAGER SORBER[310]	21	143 Inf D	B 1/17/1842 PA. R Luzerne Co., PA. E Aug 62 private. C Jul 1: wound resulting in compound fracture of the right femur. D Aug 12 (Letterman Hospital medical log noted during final days that patient was "suffering considerably with diarrhea."
R4#71	MARK BEATTY	~24	1 PRC D (30 Inf)	B ~1839 PA. 1860: R Allegheny, Allegheny Co., PA; occ clerk, cigar maker. E Jun 61 private. C Jul 2: GSW to left knee. D Aug 2.
R4#72	JOHN HARVEY JR[311]	28-29	69 Inf A	B ~1834. R Philadelphia, PA. E Aug 61 private. KIA Jul 3: shell fragment wound to the brain during pre-Pickett's charge bombardment.
R4#73	JOSEPH WERST	18-19	153 Inf C	B ~1844 PA. R Saucon, Lehigh Co., PA. Occ laborer. E Sep 62 private. KIA Jul 2.
R4#74	JOHN BOYER	31	150 Inf F	B 8/17/1831 Chester Co., PA. R Phoenixville, Chester Co., PA. E Aug 62 private. KIA Jul 1. Survivors (WC107250): W Mary 31 (M Mar 53 | ReM 1866): 5 chn: 1 ♀- Sally 8 & 4 ♂- twins Thurston and Davis 5, Nicholas 2, John 15 months.
R4#75	S M LITTLE SAMUEL M LITTLE	~21	62 Inf F	B ~1842. R Pittsburgh, PA. Occ carver. E Jul 61 private. KIA Jul 2.

---

310 **Suffering final days at Camp Letterman**. Transferring into Camp Letterman on July 24th, Major Sorber was noted to be "considerably debilitated." Over the subsequent 3½ weeks, Major began suffering considerably with diarrhea while also experiencing secondary hemorrhage from his wound site. Sorber's father, John Sorber, mustered into the army on the same September 6, 1862 date as did his son, but he had chosen to enlist into 9th Pennsylvania Cavalry. Entering the Chickamauga campaign in the West during the time of Gettysburg, John Sorber would not have been aware of his son's agonizing hospital course until he would die on August 12th.

311 **A father and son in the 69th Pennsylvania Infantry hunker down at the Angle during the July 3rd Cannonade**. On August 23, 1861, John Harvey, Sr. would enlist for the same Company A 69th Pennsylvania unit as his son had four days earlier. The father and son would serve nearly the next two years together. And likely they were attempting to shelter beside each other during the pre-Pickett's charge cannonade when John Jr. would receive a mortal head wound from a shell fragment. In what was likely a mix of PTSD and profound grief reaction, John Sr. would desert from the army on July 17. Some few months later, John Sr. would come back into army care, but in an extremely malnourished state. John Harvey, Sr would then die on November 15, 1863.

R4#76	W H DUNN WILLIAM H DUNN	~21	62 Inf F	B ~1842 PA. 1860: R Baldwin, Allegheny Co., PA. E (Pittsburgh, PA) Jul 61 private. KIA Jul 2.
R4#77	J A WALKER JOHN A WALKER	27-28	62 Inf D	B ~1835 Armstong Co., PA. R same. Occ farmer. E (Putneyville, Mahoning twp, Armstrong Co., PA) Aug 62 private. Nov/Dec 62: hospitalization in Philadelphia for an unspecified condition. KIA Jul 2.
R4#78	RICHARD LOUDMAN	~25	62 Inf H	B ~1838 England. R Allegheny Co., PA. Occ coal miner. E (Pittsburgh, PA) Jul 61 private. KIA Jul 2.
R4#79	T R WOODS THOMAS R WOODS	~20	62 Inf A	B ~1843. R Allegheny Co., PA. Occ carpenter. E Jul 61 private. KIA Jul 2.
R4#80	JOHN MATHERS	~26	62 Inf L	B ~1837. R Pittsburgh, PA. E Jul 61 private. Promoted to sergeant on 8/29/61. Reduced in rank to private on 1/1/62 for an unspecified infraction. KIA Jul 1.
R4#81	GEORGE McINTOSH GEORGE J McINTOSH	27-28	62 Inf L	B ~1835 Scotland. R Birmingham, PA. Occ laborer. E Aug 61 private. KIA Jul 2: GSW through left chest. Survivors (WC21305): W Hannah 30 residing in Philadelphia, PA (M Apr 54); 2 ♀- Hester 6, Elizabeth 2.
R4#82	SERGT J S OSBORN **ISAAC** SYLVESTER OSBORN, **SR**[312]	~34	62 Inf I	B ~1829 Rayne, Indiana Co., PA. R Jefferson Co., PA. Occ laborer. E Jul 61 sergeant. Serving as Company I color sergeant at Gettysburg. KIA Jul 2, while fighting in the Wheatfield. Survivors (WC138511): W Mary 25 (M May 58); 2 ♂- John 3, Isaac (B 10/20/63- W Mary 5-6 months pregnant at soldier's death).
R4#83	E McMAHON EDWARD McMAHON	30-31	140 Inf I	B ~1832. R Beaver Co., PA. E Aug 62 private. KIA Jul 3.
R4#84	JOHN BUCKLEY	37-38	140 Inf B	B ~1825 Sandy Lake, Mercer Co., PA. R same. Occ farmer. E Aug 62 private. KIA Jul 2. Survivors (WC38034 not online): W Harriet ~35 (M Dec 50); 6 chn: 4 ♂- George 11, Samuel 9, Job 7, Luke 2 & 2 ♀- Alice 5, Mary 3.
R4#85	JOHN LONG	22	62 Inf D	B 5/14/1841 Westmoreland Co., PA. R Armstrong Co., PA. Occ farmer. E Putneyville, Armstrong Co., PA) Aug 62 private. Sep/Oct 62: detailed to work in hospital in Frederick, MD. KIA Jul 2.
R5#13	H M KINSEL HENRY MARTIN KINSEL	25-26	110 Inf H	B ~1837. R Blair Co., PA. E (Tyrone, Blair Co., PA) Aug 62 private. KIA Jul 2.

---

312 **Soldier's widow is five-months pregnant with couple's third child at his death.** Isaac Osborn, Jr., the soldier's first son, would be born October 20, 1863.

R5#14	CHARLES T GARDNER CHARLES F GARDNER	19-20	111 Inf H	B ~1843 England. R Blair Co., PA. 1860 occ: miller (same occ as father Henry). E Oct 61 private. KIA Jul 2: GSW to head.
R5#15	HIRAM WOODRUFF[313]	~29	13 PRC G (42 Inf)	B ~1834 NY. 1860: R Keating, McKean Co., PA; occ stage driver. Occ teamster. E May 61 private. May/Jun 62: detached service as a teamster. Detached service in the ambulance train 6/30/62→12/31/62. KIA Jul 2.
R5#16	P O'BRIEN PATRICK O'BRIEN[314]	29-30	69 Inf A	B ~1833 Ireland. R Philadelphia, PA. E Aug 61 private. KIA Jul 3: wounded in the head.
R5#17	JOHN HURLEY	20-21	69 Inf H	B ~1842. E (Philadelphia) Oct 62 private. KIA Jul 3: shot in chest.
R5#18	GEORGE DUNKINFIELD[315]	22-23	72 Inf H	B ~1840 England. R Philadelphia, PA. E Aug 62 private. KIA Jul 2.
R5#19	WILLIAM EVANS	20-21	71 Inf I	B ~1842 Philadelphia, PA. R same. E May 61 private. KIA Jul 3.
R5#20	DAVID STAINROOK (MN AUGUSTUS)	21	72 Inf E	B 12/4/1841 Philadelphia, PA. R same. E Aug 61 private. KIA Jul 3.
R5#21	WILLIAM W CLARK	28-29	72 Inf A	B ~1834. R Philadelphia, PA. E Aug 61 private. KIA Jul 3: minié ball through the body. Survivors (WC17582): W Christianna 28 (M Apr 60); 1 ♂ - John 9 months.
R5#22	WILLIAM BROWN	28-29	71 Inf D	B ~1834. R Germantown neighborhood, Philadelphia, PA. E Jan 62 private. Captured 6/30/62 at White Oak/ Savage, VA. Paroled 8/5/62 at Aiken's Landing. Deserted 8/19/62 on march from Yorktown to Bethel. Returned to regiment on an unrecorded date. D Jul 3 of wounds. Survivor (WC34080): M Mrs. Abigail Brown 53 (widow of Hugh Brown).

---

[313] **Soldier's six months' detachment to the ambulance service.** Hiram Woodruff, whose pre-enlistment occupation had been as a teamster, was detached to serve in the ambulance train from July through December 1862.

[314] **The deaths of two brothers in the 69th Pennsylvania Infantry who fought at the Angle.** Patrick O'Brien fought against Pickett's charge alongside his brother William in the 69th Pennsylvania Company A. William would be wounded in the hip and would die on Jul 19. Today Williams' remains, unlike his brother's, lie buried as an unknown.

[315] **Soldier has later famous comedian as a nephew.** George Dunkinfield's brother, James, had also enlisted in the 72nd Pennsylvania infantry but James had to be discharged following a disabling wound at Fair Oaks, Virginia earlier in the war. After the war, James would have a son named William Claude Dunkinfield, who would have been George Dunkinfield's nephew. William Claude Dunkenfield would gain fame as the profane early-20th century comedian, W. C. Fields.

R5#23	ROBERT L PLATT ALONZO RICHARD PLATT	~31	150 Inf A	B ~1832 Dryden, Tompkins Co., NY. 1860: R Richmond, Crawford Co., PA; occ farmer. E Aug 62 private. KIA Jul 1: hit by shell. Survivors (WC57018): W Abigail 30 (M Jul 55); 3 chn: 1 ♀- Sibyl & 2 ♂- Hampson 3, Charles 17 months.
R5#24	D BUMGARDNER DANIEL BUMGARDNER	23-24	141 Inf A	B ~1839. 1860: R Wharton, Fayette, PA; occ farm laborer. R Bradford Co., PA. E Aug 62 private. C Jul 2: wounded in the right thigh and left knee. D Jul 23.
R5#25	GEORGE HILES	35-36	68 Inf C	B ~1827 England. R Philadelphia, PA. R same. 1850 occ weaver. E Aug 62 private. C Jul 2: wounded in left thigh. D Jul 24. Survivors (WC40518): W Ann 41 (M Jun 49); 1 ♂- James 11 and 3 non-dependent prior chn: 2 ♀- Ellen 22, Bridget 18 & 1 ♂- William 20.
R5#26	SERGT JOHN LOUGHREY	~40	26 Inf E	B ~1823 Ireland. R Philadelphia, PA. E May 61 private. Promoted to sergeant on 7/1/61. C Jul 2: wound to leg with fracture of femur. D Jul 19.
R5#27	G T BISHOP GEORGE T BISHOP	32	141 Inf I	B ~1831 PA. 1860: R Wysox, Bradford Co., PA.; occ: working as a carpenter in a saw mill. E Aug 61 private. C Jul 2: wounded in left leg→amp. D Jul 12 or 15. Survivor (WC47769): M Mrs. Bethany Bishop 60 in 1864 (widow of Israel Bishop).
R5#28	ROBERT THOMPSON	21-22	83 Inf I	B ~1841. R Erie, PA. E Sep 61 private. Promoted to corporal on 4/1/63. C Jul 2: wounded in the lung. D Jul 7.
R5#29	SERGT J MYERS JACOB MYERS	~27	62 Inf G	B ~1836. E (Pittsburgh, PA) Jul 61 private. Jul/Aug 62: promoted to corporal. Promoted to sergeant on 10/14/62. C Jul 2: wounds to head, shoulder and chest. D Jul 9.
R5#30	JOSEPH SHERRAN	~22	62 Inf f	B ~1841 PA 1860: R Pittsburgh, PA.; occ laborer. E Jul 61 private. C Jul 2: wounds to left knee and right leg. D Jul 27. Survivor (WC30089): M Mrs. Catharine Sherran ~47 (widow of David Sherran).
R5#31	J SIMONSON JOHN SIMONSON	22	28 Inf I	B 8/21/1840 Baltimore, MD. R Philadelphia, PA. E Jun 61 private. C Jul 3: wounded in the lungs. D Jul 12.
R5#32	GIDEON E BARYAR GIDEON **BURGER** or BORGER	20-21	153 Inf H	B ~1842 PA. 1860: R Quincy, Franklin Co., PA.; occ farm laborer. R Moore twp, Northampton Co., PA. E (Northumberland Co., PA) Sep 62 private. C Jul 1. D Jul 6 or 7.
R5#33	GOTFRIED HAMMON **GOTTLIEB HAMMANN**	37-38	74 Inf K	B ~1825 Germany. R Birmingham, Allegheny Co., PA. 1860 occ: stone cutter. E Sep 61 private. C Jul 2: shot through the head. D Jul 3. Survivors (WC31148): W Caroline 34 (M Sep 56); 3 chn: 1 ♀- Emma 6 & 2 ♂- Louis 4, Frederick 2.

R5#34	WILLIAM H MILLER	24-25	153 Inf E	B ~1838. R Northampton Co., PA. E (Palmer twp, Northampton Co., PA) Oct 62 private. C Jul 1: severely wounded in the left leg→amp. D Jul 9.
R5#35	LIEUT JOHN O WOODS JOHN **O'HARA** WOODS	~22	11 PRC D (40 Inf)	B ~1841 PA. 1860: R Connoquenessing, Butler Co., PA. E Apr 61 corporal. Captured 6/27/62 at Gaines' Mill, VA. Paroled on 8/5/62 at Aiken's Landing, VA. Sep/Oct 62: promotion to sergeant. Commissioned 2nd lieutenant on 12/14/62. KIA 2.
R5#36	SERGT W REYNOLDS WILLIAM REYNOLDS	29-30	142 Inf I	B ~1833 Sherman, Chautauqua Co., NY. R Venango Co., PA. E Aug 62 sergeant. C Jul 1. D Jul 10. Survivor (WC73189): 1 ♂- George 7 (PGF Orson Reynolds appointed guardian as William's wife Harriet [M Oct 51] had died 2/27/57).
R5#37	AMOS P SWEET	23-24	150 Inf H	B ~1839 PA. 1860: R Troy, Crawford Co., PA.; occ farmer. R Crawford Co., PA. E Aug 62 private. C Jul 1: wounded in right leg→amp x2. D Jul 15. Survivors (WC140116): W Atlanta 26 (M Mar 60| ReM 1866): 1 ♀- Amy 11 months.
R5#38	SERGT LORENZO HODGES	25	150 Inf G	B 2/6/1838 Allegany Co., NY. R McKean Co., PA. Occ farmer. E Aug 62 corporal. Promoted to sergeant on 9/2/62. C Jul 1: balls in chest, hip and left hand. D Jul 14. Survivors (WC103749): W Rosetta 24 (M Dec 55| ReM 1866); 2 ♀- Agnes 4, Elnora 20 months.
R5#39	LIEUT F KEIMPEL JOHANN BERNHARD KUMPEL	28	27 Inf E	B Sep 1834 Germany. R Philadelphia, PA. E Jun 61 corporal (as authorized through Pennsylvania Gov. Andrew Curtin). Commissioned 2nd lieutenant on 12/18/61. Promoted to 1st lieutenant on 11/1/62. KIA Jul 1. Survivors (WC83151): W Wilhelmine 29 (M Nov 58| ReM1865); 1 ♀- Margaret 4.
R5#41	JAMES O'NEIL	29-30	69 Inf B	B ~1833. R Philadelphia, PA. E Aug 61 private. KIA Jul 2. Survivors (WC11916): W Anna 26 (Feb 53); 1 ♂- John 9.
R5#42	LIEUT W H SMITH WILLIAM HEMRY SMITH[316]	32	106 Inf B	B 12/2/1830 Lilesville, Anson Co., NC. 1860: R Clay, Adair Co., MO; occ: farm laborer. R Philadelphia, PA. E Aug 61 private. Commissioned 2nd lieutenant on 11/24/62. KIA Jul 2. Survivors (WC13864): W Hannah 25 (M 4/1/63| ReM 1870); Hannah approximately 3 months pregnant with William, who would be born 12/23/63.

---

316 **Soldier's widow is three-months pregnant with couple's first child at his death.** On March 27, 1863, the 32-year-old lieutenant William Smith received approval for a 10-day leave, during which time he traveled back to Clark County, Missouri to marry the 25-year-old Hannah Little on April 1st. Lieutenant Smith would be killed at Gettysburg on Jul 2nd, almost 3 months to the day from his marriage. On December 28, 1863, his widow would birth a son William, named in her late husband's remembrance.

R5#44	SERGT JAMES M SHEA JAMES **McSHEA**	35-36	69 Inf B	B ~1827 Ireland. R Philadelphia Co., PA. E Oct 61 private. Promoted to corporal on 6/1/62. Sep→Dec 62: dispatched away from regiment on recruiting service. KIA Jul 2. Survivors (WC122653): 1st W Mary (M 1851| died 1858)→ 3 chn: 2 ♀- Anne 11, Mary 6 & 1 ♂- John 9; 2nd W Sarah 35 (M Nov 60| ReM 1868); 1 ♀- Sarah 22 months.
R5#45	F GALLAGHER **TIMOTHY** GALLAGHER	26-27	69 Inf B	B ~1836 Ireland. E (Philadelphia, PA) Nov 61 private. KIA Jul 2: wounded in brain.
R5#46	JOHN HENEISON JOHN **HENNEISEN**[317]	23-24	153 Inf C	B ~1839. R Philadelphia, PA. E Sep 61 private. KIA Jul 1.
R5#47	SERGT E N SOMERCAMP EDWARD NAPOLEON **SOMMERKAMP**[318] or SOMMER KAMP	~31	29 Inf I	B ~1832 MD. Occ: jeweler. R Philadelphia, PA. E Jul 61 sergeant. Jun 62→Feb 63: Dispatched away from regiment on recruiting service. KIA Jul 3. Survivors (WC12131): W Elizabeth 30 (M Apr 50); 4 chn: 1 ♀- Sophia 12 & 3 ♂- William 6, Charles 4, Edward 3 weeks.
R5#49	WILLIAM DOUGLASS	21-22	155 Inf B	B ~1841. R Allegheny Co., PA. E (Pittsburgh, PA) Aug 62 private. KIA Jul 2: GSW to the abdomen.
R5#50	GEORGE W WILCOX (MN WILSON)	18-19	155 Inf I	B ~1844 PA. R Allegheny Co., PA. Occ coal miner. E (Pittsburgh, PA) Aug 62 private. KIA Jul 2.
R5#51	PATRICK J O'CONNOR	30-31	91 Inf D	B ~1832. R Philadelphia, PA. E Sep 61 private. KIA Jul 3: hit by a shell. Survivor (WC10819): W Ann 40 (M Oct 60); no chn.
R4#52	E BERLIN ELI BERLIN	34-35	83 Inf G	B ~1828 Germany. R Tionesta, Forest Co., PA. Occ farmer. E Aug 62 private. KIA Jul 2: GSW through the heart. Survivors (WC34302): W Caty (Catharine): 29 (M Jan 54|ReM1871); 5 chn: 4 ♂- Leander 8, Orlando 6, Clements 3, Oran 2 & 1 ♀- Emily 5.
R5#54	ROBERT GRIFFIN	~22	83 Inf A	B ~1841 Canada. R Titusville, Crawford Co., PA. Occ blacksmith. E Jul 61 private. Nov/Dec 62: promotion to corporal. KIA Jul 2: head wound.

---

[317] **Identity question**. Some internet sources posit that the soldier buried in this grave is John Henneisen of the 73rd PA infantry Company C. However, there was a John Henneisen who was a member of 153rd Company C (the unit assignment inscribed on the gravestone), who was killed on July 1st.

[318] **Extended dispatch for recruiting service allows wife to become pregnant with couple's fourth child**. Sergeant Edward Sommerkamp was dispatched for recruiting from June 1862 into February 1863. At the time that this dispatch was ending, his wife Elizabeth must have known that she was five-months pregnant with what would be the couples' fourth child. Edward Sommerkamp was born on June 14, 1863. Nineteen days later, on July 3rd, his father would be killed in action at Gettysburg.

R5#60	LEWIS FRAZER **LOUIS FLOSSEN** or LOUIS FLAZER	20-21	53 Inf E	B ~1842. R Union Co., PA. E Oct 61 private. E Oct 61 private. KIA Jul 2.
R5#64	SERGT M G ISETT MATHEW G ISETT[319]	24-25	53 Inf C	B ~1838 PA. R Huntingdon Co., PA. Occ farmer. E Sep 61 sergeant. Wounded in the leg on 12/17/62 at Fredericksburg, VA. Promoted to 1st sergeant on 1/1/63. KIA Jul 2.
R5#73	JOHN R INERY JOHN RODGERS **QUEREY**	~22	2 PRC C (31 Inf)	B ~1841 Ireland. R Philadelphia, PA. E May 61 private. C Jul 2: wounded in the left arm and leg. D Jul 4 or 5.
R5#74	ISAAC EATON	~35	10 PRC B (39 Inf D)	B ~1828 Mercer Co., PA. R Clarksville, Greene Co., PA. Occ sawyer. E Apr 61 private. Hospitalized 9/10/62 through Nov/Dec 62 for an unspecified condition. C Jul 2: wounded in the back and spine. D Jul 4 or 9.
R5#75	PATRICK HUNT PATRICK **HART**	25-26	99 Inf E	B ~1837 Ireland. R Philadelphia, PA. Occ porter. E Aug 61 private. C Jul 2: wounded in right thigh. D Jul 4.
R5#76	WILLIAM DANCHY WILLIAM **DONNELLY**	~36	1 PRC H (30 Inf)	B ~1827. E (West Chester, Chester Co., PA) Jun 61 private. Wounded on 6/21/62 during the Seven Days Battle. Mar/Apr 63: promotion to corporal. C Jul 2: wounded in the chest. D Jul 5 or 7.
R5#77	THOMAS SHIELDS	~37	99 Inf H	B ~ 1826. E (Philadelphia, PA) Jul 61 into 66th PA Infantry as a private. Transfer to 99th PA Infantry on 3/25/62. C Jul 2: wounded right thigh→amp. D Jul 5. Survivors (WC31361): W Ann 36 (M Jul 47); 3 chn: 2 ♀- Bridget 9, Maggie 4 & 1 ♂- Andrew 15.
R5#78	JOHN LUSK	23	1 PRC I (30 Inf)	B 9/29/1839 PA. 1860: R North Middleton, Cumberland Co., PA; occ: farm laborer on father's farm. E (West Chester, Chester Co., PA) Jun 61 private. C Jul 3. D Jul 11.
R5#79	J KLEPPINGER JOSEPH KLEPPINGER	21	153 Inf D	B 8/28/1841 PA. R Northampton Co., PA. Occ: farmer, saddler. E Sep 62 private. C Jul 1. D Jul 7.
R5#80	LIEUT W H BEAVER WILLIAM H BEAVER	21-22	153 Inf D	B ~1841 East Allen, Northampton Co., PA. 1860: R same; occ farm laborer. Commissioned 2nd lieutenant/ mustered-in Oct 62. KIA Jul 1.

---

319 **Father hazards a visit to the unhealthy fields of Gettysburg following news of his son's death.** In the Isett family oral history, James Isett undertook to visit the Gettysburg following news of his son's death. In the course of his visit to these unsanitary fields, James Isett would contract some infectious illness, which would lead to his death back at home on August 11, 1863.

R5#81	J QUINN JAMES QUINN	~19	99 Inf K	B ~1844 PA. R Philadelphia, PA. Occ: laborer, iron bolt factory worker. E Jul 61 corporal. C Jul 2: wounded in leg→amp. D Jul 17. Survivor (WC57472): M Mrs. Mary Quinn 45 in 1864 (widow of Andrew Quinn).
R5#82	WILLIAM THOMAS	37-38	110 Inf E	B ~1825. R Philadelphia, PA. E Aug 61 private. C Jul 2: severe wounds to both thighs. D Aug 17.
R5#83	D HEMPHILL DAVID HEMPHILL	20-21	72 Inf E	B ~1842 Philadelphia, PA. R same. Occ laborer. E Aug 61 private. Sep/Oct 62: marked as a deserter following straggling 30 days. Returned to duty on 9/15/62. C Jul 2: wound fracturing right femur→amp. D Aug 20. Survivors (WC121639):M Mrs. Margaret Hemphill 45 in 1864 (widow of David Hemphill).
R5#84	H PURDY HUGH PURDY	33-34	Indpt Batt F PA LA	B ~1829. E (Pittsburgh, PA) Oct 61 private. C Jul 3: compound fracture wound of right femur. D Sep 11.
R5#85	JAMES E BEALS JAMES E **BEALES**[320]	21-22	148 Inf H	B ~1841 Centre Co., PA. E (Philipsburg, Centre Co., PA) Aug 62 private. C Jul 2: severe wound to left arm→amp. D Aug 8.
R5#86	F BORDENSTEDT FREDERICK **BEVENSTED**	42-43	69 Inf A	B ~1820 PA. R Philadelphia, PA. E Aug 61 private. C Jul 3: penetrating wound to the lung. D Aug 6.
R5#87	WILLIAM S STRAUSE WILLIAM **STRAUSS**	18	151 Inf H	B 12/5/1844 Rehrersburg, Tulpehocken twp, Berks Co., PA. R same. E Sep 62 private. Mar/Apr 63: detailed to provost guard duties at Fairfax Courthouse. C Jul 1: multiple wounds. D Aug 1.
R5#88	SERGT JAMES PARKS (MN BRATTON)	23	139 Inf C	B 3/16/1840 Armstrong Co., PA. R same. Occ farmer. E Jul 62 private. Promoted to 1st sergeant on 4/24/63. C Jul 3: wound to left leg. D Aug 8.
R5#89	JAMES KELLY	23-24	69 Inf K	B ~1839. E (Philadelphia, PA) Sep 61 private. KIA Jul 3.
R5#90	JACOB FREY JACOB **FRY**	21-22	105 Inf C	B ~1841. E (Pittsburgh, PA) Aug 61 private. D Jul 2 of wounds.

---

320 **Order for "Whiskey given freely" as soldier dies at Camp Letterman**. On August 7, 1863, James Beales was received by Camp Letterman Hospital in a very dire condition. He was reported 19 years old. His left upper arm amputated stump was gangrenous and hemorrhaging. His only treatment was beef tea and "whiskey given freely." He died the next day.

ID	Name	Age	Unit	Details
R6#1	CAPT A J SOFIELD ALFRED J SOFIELD[321]	~39	149 Inf A	B ~1824 Wellsboro, Tioga Co., PA. R same. Occ Justice of the Peace. E Aug 62: appointed captain. KIA: while stationed along Chambersburg Pike, struck by an artillery round fired from Herr Ridge, which split him in half, killing him and two other nearby soldiers instantly. KIA Jul 1. Survivors (WC19762): W Helen 32 (M Oct 50); 3 ♂- William 10, James 8, Benjamin 5.
R6#10	DANIEL F GOSS	22-23	149 Inf F	B ~1840 Huntington Mills, Luzerne Co., PA. 1860: R same; occ: farm laborer on father's farm. E Aug 62 private. KIA Jul 1.
R6#15	DAVID C KLEIN DAVID **KLINE**	22-23	149 Inf H	B ~1840. 1860: R Derry, Mifflin Co., PA; occ: farm laborer on father's farm. E Aug 62 private. KIA Jul 1.
R6#16	SERGT PHILIP PECKENS PHILIP **PECKINS**	44-45	141 Inf F	B ~1818 PA. R New Milford, Susquehanna Co., PA. Occ farmer. E Aug 62 sergeant. Mar/Apr 63: allotted days on furlough. C Jul 2: severe wounds to both legs→amp of left leg. D Jul 10. Survivors (WC115434): W Lydia 42 (M May 46| ReM 1866); 2 chn: 1 ♀- Cynthia 12 & 1 ♂- Frederick 7.
R6#17	ROBERT MORRISON[322]	22-23	69 Inf A	B ~1840 Philadelphia, PA. R same. Occ laborer. E Sep 61 private. KIA: Jul 3. Survivors (WC113048): W Catharine 22 (M Nov 61| died 9/30/67 from tuberculosis); 1 ♂- John 11 months.
R6#18	SAMUEL HAYBURN	30-31	106 Inf B	B ~1832 Philadelphia, PA. R same. 1860 occ: dealer. E Aug 61 corporal. KIA Jul 2.
R6#19	SAMUEL R GARVIN	18	72 Inf E	B 2/6/1845 PA. R Philadelphia, PA. E Sep 62 private. KIA Jul 3.
R6#20	JOHN McHUGH	23-24	72 Inf K	B ~1839 Ireland. R Philadelphia, PA. 1860 occ tailor. E Mar 62 private. KIA Jul 3.
R6#21	IRA CORBIN	20	145 Inf D	B 4/29/1843 PA. R Venango twp, Eric Co., PA. Occ laborer. E Aug 62 private. KIA Jul 2. Survivor (WC141232): M Mrs. Salley Corbin 62 in 1869 (widow of Smith Corbin).
R6#22	H S THOMAS HENRY L **TALMAGE**	32-33	145 Inf I	B ~1830 NY. 1860: R Washington twp, Eric Co., PA; occ blacksmith. E Sep 62 private. KIA Jul 2.

---

321 **Three men are instantly killed by a single Confederate shell**. The artillery shell that on July 1st struck and killed Captain Sofield at the 149th Pennsylvania Infantry position along the Chambersburg Pike, simultaneously killed Corporal Nathan Wilcox and Private Edwin Dimmick. Captain Sofield, who had been a Justice of the Peace prior to being appointed as captain, had written home wistful letters home to his wife, anticipating a return home in the future.

322 **The death of soldier's widow four years after his death means their young son's guardianship would have to be determined in Philadelphia's Orphan Court**. Robert Morrison's death at Gettysburg would be followed four years later by the death of his widow Catharine Morrison from tuberculosis. As not infrequently occurred, their now 5-year-old son, John, in the absence of a welcoming relative who stepped forward, would have his guardianship decided in the Philadelphia's Orphan's Court.

R6#23	J TAYLOR JOHN MILTON TAYLOR or MILTON JOHN TAYLOR	21-22	145 Inf B	B ~1841. R Mercer Co., PA. E (West Greenville, Mercer Co., PA) Aug 62 corporal. Left sick 11/5/62→Mar/Apr 63 at Snickers Gap, VA. Died Oct 19 in a Richmond hospital of scurvy.
R6#24	S SHOEMAKER SYLVESTER SHOEMAKER	19-20	53 Inf F	B ~1843 NY. R Dallas, Luzerne Co., PA. E Oct 61 private. Sep/Oct 62: absent sick since 8/15/62. Promoted to corporal on 11/1/62. Court martial verdict 4/13/63 of guilty with sentence of forfeiting $10 pay for infraction of leaving a picket line without orders. KIA Jul 2.
R6#25	WILLIAM H MYERS[323]	~22	62 Inf C	B ~1841 Clarion Co., PA. 1860: R same; attending school while residing on his father's farm. E Jul 61 private. Wounded seriously in chest at 6/27/62 at Gaines' Mill, VA. Promoted to corporal on 9/10/62. Jan 63: Father comes to camp with request to take his ill son home where he can receive "proper nursing." Following intercession by a junior regimental officer, the father's request is ultimately approved by John Tucker, Assist. Sec. of War, for the period 1/17/63-2/17/63 and extended into Apr 63. Returning to duty thereafter, he is KIA Jul 2.
R6#26	MAJOR W G LOWRY WILLIAM GUSTIN LOWRY[324]	27	62 Inf C	B 1/27/1836 Armstong Co., PA. 1860: R Piney, Clarion Co., PA; occ clerk. Commissioned 2nd lieutenant Jul 61. Promoted to 1st lieutenant on 11/12/61. Promoted major 9/10/62. Approval began 1/27/63 for 30 days' leave-of-absence to attend to permanent arrangements for mother who depended on him. KIA Jul 2: GSW through the head. Survivor (WC29977): W Mary Jane "Mattie" 27 (M 2/23/63| ReM 1873); no chn.
R6#27	JAMES HILL	21-22	142 Inf I	B ~1841. R Venango Co., PA. E Aug 62 private. KIA Jul 1. Survivors (WC35204→WC692885 neither online): W Deborah 21 in 1864 (M Oct 61| ReM 1865); 1 ♀- Carrie 7 months (B Dec 62, died in May 64).
R6#28	THOMAS D ALLEN	26-27	151 Inf A	B ~1836 PA. R Montrose, Susquehanna Co., PA. Occ wagon maker, mechanic. E Sep 62 corporal. C Jul 1. D Jul 7. Survivors (WC28616): 2nd W Harriet ~24 (M Aug 59| ReM 1864); 1 ♂- Edwin 4 (child of 1st wife, Mary, who died 2/22/59, seven days after giving birth to Edwin).

---

323 **Father's deep love for his son is demonstrated in his personally fetching ill son home for "proper nursing."** A father's tender care for an ill, enlisted son is not better shown than when Abner Myers appeared at the 62nd Pennsylvania infantry camp in January 1863 to take his son William back home for "proper nursing." Upon his return from furlough around May, William would be killed in action on July 2nd.

324 **Major's new wife become widow in five months.** On January 27, 1863, Major William Lowry left his regiment for a 30-day furlough that had been approved based on his expressed need to attend to certain arrangements for a mother who depended on him. Whether prearranged surreptitiously or occurring unexpectedly, on February 12, 1863 during this furlough, Lowry would marry Miss Mary Jane Stewart. Not quite five months later, on July 2nd, Mrs. Mattie Lowry would become a new war widow and thereby entitle herself to William's $25-per-month survivor's pension. Before his marriage, this generous lieutenant's pension would have gone to his mother. At least some consolation, Mrs. Rhoda Lowry, herself a widow, was already receiving a $8-per-month mother's pension following the February 12, 1862 death of her younger son, Robert, who had been a corporal in William's same 62nd Pennsylvania regiment Company C. Quite curiously, Robert's death had resulted from being "shot through the head by an accidental discharge of a pistol while in the camp (WC7390)."

R6#29	PATRICK HAYES	29-30	81 Inf D	B ~1833. R Philadelphia, PA. E Sep 61 private. C Jul 2. D Jul 5. Survivors (WC11007): W Mary 38 (M Nov 46): 3 ♀- Catharine 15; Margaret 11, Ellen 6.
R6#30	CHARLES McCARTY	26-27	72 Inf K	B ~1836. R Philadelphia, PA. E Sep 61 private. C Jul 3: wounded in arm near shoulder→amp. D Jul 12. Survivor (WC12270): M Mrs. Margaret McCarty 44 (claimed abandonment by husband Charles McCarty in 1861).
R6#31	JOSEPH NEWTON	25-26	81 Inf D	B ~1837 England. R Philadelphia, PA. Occ cotton spinner. E Sep 61 private. C Jul 2. D Jul 5. Survivors (WC162622 not online): W Jane 26 (M Jul 60| ReM 1871); 2 chn: 1 ♀- Ann 2 & 1 ♂- Joseph 15 months.
R6#32	ALEXANDER MILLS	20-21	72 Inf E	B ~1842 PA. R Philadelphia, PA. 1860 occ: apprentice locksmith. E (Philadelphia, PA) Aug 61 private. C Jul 1: wounded in chest. D Jul 9.
R6#33	D A AMMERMAN[325] DAVID ALBERT AMMERMAN	23-24	148 Inf B	B ~1839 PA. R Fleming, Centre Co., PA. Occ laborer. E (Milesburg, Centre Co., PA). Aug 62 private. C Jul 2: leg wound. D Jul 5. Survivor (WC201592 not online): M Mrs. Rachel Ammerman ~65 in 1880 (widow of William Ammerman).
R6#34	JAMES S LYNN JAMES **H LINN**	26	140 Inf G	B 3/25/1837 PA. R Washington Co., PA. E (Canonsburg, Washington Co., PA) Aug 62 private. C Jul 2. D Jul 7. Survivor (WC23502): M Mrs. Eliza Linn 62 (widow of Aaron Linn).
R6#35	WILLIAM VAN BUSKIRK[326]	39	142 Inf K	B 8/9/1823 PA. R Pottstown, Montgomery Co., PA. Occ physician. E Aug 62 private. C Jul 1: GSW to the leg. D Jul 6. Survivors (WC146375): 2 chn: 1 ♂- Joseph 12 & 1 ♀- Maria 8 [W Mary (M Sep 48)| deserted family in 1856].
R6#36	HENRY A CORNWELL	22	121 Inf A	B 1/13/1841 Allegheny twp, Venango Co., PA. R same. Occ laborer. E Aug 62 private. Promoted to corporal on 12/14/62. C Jul 1. D Jul 8.
R6#37	GEORGE YOUNG GEORGE W YOUNG	32-33	150 Inf F	B ~1830. R Philadelphia, PA. E Aug 62 private. C Jul 1. D Jul 9. Survivors (WC48070): W Martha 31 in 1864 (M Oct 51); 2 chn: 1 ♀- Margaret 11 & 1 ♂- William 7.

---

325 **Death during surgery?** An Ancestry.com public family tree reports that David Ammerman died during the surgery to amputate his wounded leg.

326 **A physician enlists as an infantry private.** William Van Buskirk reports his occupation in the 1860 U.S. Census as physician. However, his enlistment into the 142nd PA infantry regiment was not as a surgeon, but as an infantry private. His service record does not indicate whether Van Buskirk took on any ad hoc responsibilities as a regimental care provider. After William Van Buskirk's death at Gettysburg, a guardian, Mr. Andrew E. Williams, had to be court-appointed for the care of William's 12-year-old son and 8-year-old daughter. Mrs. Mary Ann Buskirk, his wife and their mother, had deserted the family in 1856 to take up residence with another man, with whom she would have two children with, while never obtaining a divorce from her husband.

R6#38	ALBERT DUSTUN ALBERT **BRESTEL**	~37	75 Inf A	B ~1826 Germany. R Philadelphia, PA. Occ laborer. E Aug 61 private. KIA Jul 1. Survivors (WC105724): W Maria 47 in 1864 (M Apr 52 | ReM 1867); 1 ♂- Charles 10.
R6#39	ALMOND M CHESBRO[327] or CHEESBRO	21	53 Inf G	B 6/22/1842 Potter Co., PA. R same. E Oct 61 private. Promoted to corporal on 12/12/61. Promoted to sergeant on 8/14/62. Detached on Recruiting Service from 8/15/62→Mar/Apr 63. C Jul 2: wounded in both legs. D Jul 10. Survivors (WC44288 not on line): M Mrs. Lavena Cheesbro ~41 (Miram Cheesbro disabled due to his blindness).
R6#40	JOSEPH KHYLE JOSEPH **KILE**[328]	24-25	53 Inf G	B ~1838 PA. 1860: R Bingham twp, Potter Co., PA; farm laborer on father's farm. E Oct 61 private. Sent to general hospital at Alexandria on 8/29/62 for an unspecified condition. C Jul 2. D Jul 5. Survivor (WC16129): W Betsey 23 (M 5/24/63); no chn.
R6#41	E A ALLEN ERASTUS A ALLEN	21-22	145 Inf I	B ~1841 PA. 1860: Girard, Erie Co., PA; occ boatman. E Aug 62 private. C Jul 2: wounded in abdomen. D Jul 5.
R6#42	RICHARD MILLER	21-22	140 Inf C	B ~1841. E (Washington Co., PA) Aug 62 private. C Jul 2: wounded in shoulder. D Jul 26
R6#43	M CHARRITY MATTHEW **GARETY**	~22	71 Inf A	B ~1841. E Jul 61 in Philadelphia as a private. C Jul 3. D Jul 13.
R6#44	LOUIS DILLE **LEWIS DILLEY**	34	140 Inf D	B 2/1/1829 PA. 1860: R French Creek, Mercer Co., PA; occ farmer on father's farm. R Washington Co., PA. E Aug 62 private. C Jul 2: severe wound to arm→ amp. D Jul 19. Survivor (WC195708 not online): W Maggie 23; no chn.
R6#45	ETHIEL A WOOD ETHIEL **C** WOOD	22-23	141 Inf B	B ~1840 Bradford Co., PA. 1860 R: Towanda, Bradford Co., PA. Occ farmer. E Aug 62 private. C Jul 2: wound to right leg→amp. D Jul 13.
R6#46	JOSEPH G FELL (MN GILLINGHAM)	21	141 Inf C	B 4/6/1842 Bradford Co., PA. R same. 1860 occ: attending school. E Aug 62 private. Promoted to sergeant major on 8/29/62. C Jul 2: wound to right thigh. D Jul 17. Survivor (WC201925 not online): M Mrs. Elizabeth Fell 62 in 1881 (Samuel Fell due to drunkenness affirmed never to have supported the family).

---

327 **Soldier's extended detachment on recruiting service.** On August 14, 1862, Sergeant Almond Chesbro was detached from the 53rd Pennsylvania Infantry on recruiting service that would extend until March or April 1863. Upon returning to his regiment, he would be mortally wounded on July 2nd and die thereafter on July 10th.

328 **Soldier's wife becomes widow in six weeks.** On May 24, 1863, Ms. Betsey Elliott married private Joseph Kile of the 53rd Pennsylvania infantry. Six weeks later to the date, the new Mrs. Betsey Kile would become a widow. On a more sanguine note, in July 1883, Mrs. Betsey Kile was dropped from the widows' pension rolls based on her failure to claim the previous three years of payments. As she became aware of being dropped, Mrs. Kile in March 1864 applied for a restoration, explaining that she was aware that the monies were safe and that she was wanted the amounts to accumulate so that she "could make a large payment on my place."

R6#47	ROBERT MICHAELS ROBERT S **MICHAEL**	18	145 Inf A	B 11/27/1844 PA. R Jefferson Co., PA. E Aug 62 private. C Jul 2: shot through lower third of both thighs→amputations of both legs. D Jul 12 or 16.
R6#48	PETER HILL	21-22	68 Inf G	B ~1841 Germany. R Philadelphia, PA. Occ molder. E Aug 62 private. C Jul 2: wound to upper femur. D Jul 17. Survivor (WC17841): M Mrs. Sybilla Hill 55 (widow of John Hill).
R6#49	SERGT GEORGE HERRICK	41-42	110 Inf H	B ~1821 Middlesex Co., MA. 1860: R Antis, Blair Co., PA; occ: inn keeper. E Sep 62 private. Promoted to 5th sergeant on 1/1/63. May/Jun 63: promotion to 1st sergeant. C Jul 2: wounded in left thigh. D Jul 18. Survivors (WC19747): W Melinda 32 (M Dec 51); 2 chn: 1 ♀- Cora 8 & 1 ♂- Frank 2.
R6#50	J W GUTHRIE JOHN W GUTHRIE	19-20	105 Inf B	B ~1843 PA. R Jefferson Co., PA. 1860 occ: day laborer. E Sep 61 private. C Jul 2: wounded in right knee. D Jul 25.
R6#51	MOSES MILLER	31-32	110 Inf B	B ~1831 Ireland. R Philadelphia, PA. Occ bricklayer. E Oct 61 private. C Jul 2: wounded in right thigh. D Aug 1. Survivor (WC34894): W Elizabeth 30 (M Feb 55); no chn.
R6#52	GEORGE ROWAND GEORGE **ROWEN**	26-27	26 Inf K	B ~1836. R Philadelphia, PA. E Aug 61 private. C Jul 2: shot in right hip and left hand. D Jul 13. Survivor (WC26238) W Mary 19 (M May 61} ReM 1873); 1 ♂ - George 17 months.
R6#53	GEORGE OSMAN	23-24	148 Inf C	B ~1839 PA. R Centre Co., PA. Occ carpenter. E Aug 62. C Jul 2. D Jul 4. Survivor (WC21738): M Mrs. Sarah Osman 64 (widow of Daniel Osman).
R6#54	SERGT P HILGERS PETER JOSEPH HILGERS	28-29	73 Inf D	B ~1834 Germany (immigrated 1854.) R Philadelphia, PA. Occ tinsmith. E Sep 61 sergeant. C Jul 1: wounded in the head and neck. D Jul 5. Survivors (WC123072): W Louisa 25 (M Nov 57| ReM 1868); 2 chn: 1 ♂- Charles 3 & 1 ♀- Catharine 20 months.
R6#55	FREDERICK HEINLEY **FRITZ HEINLE**	28-29	74 Inf K	B ~1834 Germany. Occ brewer. E (Pittsburgh, PA) Sep 61 private. Promoted to corporal on 1/28/62. Nov/Dec 62: promotion to sergeant. C Jul 2: D Jul 8.
R6#56	W GRAGLE WESLEY **CRAGLE**	20-21	143 Inf D	B ~1842 Union, Luzerne Co., PA. R Luzerne Co., PA. E Aug 62 private. C Jul 1. D Jul 15. Survivors (WC217494 not online): M Mrs. Margaret Cragle 66 in 1883 (Jacob Cragle affirmed unable to perform ordinary manual labor).
R6#57	CORP B F ULRICH **HENRY** FISHER ULRICH	26-27	143 Inf B	B ~1836 Broom Co., NY. R Susquehanna Co., PA. Occ mason. E Aug 62 corporal. C Jul 1. D Jul 12. Survivors (WC199656 not online): M Mrs. Mary Ulrich 49 (Philip Ulrich affirmed to have long before abandoned support of family).

R6#58	CHARLES CLYDE	21-22	150 Inf I	B ~1841 NY. R Crawford Co., PA. 1860 occ: farm laborer. E Aug 62 private. C Jul 1: severe wound right leg→amp. D Jul 17. Survivor (WC134322): M Mrs. Prudence Clyde 62 (widow of Hugh Clyde).
R6#59	JACOB MAUCH JOHN JACOB MAUCH	26-27	150 Inf I	B ~1836. R Crawford Co., PA. E Aug 62 private. E Aug 62 private. C Jul 1. D Jul 17. Survivors (WC30467): W Christine 22 (M Apr 58| ReM 1865); 2 chn: 1 ♂- John 4 & 1 ♀- Caroline 18 months.
R6#60	WILLIAM HOLMES WILLIAM J HOLMES	25-26	150 Inf G	B ~1837 Canada. 1860: R Keating, McKean Co., PA; occ shoemaker. E Aug 62 corporal. C Jul 1: wounded in leg. D Jul 23. Survivors (WC45235): W Jerusha 23 (M Aug 57| ReM 1875): 3 chn: 2 ♀- Zera 5, Francis 3 & 1 ♂- William Jr. 18 months.
R6#61	WILLIAM S STAMM WILLIAM S STAMM, **JR**	23	151 Inf G	B 1/1/1840 Penn twp, Berks Co., PA. 1860: R Berks Co., PA; occ laborer. E Sep 62 private. C Jul 1: wounded in right thigh→amp. D Aug 2. Survivor: (WC367228 not online) F William S. Stamm, Sr. 74 in 1890 (widower of Magdalena Stamm, who is aged and unable to support wife and himself).
R6#62	J JONES JOSEPH JONES	37-38	142 Inf A	B ~1825 Wales. R Mercer Co., PA. Occ miner. E (Middlesex, Mercer Co., PA) Aug 62 private. Mar/Apr 63: promotion to corporal. C Jul 1. D Jul 17.
R6#63	SAMUEL CRAMER	19-20	142 Inf B	B ~1843. R Westmoreland Co., PA. E (Mount Pleasant, Westmoreland Co. PA) Aug 62 private. C Jul 1: wounded in left arm and left leg→both amp. D Jul 9.
R6#64	JOHN W CRUSAN JOHN WILLIAM **CRUSAW**	20-21	56 Inf B	B ~1842 Westmoreland Co., PA. R Indiana Co., PA. 1860 occ: farm laborer. E (Blairsville, Indiana Co., PA) Sep 61 private. C Jul 1: wounded in right thigh. D Aug 10. Survivor (WC144317): M Mrs. Isabella Crusaw 49 in 1869 (widow of Joseph Crusaw).
R6#65	SOLOMON SHIRK[329]	17	107 Inf B	B ~1846 Cumberland Co., PA. E Nov 61 private. Wounded 9/17/62 at Antietam and hospitalized through Nov/Dec 62. C Jul 1. D Jul 3.
R6#66	JAMES LUKENS JAMES P LUKENS	27-28	150 Inf E	B ~1835 PA. Occ brickmaker. E Aug 62 corporal. Promotion to corporal during service. C Jul 1. D Jul 2. Survivors (WC62589): W Margaret 25 in 1864 (M Oct 57| ReM Dec 64); 1 ♂- Walter 4.

---

329 **Minor at death.** An Ancestry.com public family tree gives Solomon Shirk's birthyear as 1846. The September 1850 U.S. Census report for Cumberland County, PA gives Solomon's age as 4 (however, this Census report might be the basis for the Ancestry.com public family tree birthyear). Taking his age on the September 1850 Census to be accurate, Solomon was not 18, but no older than 16 at his November 1861 enlistment. He could have been no older than 17 when he was killed at Gettysburg.

R6#67	M KELLY MARTIN KELLY[330] 106 Inf E			Misidentified soldier in grave. A Martin Kelly of Company B 106th Pennsylvania infantry was severely wounded at Gettysburg on July 2nd, underwent a left leg amputation, but survived the injury and the war.
R6#68	SERGT JOHN O LORNER JOHN **O'CONNER**	~27	69 Inf G	B ~1836 Ireland. Occ laborer in blacksmith shop. E May 61 sergeant. KIA Jul 3: GSW to head. Survivors (WC124493): M Mrs. Margaret O'Conner 60 in 1864 | F John O'Connor receives pension after Margaret's death in 1868).
R6#69	JOHN HARRINGTON	20-21	69 Inf K	B ~1842 Camden, Camden Co., NJ. 1860: R Stockton, Camden Co., NJ; occ: laborer residing on father's farm. R Philadelphia, PA. E Aug 61 private. KIA Jul 2: GSW to the head.
R6#70	JAMES KEATINGS JAMES **GIDDONS**[331]	~35	90 Inf H	B ~ 1828 Ireland. R Philadelphia, PA. 1860 occ: weaver. E Nov 61 private. KIA Jul 2. Survivors (WC11208): W Margaret 35 (M May 54); 3 ♂ - William 8, James 6, John 3.
R6#71	ISAAC JENKINS	19-20	107 Inf G	B ~1843 PA. R Bradford Co. PA. Occ farmer. E Feb 62 private. C Jul 1: wounded in the shoulder. D Jul 9.
R6#72	J RUPPINS **GIDEON RUPPERT**	~21	107 Inf B	B ~1842 Berks Co., PA. 1860: R Rockland, Berks Co., PA; attending school residing at father Gideon Ruppert's home. E (Kutztown, Berks Co., PA) Feb 62 private. KIA Jul 1. Survivors (WC248249 not online): M Elizabeth 69 in 1886 (husband unable to support wife).
R6#73	WILLIAM BEAUMONT[332]	23-24	88 Inf A	B ~1839 PA. 1860: R St. Clair, Schuylkill Co., PA; occ coal miner. E Aug 1861 private. Desertion 11/12/62→3/18/63 due to illness. KIA Jul 1: shot in the neck. Survivor (WC105125): M Mrs. Mary Beaumont 59 (widow of William Beaumont, Sr.).

---

330 **Misidentified soldier in grave**. Martin Kelly was severely wounded in the left leg at Gettysburg, but he was one of the lucky soldiers to survive both the amputation and the war.

331 **Fighting under an alias**. In her widow's pension application, Margaret Giddons reported that her husband's enlistment under the wrong last name of Keatings had not been deliberate, but was rather the result of a clerical error he had tried unsuccessfully to have corrected. In writing to Mrs. Giddons of her husband's death at Gettysburg, a regimental officer appeared to undercut this simple explanation by noting that in his own company, Giddons was only known by the name of Keatings.

332 **Three coal mining brothers enlist into the army**. In August 1861, William Beaumont along with his other coal miner brothers would enlist into the 88th Pennsylvania infantry and all be assigned to Company A. Williams' older brother, George would be wounded at Fredericksburg but would survive the war. Williams' younger brother John would be killed at Petersburg in 1864.

R6#74	JAMES AMSLEY[333] (MN McDONALD)	30	107 Inf H	B 5/7/1833 Mercersburg, Franklin Co., PA. R same. Occ shoemaker. E Dec 61 private. C Jul 1. D Jul 9. Survivors (WC10834): W Susan 30 (M Dec 52); 4 chn: 2 ♂- William 9, James 2 & 2 ♀- Rebecca 6, Susan 4 (plus 7 months pregnant with ♀ Mary, who would be born Sep 17, 1863).
R6#75	J N BURR JOSEPH W BURR	27-28	NY 147 Inf C	B ~1835 Ellisburg, Jefferson Co., NY. 1860: R Boylston, Oswego Co., NY. Occ farmer. E Aug 62 private. KIA Jul 1. Survivors (WC137619): W Catharine 23 (M Jul 56| ReM 1868); 2 ♂- William 3, Daniel 6 months.
R6#76	JAMES W TAFT (MN WILLIAM)	26-27	142 Inf D	B ~1836 Somerset, Somerset Co., PA. R Johnstown, Cambria Co., PA. E Aug 62 private. Wounded on 12/13/62 at Fredericksburg, VA. Deserted 1/21/63 near Falmouth, VA. Brought back to company on 2/20/63. C Jul 1: GSW to right thigh →amp→typhoid fever complication. D Aug 8. Survivors (WC71200): W Louisa 26 (M Dec 54| ReM 12/6/64); 2 chn: 1 ♀- Josephine 5 & 1 ♂- James 2.
R6#77	JOSEPH MONTAGNE JOSEPH **MONTONYE** or MONTANYE	18	143 Inf D	B 10/24/1844 Luzerne Co., PA. Occ yeoman. E (Kingston, Luzerne Co., PA) Aug 62 private. D Jul 3: killed by bursting of a shell.
R6#78	ALFRED BOYDEN[334] 149 Inf A			B 5/10/1844 Tioga Co., PA. Occ farm laborer. E Aug 62 private. Promotion to corporal during service. MO 6/24/1865. D 1/13/1922 (age 77).
R6#80	CHARLES E WEBSTER[335] (MN EDWIN)	22	26 Inf C	B Jul 1841 England. R Philadelphia, PA. E May 61 private. Employed as a cook on hospital muster roll 1/30/62 until March 63 when returned to the company. May/Jun 63: employed as cook. KIA Jul 3.
R6#81	LIEUT JOHN REYNOLDS	36-37	68 Inf E	B ~1826 Ireland. Occ tailor. E (Pittsburgh, PA) Aug 62 private. Promoted to sergeant major on 2/7/63. Appointed 2nd lieutenant on 6/30/63. KIA Jul 2.
R6#82	ALONZO McCALL	20	10 PRC B (39 Inf)	B 4/7/1843 Beaver, Beaver Co., PA. 1860: R Shenango twp, Mercer Co., PA; occ: carpentry apprentice under his father, John McCall. E Jul 61 private. KIA Jul 2.

---

333 **Soldier's widow is pregnant with couple's fifth child at his death.** James Amsley's wife, Susan, would birth a 5th child, Mary On September 17, 1863.

334 **Misidentified soldier in grave.** Corp. Alfred Boyden was not a casualty of the Battle of Gettysburg. He survived the war, living into his 70's.

335 **Soldier has extended service as a hospital cook.** Charles Webster, an English immigrant, was employed as a hospital cook from February 1862 until March 1863. Returning to his infantry regiment in May or June 1863, he assumed duty in his company as the cook. Still assuming a position as an infantryman in battle, he was killed in action on July 3rd.

R6#83	SERGT J W MOLINEAUX JAMES **L MULLENEAUX**[336]	25	197 Inf K		B ~Dec 1837 PA. Commissioned 1st lieutenant Jul 64 for 100-day muster. Mustered out Nov 64. D 12/12/64, cause of death not found.
R6#86	JAMES S RUTTER **JOSEPH** SNADER RUTTER[337]	17	1 PRC E (30 Inf)		B 10/30/1845 Leacock twp, Lancaster Co., PA. R Lancaster Co., PA. Occ farmer. E Aug 62 private. KIA Jul 2. Survivor (WC242823 not online): F John Rutter 69 in 1886 (disabled widower of Caroline Rutter, who had died in 1854).
R6#88	B E TRUE BIRCHARD EZRA TRUE	23	83 Inf B		B 3/22/1840 PA. 1860: R Meadville, Crawford Co., PA. E Aug 61 private. KIA Jul 2.
R6#91	SERGT T J BELTON THOMAS J BELTON	~24	13 PRC B (42 Inf)		B ~1839 Ireland. R Duncannon, Perry Co, PA. Occ peddler. E May 61 (Harrisburg, PA) sergeant. Promotion from 3rd to 2nd sergeant on 12/12/61. Captured at 6/27/62 at Gaines' Mill, VA. Paroled 8/5/62 at Aiken's Landing, VA. Absent, in hospital through 12/31/62. Promotion to 1st sergeant on 3/1/63. KIA Jul 3.
R6#94	JAMES WALLACE	~41	26 Inf G		B ~1822 Ireland. R Philadelphia, PA. E May 61 private. Promoted to corporal on 12/1/62. C Jul 1: GSW to the back. D Jul 15.
R7#1	ROBERT LOCKHART (MN JOHN)	~27	29 Inf K		B ~1836 PA. R Philadelphia, PA. Occ stone cutter. E Jun 61 private. KIA Jul 3. Survivors (WC12352): W Mary 27 (M Jun 57| ReM 1866); 2 chn: 1 ♀- Elizabeth 3 & Robert John Jr. 16 months.
R7#2	THEO SAYLOR THEODORE SAYLOR[338] (THEODORE STRAYLINE ALIAS)	~19	72 Inf C		B ~1844 Philadelphia, PA. R same. E Aug 61 private. Promoted to corporal on 12/25/62. KIA Jul 3. Survivor (WC93101): W Mary 25 (M May 61| ReM 1866); 1 ♀- Anne 16 months.
R7#3	LIEUT J D GORDON JOHN DUNLAP GORDON	24-25	56 Inf B		B ~1838 Black Lick twp, Indiana Co., PA. 1860: R same; occ farm laborer. E (Blairsville, Indiana Co., PA) Sep 61 private. Promoted to 5th sergeant on 5/2/62. Promoted to 1st sergeant on 12/28/62. Commissioned 2nd lieutenant on 4/10/63. KIA Jul 1.

---

336 **Misidentified soldier in grave.** First lieut. James Mulleneaux was not a casualty of the Battle of Gettysburg.

337 **Minor at death.** Joseph Rutter's Mennonite birth record gives his birthdate as October 30, 1845. This birthdate is further supported by Joseph's reported ages of 4 and 14 in the successive August 1850 and July 1860 U.S. Censuses. This birthday attests to the fact that Joseph was not 18, but actually 16 at his August 1862 enlistment. Similarly, when he would be killed in action July 2nd, he would have been only 17.

338 **Fighting under an alias.** Theodore Saylor adopted the alias Theodore Strayline in joining the army.

R7#4	A CREIGHTON ALEXANDER CREIGHTON[339]	26-27	148 Inf F	B ~1836 Ireland. E (Cameron Co., PA) Aug 62 private. KIA Jul 3: struck in the head by a shell fragment and killed instantly. Survivor (WC17281): M Mrs. Mattie Creighton 53 (widow of Alexander Creighton).
R7#5	SERGT R H COWPLAND REGINALD HEBER COMPLAND	22	121 Inf I	B 4/1/1841 PA. R Philadelphia, PA. 1860 occ: clerk in the father's (Joshua Cowpland) merchant shop. E Jan 62 corporal. Promoted to sergeant on 8/9/62. KIA Jul 1.
R7#6	J J FINNEFROCK			No killed Gettysburg soldier having the same last name as the soldier buried to the left of this grave found in military sources.
R7#7	SAMUEL FINNEFROCK	21	142 Inf B	B 4/27/1842 Somerset, Somerset Co., PA. R Westmoreland Co., PA. E (Mount Pleasant, Westmoreland Co., PA) Aug 62 private. KIA Jul 1.
R7#8	CORP C WALTERS CYRUS WALTERS[340]	~18	142 Inf B	B ~1845. 1860 R: Chillisquaque, Northumberland Co., PA. R Westmoreland Co., PA. E Aug 62 corporal. C Jul 1. D Oct 30. Survivor (WC23049): M Miss Catharine Pershing 42 (never married).
R7#11	JOSEPH S GUTELIUS	21	150 Inf D	B 1/1/1842 Mifflinburg, Union Co., PA. 1860: R same; occ: apprentice coach maker. E (Lewisburg, Union Co., PA) Aug 62 corporal. KIA Jul 1. Survivor (WC126423): M Mrs. Lydia Gutelius 62 in 1866 (widow of Frederick Gutelius).
R7#12	NATHAN HILCOX NATHAN H WILCOX[341]	19-20	149 Inf A	B ~1843 PA. R Tioga Co., PA. 1860 occ: farm laborer on widowed mother's farm. E Aug 62 private. KIA Jul 1: killed by same shell that struck Capt. Sofield "splitting him in half." Survivor (WC36969): M Mrs. Abigail Wilcox 41.

---

339 **First man reported killed in his regiment.** One history of the 148th Pennsylvania Volunteers reports that Alexander Creighton was the first man killed in Company F at Gettysburg. The history recounts that the regiment had been supporting a battery to its front when a shell fragment struck Private Creighton in the head and killed him instantly.

340 **Mother's pension application is complicated by the fact of her unwed status at the time of his birth.** Miss Catharine Pershing's dependent mother's application acknowledges that her son, Cyrus Walters, had been born out of wedlock. Interestingly, in neither the 1850 nor 1860 U.S. Census is Cyrus listed with the surname of Pershing, only Walter. In the 1850 U.S. Census, the 5-year-old Cyrus is living with a young couple named Solomon and Catharine Walter, possibly reflecting Catharine Pershing's need to arrange foster care for the young child an unwed 19th-century woman would have experienced difficulty supporting.

341 **Three men are instantly killed by a single Confederate shell.** The artillery shell that on July 1st struck and killed Corporal Wilcox at the 149th Pennsylvania Infantry position along the Chambersburg Pike, simultaneously killed Captain Alfred Sofield and Private Edwin Dimmick.

R7#14	F E NORTHORP FRANK EUGENE **NORTHRUP**[342]	21	150 Inf F	B 8/4/1841 Binghamton, Broome Co., NY. R same. 1860 occ: clerk. E Aug 62 1st sergeant. Deserted during 8/2→10/31/62 detachment for recruiting service. Nov/Dec 62: arrested and placed in close confinement in the Old Capitol Prison on several charges, including desertion and breaking jail. Additionally, action taken to merge his 150th PA infantry record under alias Henry A Wiley to service record under true name of Northrup. Reduced to rank of private 6/13/63. KIA Jul 1: wound to the head. Survivors (WC14350): W Mary 26 (M May 60); 1 ♀- Fanny 2.
R7#17	WILLIAM H HARMAN WILLIAM HENRY **HARMONY**	24	149 Inf I	B 10/16/1838 Huntingdon Co., PA. E (Mount Union, Huntingdon Co., PA) Aug 62 private. KIA Jul 1.
R7#19	JAMES LOGAN	21-22	149 Inf G	B ~1841 Scotland. 1860 R: Ward, Tioga Co., PA. Occ miner. E Aug 62 corporal. C Jul 1. D Jul 3.
R7#20	ROBERT McGUIRE	31-32	53 Inf F	B ~1831 PA. R Kingston, Luzerne Co., PA. Occ molder. E Oct 61 private. KIA Jul 2. Survivors (WC102168): W Elizabeth 37 (M Nov 57| ReM 1866); 2 chn: 1 ♂- James 5 & 1 ♀- Annie 2.
R7#21	DANIEL HARRINGTON	19-20	53 Inf F	B ~1843 Ireland. R Luzerne Co., PA. E Sep 61 corporal. Promotion to sergeant during service. KIA Jul 2.
R7#22	C HERBSTER CHARLES WILLIAM HERBSTER	~20	99 Inf C	B ~1843. R Philadelphia, PA. E Jul 61 private. KIA Jul 2. Survivors (WC104003): F Michael Herbster 62 in 1866 (affirmed disabled for several years due to an arm amputation; soldier's mother, Mrs. Mary Herbster had died in 1860).
R7#23	FRANKLIN MYERS FRANKLIN **MYRES**	~22	99 Inf D	B ~1841. E (Philadelphia) Jul 61 private. KIA Jul 2.
R7#24	THOMAS KAIN THOMAS MARION **CAIN**	~40	99 Inf K	B ~1823 PA. E Aug 61 private. KIA Jul 2. A FindAGrave.com memorial identifies Thomas Cain as being a child of James and Sarah Cain of Butler County, Pennsylvania.
R7#25	JOSIAH BUTTERWORTH **JOSEPH** BUTTERWORTH	18-19	114 Inf E	B ~1844 England. R Philadelphia, PA. 1860 occ: apprentice molder. E Aug 62 private. KIA Jul 2. Survivor (WC176056 not online): M Mrs. Mary Butterworth ~54 in 1873 (widow of William Butterworth).

---

342 **Soldier deserts during a detachment for recruitment.** First sergeant Frank Northrup's service record documents a desertion during a detachment for recruiting, a subsequent confinement in the Old Capitol Prison and reduction to the rank of private. Notwithstanding this dubious record, Northrup was dutifully present with his 150th Pennsylvania regiment on July 1st when he would be killed in action.

R7#26	THOMAS BURNS[343]	~28?	2 PRC B (31 Inf)	B ~1835? Ireland. R Philadelphia, PA. Occ laborer. E oct 61 private. Jan/Feb 63: one month's pay to be forfeited for an unspecified infraction. KIA Jul 2. Survivor (WC50994): W Anne 50 (M Nov 54); no chn.
R7#27	THOMAS M SAVAGE	23-24	2 PRC H (31 Inf)	B ~1839 PA. R Philadelphia, PA. 1860 occ: tailor. E Aug 61 private. Jan/Feb 63: one month's pay to be deducted for an unspecified infraction; promotion to corporal during this period. Promoted to sergeant 6/1/63. C Jul 2. D Jul 2 or 3.
R7#28	JOHN GREENWOOD[344]	~24	109 Inf I COLOR SERGT	B ~1839. 1860: R Haycock Bucks Co., PA: occ farm laborer. R Philadelphia, PA. E Feb 62 private. Rank of corporal held Jul→Nov 62. Captured 8/9/62 at Battle of Cedar Mountain. Paroled 9/13/62 at Aiken's Landing. Promoted to sergeant during service. KIA Jul 3.
R7#29	J BAINBRIDGE JOHN BAINBRIDGE	18-19	147 Inf F	B ~1844 England. 1860 R: Kingston, Luzerne Co., PA. Occ blacksmith. E (Hazleton, Luzerne Co., PA) Aug 62 private. KIA Jul 3: GSW to the head.
R7#30	G DEISROTH GEORGE DEISROTH	21-22	147 Inf F	B ~1841 PA. 1860: R Sugarloaf twp, Luzerne Co., PA. E Aug 62 private. KIA Jul 3.
R7#31	ABRAHAM CRAWLEY[345]	48	68 Inf A	B 12/2/1814 Roxbury, MA. R Philadelphia, PA. Occ brush maker. E Aug 62 private. Aug/Sep 62: promoted to corporal. C Jul 2: wounded in lung and left arm. D Jul 7. Survivors (WC167238 not online): W Elizabeth 36 (M Mar 53| died 4/28/71 from asthma); 2 ♂- Millard 7, Abraham 5.[346]

---

343 **Identity question**. Unless accounted for by a clerical error in recorded age at enlistment, Thomas Burns, killed at about age 28, was married to a woman, aged 50, and whom, by extension, he had married in Ireland when he was 19 and she 41.

344 **A Color Sergeant is instantly killed during battle**. In Capt. Frederick Gimber's Gettysburg report, the 109th Pennsylvania Infantry lost only three men killed during the battle, one being the color sergeant John Greenwood, who was reported killed instantly.

345 **Overaged at enlistment**. One genealogical record gives Abraham Crawley's birth year as 1814. This birth year would agree with the age of 36 that he gave for the 1850 U.S. Census. Working from these two dates, Abraham Crawley's age at his 1862 army enlistment was not 43, as he claimed, but likely 47, or two years beyond the accepted upper-age for voluntary enlistment.

346 **Soldier's two young sons must be sent off to Philadelphian orphanage**. Following Abraham Crawley's wife Elizabeth's death from asthma in 1871, guardianship of their 15- and 13-year-old brothers would be granted to the Lincoln Institute, a Philadelphian orphanage begun in 1866 by a wealthy philanthropist.

R7#32	SERGT JOHN WOGAN[347]	38	69 Inf G	B ~1825 Ireland. R Philadelphia, PA. Occ weaver. E May 61 corporal. Absent, sick in hospital 5/2-8/18/62. KIA Jul 3: wounded in abdomen. Survivors (WC27857 not online); W Elizabeth 44 (M Feb 47); 5 chn: 3 ♂- Peter 14, Patrick 12, William 5 & 2 ♀- Catharine 6, Elizbeth 3.
R7#33	JAMES McINTYRE JAMES **McENTYRE**	~30	69 Inf G	B ~1833 Ireland. R Philadelphia, PA. Occ laborer. E May 61 private. KIA Jul 3. Survivors (WC11726): W Margaret 35 (M Oct 53); 3 ♂- William 9, Henry 7, James 5.
R7#34	JAMES CLARY JAMES **CLAY**[348]	~37	69 Inf G	B ~1826 Ireland. R Philadelphia, PA. Occ weaver, laborer. E May 61 private. KIA Jul 3: killed instantly by head wound from canister (friendly fire of Cushing's battery). Survivors (WC105623): W Jane 35 (M Apr 47 | died 7/28/66); 4 chn: 1 ♀- Eliza 13 & 3 ♂- James 11, George 7, William 2.
R7#35	JAMES COYLE[349]	~29	69 Inf G	B ~1834 Ireland. R Philadelphia, PA. Occ laborer. E May 61 private. KIA Jul 3: killed instantly by head wound from canister (friendly fire of Cushing's battery).
R7#36	JAMES RICE	18-19	69 Inf G	B ~1844 Philadelphia, PA. R same. Occ laborer. E Dec 62 private. Joined regiment from depot on 3/28/63. KIA Jul 3.
R7#37	WILLIAM KIKER	37-38	72 Inf K	B ~1825 Philadelphia, PA. R same. Occ curbstone setter. E Aug 61 private. KIA Jul 3. Survivors (WC22558): Phoebe W 36 (M Mar 45); 2 chn: 1 ♂- Peter 16 & 1 ♀- Mary 14
R7#38	JOHN HOPE	~46	71 Inf H	B ~1817 Ireland. R Philadelphia, PA. Occ print cutter. E Jul 61 private. KIA Jul 3. Survivor (WC162809 not online): W Sarah 60 in 1871: 1 dependent ♂- William 14.

---

[347] **Soldier's five orphaned children are split up and sent off to separate orphanages**. Eight months after John Wogan would be killed in Pickett's charge, Elizabeth Wogan, his wife and the mother of his five children, would die of phthisis, end-stage pulmonary tuberculosis. To add to this tragedy, the widow's and dependent-minors' claim she submitted one month after her husband's death was filed away without action following the Pension Office's disqualification of her agent. No monies would ever be paid out to Elizabeth as a war widow or to any of her children. Lastly, as a sad commentary on orphan services in the mid-19th century, of the three minor Wogan children, the two girls would be separated and sent to different orphan homes while the youngest boy, William, for an unreported rationale, would be placed in an asylum, where he would die six years later at age 12.

[348] **Friendly fire death from Cushing's battery**. In Lieutenant Alonzo Cushing's firing of canister to repulse Confederates converging on the Angle, both James Clay and James Coyle of the 69th Pennsylvania Infantry received friendly-fire head wounds from errant balls.

[349] **Friendly fire death from Cushing's battery**. In Lieutenant Alonzo Cushing's firing of canister to repulse Confederates converging on the Angle, both James Coyle and James Clay of the 69th Pennsylvania Infantry received friendly-fire head wounds from errant balls.

R7#39	NELSON REASER[350]	~18[351]	151 Inf B	B ~1845 PA. R Pike Co., PA. E Sep 62 private. C Jul 1: wounded in knee→amp. D Jul 23. Survivor (WC372130 not online): M Mrs. Eleanor Reaser 78 in 1893 (Phillip Reaser died in Sep 1877).
R7#40	ROBERT LESHER	~23	71 Inf D	B ~1840 PA. 1860: R Philadelphia, PA; occ carpenter. E May 61 private. Captured on 10/21/61 at the Battle of Ball's Bluff. Paroled 2/22/62. C Jul 3. D Jul 8.
R7#41	WASHINGTON LININGER	18-19	145 Inf B	B ~1844 Summit twp, Eric Co., PA. Occ farmer. E Aug 62 private. Captured on 5/3/63 at Chancellorsville and paroled subsequently. C Jul 2: wounded in leg. D Jul 10.
R7#42	WILLIAM CONLIN	30-31	140 Inf H	B ~1832. R Beaver Co., PA. E Aug 62 private. C Jul 2: severe wound to left leg→ amp. D Jul 15.
R7#43	LIEUT G H FINCH / GEORGE H FINCH	29-30	145 Inf E	B ~1833 NY. 1860: R Freehold twp, Warren Co., PA; occ mason. E Aug 62 private. Promotion to sergeant during service. Commissioned 2nd lieutenant on 12/13/62. C Jul 2: wounded in abdomen. D Jul 6.
R7#44	ISAAC E DORMAN	23-24	145 Inf A	B ~1839 PA. R Conneaut twp, Erie Co., PA. E Aug 62 private. Nov/Dec 62→ Jan/Feb 63: sick in hospital in Washington, D.C. C Jul 2: wounded in shoulder. D Jul 25.
R7#45	JOHN STOCKTON	~25	71 Inf I	B ~1838 PA. R Philadelphia, PA. E Jun 61 private. C Jul 2: wounded in leg→amp. D Jul 12.
R7#46	ROBERT W BELL	21-22	56 Inf I	B ~1841 PA. 1860 R: Haines, Centre Co., PA. R Centre Co., PA. E Nov 61 private. Sick in Harrisburg hospital from 2/28/62→Jul/Aug 62 with unspecified condition. KIA Jul 1.
R7#48	JOHN E WHITE	35-36	53 Inf D	B ~1827 Centre Co., PA. 1860: R Rush twp, Centre Co., PA; occ mechanic. E Oct 62 private. KIA Jul 2. Survivors (WC145499): W Margaret 27 (M Aug 55| ReM 1866); 5 chn: 2 ♂- Eugene 8, John 2 & 3 ♀- Emlin 6, Blanch 4, Gertrude 7 mos.

---

350 **Attempted elder scam of mother's pension monies.** In an 18th century instance of elder scam, a supposed good Samaritan named Pat Jones offered in June, 1893 to accompany Mrs. Reaser and her daughter as they traveled to cash the long-awaited, first payment on her dependent mother's pension. Emerging from the bank, Pat Jones attempted to hand over to Mrs. Reaser only $100 of the $281 in the draft. Pat Jones did not inform Mrs. Reaser and her daughter that he had deposited the greater sun in an account in his name at this bank. Mrs. Reaser refused to accept the $100 and turned to have the matter taken up with the authorities. Eventually, a full restitution of money Pat Jones had attempted to steal would be made. But it would be made to Mrs. Reaser's daughter, not Mrs. Reaser herself, as Mrs. Reaser died on August 16, 1893, barely two months after this defrauding incident had taken place.

351 **Minor at enlistment.** Nelson Reason's reported ages of 5 and 15 for the successive September 1850 and July 1860 U.S. Census reports attest to the likelihoods that Nelson was only 17 at his September 1862 enlistment and only 18 when he died of July 1st battle wounds on July 23rd.

R7#49	MATTHEW SMITH	21-22	71 Inf G	B ~1841. R Philadelphia, PA. E Sep 61 private. C Jul 3: wounded in chest. D Jul 5. Survivor (WC54225): M Mrs. Jane Smith 43 (widow of James Smith, who had died on 12/17/61).
R7#50	LIEUT MICHAEL MULLIN	~29	69 Inf G	B ~1834 Ireland. R Philadelphia, PA. Occ weaver. E May 61 sergeant. Promoted to 1st sergeant on 9/20/61. Wounded on 9/17/62 at Antietam. Promoted to 1st sergeant on 3/31/63. Commissioned 2nd lieutenant on 6/5/63. C Jul 3. D Jul 8. Survivor (WC65713): M Mrs. Ellen Mullen 52 in 1864 (widow of James Mullen, who died of tuberculosis on 8/1/64).
R7#51	SAMUEL W BARNET SAMUEL WALLACE **BARNES**	19-20	140 Inf H	B ~1843 Raccoon twp, Beaver Co., PA. R Beaver Co., PA. E Aug 62 private. C Jul 2: severe wound in right leg→amp. D Aug 2.
R7#52	ISAAC H RICH	31-32	106 Inf H	B ~1831 Philadelphia, PA. R Philadelphia, PA. Occ ship joiner. E Sep 61 corporal. Reduced to private by Col. Turner Morehead for an unspecified infraction on 5/1/62. C Jul 2: wounded in abdomen. D Jul 4. Survivors (WC42763): W Ann 31 (M Feb 52); 5 chn: 3 ♂- George 10, Robert 4, William 15 months & 2 ♀- Letitia 8, Mary 6.
R7#53	FREDERICK GILLHOUSE FREDERICK **GILHOUSEN**	41-42	148 Inf I	B ~1821 Dauphin Co., PA. R Knox twp, Jefferson Co. PA. Occ farmer. E Aug 62 private. C Jul 2: wounded in hip. D Jul 17. Survivors (WC52236): W Lavinia (M Nov 44): 4 chn: 1 ♂- Hiram 16 & 3 ♀- Rebecca 15, Rachel 11, Lavina 8.
R7#54	R J AKAM RICHARD JOHNSON AKAM	19-20	145 Inf I	B~ 1843 Chautauqua Co., NY. R Corry, Erie Co., PA. Occ laborer. E Aug 62 private. Apr 63: under arrest at Division HQ for an unspecified offense. C Jul 2: severe wound in leg→amp. D Jul 15.
R7#55	JOHN McCASLAND JOHN **McAUSLAND**	~23	72 Inf D	B ~1840 Ireland. R Philadelphia, PA. E Aug 62 private. C Jul 2 or 3: wounded in right arm→amp. D Jul 21. Survivors (WC48234): W Sarah 28 (M May 60): 2 chn: 1 ♀- Mary 2 & 1 ♂- John 2 months.
R7#56	HARRISON LONG	18-19	148 Inf I	B ~1844. R Brookville, Jefferson Co., PA. Occ farmer. E Aug 62 private. C Jul 2: severe wound in left leg→amp. D Jul 21.
R7#57	JOHN KUNKLE	20-21	148 Inf E	B ~1842 Indiana Co., PA. R same. Occ blacksmith. E Aug 62 private. C Jul 2: wounded in thigh→leg amp. D Jul 24. Survivor (WC380881 not online): M Mrs. Agnes Kunkle 81 in 1891 (widow of Adam Kunkle).
R7#58	JOHN WEIDNER JOHN **WEDNER**	28-29	68 Inf B	B ~1834 Germany. R Philadelphia, PA. Occ brickmaker. E Aug 62 private. C Jul 2. D Jul 8. Survivors (WC89097): W Anna 24 (M Jun 60| ReM 1865); 2 chn: 1 John 2 & 1 ♀- Mary 3 months.

R7#59	THOMAS B McCULLOUGH	19-20	148 Inf I	B ~1843 Jefferson Co., PA. 1860: R Pine Creek, Jefferson Co., PA. Occ farmer. E Aug 62 private. Promoted to corporal on 11/1/62. C Jul 2: wounds to arm and groin. D Jul 13 or 24.	
R7#60	JEREMIAH DORMANDY 19 Inf C			No killed Gettysburg soldier with this or similar name found in military sources.	
R7#61	WILLIAM MUNSEN WILLIAM HENRY **MENCER**	~20	Batty G 1st Res LA	B ~1843 PA. R Surveyor Run, Clearfield Co., PA. E Aug 61 private. Mar/Apr 63: absent for 10-day furlough begun April 23rd. KIA Jul 2.	
R7#62	CHARLES CARMER CHARLES W **McCORMICK**	21-22	57 Inf A	B ~1841. E Nov 61 private. C Jul 2: wounded in shoulder and left knee. D Jul 12.	
R7#63	CORP MARTIN BERRY **MORTON** BERRY	25-26	140 Inf D	B ~1837. R Bradford Co., PA. E Aug 62 private. Promoted to corporal on 1/7/63. C Jul 2: severe wounds to the knee, hip and shoulder. D Jul 10. Survivors (WC24436→WC726356 neither online); W Lydia 21 (M Dec 56| ReM 1866); 2 chn: 1 ♀- Mary 4 & 1 ♂- George 2	
R7#64	ABSALOM LINK	26-27	Indpt Batty C PA LA	B ~1836 PA. E (Pittsburgh, PA) Oct 61 private. C Jul 2. D Jul 13. Survivors (WC103408): W Dinah 23 in 1865 (M May 58); 1 ♀- Martha 5.	
R7#65	SERGT J HUNTER JAMES HUNTER[352]	40-41	57 Inf B	B ~1822 PA. R Mercer Co., PA. Occ farmer, grocer. E (Clarksville, Mercer Co., PA) Nov 61 private. Nov 61: promotion to corporal. Promoted to sergeant during service. Detailed on recruiting service 10/24/62→5/16/63. C Jul 2: wounded in left leg→amp. D Jul 13. Survivors (WC29702 not online): W Nancy ~34; 3 chn: 1 ♀- Caroline 10 & 2 ♂- William 2 (plus 5-months pregnant with James, who would be born 11/4/63).	
R7#66	LAWRENCE BENNETT **LOREN** BENNETT or LORIN BENNETT	41-42	141 Inf B	B ~1821 Bradford Co., PA. R Towanda, Bradford Co., PA. Occ farmer. E Aug 62 private. Mar/Apr 63: absent sick, sent home by order of surgeon. Jul 2: severe wound in leg→amp. D Jul 10. Survivors (WC173823 not online): W Sarah 38 (M Jun 48| died 1/25/76); 5 chn: 4 ♀- Sarah 11, Alice 8, Nancy 7, Mary 18 months & 1 ♂- Jonathan 3.	

---

352 **Soldier's widow is five months pregnant with the couple's third child at his death.** On May 16, 1863, Sergeant James Hunter returned from a six-month recruiting trip for the regiment. When he died of a Gettysburg wound eight weeks later on July 13th, he would leave behind two young children and a wife five-months pregnant with a third, James, who would be born on November 3rd.

R7#67	J RHODES JEREMIAH RHODES	23	105 Inf C	B 4/11/1840 PA. R Redbank, Clarion Co., PA. Occ farmer. E Aug 61 private. May/June 62: wounded at Battle of Fair Oaks, VA. C Jul 3: GSW to left shoulder and lung. D Jul 16. Survivors (WC54307): W Silvina 23 (M Jun 60│ ReM Jun 64); 1 ♀- Margaret 2.
R7#69	GEORGE HOWARD	19-20	110 Inf G	B 1843. E Aug 61 private. Captured on 6/9/62 at the Battle of Port Republic, VA. Paroled 9/13/62 at Aiken's Landing. C Jul 2: wounded in left thigh. D Jul 28.
R7#70	FRANCIS M BURLEY[353]	28-29	110 Inf A	B ~1834 PA. R Tyrone, Blair Co., PA. Occ saddler. E Apr 61 to 3rd PA infantry Co D as a private. Transferred to 110th PA infantry as 4th sergeant on 10/24/61. Promoted to 2nd sergeant on 10/26/61. Survivor (WC87719) W Margery ~ 21 (M Dec 58); 1 ♂- William 2 (John Burley 34 appointed guardian in 1866).
R7#71	GEO W INGRAHAM GEORGE W INGRAHAM	27-28	68 Inf A	B ~1835 Philadelphia, PA. R same. Occ shoemaker. E Aug 62 corporal. C Jul 2: wounded in both legs→one amp. D Jul 24. Survivors (WC138699): W Anna 23 (M Oct 56│ died 7/23/69 of erysipelas, a toxemia associated with a virulent streptococcal skin infection); 3 chn: 2 ♀- Anna 9, Sarah 3 & 1 ♂- George 21 months.
R7#72	CORP DAVID STOUP[354]	25	63 Inf E	B 1/30/1838 PA. 1860: R East Deer, Allegheny Co., PA; occ: farm laborer. R Pittsburgh, PA. E Aug 61 private. Promotion to corporal during service. Jul 63: suffered non-combatant post-battle injuries. D Jul 20.
R7#73	JOHN DEVON[355]	~36	26 Inf F	B ~1827. R Philadelphia, PA. E May 61 private. Confinement Feb 63 and court martial sentence from Mar 63→May 64 (projected) for the offense of a penknife attack on a HQ Commissary sentry during a midnight raid in search for whiskey. C Jul 2: GSW to right thigh→amp. D Jul 10.
R7#74	WILLIAM CALLAN	21	26 Inf C	B 7/23/1841 Philadelphia, PA. R same. 1860 occ: cordwainer. E May 61 private. C Jul 2: GSWs to chest, leg and arm. D Jul 12. Survivor (WC11209): M Mrs. Margaret Callen 45 (widow of David Callan).

---

353 **Soldier's young son is removed from widow's care due to morals charge**. In 1866, the State Court of Blair County, Pennsylvania, awarded guardianship of 5-year-old son William to John Burley, Francis Burley's brother. The court had taken care of the child away from his mother, Mrs. Margery Burley, based on allegations that Mrs. Burley had entered into the profession of public prostitution.

354 **Soldier's death following assault on wagon**. David Stoup's death at Gettysburg did not result from battle. As he lay in a hospital, David confided to a fellow soldier that his injuries had followed being pushed off the wagon buggy seat by an intoxicated driver and then being run over by the wagon's wheels.

355 **Soldier is court martialed for a Commissary raid he undertook while seeking whiskey**. On March 26, 1863, John Devon was brought to a court martial proceeding on account of an attempted larcenous raid on the Divisional Commissary February 3, 1863 at midnight. Devon was intercepted by two Commissary attendants, one of whom he stabbed on the hand and wrist before attempting to run away. At his court martial hearing, Devon explained that he had been "drunk the whole day" and that he had attempted to raid the Commissary for whiskey in storage there. Devon was, of course, found guilty and his sentence was to "forfeit all pay and allowances now due or that may be due him and to be confined at hard labor for the remainder of his term of enlistment at such place as proper authority may appoint." However, one of these places as the proper authority thought to appoint was to place him on the battle line on July 2nd, during which deployment he would be mortally wounded.

R7#75	J HAYMAN JOSHUA V HAYMAN	~30	26 Inf A	B ~1833 Baltimore, MD. R Philadelphia. PA. Occ artist. E (Philadelphia) Jul 62 private. C Jul 2: wounded in chest and abdomen. D Jul 9. Survivors (WC14829): W Elizabeth 25 (M Sep 61); 1 ♂- James 11 months.
R7#76	W H KNICHENBOCHER WILLIAM KNICKERBOCKER[356]	40-41	141 Inf K	B ~1822 Smithville, Chenango Co., NY. R same. Occ farmer. E Aug 62 private. Jan/Feb 63: absent, sent to Division hospital near Falmouth, VA. KIA Jul 2. Survivors (WC21003): W Alma 33 (M Aug 49| ReM 1865); 5 chn: 3 ♂- Marion 13, Joseph 9, Oliver 4 & 2 ♀- Lucinda 11, Ellen 2.
R7#77	CORP W GORDON WILLIAM A GORDON	~35	26 Inf I	B ~1828. R Philadelphia, PA. E May 61 private. Promoted to corporal on 1/18/63. Sep/Oct 62: $6 to be deducted from pay by sentence of court martial for an unspecified infraction. C Jul 2: fracture of leg. D Jul 4. Survivors (WC58049): W Margaret 34 (M Feb 49); 3 chn: 2 ♀- Jane 13, Elizabeth 11 & 1 ♂- William 4.
R7#78	JOHN C DOWNING	19-20	57 Inf C	B ~1843 PA. 1860: R Hickory, Mercer Co., PA; occ farm laborer on his father's farm. E Oct 61 private. C Jul 2: struck by a solid shot which fractured both legs. D Jul 4 or 5. Survivors (WC335662 not online): M Mrs. Phoebe Downing 68 in 1890 (widow of Thomas Downing).
R7#79	J J WOOD JOSHUA JAMES WOOD or JAMES JOSHUA WOOD	26-27	114 Inf I	B ~1836. E (Philadelphia, PA) Aug 62 private. C Jul 2. D Jul 3.
R7#80	SERGT VONDERFEER FRITZ VON DER FEHR or VONDERVEHER	~36	71 Inf H	B ~1827 Germany PA. R Philadelphia, PA. E (Washington, D.C.) Aug 61 private. Promoted to corporal on 10/31/61. Promoted to sergeant on 2/14/62. C Jul 2: wounded in the chest. D Jul 3. Survivor (WC6653): W Margaret 31 (M Apr 55): no chn.
R7#81	A DELINGER LEVI DILLINGER	~25	71 Inf K	B ~1838. R Philadelphia, PA. E June 61 private. C Jul 3. D Jul 3 or 5.
R7#82	JOSEPH A FURGUSON JOSEPH A FERGUSON	19-20	139 Inf A	B ~1843 Canada. Occ blacksmith. E (Mercer Co., PA) Sep 62 private. C Jul 2. D Jul 15.
R7#83	BENJAMIN HASSLER	31	93 Inf D	B 10/22/1831 Berks Co., PA. E Sep 62 private. D Jul 21 from chronic diarrhea. Survivors (WC89582): 2 chn: 1 ♀- Martha 10 & 1 ♂- Franklin 6; W Martha (M Jul 51| had died 12/6/60).

---

356 **Widow makes dubious request for pension back payment.** On June 11, 1865, Mrs. Alma Knickerbacker married Stephen Price, ending her entitlement to a widow's pension. Fifteen years later, she learned that Stephen Price had never been divorced from his first wife. Subsequent to this discovery, the former Mrs. Knickerbacker made an appeal not to just have her widow's pension reinstated, but as well, to receive a back payment to cover the years that she was not legally remarried. Mrs. Knickerbacker's request for pension reinstatement was granted. Her request for the back payment was not.

R7#84	JAMES RAY JAMES **RAE**	20-21	91 Inf E	B ~1842. R Philadelphia, PA. E (Philadelphia) Oct 61 private. C Jul 3: wounded in the thigh. D Jul 4.
R7#85	G W STALKER GEORGE W STALKER	20-21	83 Inf I	B ~1842 Lower Merion twp, Montgomery Co., PA. R Erie Co., PA. E Aug 61 private. Wounded on cheek and captured 7/1/62 at the Battle of Malvern Hill. Paroled 7/25/62. Jan/Feb 63: returned to duty. C Jul 1: wound to right leg. D Jul 7 or 10.
R7#86	LIEUT P MORRIS PATRICK MORRIS	41-42	62 Inf M	B ~1821 Ireland. 1860: R Altoona, Blair Co., PA; occ brakeman. E Aug 61 sergeant. Commissioned lieutenant on 12/15/62. C Jul 2. D Jul 11. Survivors (WC36140): W Catharine 37 in 1864 (M Oct 55); 2 ♂ - James 6 and Samuel 11 (from 1st wife Elizabeth who died Mar 52).
R7#87	DARIUS COYLE	25-26	83 Inf D	B ~1837 Eric Co., PA. R Edinboro, Eric Co., PA. Occ laborer. E Sep 61 private. Wounded 7/1/62 at the Battle of Malvern Hill, VA. Absent, in the hospital: Jul 62→Nov/Dec 63. C Jul 2: wounded in the head. D Jul 14.
R7#89	T P SWOOP THERON P **SWAP**	21	111 Inf H	B 1/22/1842 NY. 1860: R Spring twp, Crawford Co., PA; occ cabinet maker. E Dec 61 private. C Jul 3: wounded in abdomen. D Jul 6.
R7#91	D HANNA DAVID HANNA	~21	29 Inf A	B ~1842 Philadelphia, PA. R same. 1860 occ: laborer. E Jun 61 private. C Jul 3: wounded shoulder/neck. D Jul 7. Survivor (WC30963): M Mrs. Ann Hanna 56 (widow of Samuel Hanna).
R7#92	PATRICK FURY[357] 115 Inf F			Misidentified soldier in grave. Patrick Fury, a private in the 115th PA infantry was not killed at Gettysburg but went on to enlist in a Veteran Volunteers regiment in 1864.
R7#93	BENJAMIN SCHLABACH	20-21	153 Inf D	B ~1842 PA. R East Allen twp, Northampton Co., PA. 1860 occ: laborer. E Sep 62 private. C Jul 1: wounds in left hip and right hand. D Aug 1.
R7#94	CORP U McCRACKEN URIAH McCRACKEN	23-24	153 Inf C	B ~1839 PA. R Upper Mount Bethel twp, Northampton Co., PA. 1860 occ: miller's apprentice. E Sep 62 corporal. C Jul 1. D Jul 8.

---

[357] **Misidentified soldier in grave.** Patrick Fury was not killed at Gettysburg but went on to enlist in a Veteran Volunteers regiment in 1864.

R7#95	JAMES IRVING JAMES **ERWIN**[358]	36-37	73 Inf G	B ~1826. E Oct 61 private. KIA Jul 3. Survivors (WC29569): W Catharine 30 in 1864 (M Jan 48); 3 chn: 1 ♂- Charles 14 & 2 ♀- Rosanna 9, Margaret 7 (Catharine dropped in 1876 due to fraud). Dropped in 1876 for fraud. (WC12271 not online) 2nd W Martha 30 (M Mar 61): no chn (dropped in 1865 based on ineligibility due to bigamy).
R7#96	JOHN REIMEL[359]	30-31	153 Inf K	B ~1832 PA. R Lower Mount Bethel twp, Northampton Co., PA. Occ carpenter. E Sep 62 corporal. C Jul 1. D Jul 9. Survivors (no approved WC found in pension records): W Hannah (D 1863); 1 ♀- Mary (B 1862→?).
R7#97	FRITZ SMITTLE **FRANZ SCHMITTEL**	29-30	74 Inf H	B ~1833 Germany. R Allegheny Co., PA. Occ watchmaker. E Aug 62 private. KIA Jul 3. Survivor (WC17560): W Philipina 25 (M Mar 60): no chn.
R7#98	EMIL PREIFER EMIL **PREISER**[360]	~19	27 Inf E	B ~1844 Germany. 1860: R Philadelphia, PA; occ confectioner apprentice. E May 61 private. Promoted to corporal on 3/1/62. C Jul 1. D Aug 21.

---

358 **The soldier's previous wife bumps his widow from the pension rolls**. In August 1863, Mrs. Martha Erwin filed a pension application following the death of Private James Erwin, her husband of 2½ years. Following initial acceptance, she was dropped in 1865 following a determination that James Erwin had committed bigamy in his marriage to her. This situation had come to light with the 1864 filing of a pension application by a Mrs. Catharine Erwin for herself and three children. In this pension application, Mrs. Catharine Erwin reported a marriage to James Erwin in January 1848 but stated that in the Spring of 1858 he had abandoned her and their children. She reported that since this time she had not divorced or remarried. Following the acceptance of her pension application, Mrs. Catharine Erwin continued to execute vouchers for payments into 1876. However, In July 1876, a Patrick Ward contacted a local U.S. Pension agent to inform him that "Mrs. Erwin" had been his wife since September 1875, but that she was continuing to fraudulently execute vouchers for the Erwin pension. The U.S. Pension Office responded to this serious charge by contacting the clerk of the Blue County District Court, who confirmed the Ward marriage. The clerk further informed the Pension Office that prior to Ward marriage that this woman had not known as Mrs. Erwin, but as "Mrs. Brink," due to her cohabitation with this man whom it was locally presumed she was unmarried to. The clerk further volunteered that he had attempted to dissuade Patrick Ward from marrying the Erwin woman, whom the clerk characterized as a "hard drinker" and an "old reprobate." But, as concerned the Pension Office, a full investigation of this fraud allegation ended with Mrs. Catharine Ward being dropped from the pension rolls and criminal prosecution being entertained.

359 **No widow's pension approval found in records**. No approved Widow's Certificate is found in the U.S. Pension files for John Reimel's widow, Hannah, and his daughter, Mary, who would have been about one-year-old at his father's death.

360 **Accepted at seventeen for enlistment**. On May 5, 1861, Emil Preiser was allowed to enlist as a private into 27th Pennsylvania Infantry. This was despite his honest acknowledgement that he was a minor at 17 years of age.

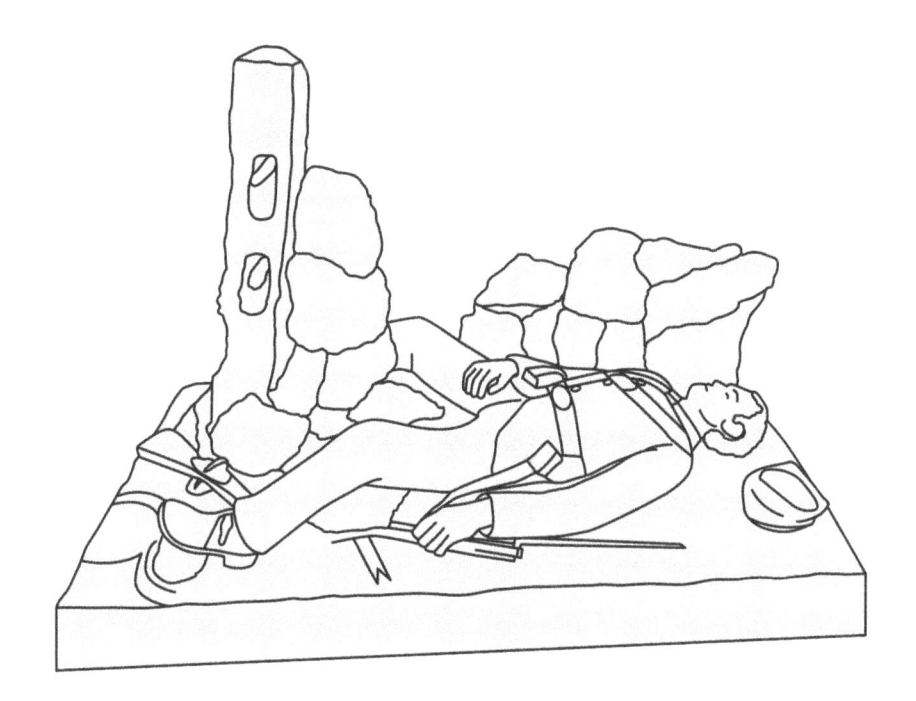

116th Pennsylvania Infantry Monument on the Stoney Hill

★ ★ ★ ★ ★

The Good Death: A scene reported to Major St. Claire Mulholland of an "at peace" appearing soldier dead at a barricade, remembered and memorialized in their regimental monument.

Rhode Island

ID	Name	Age	Unit	Details
R1#1	WILLIAM BEARD[361]	32-33	Battery E 1 LA	B ~1830 England. R Johnston, Providence Co., RI. Occ weaver, operator. E Aug 62 private. KIA Jul 2. Survivor (WC8703): W Isabella 33 (M Jun 61); no chn.
R1#2	CORP HENRY H BALLOU	20-21	Battery B 1 LA	B ~1842 RI. R Providence, RI. Occ farm laborer. E Aug 61 private. Promoted to corporal on 1/31/63. C Jul 2: shot in thigh. D Jul 2 or 3.
R1#3	ALFRRED G GARDNER[362]	41	Battery B 1 LA	B 12/25/1821 Swansea, Bristol Co., MA. R Providence, RI. Occ farmer and gardener. E Aug 62 private. KIA Jul 2: struck in left shoulder by cannonball which nearly severed his arm from the shoulder and causing his death within a few minutes. Survivors (WC7995): W Adelia 35 (M Feb 45); 4 chn: 3 ♀- Ida 13, Lillian 12, Margaret 4 & 1 ♂- Alfred D. 7.
R1#4	WILLIAM JONES (ALIAS) JOHN MAHONEY[363]	25	Battery B 1 LA	B 12/6/1837 Boston, MA. E (Providence, RI) Aug 61 private. Promoted to corporal on 11/1/61. Reduced to private on 7/11/62 for an unspecified offense. KIA Jul 3: killed instantly by a shell fragment striking him in the head. head. Survivor (WC382553 not online): M Mrs. Margaret Nott 72 in 1890 (twice widowed).
R2#1	IRA BENNETT ZELAH IRA BENNETT	32	Battery B 1 LA	B 1/20/1831 Troy, Waldo Co., ME. R Montville, Waldo Co., ME. Occ farmer. E Jul 62 into the 19th ME Co. B as a private. Detached 12/24/62 to Battery B 1st RI LA. KIA Jul 2. Survivors (WC16377): W Lucinda 23 (M Sep 56| died 10/25/64); 3 chn: 1 ♀- Mary 5 & 2 ♂- John 3, Zela 10 months.
R2#2	DAVID B KING	~27	Battery B 1 LA	B ~1836 RI. R Scituate, Providence Co., RI. E Aug 61 private. KIA Jul 2 or 3. Survivors (WC20078→WC776895 neither online): W Mary 18 (M Dec 60| ReM 1866); 1 ♂- David 15 months.

---

361 **Soldier remembered as industrious fellow always willing to accept chores to earn extra money.** William Beard was remembered by his regiment as a very industrious individual, who was almost constantly employed in washing clothes for fellow soldiers, for which he earned extra money.

362 **Artilleryman undergoes delirious reaction to mortal wounding by a cannonball.** Evidencing the extreme tension of working a cannon during an artillery duel, Alfred Gardner is reported to have experienced a delirious reaction to his mortal wounding by a cannonball. While presumably prostrate, he is reportedly immediately exclaimed: "Glory to God. I am happy. Hallelujah. Tell my wife I died happy." He then died within a few minutes of being struck.

363 **Fighting under an alias.** By the testimony of a half-brother, John Mahoney left his Irish-born parents in Boston, and without telling them of his plans, wrote later to inform them that he had joined 1st RI Light Artillery. Mahoney at that writing instructed all family members to write to him under the alias William Jones. There was speculation that John Mahoney employed an alias with the intent of personally sidestepping the prevailing prejudices of the day against the Irish.

R2#3	JOHN ZIMMILA	~32	Battery A 1 LA	B ~1831. R Providence, RI. E Jun 61 private. Wounded in leg on 9/17/62 at Antietam. KIA Jul 3: killed instantly by wound to the head.
R2#4	ERNEST SIMPSON[364]	23-24	Battery E 1 LA	B ~1839 Germany. E Sep 61 private. Hospitalized Jul/Aug→9/30/61 for an an unspecified condition. Promoted to corporal on 1/26/62. Hospitalized 8/10/62 for an unspecified condition. KIA Jul 2.
R2#5	JOHN BREEN JOHN **GREENE**[365]	~38	Battery B 1 LA	B ~1825 Cumberland, Providence Co., RI. R same. Occ manufacturer. E Feb 62 private. C Jul 3: severe wound in right thigh→amp. D Jul 16.
R2#6	JOHN HIGGINS	~22	2 Inf K	B ~1841 Ireland. R Smithfield, Providence Co., RI. Occ day laborer. E Jun 61 into 2nd RI Infantry as a private. Detached on 7/1/61 to Battery A of 1st RI LA. C Jul 3: severe wound in arm→amp. D Jul 8. Survivor (WC12264): M Mrs. Ann Higgins 56 (widow of Dennis Higgins).
R2#7	ALVIN HILTON	19	4 ME Inf K	B 11/29/1843 Appleton, Knox Co., ME. R same. E Sep 61 into 4th ME Infantry as a private. Detailed to Battery E of 1st RI LA. C Jul 2. D Jul 10.
R2#8	FRANCIS H MARTIN	~20	99 PA Inf B	B ~1843. E Jul 61 into 99th PA Infantry Company B as a private. Detached to serve with 1st RI LA on 2/5/63. C Jul 2. D Jul 2 or 10.
R2#9	PATRICK LONNEGAN	~21	Battery A 1 LA	B ~1842 Ireland. R Providence, RI. E Jun 61 private. KIA Jul 2: shot in groin while holding artillery horses.
R2#10	CHARLES POWERS	20-21	2 Inf C	B ~1842 Providence, RI. R same. Occ laborer. E Dec 61 private. KIA Jul 3: killed by a shell.

---

364 **Soldier shows death wish?** Reportedly, Ernest Simpson jointed the battery with the expectation of being killed. A lieutenant with his battery reported that Simpson implored to leave the relative safety of serving as a company clerk and to take charge of one of the cannons. Within a few minutes of taking charge of a gun, his death premonition was realized when a shot nearly decapitated him.

365 **Gallows humor in an artillery unit.** When at Malvern Hill John Greene was struck that day by a second glancing blow of a shell fragment, he hopped up and unleashed a string of profanities: "The damn rebels has got the dead range on me sure." Greene's reaction apparently caused some bemusement in his battery, as in subsequent artillery engagements, a frequent jest from his mates was: "Look out, John, the rebels has got a dead range on you." Tragically, all jesting stopped for the 1st RI Artillery Battery B due to its carnage suffered in the July 3rd cannonade duel.

9th Pennsylvania Reserves (38th Infantry) Monument at the base of Little Round Top

★ ★ ★ ★ ★

As an exception to most 19th century monuments showing no emotion, the soldier here casts his head down at a comrade's grave in mourning.

222 Abraham Lincoln's Honored Dead at the Gettysburg National Cemetery

Vermont

R1#4	EDMOND P DAVIS[366]	18	16 Inf H	B 10/3/1844 Claremont, Sullivan Co., NH. R Reading, VT. Occ farmer. E Sep 62 private. KIA Jul 3. Survivor (WC18783): M Mrs. Martha Davis 62 (widow of Joshua Davis).
R1#5	PHILLIP HOWARD	19	16 Inf A	B ~Dec 1843 Potsdam, St. Lawrence Co., NY. Occ farmer. E Aug 62 private. A fine of $5 on 1/24/63 as sentenced by a court martial for an unspecified infraction. C Jul 3: wounded in the shoulder by a bursting shell. D Jul 10.
R2#1	LIEUT W H HAMILTON WILLIAM HARRISON HAMILTON[367]	29	14 Inf I	B 10/19/1833 Montgomery, Franklin Co., VT. Occ lawyer. E (Castleton, Rutland Co., VT) Aug 62 sergeant. Commissioned 2nd lieutenant on 1/22/63. Leave of absence 4/1-7/63, during which time he got married. C Jul 3: shell took off one leg and nearly the other. D Jul 3 or 5. Survivor (WC35977): W Harriet 20 (M 4/3/63); no chn.
R2#2	WILLIAM G (or C) JEFFREY 1 Inf A			Killed Gettysburg soldier with this or similar name not found in military sources.
R2#3	W FLETCHER GEORGE WASHINGTON FLETCHER	32-33	13 Inf D	B ~1830 Richford, Franklin Co., VT. R same. Occ farmer. E Sep 62 corporal. May 63: absented with measles. Hospitalized at Gettysburg field hospital on July 11, 1863 with chronic diarrhea. D Jul 13. Survivors (no approved WC found in pension records) W Julia 35 (M Mar 53): 2 ♀- Lonia 8, Flora 16 months.
R2#4	WILLIAM MARCH (MN JOHN)	18	13 Inf D	B 7/7/1844 Quebec, Canada. R Colchester, Chittenden Co., VT. Occ: mechanic. E Aug 62 private. KIA Jul 3: reported to have lived about two hours after "having had both of his legs being shot off." Survivor (WC87220): M Mrs. Sarah March 39 (widow of Edward March).
R2#5	ORSON S CARR	21-22	13 Inf E	B ~1841 Underhill, Chittenden Co., VT. R Stowe, Lamoille Co., VT. Occ cooper. E Sep 62 private. KIA Jul 3: killed by a piece of shell that took off one leg. Survivors (WC18885): W Nancy 24 (M Oct 60| ReM Sep 64); no chn.

---

366 **Soldier's father dies back home in Vermont three months after he enters the army.** On October 23, 1862, the just-turned 18-year-old Edmund Davis reported for duty with the 16th Vermont Infantry. Just three months later, on January 21, 1863, Edmund's father, Joshua Davis, would die back in Cavendish, Vermont.

367 **Woman marries a lieutenant and three months later is widowed.** During an approved leave from his regiment the first full week of April 1863, Lieutenant William Hamilton married Ms. Harriet Smith on April 3, 1863. Three months later, Mrs. Hamilton would be a war widow.

R2#6	PLINY F WHITE[368]	25	14 Inf E	B 4/2/1838 Starksboro, Addison Co., VT. R Whiting, Addison Co., VT. Occ farmer. E Aug 62 private. C Jul 3: wounded by a shell fragment in the right arm→amp. D Aug 5: wound healing complicated by fever and diarrhea. Survivor (WC41847): M Mrs. Julia Morrill (widow of Augustus White and of 2nd husband Hibbard Morrill).
R2#7	ANTOINE ASH	25-26	2 Inf C	B ~1837 Charlotte, Chittenden Co., VT. R Hinesburg, Addison Co., VT. Occ farmer. E Aug 62 private. D Jul 13: inflammation disease of the lungs. Survivors (WC140477 not online): M Mrs. Elenora Ash 65 in 1864 (Barzilla Ash affirmed unable to support wife).
R2#8	CHARLES W WHITNEY (MN WALLACE)	18	13 Inf E	B Oct 1844 Turnbridge, Orange Co., VT. R Wolcott, Lamoille Co., VT. Occ farmer. E Aug 62 private. C Jul 3: wound to left thigh. D Jul 15.
R2#9	BENJAMIN N WRIGHT	32	13 Inf I	B 1/30/1831 St Albans, Franklin Co., VT. R Montpelier, Washington Co., VT. Occ carpenter and joiner. E Aug 62 private. KIA: Jul 3. Survivor (WC75905): W Julia 41 in 1865 (M Apr 60); no chn.
R2#10	LESTER L BAIRD	39-40	14 Inf H	B ~1823 Chittenden, Rutland Co., VT. R Pittsfield, Rutland Co., VT. Occ millwright. E Sep 62 private. C Jul 3. D Jul 12. Survivors (WC17096): W Lucy 38 (M Jun 45); 5 chn: 3 ♀- Lucy 18, Martha 13, Maria 10 & 2 ♂- Edwin 16, Elwin 9.
R2#11	RICHARD C ARCHER	32	14 Inf B	B 7/27/1830 Plymouth, Windsor Co., VT. R Wallingford, Rutland Co., VT. Occ sawyer. E Aug 62 private. C Jul 3: wounded on the left side and left leg by shell fragments. D Jul 14. Survivor (WC15557): W Adeline 28 (M Dec 53); no chn.
R2#12	HENRY C WHITE[369]	19-20	16 Inf E	B ~1843 Bridgewater, Windsor Co., VT. R Weathersfield, Windsor Co., VT. Occ preacher. E Aug 62 private. C Jul 3: wound fracturing femur→amp. D Jul 14. Survivor (WC225301 not online): M Mrs. Mary White ~76 in 1886.
R2#13	ZENAL C LAMB	29	16 Inf C	B 6/14/1834 Stockbridge, Windsor Co., VT. R Ludlow, Windsor Co., VT. Occ farmer. E Aug 62 private. C Jul 3. D Jul 4. Survivors (WC78225): W Sarah 26 (M Jun 57| ReM 1865); 3 chn: 2 ♂- Willie 4, Elmer 6 months & 1 ♀- Isadore 2.

---

368 **Soldier avows patriotic motivation for enlisting into the army.** Pliny White's Vermont death notice recounted what he had avowed as his patriotic motivation for enlisting in the army. "If this rebellion is put down and I do not help do it, I shall feel that I have no right to enjoy the blessings of the Government."

369 **Prior occupation a preacher.** Henry C. White's service record reports that his pre-enlistment occupation was as a preacher.

R2#14	JOHN DYER	26	16 Inf D	B May 1837 Townshend, Windham Co., VT. R same. Occ farmer. E Aug 62 private. KIA Jul 3.
R2#18	COPORAL _____ WARREN[370]			Likely misidentified soldier in this grave.
R2#19	RUFUS D THOMPSON	18-19	1 Cav L	B ~1844 Chittenden, Rutland Co., VT. R Colchester, Chittenden Co., VT. Occ farmer. E Aug 62 private. C Jul 3. D Jul 6. Survivors (WC19022): W Amelia 22 (M Jan 62| ReM 1870); 1 ♂- Ellsworth 6 months.
R2#20	CHARLES CORLEY CHARLES **COWLEY**[371]	19-20	1 Cav K	B ~1843 St. Albans, VT. R same. Occ farmer. E Aug 62 private. C Jul 3: wound to left shoulder. Sent to hospital and received a pass on 8/3/63. Desertion afterwards?
R2#21	JOEL J SMITH[372]	34	1 Cav C	B ~Jan 1829 Lebanon, Grafton Co., NH. R Duxbury, Washington Co., VT. Occ farmer. E Sep 61 private. Employed as company cook Sep 62→Jun 63, KIA Jul 3: GSW to the head. Survivors (WC129079): W Loease 32 (M Oct 50| ReM 1867); 1 ♀- Clara 6.
R2#27	WILLARD M PIERCE	20	16 Inf I	B 12/6/1842 Putney, Windham Co., VT. R same. Occ farmer. E Sep 62 private. KIA Jul 3.
R3#2	JOSEPH ASHLEY	24	16 Inf C	B 4/30/1839 Quebec, Canada. R Cavendish, Windsor Co., VT. E Aug 62 private. Captured in May 63 and paroled 5/11/63. Held at Camp Convalescent 5/29/63. KIA Jul 3: killed by a shell fragment passing through his left side. Survivors (WC69682): W Phebe 19 in 1864 (M Feb 59); the two children from this marriage had died by the time of soldier's death.
R3#3	CHARLES W ROSS[373]	17	14 Inf G	B ~1846 Huntington, Chittenden Co., VT. R Starksboro, Addison Co., VT. Occ farmer. E Sep 62 private. KIA Jul 3.

---

370 **Identity question**. This grave of a Corporal Warren lies amidst a row of 1st Vermont Cavalry graves. A Corporal Daniel Warren of Company K 1st Vermont Cavalry was present at Gettysburg, was captured July 3rd, then taken as a prisoner-of-war to Richmond. It is possible in some way that an otherwise unidentified corpse became suspected of being this Corporal Warren and a field burial marker so engraved. However, Corporal Warren survived imprisonment in Richmond and returned to active duty eleven months after his capture.

371 **Misidentified soldier in grave**. It appears likely that there is a misidentified soldier and not Charles Cowley buried in this grave. His service record includes documentation that while hospitalized at the Marine Hospital in Burlington, Vermont, he received an August 3, 1863 pass from which he never returned. A 1912 final review concluded that Cowley's Civil War service ended as a deserter.

372 **Soldier serves extended period as company cook**. Following Joel Smith's enlistment in September 1861, one year later he began service as the company cook which extended into June 1863. Serving as company cook did not excuse Smith from the battle line and he would be killed in action July 3rd.

373 **Minor at death**. Charles Ross's reported ages of 4 and 14 on the successive October 1850 and July 1860 U.S. Censuses attest to the likelihood that he was not 18, but 16 at his September 1862 enlistment. The implied birthyear of 1846 means that Charles was likely only 17 when he was killed in action on July 3rd.

R3#4	CHARLES E MEAD	26	14 Inf G	B 10/25/1836 Hinesburg, Chittenden Co., VT. R same. Occ farmer. E Sep 62 corporal. KIA Jul 3.
R3#8	MARTIN J COOK (MN JEFFERSON)	18	16 Inf D	B 3/5/1845 Alstead, Cheshire Co., NH. E Aug 62 private. KIA Jul 3.
R3#9	JOSEPH M MARTIN[374] (MN MICAJAH)	22	16 Inf D	B 1/27/1841 Weston, Windsor Co., VT. R Jamaica, Windham Co., VT. Occ farmer. E Aug 62 private. KIA Jul 3.
R3#10	WILLIAM E GREEN	21-22	14 Inf G	B ~1841 Lincoln, Addison Co., VT. R same. Occ farmer. E Sep 62 private. KIA Jul 3. Survivor (WC139685): F Philander Green 58 in 1868 (disabled from spinal injury sustained in 1866 fall from a building).
R3#13	DYER ROGERS	34-35	14 Inf D	B ~1828 Edinburg, Saratoga Co., NY. R Orwell, Addison Co., VT. Occ: ship carpenter. E Aug 62 private. KIA Jul 3. Survivors (WC19273): W Susan 30 (M May 49| ReM 1874); 4 chn: 2 ♀- Esther 13, Emma 10 & 2 ♂- Jesse 7, Freddy 5.
R3#15	ALBERT A WALKER (MN ALLEN)	18-19	14 Inf D	B ~1844 Bridport, Addison Co., VT. R same. Occ farmer. E Aug 62 private. KIA Jul 3.
R3#16	CHARLES MOREE JR CHARLES **MORSE** JR	40	16 Inf A	B 1/3/1823 Rochester, Windsor Co., VT. R same. Occ farmer. E Aug 62 private. Promoted to corporal on 12/10/62. KIA Jul 3. Survivors (WC19025): W Sarah 39 (M Jun 46| ReM 1866); 4 chn: 3 ♂- Charles 14, Summer 5, Kimball 4 & 1 ♀- Lizzie 8.
R3#17	GARRETT L ROSEBOOM	26-27	14 Inf D	B ~1836 Albany, NY. R Benson, Rutland Co., VT. Occ tinsmith. E Aug 62 private. KIA Jul 3.
R3#18	IRA EMERY JR[375]	23	16 Inf A	Remains relocated from grave on 1/8/64
R3#19	WILLIAM O DOUBLEDAY	44-45	14 Inf H	B ~1818 Sharon, Windsor Co., VT. R Sherburne (Killington), Rutland Co., VT. Occ farmer. E Oct 62 private. C Jul 3: wound fracturing left tibia→amp→ complication of dysentery. D Aug 12. Survivors (WC25222): W Emma 38 (M Nov 46); 3 ♂- Otto 11, George 8, Fred 2.

---

374 **Soldier's father a physician.** Joseph Micajah Martin's father, Franklin Martin, was a physician. His son's middle name was the first name of his father.

375 **Empty grave.** Ira Emery, Jr., a private in the 16th Vermont, would be killed in action on July 3rd. He would leave behind a 20-year-old wife, Ellen, and a 6-month-old daughter, Clara Belle. As not uncommonly occurred, the new, young widow would remarry within a few short years—in Ellen's case, by the end of 1865. Ira Emery, Sr. would outlive his sacrificed namesake by 20 years.

R3#20	ANDREW E OSGOOD	20	13 Inf H	B 11/14/1842 Cabot, Washington Co., VT. R same. Occ farmer. E (Calais, Washington Co., VT) Sep 62 private. C Jul 3. D Jul 7.
R3#21	GEORGE L BALDWIN	23	14 Inf F	B 3/9/1840 Shelburne, Chittenden Co., VT. R Williston, Chittenden Co., VT. Occ farmer. E Aug 62 private. Promoted to corporal on 3/3/63. C Jul 3: GSW to hip. D Aug 2. Survivor (WC61289): W Lucy 23 (M Aug 62| ReM Jul 64); no chn.
R3#22	G F SIMMONS **JOSEPH** SIMMONS	40-41	13 Inf C	B ~1822 Canada. R Marshfield, Washington Co., VT. Occ farmer. E Sep 62 private. C Jul 3. D Jul 14.
R3#23	SYLVANUS A WINSHIP	25-26	16 Inf C	B ~1837 Weston, Windsor Co., VT. R same. Occ farmer. E Aug 62 private. KIA Jul 2. Survivor (WC23988): W Jane 23 (M May 60| ReM 1866); no chn.
R3#24	SERGT M P BALDWIN MOSES POLLARD BALDWIN	29	16 Inf C	B 2/25/1834 Plymouth, Windsor Co., VT. R same. Occ farmer. E Aug 62 corporal. Promoted to sergeant on 4/14/63. KIA Jul 2. Survivors (WC25217): W Lorinda 31 (M Jul 57); 2 chn: 1 ♂- Charles 2 (B Jan 61| died Nov 64) & 1 ♀- Lora Abby 7 weeks.
R3#25	MAJOR H H SMITH HENRY H SMITH	21-22	13 Inf	B ~1841 Marshfield, VT. R Stowe, Lamoille Co., VT. Occ trimming carriages, mechanic. E Sep 62 1st sergeant. Promoted to sergeant major on 2/23/63. KIA Jul 3.
R3#26	CORP IRA E SPERRY (MN EMERSON)	24	1 Cav L	B 12/12/1838 VT. R St. Albans, Franklin Co. VT. 1860: occ confectioner. E Aug 62 corporal. C Jul 3: wound to right thigh→amp. D Jul 22. Survivors (WC27014 not online): W Mary (M May 61); 1 ♀- Lucy.
R3#27	JOHN L MARSHALL	23-24	4 Inf K	B ~1839 Chester, Windsor Co., VT. R same. Occ farmer. E Sep 61 private. C Jul 2: wounds to right forearm and fracturing left knee joint→amp. D Aug 8.
R3#28	SERGT THOS BLAKE THOMAS BLAKE	23-24	13 Inf A	B ~1839 Ireland. R Rutland Co., VT. Occ marble work. E Aug 62 sergeant. KIA Jul 3.
R3#29	CORP MICHAEL McENERNY MICHAEL **McINERNEY**	30-31	13 Inf A	B ~1832 Ireland. R Rutland Co., NY. Occ farmer. E Aug 62 sergeant. Reduction to rank of private on 11/3/62 for an unspecified offense. KIA Jul 3. Survivor (WC19594): W Ellen 35 (M Aug 55); no chn.

Bas-relief on base of William Wells statue at base of Big Round Top, memorializing charge of the 1st Vermont Calvary at end of July 3rd day.

★ ★ ★ ★ ★

BG Elon Farnworth relented to the order by BG Hugh Judon Kilpatrick to lead his brigade on what he felt would be a futile and costly charge only after Kilpatrick questioned whether his reluctance to follow the order might be due to cowardice. Farnworth would be killed during this charge along with several Vermont cavalrymen, while Wells, then a major, although riding beside Farnsworth, would escape injury.

West Virginia

R1#1	SERGT GARRET SELBY **GARRETT** C SELBY	36-37	1 Cav F	B ~1826 Harrison Co, VA (now WV). R Decator Twp, Washington Co., OH. Occ mechanic. E (Athens Co., OH) Aug 61 sergeant. KIA June 30 at Hanover, PA. Survivors (WC102950): W Eveline 29 (M Jan 51| died 12/15/66); 4 chn: 1 ♀- Fanny 10 & 3 ♂- Edward 9, Richard 5, Garrett H 3.
R1#2	SERGT GEORGE COLLINS[376]	23-24	1 Cav L	B ~1839 OH. R Steubenville, Jefferson Co., OH. 1860: occ laborer. E Oct 61 private. Promotion to corporal in Apr 62. Promotion to 3rd sergeant 6/17/62. Court martialed 10/10/62 and sentenced to 6-months confinement at the Brooklyn Navy (offense not specified). Released following appeal to the Secretary of War and returned to duty 11/20/62 as private. KIA June 30 at Hanover, PA.
R1#3	CHARLES LACEY[377] 1 Cav Co C			Likely misidentified soldier in grave.
R1#4	WILLIAM BAILEY WILLIAM **BAILY**	23-24	1 Cav E	B ~ 1839 Pickaway Co., OH. R Orange, Meigs Co., OH. Occ farmer. E (Parkersburg, Wood Co., VA [now WV]) Nov 61 private. KIA Jul 3. Survivors (WC35517): W Judith 32 (M Apr 50| ReM 1886); 5 chn: 3 ♂- Henry 10, John 7, William 3 & 2 ♀- Louisa 9, Sarah 5.
R2#1	SIMON MAINE SIMON **MAIN**	21-22	7 Inf F	B ~1841 Greene Co., PA. 1850 R: Jackson, Greene Co., PA. Occ farmer. E (Morgantown, Monongalia Co., VA [now WV]) Sep 61 private. Hospitalizations in Dec 61 and Oct/Nov 62→Dec/Jan 63 for unspecified condition. C Jul 3: shell wound to thigh. D Jul 4. Survivor (WC147777): W Elsie 19 in Jan 1867 (M Jul 61); no chn.
R2#2	JOHN BROWN 7 Inf Co E			Killed Gettysburg soldier with this common name or similar name in this regiment not found in military sources.
R2#3	AARON AUSTIN	~25	7 Inf E	B ~1838 Monongalia Co., VA (now WV). Occ farmer. E Jul 61 private. Sep/Oct 62: hospitalized at Alexandria, VA. Nov/Dec 62: convalescent camp. C Jul 2 or 3. GSW to abdomen. D Jul 10.

---

[376] **Harsh court martial sentence.** As an unusually harsh court martial sentence, George Collins was stripped of his sergeant's rank and sent to the Navy Yard in Brooklyn for six months of confinement. The specific offense for which he was sentenced is not specified in his service record file.

[377] **Misidentified soldier in grave.** A Private Charles Lacey does appear in the muster of the 1st MD Infantry Company C. However, his service record documents that he deserted during an April 1863 hospitalization in Baltimore.

R2#4	THEODORE STEWART	20-21	7 Inf C	B ~1842 Tyler Co., VA (now WV). R same. Occ farmer. E (Sistersville, Tyler Co, VA [now WV]) Aug 61 private. Nov/Dec 61: promoted to corporal. Promoted to sergeant on 10/18/62. Wounded in Dec 62 at Fredericksburg, VA: flesh wound through right thigh. Dec 62/Jan 63: hospitalized in Washington, D.C. Mar/Apr 63: absent, sick at hospital in Grafton, VA (now WV). KIA Jul 3.
R2#5	GEORGE BERGER[378]	34-35	7 Inf F	B ~1828. Occ farmer. E (Woodsfield, Monroe Co., OH) Sep 61 private. Absent sick and hospitalized with an unspecified condition at Alexandria, VA: Jun 62→Oct 62. Nov/Dec 62→Apr 63: held in confinement at Fort Delaware after arrest for desertion. Lieutenant Alonzo Conaway secures Berger's release with 4/14/63 letter affirming that Berger had not been deserting, but was attempting to return to the regiment from the hospital when arrested. KIA Jul 2 or 3.
R2#6	MARTIN L SCOTT (MN LUTHER)	24-25	7 Inf B	B ~1838 Marshall Co., VA (now WV). Occ farmer. E (Cameron, Marshall Co., VA [now WV]) Aug 61 private. Jan/Feb 62: hospitalized at Cumberland, VA (now WV). Aug 62→Jan/Feb 63: hospitalized at Alexandria, VA with unspecified condition. KIA Jul 2.
R2#7	CAPT W N HARRIS WILLIAM NELSON **HARRISS**	36-37	1 Cav E	B 1826 Wood Co., VA (now WV). 1860 R: same. Occ: farm laborer. E (Parkersburg, Wood Co., VA [now WV]) Sep 61. Commissioned Captain after after recruiting his company. C Jul 3. D Jul 4.

---

378 **A lieutenant from soldier's regiment intervenes to have released from confinement only for the soldier to be killed eleven weeks later.** In April 1863, a lieutenant in 7th West Virginia Infantry regiment intervened to have George Berger released from an unjust confinement for desertion. Eleven weeks after returning to his regiment, Berger would be killed in action at Gettysburg.

230 *Abraham Lincoln's Honored Dead at the Gettysburg National Cemetery*

Color sergeant Ben Crippin memorialized on the 143rd Monument on the Chambersburg Pike

★ ★ ★ ★ ★

As enemy fire was succeeding July 1st in driving the 143rd Pennsylvania regiment from its position on McPherson Ridge, Color Sergeant Ben Crippin was killed as he lagged behind to turn with his flag and impetuously shake his fist at the advancing Confederates. Today, Crippin's remains most probably lie buried as an unknown.

Wisconsin

R1#1	LIEUT MARTIN YOUNG	32	26 Inf A	B 5/20/1831 France. R Alexandria, Douglas Co., WI. Occ merchant. E Aug 62 sergeant. Commissioned 2nd lieutenant on 2/1/63. Promoted to 1st lieutenant on 3/15/63. KIA Jul 1. Survivors (WC15312): W Margaretha 34 (M Aug 57| ReM 1871): 1 ♂- Charles 5.
R1#2	SPENCER M TRAIN[379]	~28	2 Inf C	B ~1835 Erie County, NY. R Muscoda, Grant Co., WI. Occ farmer. E Apr 61 corporal. Wounded and captured on 8/28/62 near Gainesville, VA. Paroled and sent to Washington on 9/29/62. Promoted to sergeant on 10/1/62. Wounded severely on 12/13/62 near Fredericksburg, VA. C Jul 1: wound involving compound fracture wound of left leg. D Aug 25.
R1#3	URIAH PALMER	~20	6 Inf A	B ~1843. 1860: R Montrose, Dane Co., WI; occ day laborer. R Leicester, Dane Co., WI. E Jun 61 private. Detached to Battery B 4th US Light Artillery on 9/12/62 by order of General Gibbons. C Jul 1: wounds to left arm and one hip→arm amp on Jul 12. D Jul 21 or 29.
R1#4	SERGT WALKER S ROUSS **WALKER** S **ROUSE**	23	2 Inf E	B 7/4/1840 Litchfield, Litchfield Co., CT. R Oshkosh, Winnebago Co., WI. E Apr 61 corporal. Wounded on 7/21/61 at 1st Bull Run. Promoted to sergeant on 12/31/61. Captured on 8/28/62 at Gainesville, VA. Paroled on 9/6/62. Sent to regiment on 12/14/62. Departed 4/5/63 on 15-day furlough. C Jul 1: wounded in the leg. D Jul 12.
R1#5	SERGT ANDREW MILLER	~27	6 Inf I	B ~1836 Ireland. R De Soto, Vernon Co., WI. E Jul 61 corporal. Promoted to sergeant on 11/21/61. Hospitalized 10/30/62 with an unspecified condition. KIA Jul 1.
R1#8	ERNT SCHERENBACH **ERNEST SCHIERENBOCKEN**	~26	6 Inf H	B ~1837. R Fountain City, Buffalo Co., WI. E Apr 61 private. May/Jun 62: detached to Provost Guard duty. Hospitalized Jul→Oct 62 in US Hospital at Philadelphia with an unspecified condition. KIA Jul 1.
R1#9	CHARLES HASSE CHARLES **HARRE**[380]	~19	6 Inf F	B ~1844. R Milwaukee, WI. E Jun 61 private. Aug 62: sick at Alexandria, VA. KIA Jul 1.

---

379 **Army makes a contemptible seven-cents deduction on dead soldier's final statement.** Spencer Train's mortal wound at Gettysburg had been his third battle wound serving with the 2nd Wisconsin Infantry. While Train was fighting for his life in a Gettysburg hospital, a contemptible note was being appended to his service record to deduct 7¢ deducted from his pay to cover the cost of his cartridge box plate lost in the field.

380 **Accepted at seventeen for enlistment.** On June 3, 1861, Charles Harre was allowed to enlist as a private into 6th Wisconsin Infantry. This was despite his honest acknowledgement that he was a minor at 17 years of age.

R1#10	LIEUT COL GEO H STEVENS GEORGE HENRY STEVENS[381]	31	2 Inf	B 12/3/1831 NYC. R Fox Lake, Dodge Co., WI. Occ grocer. E Aug 62 captain. Commissioned major on 8/30/62. Promoted to lieutenant colonel on 1/26/63. C Jul 1: wounded in left side. D Jul 5. Survivors (WC26641): W Harriet 25 in 1864 (M Mar 59); 2 chn: 1 ♂ Walter 3 & 1 ♀ Lucy 2.
R2#1	ABRAM FLETCHER **ABRAHAM** GREENLEAF FLETCHER[382]	28	6 Inf K	B 1/10/1835 Mount Vernon Kennebec Co., ME. R Lemonweir, Juneau Co., WI. Occ common laborer. E Jun 61 corporal. C Jul 1: wounded in left thigh. D Jul 18. Survivors (WC76292): W Sarah 25 (M Jun 56| ReM 1866); 2 chn: 1 ♂- Ira 4 & 1 ♀- Eliza 19 months.
R2#2	WILLIAM H BARNUM	~25	7 Inf K	B ~1838 IN. R Newark, Rock Co., WI. Occ farm laborer. E Aug 61 corporal. C Jul 1: GSW to bowels. D Jul 16.
R2#3	GEORGE H HAWES GEORGE H H HAWES	~23	7 Inf B	B ~1840 Weld, Franklin Co., ME. R Lowville, Columbia Co., WI. Occ farmer. E Aug 61 private. C Jul 1. D Jul 26.
R2#4	JOHN B STRAIGHT[383]	21	7 inf E	B 12/21/1841 Greene, Chenango Co., NY. R Westfield, Marquette Co., WI. E Feb 62 private. Hospitalized 9/16/62→Jan/Feb 63 with an unspecified condition. C Jul 1: wounded in the head. D Jul 22. Survivors: W Mary 19 (M 1862); 1 ♂- Ollie (B 1863).
R2#5	WILLIAM RAMTHEN **WILHELM RAMPTHON**	24-25	2 Inf K	B ~1838 Germany. R Ashford, Fond du Lac Co., WI. E Nov 61 private. Wounded on 9/4/62 at the Battle of South Mountain. C Jul 1: GSW fracture of right arm→ amp. D Jul 31 with complicating pneumonia.
R2#6	SILAS COSTER[384] **SAKE KOOISTRA**	22	2 Inf B	B 2/18/1841 Holland. R New Amsterdam, La Crosse Co., WI. Occ farm laborer. E Mar 62 private. C Jul 1: severe wound to right leg→amp. D Jul 3.
R2#7	PHILIP BENNETTS PHILIP **BENNETT**	20-21	7 Ind F	B ~1842 England. R Potosi, Grant Co., WI. E Aug 61 private. C Jul 1. D Jul 4.

---

381 **One of the two highest ranking officers in the Cemetery.** George Stevens and Max Thurman, the two sharing the rank of lieutenant colonel, are the two most senior Gettysburg officers buried in the National Cemetery.

382 **Soldier had lost younger brother to typhoid following 1st Bull Run.** Like occurred for unknown numbers of soldiers killed at Gettysburg, Abraham Fletcher had a brother who would also be killed or experience a disabling injury during the war. In Abraham Fletcher's case, Charles Fletcher was a brother, eleven years his junior, who in April 1861 and just after his 18th birthday, enlisted into the 2nd Wisconsin Infantry. Charles Fletcher would fight with this regiment at 1st Bull Run. He would come through this battle. However, his service comporting with the other Civil War reality that more soldiers would die of disease rather than of battle wounds, Charles Fletcher would contract typhoid fever and would have predeceased his older brother Abraham in May 1862.

383 **No widow's pension approval found in records.** Ancestral records report that John Straight's infant son, Ollie, died July25th, or 3 days after his own death. For an unknown reason, Mary Straight is not found to have procured a widow's pension, although she did not marry again until 1875.

384 **Soldier as a young teenager lost father and family members on a shipwreck while immigrating from Holland.** A FindAGrave posting reports that Silas Coster's father and several other family members were killed in an 1854 shipwreck as the family was emigrating from Holland.

R2#8	JOHN SCOTT JOHN W SCOTT	20-21	2 Inf D	B ~1842 WI. 1860: R Bristol, Kenosha Co., WI. E Dec 62 private. C Jul 1: severe severe wound to right leg→amp. D Aug 5.
R2#9	WILLIAM D McKINNEY	20-21	7 Inf K	B ~1842. R Allen's Grove, Walworth Co., WI. E (Beloit, Rock Co., WI) Aug 61 private. C Jul 1. D Jul 13.
R2#10	A FOWLER 7 Inf A			No Wisconsin soldier killed at Gettysburg with this name found in military sources. A Francis A Fowler of the 7th WI Infantry Company A was a prisoner of war at Antietam and died there on 7/31/64.
R2#11	ERNST SHUHART ERNST **SCHUCKART** or SCHUCHARDT	~32	2 Inf K	B ~1831 Germany. R Roxbury, Dane Co., WI. Occ laborer. E Oct 61 private. Promotion to corporal during service. C Jul 1: wounded in chest. D Jul 6.
R2#12	WILLIAM WAGNER (MN FREDERICK)	24	3 Inf F	B 9/26/1838 Germany. R Liberty, Grant Co., WI. E May 61 private. KIA Jul 3. Survivor (WC26642): M Mrs. Margaret Wagner 53 in 1864 (widow of Johannes Wagner, who was residing in Germany when he died in April 62).
R2#13	THOMAS BARTON	~23	3 Inf F	B ~1840. R Grant Co., WI. E Apr 61 private. Prisoner of war on 5/4/62 at Front Royal, VA. Paroled 9/8/62 at Aiken's Landing. Court martial sentence on 1/25/62 to forfeit $2 pay each month for three consecutive months, infraction not specified. KIA Jul 3.
R2#14	PHILONAS KINSMAN[385]	51	7 Inf K	B 7/7/1812 Landaff, Grafton Co., NH. R Beloit, Grant Co., WI. E Aug 61 private. Aug→Dec 62: sick in hospital. C Jul 1. D Jul 26. Survivors (WC14927): W Adeline 53 (M Mar 39); 3 chn: 1 ♂- Henry 22 & 2 ♀- Sarah18, Rosanna 15.
R2#15	LEWIS H EGGLESTON[386] (MN **WINCHELL**)	~26	6 Inf H	B ~1837 North East, Dutchess Co., NY. R Shiocton, Outagamie Co., WI. E June 61 musician. Rank change to private as of 7/20/62. C Jul 1: gunshot wounds both arms during his July 1st attempt to capture the 2nd Mississippi flag at the Railroad Cut. D Jul 26.
R2#16	JOHN KRAUSS JOHN **KRAUS**	24-25	26 Inf A	B ~1838 Germany. R Milwaukee, WI. Occ laborer. E Aug 62 private. Promoted to corporal on 2/1/63. KIA Jul 1.

---

385 **Overaged at enlistment.** At his August 1861 enlistment Philonas Kinsman reported his age to be 44, or one year below the upper-age limit for army acceptance. Genealogical sources agree that he was actually 49 at this enlistment and that he would be killed when he was 51. .

386 **Soldier was mortally wounded in an unsuccessful dash to capture a rebel flag.** Private Lewis Eggleston is one of two 6th Wisconsin soldiers buried here, who would receive mortal wounds during a heroic and unsuccessful dash to capture the 2nd Mississippi colors Jul 1st at the railroad cut. Moments later, 6th Wisconsin Corporal Francis Wallar would earn the Congressional Medal of Honor by successfully wrestling away this flag.

ID	Name	Age	Unit	Details
R2#17	FRANK KING	~21	6 Inf E	B ~1842 Germany. 1860: R Bear Creek, Sauk Co., WI; occ: farm laborer on father's farm. R Fond du Lac, Fond du Lac Co., WI. E Jun 61 private. KIA Jul 1.
R2#18	JAMES C PERRINE	~29	2 Inf I	B ~1834. R Dodgeville, Iowa Co., WI. E (Mineral Point, Iowa Co., WI) Apr 61 private. Performed extra duty service as a hospital nurse 11/4/61→2/5/62 and 3/01→4/03/62. C Jul 1: wounded in one arm. D Aug 19.
R2#19	FRANTZ BENDA	19	26 Inf F	B 8/18/1844 Czech Republic. R Manitowoc, Manitowoc Co., WI. Occ farmer. E Aug 62 private. C Ju1: GSW hip and pelvis. D Aug 28.
R3#3	MARCELLOUS CHASE / **MARCELLUS** CHASE	~26	7 Inf A	B ~1837. R Chippewa Falls, Chippewa Co., WI. E Jul 61 private. Wounded on 8/28/62 at Gainesville, VA. Promoted to corporal on 3/12/63. KIA Jul 1: GSW to head.
R3#6	JOHN T CHRISTIE / JOHN T **CHRISTY**	~20	2 Inf F	B ~1843 R Waterford, Racine Co., WI. E Apr 61 private. Promoted to corporal on 1/20/63. C Jul 1: wounded in right foot→amp. D Jul 11 or 12.
R3#7	FRANK M BULL / **FRANCIS** M BULL	19-20	7 Inf D	B ~1843. R Muscoda, Grant Co., WI. E Aug 61 private. Sick in the hospital 9/2/62→1/15/63 with an unspecified condition. Promoted to corporal on 3/19/63. C Jul 1: wounded in thigh and ankle. D Jul 9.
R3#8	EDWARD LEAMAN / EDWARD **LEEMAN**	21	6 Inf E	B 6/25/1842 England. R Taycheedah, Fond du Lac Co., WI. E May 61 private. KIA Jul 1.
R3#9	SERGT FRED A NICHOLS / FREDERICK A NICHOLS	25	2 Inf A	B 3/10/1838 Charlemont, Franklin Co., MA. 1860 R: Fox Lake, Dodge Co., WI; occ: day laborer. E Apr 61 private. Promotion to corporal on 1/1/62. Promotion to 1st sergeant on 7/30/62. C Jul 1: GSW to left brain. D Jul 2.
R3#10	JOHN McDONALD	~25	2 Inf A	B ~1838 Canada. R Columbus, Dodge Co., WI. Occ farm laborer. E April 61 private. Wounded on 8/30/62 at 2nd Bull Run. Promotion to corporal on 11/1/62. C Jul 1: GSW to left brain. D Jul 2.
R3#11	CHARLES BRANSTELLER / CHARLES **BRANDSTETTER**[387]	~29	2 Inf A	B ~1834. R Kingston, Green Lake Co., WI. E Nov 61 private. Captured on 8/6/62 while on return for reconnaissance. C Jul 1: shot in left side. D Jul 9.

---

[387] **Volunteer earned a pay bonus for reportedly traveling over 50 miles to reach the Enrollment Office.** New recruit Charles Brandstetter was purported to have traveled over 50 miles to arrive at the enrollment office at Madison, Wisconsin. In so doing, he earned himself the recommendation that he be paid for his travel and additionally for his six days' sustenance in travel.

R3#12	SERGT JAMES GOW[388]	~23	2 Inf C	B ~1840 Scotland. R Lancaster, Grant Co., WI. Occ carpenter. E Apr 61 private. Promoted to sergeant on 3/10/62. May/Jun 62: serving on daily duty as color bearer. Wounded at Gainesville, VA on 8/28/62→hospitalized at Alexandria, VA. Promoted to 1st sergeant on 1/31/63. Mar/Apr 63: sprained ankle accidentally on the march. KIA Jul 1: GSW to abdomen. Survivor (WC48303) M Mrs. Jeannette Gow 52 in 1864 (claimed abandonment by husband, Jacob Gow in 1852).
R3#13	HENRY R McCOLLUM[389] (MN RANDALL)	22	2 Inf H	B 8/6/1840 IN. R Dekorra, Columbia Co., WI. E Jun 61 private. KIA Jul 1: GSW to abdomen.
R3#14	HANFORD C TUPPER (MN COLBURN)	19-20	2 Inf G	B ~1843 Binghamton, Broome Co., NY. R Leeds, Columbia Co., WI. E Sep 61 private. C Jul 1: GSW to abdomen. D Jul 2.
R3#15	SERGT WILLIAM GALLUP	~23	6 Inf D	B ~1840 LeRoy, Dodge Co., WI. R Milwaukee, WI. E May 61 corporal. Promotion to sergeant during service. KIA Jul 1.
R3#16	HENRY ANDERSON	~30	6 Inf B	B ~1833 Sweden. R Stillwater, Washington Co., MN. Occ millman. E (Prescott, Pierce Co., WI) Jun 61 private. Wounded 9/4/62 at the Battle of South Mountain. KIA Jul 1.
R3#17	PETER KRAISCHER PETER **KRENSCHER**	19	26 Ing C	B 8/20/1843 Germany. R Paris, Kenosha Co., WI. E Aug 62 private. C Jul 1: GSW to left side. D Jul 12.
R3#18	PETER KUHN	19-20	26 Inf G	B ~1843 Germany. R Wayne, Washington Co., WI. Occ carpenter. E Aug 62 private. C Jul 1: compound fracture wound of right leg. D Jul 9.
R3#19	JOSEPH BALMES	19-20	26 Inf C	B ~1843 Germany. R Milwaukee, WI. Occ wagon maker. E Aug 62 private. C Jul 1: wounded in right hip. D Jul 14. Survivors (WC90579): M Mrs. Anna Balmes 52 in 1866 (Joseph Balmes, Sr. affirmed incapable of supporting wife).
R3#20	MATHIAS SCHEIVESTER MATHIAS **SCHWISTER**	20-21	26 Inf E	B 1842 Germany. E Aug 62 private. R Granville, Milwaukee Co., WI. Occ laborer. C Jul 1. D Jul 9.

---

[388] **Soldier's mother makes dubious claim of husband's abandonment on pension application.** In Mrs. Jeannette Gow's 1864 application for a dependent mother pension, she reported that her husband, Jacob Gow, had deserted her in 1852. This claim appears contradicted by the 1860 U.S. Census, which shows Jacob Gow heading the household, while holding employment as a stone mason.

[389] **Soldier's father a physician.** The 1860 U.S. Census shows Henry McCollum residing at the home of his father, Dr. James McCollum, a physician.

R3#21	LEION STEDOMAN **LEVI STEDMAN**	~21	6 Inf I	B ~1842. R Brookville, Waukesha Co., WI. E Jun 61 private. Wounded on 9/17/62 at Antietam. C Jul 1. D Jul 17.
R4#4	EDWARD H HEATH	~20	2 Inf H	B ~1843 Racine, Racine Co., WI. R Madison, Dane Co., WI. Occ farm laborer. E May 61 private. Wounded and captured on 8/28/62 at Groveton, VA. Returned to duty from parole camp on 3/23/63. Promoted to corporal on 4/1/63. KIA Jul 1: GSW to right lung.
R4#8	LIEUT WM S WINEGAR WILLIAM SEWARD **WINNEGAR**	22	2 Inf H	B 10/27/1840 Stark, Herkimer Co., NY. R Milton, Rock Co., WI. E Apr 61 private. Promoted to sergeant on 6/11/61. Severely wounded on 8/28/62 at Groveton, VA. Commissioned 2nd lieutenant on 9/1/62. Mar/Apr 63: returned to duty. Departure on 4/19/63 on fifteen-day leave-of-absence. KIA Jul 1: GSW to right lung.
R4#13	SERGT MAJOR LEGATE GEORGE H LEGATE	26-27	2 Inf	B ~1836 RI. R Mineral Point, Iowa Co., WI. E Apr 61 private. Promotions to corporal, then sergeant during service. Promoted to sergeant major on 4/1/63. C Jul 1: GSW to knee. D Jul 1. Survivor (WC196136 not online): M Mrs. Emeline Legate 73 in 1880 (widow of Charles Legate).
R4#16	LIEUT CHAS BROKET CHARLES **BRUCKERT**	43	26 Inf I	B ~Feb 1820 Germany. Occ dyer. E (Milwaukee, WI) Aug 62 sergeant. Promoted to 1st sergeant on 3/15/63. Commissioned lieutenant (had been previously acting at this rank) effective 5/30/63. C Jul 1: severely wounded in right leg→amp. D Jul 16.
R4#17	CHRISTIAN STIER	25-26	26 Inf F	B ~1837 Germany. R Newton, Manitowoc Co., WI. Occ farmer. E (Manitowoc, Manitowoc Co., WI) Aug 62 private. C Jul 1: penetrating wound to the back. D Jul 16.
R4#18	JAMES KELLY[390]	32-33	6 Inf B	B ~1830 Ireland. R Prescott, Pierce Co., WI. Occ laborer. E May 61 private. Promotion to corporal during service. C Jul 1: GSW to left chest. D Jul 21.
R4#19	WILLIAM E EVANS[391]	~20	6 Inf B	B ~1843 Bradford Co., PA. R Prescott, Pierce Co., WI. E May 61 private. Promoted to corporal on 9/5/62. C Jul 1: gunshot wounds through both thighs during his July 1st attempt to capture the 2nd Mississippi flag at the Railroad Cut. D Jul 3.

---

[390] **Plea from a soldier after being shot in the chest: "Colonel, won't you tell my folks I was a good soldier?"** A FindAGrave.com memorial carries a story of James Kelly's mortal wounding at Gettysburg. "After being hit, he grabbed Col. Dawes' coat sleeve, displayed his wound and asked 'Colonel, won't you tell my folks I was a good soldier?' To which Dawes replied, 'Yes, Kelly, I will.'"

[391] **Soldier was mortally wounded in an unsuccessful dash to capture a rebel flag.** Private William Evans is one of two 6th Wisconsin soldiers buried here, who would receive mortal wounds during a heroic and unsuccessful dash to capture the 2nd Mississippi colors July 1st at the railroad cut. Moments later, 6th Wisconsin corporal Francis Wallar would earn the Congressional Medal of Honor by successfully wrestling away this flag.

**Monument of Berdan's U.S. Sharpshooters Company G (1st Wisconsin)
on the Emmitsburg Road**

★ ★ ★ ★ ★

The morning of July 2nd a detachment of 100 Wisconsin sharpshooters was advanced to the crest of a hill 200 yards west of this monument in order to reconnoiter Confederate movements while simultaneously keeping up a constant fire on Confederate troops to their front.

U. S. Infantry

R1#1	LIEUT SILAS A MILLER[392]	~33	12 Inf A	B ~1830 NYC. R Piermont, Rockland. Occ former railroad conductor, clerk. E Aug 61. Commissioned 2nd lieutenant on 2/19/63. Promoted to 1st lieutenant on 6/3/63. KIA Jul 2: shot through chest. Survivors (WC28717): Silas Miller, PGF and guardian, 60; 3 ♀- Ella 11, Emma 9, Annie 6; W Margaret (M Sep 50 | died Mar 1861).
R1#2	H GAERTNER			Killed Gettysburg soldier with this name not found in military sources.
R1#4	WILLIAM REYNOLDS	25	6 Cav C	B 10/29/1837 Bradleytown, Venango Co., PA. E Aug 62 private. KIA Jul 3.
R1#5	AUGUSTUS NELSON	20-21	6 Cav E	B ~1842 Cleveland, OH. Occ painter. E Aug 61 private. C Jul 3: mortally wounded in cavalry battle in Fairfield, PA. D Jul 3.
R1#6	WILLIAM S MOTTERN WILLIAM **MATTERN**	29-30	6 Cav H	B ~1833 Berks Co., PA. R Schuylkill Co., PA. Occ boatman. E Aug 61 private. C Jul 3. D Jul 4. Survivors (WC16250): W Elizabeth 21 (M Oct 58); 1 ♂- William 2.
R1#7	JOHN PATTINSON	23-24	6 Cav H	B ~1839 England. Occ farmer. E Sep 61 private. D Jul 3 of wounds.
R1#12	CHARLES BODMAN	23-24	11 Inf G	B ~1839 Williamsburg, Hampshire Co., MA. Occ farmer. E Oct 61 private. C Jul 2: wounded in right leg→amp. D Aug 15.
R1#13	C F SMETZER CHRISTIANA F **SCHMIDTZER**	~36	6 Inf G	B ~1827 Germany. E Feb 61 private. C Jul 2: wound fracturing left leg. D Aug 23.
R1#14	J CONWAY JOHN CONWAY	~28	11 Inf F	B ~1834 Ireland. R Morristown, St. Lawrence Co., NY. Occ laborer. E Mar 62 private. C Jul 2 or 3. E Aug 18 private. Survivor (WC116256): F Patrick Conway aged over 70 in 1867 (aged widower of Catharine Conway who was affirmed unable to support himself).
R1#15	JAMES STANTON	~35	2 Inf H	B ~1828 Ireland. 1860 R: Pittston, Luzerne Co., PA. Occ boatman. 1st E Jul 58 private. C Jul 2: wound fracturing left leg. D Aug 11.

---

392 **"Oh, God, I am shot!"** On July 18th, the adjutant of 12th Infantry wrote to Charles Miller to inform him of his brother's death from sharpshooter action. Exerted from that letter is a rare, intimate account of soldier being killed in action. "He was shot through the body, near the heart and said, oh! God, I am shot— was moved to a rock near, and only lived about ten minutes, he spoke no more, was unable, & evidently expected death…"

ID	Name	Age	Unit	Details
R1#16	D WALLACE DENNIS WALLACE *or* WALLIS	~28	Batty I 5 Art	B ~1835 Montreal, Canada. E Jan 62 private. C Jul 2: severe wounds in both legs →both legs amp. D Aug 2. Survivors (WC138951): W Abby (M Aug 53 | ReM 1867); 1 ♂- Thomas 8.
R1#17	GEORGE SMITH	~28	7 Inf I	B ~1835 Germany. Occ laborer. E May 60 private. C Jul 2. D Aug 7. Survivors (WC117276): W Theresa (M Mar 62 | died 7/17/65); 1 ♀- Georgiana 6 months.
R1#18	C MILLER CHRISTIAN MILLER	~38	7 Inf E	B ~1825. E (Cleveland, OH) Jul 62 private. C Jul 2: GSW to right foot. D Oct 11.
R1#19	P McGRINITY PATRICK McGRINITY	~24	Batty I 1 LA	B ~1839 Ireland. R Milford, Worcester Co., MA. Occ bootmaker. E Jun 61 private. C Jul 3. D Sep 5.
R1#20	F ROVEY **MARTIN RONEY**	20	14 Inf G	B ~Mar 1843 Ireland. Occ laborer. E Nov 61 private. C Jul 2: wounded in left arm →amp. D Aug 2.
R1#21	SERGT ALFRED E COOK ALFRED ETHINGTON COOK	24	11 Inf C	B 5/16/1839 Plainfield, Hampshire Co., MA. R same. Occ laborer. E Sep 61 private. Promotion to sergeant during service. D Aug 10 of wounds
R1#23	LIEUT G W SHELDON GEORGE W SHELDON	23-24	Berdan's 1 USSS C	B ~1839. R Kalamazoo, MI. E Aug 61 private. KIA Jul 2.
R1#24	WILLIAM H WOODRUFF[393]	~22	Berdan's 1 USSS G	B ~1841 Illinois. R Fox Lake, Dodge Co., WI. E Oct 61 private. KIA Jul 2.
R1#25	GEORGE VAN BUSKIRK	23-24	11 Inf D	B ~ 1839 Monroe twp, Clermont Co., OH. E Nov 60 private. KIA Jul 2.
R1#26	EDMUND W HOWARD[394]	~18	14 Inf C	B ~1845 RI. Occ farmer. E Jul 61 private. C Jul 2: GSW to right leg. D Jul 15.
R1#29	LIEUT WESLEY F MILLER[395]			Removed

[393] **Soldier's father a physician.** Census reports show William Woodruff's father, John Woodruff, was a physician.

[394] **Minor at enlistment.** The June 9, 1860 U.S. Census report Foster, RI shows Edmund W. Howard as being 15-years-old, an age in agreement with an Ancestry.com family tree reporting his birth year as 1845. Likely, then, Edmund was 16 when he enlisted into the army in July 1861 and 18 when he was mortally wounded at Gettysburg in 1863.

[395] **Empty grave.** Lieutenant Wesley Funk Miller was the oldest son of Stephen Miller, who during the Civil War had distinguished himself by rising from private to colonel of the 1st Minnesota Infantry. However, prior to its engagement at Gettysburg, Stephen Miller had left the regiment and was trading on his Civil War renown to run for Governor of Minnesota. Stephen Miller would win this election on July 10, 1863. However, he would have known that he had lost his son, a lieutenant in the 7th U.S. Infantry, on July 2nd. Apparently, the decision was made initially to let Wesley lay with others of the honored dead sacrificed at Gettysburg. However, some years after the dedication of the Gettysburg National Cemetery, family members would have Wesley Miller's remains relocated to the Harrisburg City Cemetery in Pennsylvania.

R1#30	HENRY GOODEN 127 USCT C			B ~1821 York Co., PA. This United States Colored Troop soldier was not a casualty of Gettysburg. He enrolled in Aug 64 for a one-year term. He would die in 1876 and be reburied in the national military cemetery in November 1884 (age ~45).
R1#31	JAMES I BRIDGES	41-42	5 Inf C	B ~1821 England. Occ farmer. E Aug 48 private. Date died not found.
R2#1	LEVI STRICKLAND	19-20	11 Inf C	B ~1843 Philadelphia, PA. Occ farmer. E (Harrisburg, Dauphin Co., PA) Dec 62 private. KIA Jul 2.
R2#2	JAMES AGIN JAMES **EAGIN**	22-23	14 Inf D	B ~1840 Ireland. Occ laborer. E (Hartford, CT) Aug 61 private. C Jul 2: wounded in abdomen. D Jul 4 or 29.
R2#7	CHARLES WILSON	22	11 Inf G	B 10/31/1840 Sherburne, Chittenden Co., VT. R Rutland Co., VT. Occ farmer. E Dec 61 private. KIA Jul 2. Survivor (WC36595): M Mrs. Lucy Wilson 63 (widow of Otis Wilson).
R2#8	CHARLES SCHMIDT	?	14 Inf E	B ? E ? private. C Jul 2: wound to left thigh. D Jul 3.
R2#9	D A McKEAN **ALCOTT D McKEEN**	19	11 Inf D	B ~ Mar 1844 Ontario, Wayne Co., NY. Occ laborer. E (Palmyra, Wayne Co., NY) May 62 private. C Jul 2. D Jul 3.
R2#14	M KENNEDY MICHAEL KENNEDY	~27	10 Inf D	B ~1836. Occ soldier. ReE Mar 62 private. KIA Jul 2.
R2#15	W R DAVIS WILLIAM R DAVIS	`~29	10 Inf H	B ~1834 Ireland. Occ house painter. E (Detroit, MI) Aug 55 private. KIA Jul 2.
R2#16	S CORRELL SOLON L **CORNELL**	22	17 Inf A 2nd Bat	B ~Feb 1841 Knox Co., OH. Occ wood turner. E May 62 private. KIA Jul 2.
R2#17	JULIUS FURGESON JULIUS **FERGUSON**	19-20	74 Inf A	B ~1843 Albany, NY. Occ laborer. E Aug 62 private. C Jul 2. D Jul 3.
R2#18	B M M BARNEY McNAMEE	35-36	17 Inf B	B ~1817 Ireland. Occ laborer. E Jul 62 private. D Jul 2 of wounds.
R2#20	E M WILLIAMS EDWARD MARCELLUS WILLIAMS	19	3 Inf I	B 9/14/1843 Rochester, Monroe Co., NY. R same. Occ carpenter. E Jun 62 private. KIA Jul 2. Survivor (WC113427): F Edward E Williams 50 in 1867 (disabled widower of Mary Ann William).

R2#21	CASPER KUPFERLY **CASPARD KUPFERLE**	~25	3 Inf G	B ~1838 France. Occ painter. E (NYC) Jan 61 private. KIA Jul 2.
R2#22	ROBERT FURLONG (ALIAS) SEXTON, DENNIS[396]	25-26	3 Inf C	B ~1837 London, England. Occ laborer. E (NYC) Jul 58 private. KIA Jul 2: wounded in the chest. Survivor (WC24740): W Mary 22 (M Oct 62).
R2#24	WILLIAM A MASON	21-22	7 Inf I	B ~1841 Atlantic Co., NJ. Occ sailor. E (Washington, D.C.) Nov 62 private. C Jul 2: wounded in the head. D Jul 4.
R2#25	DANIEL KINNEY DANIEL **KENNY**	27	12 Inf C 1st Bat	B ~Jun 1836 Ireland. Occ farmer. E (Albany, NY) Dec 61 corporal. KIA Jul 2.
R2#26	SERGT H ROGERS HUGH ROGERS	30-31	12 Inf D	B ~1832 Ireland. Occ soldier. ReE Sep 1861 sergeant. KIA Jul 2
R2#27	ROBERT MORRISON	23-24	Batty C 5 US Art	B ~1839 Ireland. Occ laborer. E (Allentown, PA) Aug 62 private. KIA Jul 2.
R2#32	LIEUT CHRISTIAN BALDER	~31	6 Cav A	B~ 1832 Germany. E Apr 1855 into 1st US Cavalry as a private. Promoted to sergeant during service. Commissioned 2nd lieutenant into the 6th US Cavalry on 10/23/61. Promoted to 1st lieutenant on 12/23/62. Mortally wounded at at Fairfield, PA Jun 30. D Jul 3.
R2#34	J MOLES JOHN MOLES, JR	~20	12 Inf C	B ~1843 Ireland. 1860 R: Oswegatchie, St. Lawrence Co., NY. Occ farm laborer. E date not found. KIA Jul 2: GSW to head and back. Survivor (WC84521): M Mrs. Mary Moles 50 in 1866 (widow of John Moles, Sr).
R2#35	C T RIDDER CHARLES T RIDDER	~26	Battery D 5 US LA	B ~1837 Wayne Co., NY. Occ sailor. E Apr 61 private. KIA Jul 3: struck by a Confederate shell while serving his Union battery.
R2#36	E DENNIS FRANK W DENNIS	21-22	Battery D 5 US Art	B ~1841 New Milford, Litchfield Co., CT. Occ seaman. E Aug 62 into 146th NY Infantry Co D as private. Detached to the 5th NY Artillery on 5/9/63. KIA Jul 3.
R3#1	THOMAS WHITFORD THOMAS **WHITEFORD**	23-24	Battery F 3 US LA	B ~1839 Scotland. Occ clerk. E Aug 60 private. Promotion to corporal during service. C Jul 2: mortally wounded. Date died not found.

---

[396] **Fighting under an alias**. Dennis Sexton, under the alias of Robert Furlong, had enlisted into the 3rd U.S. Infantry in 1858 and had continued to serve under this alias until in January 1863 he was discovered and apprehended in New York City by a captain from his regiment. Fortunately for his soon-to-be widow, Sexton had married under his real name.

R3#2	AMEST FASSETTE **ANSEL SHEPHERD FASSETT**[397]	~20	Battery A 4 US Art	B ~1843 Wyoming Co., PA. 1860: R Monroe, Wyoming Co., PA; occ farm laborer. E private. C Jul 3: wounded in the right hip by an artillery shell. D Jul 13.
R3#4	JOHN PORTER	33-34	Battery C 5 US LA	B ~1829 England. Occ coal miner. E Aug 61 private. C Jul 2: wounded in spine. D Jul 9.
R3#5	MARTIN SLOGRAT MARTIN **SCANLON**[398]	18-19	Battery A 4 US Art	B ~1844 Ireland. Occ laborer. E Oct 62 private. C Jul 3. D Jul 5.
R3#6	THOMAS PADGETT	~27	Battery I 1 US Art	B ~1836 England. Pre-war occ: laborer. ReE May 60 private. C Jul 3: wounded in leg→amp. D Jul 26.
R3#7	JOSEPH W ERWIN[399]	21-22	Battery A 4 US Art	B ~1841 Guilford Co, NC. Occ carpenter. E (Bolivar, Jefferson Co., VA) Oct 62 private. Presumed KIA Jul 3. Dropped from rolls 10/24/63.
R3#8	WILIAM PATTON[400]	22-23	Battery A 4 US Art	B ~1840 Ireland. R Beaver Co., PA. Occ laborer. E Mar 62 private. KIA Jul 3.
R3#9	JAMES MURPHY[401]	25-26	Battery A 4 US Art	B ~1837 Ireland. Occ: laborer. E (NYC) Aug 58 private. KIA Jul 3. Survivor (WC37817): M Mrs. Catherine Murphy 60 in 1864 (widow of Patrick Murphy).
R3#10	JOHN MARKLEIN	22-23	Battery H 1 US Art	B ~1840 Germany. Occ teamster. E (Cincinnati, OH) Aug 61 private. KIA Jul 3.
R3#11	WILLIAM BECKER	~34	4 Inf K	B ~1829 Germany. Occ farmer. E (Milwaukee, WI) May 63 private. C Jul 2: wounded in left chest. D Jul 9.
R3#12	SERGT CHARLES GILES	27-28	11 Inf B	B ~1835 Shapleigh, York Co., ME. Occ shoemaker. E (Dover, DE) Aug 61 private. Promotion to sergeant during service. C Jul 2: wound to left arm. D Jul 16: gangrene complication.

---

397   **One of Lieutenant Alonzo Cushing's five Battery A 4th U.S. artillerymen lost July 3rd.** The grave of Ansel Fassett lies to the right of those of four other enlisted men of Lieutenant Alonzo Cushing's Battery A 4th US Artillery, men who would lose their lives from wounds incurred in the July 3rd cannonade duel. These men are Martin Scanlon, Joseph Erwin, William Patton and James Murphy. Ansel Fassett received a shell injury on this date and die on July 13th.

398   **One of Lieutenant Alonzo Cushing's five Battery A 4th U.S. artillerymen lost July 3rd.** Martin Scanlon was wounded July 3rd and would die July 5th.

399   **One of Lieutenant Alonzo Cushing's five Battery A 4th U.S. artillerymen lost July 3rd.** Joseph Erwin was presumed killed on July 3rd.

400   **One of Lieutenant Alonzo Cushing's five Battery A 4th U.S. artillerymen lost July 3rd.** William Patton was killed July 3rd.

401   **One of Lieutenant Alonzo Cushing's five Battery A 4th U.S. artillerymen lost July 3rd.** James Murphy was killed July 3rd.

R3#13	SERGT JUDAS THETART **JULIUS THETARD**	~39	6 Inf I	B ~1824 Germany. Occ soldier. 2nd ReE Jun 60. C Jul 2: wounded in right thigh→ amp. D Jul 13.
R3#14	PLAYFORD WOODS	24-25	14 Inf B	B ~1838 Warrenville, Cuyahoga Co., OH. Occ farmer. E Oct 60 private. C Jul 2: wounded in the abdomen. D Jul 5 or 8.
R3#15	WILLIAM BYRNE	21-22	17 Inf D	B ~1841 Centerport, Long Island, NY. Occ yeoman. E Dec 61 private. C Jul 2: wounded in thigh. D Jul 21.
R3#16	BENJAMIN WAY **SIDNEY** WAY	22-23	14 Inf A	B ~1840 Alburgh, Grand Isle Co., VT. Occ farmer. E Aug 61 private. C Jul 2: GSW fracturing right knee joint. D Jul 9: pyemia complication.
R3#17	JOHN WILLIS	~27	2 Inf K	B ~1836 Ireland. Occ laborer. E (Boston, MA) Jun 61 private. C Jul 2: wound to right thigh→amp. D Jul 26.
R3#18	MILLS JAMESON **MILES** JAMESON	~24	14 Inf H	B ~1839 Cold Spring, Putnam Co., NY. Occ farmer. ReE May 62 corporal. C Jul 2: wounded in both legs. D Jul 17: gangrene complication.
R3#19	FRANK BERCHARD **FRANCIS BURCHARD**	~23	14 Inf G	B ~1840 Burrillville, Providence Co., RI. Occ laborer. E Jul 61 private. Promotion to corporal during service. C Jul 2: wounded in head. D Jul 5 or 9.
R3#20	J REEMAN JOSEPH **LINEN** or LENNON	~35	6 Inf K	B ~1828 Ireland. Occ laborer. E (St. Louis, MO) Jun 56 private. C Jul 2. D Jul 25.
R3#21	JOHN W JONES[402] QR MR SERGT	~20	7 Inf E	B ~1843. R South New Market, Rockingham Co., NH. E May 61 private. Promotions to corporal and to sergeant, dates? C Jul 2. Date died not found.
R3#22	JOHN HARE	~32	2 Inf I	B ~1831 Ireland. Occ laborer. E (Philadelphia, PA) Feb 63 private. C Jul: 2 wounded in chest. D Jul 4.
R3#23	M CARROLL MICHAEL CARROLL	~34	14 Inf H	B ~1829 Ireland. Occ soldier. E Jul 59 private. C Jul 2: wounded in both legs. D Jul 5.
R3#24	G MORAN **PATRICK** MORAN	30-31	2 Inf B	B ~1832 Ireland. Occ laborer. 1st E (NYC) Dec 53 into 3rd US Artillery as a private. ReE into 2nd Inf Co B. C Jul 2. D Jul 4.

---

402 **Identity question**. It is no easy task to hit upon the true vein of a military and personal history for a soldier with so common a name as "John Jones." The John Jones profiled here appears to the 7th U.S. Infantryman sergeant who fought at Gettysburg and who was wounded on July 2nd. Arguing against the possibly that this John Jones is buried here, his service record further records that he was captured at Gettysburg and thereafter taken to Andersonville Prison, where he is recorded to have died in November 1864.

R3#25	_____ SULLIVAN PATRICK SULLIVAN	22-23	3 Inf I	B ~1840 Ireland. Occ peddler. E (NYC) Sep 61 private. KIA Jul 2: wounded in the chest and left leg.
R3#27	LIEUT WM CHAMBERLAIN WILLIAM **CHAMBERLIN**	22-23	17 Inf A	B ~1840 Lisbon, Androscoggin Co., ME. E (Lewiston. Androscoggin Co., ME. Aug 61 private. Promotions to corporal and to sergeant, dates not-noted. Commissioned 2nd lieutenant on 7/19/62. Promoted to 1st lieutenant on 8/2/62. Promotion for captain 7/2/63. KIA Jul 2.
R3#28	PATRICK TIGHE	36-37	3 Inf I	B ~1826 Ireland. R NYC. Occ laborer. E Aug 61 private. KIA Jul 2. Survivor (WC85236): W Catherine 41 in 1866 (M Dec 46); no chn.
R3#29	L GRISWOLD **LEWIS CASS GRISWOLD**[403]	20	Battery D 5 US LA	B 4/13/1843 Hartland, Livingston Co., MI. Occ farmer. E Oct 62 private. C Jul 2. D Jul 3.
R3#30	E BROWSER EUGENE **BROWER**	~20	Battery D 5 US LA	B ~1843 MI. Occ student. E May 61 private initially into 4th Michigan Infantry Company K. Transferred on 10/9/62 to Battery D of the 5th U.S Light Artillery unit. C Jul 2. D Jul 3.
R3#31	O F DRAKE OSCAR F DRAKE	23-24	16 MI Inf D	B ~1839 Oakland Co., MI. R East Saginaw, MI. 1860 occ: engineer. E Aug 61 private. Detached to Battery D US Artillery (Hazlett's Battery) on 1/1/62. KIA Jul 3.
R3#32	G H WHITE GEORGE H WHITE	22-23	2 SS Inf G	B ~1840. R Antrim, Hillsborough Co., NH. E Nov 61 private. KIA Jul 3.
R3#33	SERGT J GRAY JOSIAH GRAY[404]	27	2 SS Inf D	B 5/7/1836 Prentiss, Penobscot Co., ME. R same. Occ farmer. E Nov 61 sergeant. D Jul 4 or wounds. 1860 family: W Sarah ~29: 3 ♀: Emma ~16, Sarah ~13, and Anna ~11 (no approved WC found in pension records).
R3#34	SERGT HENRY LYE[405]	25	1 SS Inf G	B 5/18/1838 England. R Madison, WI. E Sep 61 bugler. Promotion to sergeant during service. C Jul 2. D Jul 3.

[403] **Soldier had been orphaned as a very young child.** Lewis Griswold's life was steeped in tragedy even before he was old enough to appreciate it. When he had just turned one-year-old, his mother Lucinda experienced the loss of his newborn brother Melvin. As likely an obstetrical complication, his mother died the day after his newborn brother's delivery. Then when Lewis was only 21 months, his father Daniel Griswold died. Hence, Lewis, having never really knowing his parents and having no surviving siblings, had to be subsequently taken in and raised by his maternal grandparents, the Beidelman's, who resided in Livingston Co., Michigan.

[404] **No widow's accepted pension found in records.** Possibly widow remarried prior to filing for widow's pension.

[405] **Engagement Broken by Death.** At the time of his death, Henry Lye was engaged to a Ms. Almira Shearer. A fellow soldier, William Isham, who had witnessed Lye's mortal wounding, wrote on July 28th to inform her of his death.

R3#35	BENJAMIN HAMLET BENJAMIN OLIVER **HAMBLET** III[406]	22-23	2 SS Inf A	B ~1840 Illinois. 1860: R Chanhassen, Carver Co., MN; occ farm laborer. E Oct 61 private. C Jul 3: severe wound to left leg→amp. D Jul 20. Survivor (WC194552 not online) M Mrs. Fanny Abbott 69 in 1880 (widow of Benjamin Hamblet, Jr. and of 2nd husband Nirum Abbott).
R3#36	ELI S B VINCENT ELI S BAILEY VINCENT	33	1 SS Inf G	B 6/6/1830 Almond, Allegany Co., NY. 1860: R Milton, Rock Co., WI; occ laborer. E Oct 61 private. C Jul 2. D Jul 16.
R3#37	CHARLES THATCHER (MN BENJAMIN)	38	1 SS Inf E	B 8/7/1824 Roxbury Center, Cheshire Co., NH. R Marlborough, Cheshire Co., NH. E Aug 61 private. C Jul2: wounded in left thigh. D Jul 22.
R4#1	T E SHEETS THOMAS E SHEETS	~20	14 Inf G	B ~1843 Montoursville, Lycoming Co., PA. Occ farmer. E (Williamsport, Lycoming Co., PA) Mar 62 private. KIA Jul 2.
R4#9	SERGT D W CLOCK **FRANK** W CLOCK	28-29	11 Inf D	B ~1834 Madison Co., NY. Occ: hotel clerk. E (Syracuse, Onondaga Co., NY) Jan 62 sergeant. KIA Jul 2.
R4#11	CHRISTIAN ENGERS	24-25	4 Inf H	B ~1838 Germany. Occ soldier. ReE (NYC) Aug 59 private. KIA Jul 2.
R4#12	PETER McMANIMUS PETER **McMANAMAN**	~41	4 Inf H	B ~1822 Ireland. ReE Jan 54 private. KIA Jul 2.
R4#13	_____ BARRINGTON HENRY **BOYNTON**	~37	4 Inf C	B ~1826 Pittstown, Rensselaer Co., NY. Occ: cooper. E (Rochester, Monroe Co., NY) Jul 58 private. Promotion to corporal during service. KIA Jul 2.
R4#14	PETER ROBINSON **BENNETT** ROBINSON	~33	4 Inf F	B ~1829 Sebago, Cumberland Co., ME. Occ mariner. E (Boston, MA) Dec 56 private. KIA Jul 2.
R4#15	ROGER McDONALD	~32	4 Inf H	B ~1831 Ireland. Occ shoemaker. E (NYC) Apr 60 private. KIA Jul 2.
R4#16	CHRISTIAN ALBETT CHRISTIAN **ABERT**	38-39	4 Inf H	B ~1824 Germany. Occ soldier. E Oct 53 private. KIA Jul 2.
R4#17	SERGT JOHN RILEY JOHN **RIELY**	~31	4 Inf K	B ~1832 Ireland. Occ soldier. E Jun 60 sergeant. KIA Jul 2.

---

406 **Grandson of a Revolutionary War Soldier**. Benjamin Oliver Hamblet, Sr., Benjamin's paternal grandfather, had been a soldier in the Revolutionary War.

R4#19	W MARE 4 Btn 1 Inf			No killed soldier with this or similar name found in military sources.
R4#21	T H MULLIGAN THOMAS H MULLIGAN	26-27	14 Inf A	B ~1836 Ireland. Occ mason. E (Oswego, Oswego Co., NY) Aug 61 private. C Jul 2: wound to left leg→amp. D Jul 16.
R4#22	JOHN CRERIDON JOHN **CREARDON**	~27	11 Inf B	B ~1836 Cambridge, Dorchester Co., MA. R same. Occ stone cutter. E Dec 61 private. Deserted on 1/20/63 but apprehended on 1/42/63. C Jul 2: wounded in right knee. D Jul 14. Survivors (WC94606): W Annabelle 31 (M Mar 57| died 9/21/66 of dysentery); MGM Mrs. Nancy Creardon 60 in 1867; 2 ♀- Annie 5, Margaret 3.
R4#23	RANSOM B RUSSELL	~24	6 Inf F	B ~1839 Broome Co., NY. Occ soldier. ReE (NYC) Jan 63 private. C Jul 2: GSW through left hip lodging in the spine. D Jul 15. Survivor (WC88672); W Delia 19 (M Feb 61); no chn.
R4#24	JOHN SMALL JOHN W M SMALL	29-30	17 Inf B	B ~1833 Abbot, Piscataquis Co., ME. Occ lumberman. E (Dover, DE) Nov 61 private. C Jul 2: wounded in left knee→amp. D Jul 14 of pyemia complication.
R4#25	WILLIAM CURTIS WILLIAM HENRY **CURTISS**	31-32	7 Inf A	B ~1831 NY. E Jun 62 private. C Jul 2: wounded in the back and lung. D Jul 15. Survivor (WC191162 not online): M Mrs. Luna Curtiss 62 in 1869 (William Curtiss, due to advanced age, affirmed unable to support wife and self).
R4#26	JOHN KEENAN	~31	7 Inf A	B ~1832 Ireland. Pre-war occ: laborer. ReE May 60 private. C Jul 2. D Jul 11 or 15.
R4#27	CORP JOHN FALLBRIGHT JOHN **FULLBRIGHT**	~29	2 Inf B	B ~1834 Jefferson Co., KY. Occ carpenter. E Jul 60 corporal. C Jul 2: shot in right foot and leg. D Jul 23: gangrene complication.
R4#28	WILLIAM D HAMMOND WILLIAM D **HAMMONDS**	21-22	14 Inf F	B ~1841 Canada. Occ farmer. E Mar 62 private. C Jul 2: penetrating wound to left side. D Jul 15.
R4#29	SERGT S P BLANCHARD SILAS P BLANCHARD	19	17 Inf B	B ~Jan 1844 Canada. R Houlton, Aroostook Co., ME. Occ clerk. E Jul 62 private. Promotion to sergeant during service. C Jul 2: wounded through both calves. D Jul 31: gangrene complication.
R4#30	C H WHITNEY CHARLES HENRY WHITNEY	20	17 Inf C	B 1/30/1843 Canandaigua, Ontario Co., NY. Occ printer, painter. E (Detroit, MI) Jul 62 private. C Jul 2: wounded in the right thigh. D Jul 16.
R4#31	WILLIAM DUFFY	27-28	17 Inf D	B ~1835 Ireland. Occ laborer. E (Hamilton, Aroostook Co., ME) Sep 61 private. C Jul 2. D Jul 23.

R4#32	JOHN O KEEFER JOHN **O'KEAFFE**	21-22	11 Inf F	B ~1841 Ireland. Occ laborer. E (Ogdensburg, St. Lawrence Co., NY) Dec 62 private. C Jul 2: GSW causing compound fracture of left femur. D Jul 28.
R4#33	THOMAS MURRAY	33	14 Inf F	B ~Feb 1830 Ireland. Occ carpenter. E (New Haven, CT) Sep 61 private. C Jul 2: wounded in arm and left leg→leg amp. D Jul 17: gangrene complication.
R4#34	CHARLES HORTON	20-21	11 Inf G	B ~1842 Savoy, Berkshire Co., MA. 1860: R same; occ farm laborer residing on father's farm. E Sep 61 private. C Jul 2: wounded in the chest. D Jul 12.
R4#35	J LUTZ MARTIN **LUHTZ**		14 Inf E	B ~? E Feb 62 private. C Jul 2: wounded in left knee. D Jul 27: pyemia complication.
R4#36	LIEUT N ROCKFORD **HENRY H ROCHFORD**	27-28	11 Inf E	B ~1835 Ireland. 1860: R Boston, MA; occ laborer. E Oct 56 into the 4th U.S. LA Battery I as 1st sergeant. Mustered Oct 61 into 2nd U.S. Infantry company A. Commissioned 2nd lieutenant in the 11th U.S. Infantry Company A on 2/19/63. KIA Jul 2.
R4#37	CAPT THOMAS O BARRI[407] (MN OLIVER)	41	11 Inf	B 11/16/1821 Norwich, New London Co., CT. Commissioned 5/1/1861 as 1st lieutenant and adjutant. Commissioned Captain on 5/4/61. C Jul 2: wounded in abdomen. D Jul 3. Survivors (WC139587): W Fanny 31 (M Jun 56|ReM 1869); 3 chn: 1 ♀-- Fanny 5 & 2 ♂- John 8, Thomas 9 months.

---

407 **Death on tenth wedding anniversary**. In a succession of tragic events, Mrs. Fanny Barri first would learn that her husband had been killed at Gettysburg, not just on any day, but on what would have been the couples' tenth wedding anniversary. The following year, her youngest son, Thomas, would die at two years of age. In 1869, Mrs. Barri would unite in marriage, on this occasion with her deceased husband's younger brother, John. However, three years later, she would again be widowed when John would die of tuberculosis.

Mason Memorial monument in the National Cemetery

★ ★ ★ ★ ★

A Union officer attends to the wounded Confederate General Armistead at the Angle based on Armistead's speculated appeal as a fellow mason.

Milton Keynes UK
Ingram Content Group UK Ltd.
UKHW051825011224
451756UK00009B/38